# The Rational Mind

**Scott Sturgeon** is Professor of Philosophy at the University of Birmingham. He has published numerous articles in journals such as Mind, Journal of Philosophy, Noûs, Philosophers' Imprint, and Philosophy and Phenomenological Research. He is the author of *Matters of Mind: Consciousness, Reason and Nature* (Routledge 2001). He has also contributed to many edited collections, including *Identity and Modality* (Oxford 2006), *Modality: Metaphysics, Logic, and Epistemology* (Oxford 2010), and *Conditionals, Paradox, and Probability: Themes from the Philosophy of Dorothy Edgington* (Oxford 2020).

"*The Rational Mind* ranges over a broad landscape of topics, problems and concepts, drawing links between different areas and offering, as Sturgeon aimed, a 'deep and pleasing vision' over the whole."

Anna Mahtani, *Journal of Philosophy*

"There is no doubt that this book would serve as an excellent textbook in formal epistemology. And researchers in formal epistemology will surely benefit from the book's intricate discussion of the philosophical motivations and significance of formal models, as well as its brand new, force-based picture of cognitive states."

Ru Ye, *MIND*

"Those familiar with Sturgeon's work will find the usual Sturgeonian elements: novel diagrams, imaginative examples, ways of talking about models that you simply will not find in anyone else's work. These are largely meant to help the beginner, but Sturgeon's unique creative vision meant that I turned things over in new and unexpected ways, too. In the early parts of the book, chapter 4 stood out for me as one of the most philosophically rich discussions of Bayesian updating I've read, digging into its relation to inference and basing and the somewhat strange rigidity of conditional credence....Sturgeon says that a major goal of *The Rational Mind* is to provide something useful for budding undergraduates, his colleagues working in epistemology, and everyone in between. Amazingly, he has managed to pull this off."

Jane Friedman, *Analysis*

"Sturgeon's book contains a masterful critical exposition of Bayesianism as a formal model of graded confidence and of the AGM model of belief revision, as well as being chock-full of original and interesting contributions.... [It] is both a pleasure to read and a source of many, many interesting and insightful points. I will continue to think about it for a long time."

Juan Comesaña, *Philosophical Studies*

# The Rational Mind

Scott Sturgeon

# OXFORD
UNIVERSITY PRESS

Great Clarendon Street, Oxford, OX2 6DP,
United Kingdom

Oxford University Press is a department of the University of Oxford.
It furthers the University's objective of excellence in research, scholarship,
and education by publishing worldwide. Oxford is a registered trade mark of
Oxford University Press in the UK and in certain other countries

© Scott Sturgeon 2020

The moral rights of the author have been asserted

First published 2020
First published in paperback 2024

All rights reserved. No part of this publication may be reproduced, stored in
a retrieval system, or transmitted, in any form or by any means, without the
prior permission in writing of Oxford University Press, or as expressly permitted
by law, by licence or under terms agreed with the appropriate reprographics
rights organization. Enquiries concerning reproduction outside the scope of the
above should be sent to the Rights Department, Oxford University Press, at the
address above

You must not circulate this work in any other form
and you must impose this same condition on any acquirer

Published in the United States of America by Oxford University Press
198 Madison Avenue, New York, NY 10016, United States of America

British Library Cataloguing in Publication Data
Data available

Library of Congress Cataloging in Publication Data
Data available

ISBN 978-0-19-884579-9 (Hbk.)
ISBN 978-0-19-891225-5 (Pbk.)

DOI: 10.1093/oso/9780198845799.001.0001

Links to third party websites are provided by Oxford in good faith and
for information only. Oxford disclaims any responsibility for the materials
contained in any third party website referenced in this work.

For Boysie, the Bear, and the Sun around whom we flourish.

# Preface

This book is the result of more than two decades' reflection on the intersection of epistemology and philosophy of mind. Chapter 7 appeared as 'Conditional Belief and the Ramsey Test' (*Royal Institute of Philosophy* 2002), bits of chapters 8 and 9 derive from 'Reason and the Grain of Belief' (*Nous* 2008), bits of chapters 11 and 12 derive from 'Confidence and Coarse-grained Attitudes (*Oxford Studies in Epistemology* 2010), and the rest of it is new material. Needless to say, the work contains many mistakes—there is a whole lot of it, after all, and I'm as fallible as the next chap in philosophy—but I've done my best to minimize error in what follows.

Writing the book was an experience: everything would go fine for a while, then I'd get bogged down with a change of mind about something; then everything would go fine for a while, then I'd get bogged down with another shift of opinion; and so on. The journey began when I foolishly asked two colleagues what they were working on. Dorothy Edgington kindly replied with a typescript which eventually became her masterpiece 'On Conditionals'; and Mark Kaplan so replied with a manuscript which eventually became his path-breaking book *Decision Theory as Philosophy*. What luck! Dorothy's work drew me into the world of conditional thought and Mark's into debate about the grain of our epistemic attitudes. Interaction with them both set my general work direction for years to come, for which I'm more grateful than I could ever articulate here...er.... especially now that the book is done. (For a long while there I cursed them for getting me into this mess.)

The book owes a larger-than-normal debt to Hartry Field, Paul Horwich, and Stephen Schiffer. I studied Hartry's 'Mental Representation' in grad school, along with other classic papers by him, and they had a powerful impact on my thinking. I also studied Stephen's formidable *Remants of Meaning*, which likewise shaped how I think about the rational mind. Years later I had lunch with Paul Horwich, author of *Probability and Evidence*, at which I was stunned when he outed himself as a belief-only epistemologist. That lunch prompted a serious re-think of many of topics in the book. In turn the re-think contributed greatly to the theoretical equilibrium in which I came to rest. For all of this (and more) I am deeply grateful to Hartry, Stephen, and Paul.

I am also extremely grateful to the following for comments on the manuscript, philosophical discussion over the years, and other groovy forms of support: Jackson Allen, Frank Arntzenius, Selim Berker, Paul Boghossian, Aaron Bronfman, Dave Chalmers, David Christensen, Justin Clarke-Doane, Tim Crane, Rob Cummins, Marian David, Josh Dixon, Cian Dorr, Ant Eagle, Kenny Easwaran, Bo Elliott, Kati Farkas, Kit Fine, Branden Fitelson, Miranda Fricker, Jane Friedman, Ken Gemes, Allan Gibbard, Dan Greco, Barbara Hager, Walter Hager, John Hawthorne, Anna Mahtani, Jenn McDonald, Matt Hewson, Jen Hornsby, Sophie Horowitz, Nick Jones, Jim Joyce, Tom Kelly, Kobi Kremnitzer, Jon Kvanvig, Maria Lasonnen-Arnio, Chuck Latting, Iris Latting, Keith Lehrer, Hannes Leit-saber, Eric Lormand, Ofra Magidor, Mike Martin, Elizabeth Miller, Jessica Moss, Bernhard Nickel, Greg Novack, David

Papineau, Alex Paseau, Richard Pettigrew, Jim Pryor, Sherri Roush, Ian Rumfitt, Mark Sainsbury, Mim Schoenfield, Armin Schulz, Teddy Siedenfeld, Susanna Siegel, Wolfgang Spohn, Jussi Suikannen, Mike Teitelbaum, Jonathan Vogel, Brian Weatherson, Ralph Wedgwood, Jonathan Weisberg, Greg Wheeler, Roger White, Robbie Williams, Tim Williamson, Cookie Wilson, Alexandra Zinke, and two anonymous referees for OUP.

Mostly I am grateful to the inner sphere—Maja, Sascha, and Fritz—for all that is best in my life.

# Contents

1. Guided Tour ............................................................. 1
   1.1 Structuring the Project ............................................ 1
   1.2 Starting Assumptions ............................................... 3
   1.3 Synopsis of Part I: Formal and Informal Epistemology ............... 9
   1.4 Synopsis of Part II: Coarse- and Fine-grained Attitudes ........... 11

## Part I. Formal and Informal Epistemology

2. The Bayesian Model (Probabilism) ...................................... 19
   2.1 Preview ........................................................... 19
   2.2 The Bayesian Theory of States ..................................... 19
   2.3 The Partition Principle and the Ball Game ......................... 25
   2.4 The Ball Game ..................................................... 29
   2.5 Conditional Credence .............................................. 45
   2.6 The Marble Game ................................................... 48
   2.7 The Bayesian Transition Theory: Jeffrey's Rule .................... 53
   2.8 A Matching Psychology: Creda ...................................... 58

3. The Bayesian Theory of States: Critical Discussion .................... 61
   3.1 Preview ........................................................... 61
   3.2 Contra Bayesian States: One Type of Fine-grained Attitude? ........ 61
   3.3 Contra Bayesian Conditional Credence .............................. 75
   3.4 Generalizing Bayesian States I: Intervals and Midpoints ........... 82
   3.5 Generalizing Bayesian States II: Intervals and Tertiary Attitudes . 87
   3.6 Generalizing Bayesian States III: Representors .................... 91

4. The Bayesian Transition Theory: Critical Discussion .................. 101
   4.1 Preview .......................................................... 101
   4.2 Bayesian Transition: Inference or What? .......................... 101
   4.3 Conditional and Indicative Credence .............................. 107
   4.4 Rigidity and Conditionality in the Bayesian Model ................ 111
   4.5 Conditionality and Restricted Vision ............................. 116
   4.6 Conditionality and Bayesian Kinematics ........................... 124
   4.7 The Nozick–Harman Point, *Modus Ponens*, and Supposition ......... 129
   4.8 Restricted-Vision Conditionality and Bayesian Kinematics ......... 142

5. The Belief Model (AGM) .............................................. 155
   5.1 Preview .......................................................... 155
   5.2 The Belief Model's Theory of States .............................. 155
   5.3 The Belief Model's Transition Theory ............................. 158
   5.4 Further Claims About Rational Transition ......................... 163
   5.5 Contraction ...................................................... 165

|   |   |
|---|---|
| 5.6 Postulates | 173 |
| 5.7 Linking States and Transitions: Conditional Belief | 175 |
| 5.8 A Matching Psychology: Bella | 177 |
| 6. Critical Discussion of the Belief Model | 180 |
| 6.1 Preview | 180 |
| 6.2 States in the Belief Model: Only One Coarse-Grained Attitude? | 180 |
| 6.3 Coarse-Grained Attitudes | 183 |
| 6.4 The Belief Model's Transition Theory | 189 |
| 7. Conditional Commitment and the Ramsey Test | 197 |
| 7.1 Linking Theory and Conditional Commitment | 197 |
| 7.2 The Issue | 198 |
| 7.3 The Coarse-Grained Bombshell | 199 |
| 7.4 The Fine-Grained Bombshell | 200 |
| 7.5 Diagnosing Gärdenfor's Bombshell | 202 |
| 7.6 Diagnosing Lewis' Bombshell | 206 |
| 7.7 The Rumpus | 209 |
| 7.8 Conditionals and Lewis' Bombshell | 210 |

## Part II. Coarse- and Fine-Grained Attitudes

|   |   |
|---|---|
| 8. Puzzling about Epistemic Attitudes | 221 |
| 8.1 Two Questions about Epistemic Attitudes | 221 |
| 8.2 A Puzzle in Three Easy Pieces: the Lottery and the Preface | 222 |
| 8.3 A Troika of Extreme Reactions | 226 |
| 8.4 Critical Discussion | 228 |
| 9. Belief-First Epistemology | 233 |
| 9.1 Two Strategies | 233 |
| 9.2 Credence as Update-Disposition | 234 |
| 9.3 Credence-as-Belief | 235 |
| 9.4 A Dilemma | 248 |
| 9.5 The Marching-in-Step Problem | 252 |
| 10. Credence-First Epistemology: Strengths and Challenges | 255 |
| 10.1 The Basic Picture | 255 |
| 10.2 The Strengths of Credal-Based Lockeanism | 256 |
| 10.3 Answerable Challenges for Credal-Based Lockeanism | 260 |
| 10.4 Deeper Challenges for Credal-Based Lockeanism | 268 |
| 11. Force-based Attitudes | 272 |
| 11.1 Building Epistemic Attitudes | 272 |
| 11.2 Cognitive Force | 273 |
| 11.3 Picturing Force-Based Confidence | 276 |
| 11.4 Modelling Force-Based Confidence | 279 |
| 11.5 Force-Based Lockeanism | 282 |

| | | |
|---|---|---|
| 12. | Force-Based Confidence at Work | 288 |
| | 12.1 Preview | 288 |
| | 12.2 Thick Confidence and Representors: Pesky Dilation | 288 |
| | 12.3 Force-Based Confidence and Rational Kinematics | 298 |
| | 12.4 Force-Based Confidence and Evidence | 308 |
| | 12.5 Force-Based Confidence and Content-Based Accuracy | 313 |
| 13. | Inference and Rationality | 321 |
| | 13.1 Preview | 321 |
| | 13.2 Rational Shift-in-View: a Space of Theories | 321 |
| | 13.3 Rational Steps | 328 |
| | 13.4 Inference and the Basing Relation | 330 |
| | 13.5 A Puzzle about Shift-in-View: Visual Update and Inference | 336 |
| | 13.6 A Deeper Puzzle: Inference and Confidence | 340 |
| | 13.7 Inference, Causation, and Confidence-Grounded Belief | 342 |
| | 13.8 Rational Architecture | 346 |
| | 13.9 Rational Shift-in-View | 353 |

*Bibliography*   357
*Index*   363

# 1
# Guided Tour

## 1.1 Structuring the Project

I have wide-ranging ambitions for this work. I hope the book contributes to scholarship in its many areas of concern, of course, but I also hope it proves useful as a teaching tool in formal epistemology and the philosophy of mind. The book does not aim to establish a single major hypothesis or perspective, nor even manifest a single spirit to be summed up in a snappy slogan. Instead the book's major goal is to help readers build a deep and pleasing vision across a broad range of philosophical topics. Everyone from colleague to undergraduate should get something useful out of the book.

Despite epistemology being on the cutting-edge of analytic philosophy, there is no agreement within it about where to start, about what basic elements of theory to use, or much else. One reason for this is the existence of two large and pernicious splits in the literature, splits which make for great mischief. They push epistemologists in opposite directions, blinker their vision, desensitize them to considerations that should play a central role in their work, and in various other ways mess things up in epistemology. The result is a literature tethered together more by institutional tie than theoretical agreement. Our first order of business, then, is to clarify the fault lines in question and elucidate the theoretical landscape they help to create. After doing that we'll unify the landscape over the remainder of the book, with success in that project being its major goal.

To begin, there is a gulf in the literature between formal and informal work on rationality. The former is often done in specialized languages—languages for mathematical logic, for instance, or set theory—it is theorem oriented, proof driven, sometimes axiomatized. This makes epistemology smells more like mathematics than Plato, and, as a result, often makes formal epistemology alienating to traditional workers in the field. For their work is informal in character, carried out in natural languages, normally driven by quotidian intuition and thought-experiment, never axiomatized. Informal work on rationality often smells more like Plato than mathematics, and, as a result, often alienates those naturally drawn to technical work. In my experience the sad truth is that informal epistemologists often see formal work in the area as not really epistemology *propre*, and formal epistemologists often see informal work in the area as obsolete or inchoate. This book aims to show that neither perspective is correct.

There is also a large gulf between work on the rationality of coarse-grained mental states and work on the rationality of fine-grained mental states. The former makes use of belief, disbelief, and suspended judgement as target psychological phenomena. And for this reason the work alienates those who focus on the rationality of

*The Rational Mind.* Scott Sturgeon, Oxford University Press (2020). © Scott Sturgeon.
DOI: 10.1093/oso/9780198845799.001.0001

confidence. The latter typically make use of credence or comparative confidence or something like that as target psychological phenomena. And for this reason the work alienates those who focus primarily on the rationality of belief (say). In my experience the sad truth is that theorists who focus on coarse-grained attitudes see work on the epistemology of confidence as overly nuanced, psychologically unrealistic, and little more than a side concern; and theorists who focus on fine-grained attitudes see work on the rationality of belief, disbelief, or suspended judgement as undernuanced, needlessly blunt, at best focused on derivative psychological phenomena This book aims to show that neither perspective is correct.

There is a deep and difficult four-way split, then, in literature on rationality. It can be mapped in a two-by-two matrix:

|  | Coarse-grained | Fine-grained |
| --- | --- | --- |
| Informal | Informal work on rational belief and its revision (A) | Informal work on rational confidence and its revision (B) |
| Formal | Formal work on rational belief and its revision (C) | Formal work on rational confidence and its revision (D) |

Cell (A) contains informal work on the rationality of coarse-grained states. Chisholm's work on justified belief is classic literature in the area. Cell (B) contains informal work on the epistemology of fine-grained states, and Lehrer's work on comparative confidence is influential work in this vein. Cell (C) contains formal work on the rationality of coarse-grained states, with Pollock's work on non-monotonic reasoning being classic in the area. And cell (D) contains formal work on the epistemology of fine-grained states, with Ramsey's work on subjective probability being a classic example.[1]

Eventually we'll consider work drawn from every cell of the partition, for our fundamental task is to see what formal work on rationality can learn from informal work and vice versa. I want to know what the epistemology of coarse-grained states can *teach* its fine-grained counterpart, and vice versa. The overall aim is to put forward a unified approach to all major topics in the field, with elements of the grand vision being drawn from the very best work in all of its traditions.

This means doing a good bit of philosophy of mind as well as a lot epistemology. And so it goes in the book. As the detailed chapter synopses to follow make clear, we spend as much time on the metaphysics of attitudes as we do on their rationality; and for this reason, both major words in the title of this book deserve emphasis: it is a book about mind as much as rationality, a book about rationality as much as mind. By the end of our story we should have a solid grip on what mental states (and their transitions) are like in themselves, and an equally solid grip on what it is for mental states (and their transitions) to be rational.

---

[1] See (Chisholm, 1966), (Lehrer, 1974), (Pollock, 1986), and (Ramsey, 1925).

We begin with a presentation of the best-known formal model of fine-grained mental states. This is the Bayesian Model created over centuries by Thomas Bayes, F. P. Ramsey, Richard Jeffrey, and others. The story also contains a presentation of the best-known formal model of coarse-grained mental states. This is the Belief Model created by Carlos Alchourrón, Peter Gärdenfors, and David Makinson (also known as the AGM model). Part I of the book presents the models from scratch—in a way suitable for genuine beginners—and subjects each model to vigorous informal scrutiny. Chapters which explain the models are self-contained introductions to the basic mathematics of formal epistemology. Chapters which critique the models presuppose notation introduced in the introductory chapters, but that notation will be immediately understood by anyone with even a nodding acquaintance with the area. Since Belief and Bayesian Models are critiqued informally rather than formally, Part I of the book is much more than an introduction to formal epistemology. It is also a gateway to its philosophical foundation.

As we'll see, there are strong pre-theoretic reasons to think similar things about each formal model discussed. Three of them stand out as take-home messages:

1. the theory of mental states in each model misrepresents its target domain;
2. the theory of mental-state transitions in each model is unacceptable; and
3. the story about how the former two aspects of theory link in together itself leads to technical bombshells due to its take on conditional commitment.

Similar problems crop up time and again for Belief and Bayesian Models. This motivates scrutinizing the assumptions which generate the other divide in our matrix, not the one between formal and informal work, but the one between work on coarse- and fine-grained attitudes.

Part II of the book examines that topic directly. On largely functionalist grounds it argues that coarse- and fine-grained attitudes must be unified deep down, somehow, and it provides a space of options for how that unification might work. As it happens there are two major approaches in the space developed: the belief-first approach tries to reduce fine-grained states to the coarse-grained attitude of belief, and the credence-first approach tries to reduce the coarse-grained states to the fine-grained attitude of credence. Strengths and weaknesses of each approach are examined in detail, and, in the end, a new position is put forward. This position is meant to capture the pros of each style of unification—plus manifest a few signature pros of its own—while leaving behind cons of each approach discussed.

## 1.2 Starting Assumptions

Most philosophers begin practicing their craft by imitating other philosophers. Only later do methodological worries creep in: Why am I doing philosophy this way? Do my methods hinder or raise prospects for success? Is a topic-neutral method even possible in philosophy? Many aspects of this book are explained by the answer I hold to this last question. Throughout its pages I construct arguments for various positions, for instance, but this sort of activity proves useful only if arguments _help_ in the pursuit of philosophical ends.

Why think that?

The belief that arguments are helpful when doing philosophy is itself a philosophical position if ever there were one. When you begin philosophizing by constructing arguments, therefore—as I am right now—you thereby rely on a substantive philosophical assumption. And the point generalizes from the particular case: it is not possible to divorce philosophical method from philosophical commitment. There is no free ride in philosophy, no neutral methodology, no assumption-free method to be used in one's work. Let me be clear, then, about some of the major assumptions made in this work.

We start with the thought that humans manifest features. Some of those features are physical in nature, others biological, still others psychological. And we take for granted what certain of the psychological features are like when investigating epistemic rationality—henceforth just rationality—but other psychological features will be investigated at length. In effect we begin with a few specific assumptions about our psychology, just to get the ball rolling, and then we use our assumptions to investigate rationality. This will prove useful in both directions—in developing our take on the human mind, and in developing our take on its rationality—as our overall picture moves from its starting position to theoretical equilibrium. In this way the book is equal parts philosophy of mind and epistemology.

It does not proceed, though, as if these areas are on an equal footing. Just as it would be foolish—in my view at least—for an action theorist to take her primary metaphysical cue, when putting forward a theory of human action, from approaches to the moral or political status of action, so, it is assumed here without argument, it would be foolish for a philosopher of mind to take her primary metaphysical cue, when putting forward a theory of our mental states, from approaches to when those states are rational, or well produced, or wise. The driving assumption is that nature comes first and epistemic normativity follows on.

This does not mean that epistemic theory is of secondary importance, any more than moral or political theory is of such importance simply because normativity in them follows on from action theory. The assumption has nothing to do with the importance of theory or fact. It is has to do with nature coming first in some recognizable sense, and normative fact about how nature should be, or is permitted to be, or anything like that, coming second. For our purposes this is the:

**Nature-before-Norms Assumption**   The nature of mind comes first, its rationality follows suit.

In line with this thought I'll make two further assumptions about the nature of mind, as well as a pair of normative assumptions which follow on from them.

First, I assume that *propositional attitudes* are of primary concern in the theory of rationality. Nothing of interest in this work will turn on how propositions are construed, so long as we think of them as entities which cut logical space into sections—basically, sections where they are true, and sections where they are not true.[2] Our initial assumption about the nature of mental states is then the:

---

[2] This will be fully explained later. There are deep connections between the theory of mental content and the theory of rationality. Those connections have prompted the very best work in analytic philosophy since its inception. See, for instance (Frege, 1948) or (Kripke, 1980). A major concern in all work like this is

**Binary-Attitude Assumption**  Propositional attitudes are binary relations between thinkers and propositions.

On this view, when Sascha believes that Brexit is a disaster, two things are related in a particular way: there is Sascha the believer, there is the proposition believed by her—namely, the proposition that Brexit is a disaster—and there is the situation consisting of the former being related to the latter in the belief-y way, via the psychological relation of belief. We'll see that this way of thinking about mental states proves useful for a number of reasons.

In making the Binary-Attitude Assumption, though, we're not merely thinking that it is useful to construe propositional attitudes as binary relations to propositions. We're thinking that propositional attitudes *really are* binary relations to propositions. In effect we're taking the attitudes fully seriously as well as at face value. This involves taking a stand on both the structure and the elements of propositional attitudes. The binary part of our assumption does the first thing—it specifies the structure of the mental states in question—and the person and proposition parts of our assumption do the second thing—they specify elements which slot into that structure. The intended result is a robustly realistic stance on the attitudes.[3]

We won't, though, be drawing needless distinctions between propositional attitudes. If it turns out that notionally distinct attitude types A and A* are such that it makes no difference to the *functioning* of an agent whether she lends A to claim C rather than A* to claim C, then, we'll assume that the difference between A and A* is merely notional, that there is no genuine difference between the attitudes. This amounts to a:

**Cash-Value Assumption**  There are no differences in attitude type which make no difference to the functioning of an agent.

This amounts to a kind of functionalism about propositional attitudes. The assumption in play is that there are no differences in such attitudes which make no difference to the functionality of their owners. And the key payoff of the assumption is simple: once it is established that the content of a particular propositional attitude state S is the same as the content of a particular propositional attitude state S*, we'll know that S and S* are distinct attitude types only if they lead to different functioning on the part of their owner. The Cash-Value Assumption insists that we individuate propositional attitude types by their cash value, by the difference their manifestation makes to the functioning of an agent.

So we begin with a robust realism about propositional attitudes and a functionalist take on their nature. These are descriptive assumptions about the mind, about what it

---

to defend a conception of propositions (i.e. contents) that makes sense of them when rationality is taken at face value. We set that issue aside in this work, focusing instead on how to construe the attitude part of propositional attitudes when rationality is taken at face value.

[3] I mean this stance to be incompatible with (what is known as) a measure-theoretic approach to propositional attitudes. To a rough first approximation, this approach sees the relation between propositions and our propositional attitudes as measure theory sees the relation between numbers and phenomena (such as length or weight) measured by them. See (Matthews, 1994) for details.

is like and how it works. We'll also begin with assumptions about how the mind should be from an epistemic point of view. The first of them is the:

**Rationality-of-States Assumption**   Certain of our propositional attitudes are subject to epistemic appraisal.

The thought here is not just that certain of our mental states can be rational or otherwise, it's that certain of our propositional attitudes can be rational or otherwise. These are our "epistemic attitudes", so to say, propositional attitudes which can be better or less-well taken in light of our evidence. That we manifest such mental states is a non-trivial assumption, to be sure, for it points to resources which can be used in developing a theory of rationality. If propositional attitudes can be more or less rational, after all, their rationality is likely to do with their attitudinal and content-theoretic natures. As we'll see, this is precisely how various approaches see the matter.

Finally, we assume not only that our epistemic attitudes can change, but that changes in them are likewise subject to epistemic appraisal. This is a:

**Rationality-of-Transitions Assumption**   Shifts in epistemic attitude are subject to epistemic appraisal.

The thought here is not just that certain shifts in our mental states can be rational or otherwise, it's that certain shifts in our propositional attitudes can be rational or otherwise. These are our "epistemic transitions", so to say; shifts in view which can be better or less-well taken in light of the evidence. That we manifest such shifts is a non-trivial assumption, to be sure, for it likewise points to resources which can be used in developing a theory of rational shift-in-view. If change in propositional attitude can be more or less rational, after all, its rationality is likely a function of the attitudes and contents involved in the shift. As we'll see, this is precisely how various approaches to rational shift-in-view see the matter.

On the picture to be fleshed out and revised, then, norms of rationality play two roles at once. They constrain epistemic attitudes *at* a time, and they constrain shift in epistemic attitudes *across* time. For this reason, a full-dress theory of rationality will have at least three moving parts: a theory of states, a transition theory, and a linking theory. The first theory says how epistemic attitudes should be at a moment if they're to be configured rationally. The second theory says how epistemic attitudes should shift across moments if they're to be shifted rationally. The third theory says how the first two stories fit together, how epistemic attitudes relate to their shift if such attitudes are to stitch together into a sensible life.

Think of it this way. We can depict the mental life of an agent with a cylinder built from segments:

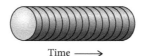

Time ⟶

**Figure 1.1**

Segments represent moments in an agent's mental life and contiguous sequences of them represent continuous intervals in that life. The cylinder as a whole represents the mental existence of the agent.

Epistemic norms can then be thought of as constraining things in three ways:

1. they make for a guide to packages of mental states in a segment of the cylinder (i.e. collections of epistemic attitudes at a moment);
2. they make for a guide to how packages should change across moments; and
3. they make for a guide to how 1. and 2. fit together.

These roles correspond to the theory of states, the transition theory, and the linking theory respectively. The full-dress theory of rationality will have at least this much structure:

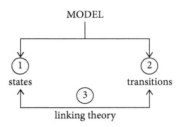

**Figure 1.2**

Formal models of rationality discussed in Part I of the book have exactly these moving parts. Aficionados will know, for instance—but don't worry if this makes no sense yet, since everything will be explained from scratch as we go!—the Belief Model (otherwise known as AGM) fleshes out the template as follows:

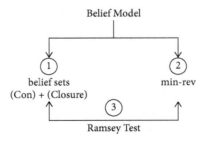

**Figure 1.3**

And the Bayesian Model (otherwise known as Probabilism) fills out the template as shown in Figure 1.4.

Moreover, whenever a formal model targets a domain of fact, the most useful way for it to do so is for three conditions to hold:

8  GUIDED TOUR

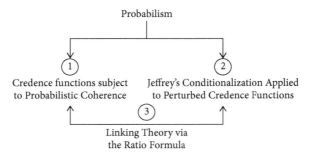

**Figure 1.4**

1. basic facts in the target domain are explicitly marked by basic elements of the model;
2. derivative facts in the target domain are explicitly marked by derivative elements of the model; and
3. derivative facts in the target domain are grounded in basic facts in that domain in such a way that their explicit marks in the model stand to one another in analogue grounding relations.

When these conditions hold we say that a model *matches* its target, and we'll see that matching turns out to be useful in a model. After all, whenever matching occurs one can *read off* from the very surface of a model how derivative and basic facts in its target domain fit together, for they do so in a way which exactly mimics their explicit marks in the model. Examples of this will be discussed as we go.

To sort out when 1.-thru-3. are satisfied by a model, four questions need to be answered:

1. what are the basic facts in the target domain?
2. what are the derivative facts in that domain?
3. which go with which grounding-wise?
4. is that relationship mirrored by marking elements in the model?

When the target domain of a model is human rationality, answering these questions is difficult. Nonetheless our discussion of formal epistemology shall make the:

**Matching-Models Assumption**  A formal model of rationality is fully acceptable only if it matches its target domain.

As we'll see, neither of the formal models discussed in Part I of the book match their target domain. We'll also see reason to suppose that no extant model revising them seems to do so either. This will become clear only after a good deal of progress has been made in our journey, though, and its significance will likewise become clear only after that progress has been made. Suffice it to say the following for now: often structural rules on offer in a model—either for states or for transitions between them—are motivated precisely by the manner in which explicit and implicit elements of the model fit together. If those elements do not match how explicit and implicit aspects of mind fit together, structural motivations end up in misalignment, resulting in confusion about what the model really means, and confusion about what kind of phenomena it can well model.

## 1.3 Synopsis of Part I: Formal and Informal Epistemology

Chapter 2 is a basic introduction to the Bayesian Model. The mathematical properties of classic probability are explained—linearity, cardinality, and so on—and the use of probability functions to model mental states is discussed. The idea that confidence should sum to unity across cells of a partition is explained. A game with balls is created and diagrammed to make visually vivid how probability works. Venn diagrams and truth-tables are used to illustrate everything for the absolute beginner. Conditional Credence is explained with intuitive examples and the standard ratio formula is introduced. A simple game with marbles is created and diagrammed to create intuition about *change* of probability; and it is shown how natural thoughts about this game lead directly to Jeffrey's rule for the update of credence. It is then shown how the Bayesian Model fits into the three-part template sketched in the previous section. The chapter closes by describing a notionally possible agent, Creda, whose psychology matches the Bayesian Model in the sense of matching discussed here. This helps to make clear what's going on when rationality in an agent matches the Bayesian Model—or fails to do so in various ways! Creda will play a starring role in Part II as well, when the relation between coarse- and fine-grained attitudes is investigated.

Chapter 3 is a critical discussion of the Bayesian theory of states. It argues that our psychological repertoire includes a great many more types of confidence than one finds in the Bayesian model. There is an extended discussion of how to think about the missing types of confidence—from a functionalist point of view, of course, but also from an intuitive point of view—and how the new types of confidence relate to a good understanding of the types of confidence explicitly marked in the Bayesian model. The discussion makes clear that Bayesian credence is a limit-case instance of a much larger psychological phenomenon. Conditional credence is then discussed at length, and it is shown that the standard Bayesian way of thinking about it—baked into the formalism—is mistaken. It is then argued that conditional credence is a fundamental moving part of our rational psychology. Three attempts are considered to generalize the Bayesian approach to confidence and conditional confidence: one makes use of the midpoints of mathematical intervals alone, one makes use of them along with 3-place (rather than 2-place) psychological attitudes, and one makes use of so-called 'representors' (i.e. sets of probability functions). Everything is explained for the genuine beginner. Then it is argued that none of the generalizations work very well—indeed the most popular one, the representor approach, isn't even clear about how it sees the link between technical aspects of the model and the mind being modelled. Both the Matching-Model and Binary-Attitude Assumptions take centre stage in the discussion.

Chapter 4 is a critical discussion of the Bayesian transition theory. The crucial distinction between a theory's dynamics and its kinematics is explained from scratch. It is argued that an approach to rational inference belongs to epistemology's dynamics rather than its kinematics, and that Jeffrey's rule for updating confidence in the Bayesian model—as his own label for it suggests—is part of epistemology's kinematics rather than its dynamics. Hence the Bayesian update rule is not a rule of rational inference (not even idealized rational inference). Credence lent to a certain kind of 'if'-sentence is explained—via the work of F. P. Ramsey—and compared to conditional credence found in the Bayesian model. Two prima facie problems for Bayesian updates are then made explicit: one turns on the fact that conditional credence never changes in Bayesian updating, and the other turns on the failure of the Bayesian model to permit conditional credence itself from being the contact point of rational shift-in-view. If conditional credence is a non-reductive part of our psychological architecture, though—as Chapter 3 has argued—both these aspects of the Bayesian transition theory are puzzling. A natural conception of conditional commitment is then motivated via the link between conditional commitment and unconditional credence, namely, the link found in the ratio formula for conditional credence. I call the natural conception of conditional commitment brought on by this link a 'restricted-vision' approach to conditionality, since it ensures that conditional credence is itself a function of what is going on in a restricted portion of an agent's perspective. Several formal consequences of this fact are explained from scratch and used to show that the most natural way of dealing with the two canvassed worries for the Bayesian model is hopeless. It is then argued that *modus ponens* style arguments do not function in thought like normal logical syllogisms, since *modus ponens* style arguments *do* specify obligatory paths forward in rational thought. This fact about them is put together with a restricted vision take on conditionality to create an approach to conditional commitment which is at odds with one of the starting assumptions of the book, namely, the Binary-Attitudes Assumption. On this approach to conditional commitment, what it is to be committed to one claim on condition another claim is true is not itself to be committed to the truth of any particular claim. Instead it is to stand in a basic conditional relationship to two claims at once. Such a 3-place approach to conditional commitment is then used to handle both major problems raised for the Bayesian Model. It is shown how the approach makes it sensible that conditional credence should never change in Bayesian updating, and, therefore, why a widely accepted point about the difference between rules of logic and rules of inference fails for *modus ponens*. The 3-place approach to conditionality is then used to motivate a new update rule, one for how an agent should update when the contact point of rational shift is conditional commitment. Finally, it is shown that the new update rule is motivated in exactly the same way as Jeffrey's rule in the Bayesian Model, namely, by a certain kind of epistemic conservatism about updating one's view.

Chapter 5 is a basic introduction to the Belief Model. It begins with an explanation of sets and how they work, then spells out sentences in a formal language and how they work, and then turns its attention to the use of sets of formal sentences to model belief-states of an agent. The idea that an agent's belief-states should harbour no conflict is explained, along with the view that logic should fully inform an agent's belief-states. These ideas are grounded in Jamesian thoughts to the effect that inquiry is aimed at securing truth and avoiding mistakes. Time is spent on the idea that both suspended judgement and disbelief reduce to belief in the Belief Model. This idea is used to spell out the Model's transition rules. Revision, expansion, and contraction rules are explained from scratch, along with the so-called 'Levi identity', and the model's conception of being economical with information. Slowly and carefully the main technical idea—known as 'partial meet contraction'—is explained for the beginner. The Model's postulates are then listed, its revision theorem is explained, and its approach to conditional belief is spelled out by appeal to the work of Ramsey. The chapter closes by describing a notionally possible agent, Bella, whose psychology matches the Belief Model in the sense of match discussed earlier. This helps to make vivid what's going on when rationality in an agent matches the Belief Model—or fails to do so in various ways! Bella will play a starring role in Part II as well, when the relation between coarse- and fine-grained attitudes is investigated.

Chapter 6 is a critical discussion of the Belief Model. It argues against most of the reductive assumptions puts forward by the model concerning our epistemic states. It rejects the view that suspended judgement reduces to belief and disbelief, for example, and likewise rejects the view that disbelief reduces to belief-in-negation. Thought experiments are used to motivate the idea that all three types of coarse-grained attitude—belief, disbelief, and suspended judgement—are self-standing psychological elements of our rational architecture. There is a discussion of how to revise the Belief Model's theory of states in light of this fact about our psychology; and it is shown that norms for belief-sets put forward by the model do not morph automatically into norms for disbelief- or suspended-judgement-sets. The Belief Model's transition theory is then critiqued at length. It is shown that its main transition rule—partial meet contraction—does not function like rational shift of belief functions in ordinary life. And the guiding principles of conservatism in the Belief Model—the way it thinks about size or importance of a given shift in belief—is fingered as the culprit for the model's difficulties.

Chapter 7 is a critical discussion of conditional commitment in both the Bayesian and the Belief model. Both use their treatment of conditional commitment as something to connect their theory of states with their respective transition theory. In doing so both models are immediately hit with technical difficulties. The Belief Model generates the 'impossibility theorem' first proved by Peter Gärdenfors, and the Bayesian model generates 'triviality results' first proved by David Lewis. Each of these technical areas is explained from scratch and diagnosed philosophically. It is argued that the bombshells discussed are best seen as showing (a) that the Binary-Attitude Assumption is false when it comes to conditional commitment, and (b) that there is no essential tie between conditional commitment and rational shift-in-view. Throughout the discussion the 3-place theory of conditionality is related back to Chapter 4's restricted-vision approach to conditionality.

## 1.4 Synopsis of Part II: Coarse- and Fine-grained Attitudes

Chapter 8 begins an extended argument about the relation between coarse- and fine-grained attitudes. The argument spreads through most of Part II of the book and begins with a pair of framing questions: how do elements within a given attitudinal space relate to one another? And how do elements across attitudinal spaces do so? Building on Chapter 6 the case is made for the view that coarse-grained attitudes do not reduce to one another any more than do their fine-grained cousins; that both coarse- and fine-grained attitudes are *sui generis* operators within their own spheres of influence. A contradiction is then generated by placing natural norms for belief and credence together with a natural story about how these attitudes relate to one another. A space of reactions is laid out to the contradiction, and its most extreme elements are rejected (basically because that they are too revisionary about how the mind works). Two options are left on the table: one says the coarse-grained attitude of belief is fundamental, with its fine-grained cousins reducing to belief; the other says the fine-grained attitude of credence is fundamental, with belief, disbelief, and suspended judgement reducing to credence. These are belief-first and credence-first epistemologies. Each gets a chapter of its own.

Chapter 9 critically discusses the belief-first approach. Two main strategies for reducing credence to belief are explained and critiqued. One tries to ground strength of credence in the functional role of belief, the other tries to ground strength of credence in the content of belief. These are the strength-as-role and strength-as-content approaches, respectively. It is argued that the former—the strength-as-role approach—cannot really get off the ground, that it's basically a non-starter. A well-known debate between Popper and Jeffrey is used to illustrate why the approach does no more than elide the important distinction between having a state and being disposed to change one. Since the strength-as-role approach ignores this important distinction, it is unacceptable. On the other hand—and very much to my initial surprise, at least—the chapter shows that the second strategy for reducing credence, the strength-as-content strategy, is much more robust than one might have supposed. The view does not fall prey to old-fashioned worries about specifying truth-conditions for its claims about probability. The view does not fall prey to worries about the agent's lack of beliefs about probability. And nor does it trivialize debate between belief- and credence-first theories in light of functionalism about the attitudes. Most importantly of all, though, the strength-as-content approach makes very good sense of reasoning with states of belief and states of credence, all within a unified approach to the attitudes. This is no mean feat as we'll see; so there is serious good news surrounding the strength-as-content approach to credence. But at the end of the day it is argued that the approach faces a nasty dilemma. In clarifying its explanatory resources, the view must either reference the signature function of credence or fail to do so. In the former case, it is argued that the strength-as-content theory turns out not to reduce credence after all (contrary to its own ambitions). In the latter case, it is argued that the strength-as-content approach entails that credal states do not function in their normal way. The chapter closes by arguing that the strength-as-content view conflicts with the fact that belief and credence march in step in the production of action, a very-bad-making feature of the view.

Chapter 10 critically discusses the credence-first approach to coarse-grained attitudes. The position's considerable strengths are canvassed from the outset. It is explained why the view underwrites a robust realism about the attitudes, in line with common sense, and why it bolsters the idea that belief, disbelief, and suspended judgement are self-standing states within their own sphere of influence, also in line with common sense. It is explained how credence-first epistemology dovetails with how we ordinarily describe coarse- and fine-grained attitudes, and, most importantly, how it makes good sense of the ways in which coarse- and fine-grained attitudes march in step when they cause and rationalize action. Further, it is explained how credence-first epistemology fits well—initial appearances to the contrary notwithstanding—with the ways in which *reductio*-based arguments work in debate, and also why we end-up chunking fine-grained states into coarse ones to begin with. This is a *lot* of good news. It is certainly enough to prompt the thought that something is deeply right in the credence-first approach. The chapter closes, though, with a descriptive and a normative problem for the approach. It is observed not only that credence is very often absent in the presence of coarse-grained attitudes—as a matter of descriptive fact—but also that credence is very often misplaced in the presence of everyday evidence—as a matter of normative fact. The chapter thus ends with a puzzle: there must be something right about credence-first epistemology, but the view can't be right as it stands.

Chapter 11 presents a new metaphysics of confidence meant to solve the puzzle. The view maintains that all types of confidence—those found in the Bayesian Model, functionally thicker types of confidence like those discussed in Chapter 3, and so on—are all built from mixtures of *cognitive force*. Just as one might be attracted to a piece of food, or repulsed by a piece of food, or manifest a feeling of genuine indifference to a piece of food after smelling it, say, it is argued that one might similarly be intellectually attracted to a claim, or repulsed by a claim, or manifest genuine intellectual indifference to a claim after considering it. Examples from everyday life are given of each type of cognitive force, so it's argued that such force is a recognizable element of the everyday conception of mind. Over the remainder of the chapter (and the next) it is shown that by grounding all types of confidence in cognitive force many useful things can be done theoretically. First it is shown how to picture and then formally model the reduction of confidence to cognitive force (with open rays in a three-dimensional volume). The force-based conception of confidence is then used to reduce belief, disbelief, and suspended judgement. And it is shown that the resulting view has all the good-making features of its credal-based cousin—indeed often to a higher degree or in greater detail—as well as good-making features not had by that cousin. Specifically, it is shown that the force-based reduction of confidence can specify a functionally minimal sufficient condition for belief and for disbelief—something the credal-based reduction of them cannot do—and the force-based view can give a *much* better explanation of suspended judgement than its credal-based cousin. It is likewise shown how the force-based view can make good sense of mental 'compartmentalization', by locating pockets of intellectual space where differing cognitive forces dominate.

Chapter 12 then puts the force-based view to even more systematic explanatory work. We saw earlier in the book that a popular transition theory uses sets of probability functions to model shifts in confidence. This approach suffers difficulties surrounding a technical aspect of its sets, namely, their tendency to 'dilate' in certain settings. This well-known phenomenon is explained from scratch and placed within a larger theoretical setting. The result unearths systematic and puzzling patterns of intuition about the acceptability (or otherwise) of the representor-based model's consequences. It is shown that the force-based view of confidence explains those patterns of intuition well. Then new types of counter-example to the representor approach are presented, ones which having nothing to do with dilation, and the force-based view is used to explain them too. Indeed it is used to explain these new intuitions in a manner in line with its explanation of better-known dilation-based worries. The full story exposes deep links between the force-based metaphysics of confidence and a triplet of Big Issues, namely, the forward-looking or ahistorical nature of transition theory, the ways in which the character of confidence should match the character of evidence, and the circumstances in which confidence is subject to content-based accuracy. Each of these Big Issues is explained from scratch and handled gracefully by the force-based view. The fact that all of this *can* be dealt with—in a relatively short space, in a relatively straightforward way, solely by appeal to cognitive force—is itself the most powerful reason to accept the force-based view. Yet there is one glaring hole in the story, a hole which turns crucially on the spot where belief-first epistemology is at its strongest. After all, nothing in the force-base story told to this point covers the nature of rational inference. That is our final topic.

Chapter 13 develops a theory of rational inference as well as a picture of the human mind to go with it. The picture is meant as an empirical hypothesis about how rationality in humans actually works, its major moving parts, how they fit together, and so on. The story begins with four questions faced by any theory of rational shift-in-view. One has to do with whether shifts within its domain are events brought about by agents or rather events which merely happen to them. One has to do with whether the approach to rational shift-in-view is meant to be part of a theory's dynamics—in which case rational and causal forces come into play—or part of a theory's kinematics—in which case only structure or pattern in the phenomena is relevant. One question has to do with whether the rationality of shift-in-view is meant to be everyday rationality (like we see in real human beings), or, instead, whether it's meant to be ideal rationality (of some sort we never see in the real world). And the final question canvassed has to do with whether mental states in the target domain are coarse- or fine-grained. Since each of these questions is to be answered in one of two ways, and since there are four questions in total, the discussion generates a sixteen-fold classification of approaches to rational shift-in-view. Well-known theorists are located within that classification and focus is placed on what's called 'doxastic' rationality in the literature. It is argued that this kind of rationality requires a special sort of blend between causal efficacy and epistemic relevance. The discussion leads to what I call a *coordinated epistemic reason*: roughly, a reason where causal-efficacy and epistemic-relevance fuse into one sort of thing. This is explained from scratch and illustrated with everyday examples. The view is defended that coordinated epistemic reasons are central to the nature of rational inference, and, as a result, that the theory of rational inference primarily concerns the non-ideal rationality of agential dynamics. This leads to a pair of puzzles discussion of which closes the book.

1. *The Dovetail Puzzle*: norms for rational inference should dovetail with those for our reaction to perceptual experience. Yet our reaction to perceptual experience looks non-agential—it looks like something which happens to us rather than something we do—so norms for rational inference and those for perceptual update seem parts of different aspects of theory. The puzzle is to make sense of how they can dovetail if this is so.

2. *The Inference Puzzle*: rational inference turns essentially on belief, which looks to be nothing but confidence deep down. Yet we do not seem to infer with our states of confidence. So the puzzle is to see how we can reason with our beliefs given they are states of confidence.

The chapter ends with thoughts on each puzzle. The relationship between agential and non-agential aspects of life is discussed, and it's emphasized that certain aspects of life 'switch hit'. This occurs when something we find in everyday life is part of its agential side one moment and its non-agential side the next, or vice versa. Examples of this are given from everyday life. It is argued that switch-hitting anchors the possibility that norms for inference and those for perceptual update dovetail with one another. But it is also argued that no simple strategy like this is available to handle the inference puzzle. A detailed sketch of our rational architecture is then put forward to tackle that puzzle directly. The sketch involves the idea that inference takes place within a dedicated reasoning faculty. It is then argued that the sense in which we reason with our beliefs is really no more than the following: we reason with the thing we believe, not with our states of belief. The book ends with a discussion of its picture of rational architecture and work left to be done if it's on the right track.

PART I

# Formal and Informal Epistemology

# 2
# The Bayesian Model
(Probabilism)

## 2.1 Preview

In this chapter we explain the best-known formal model of rational fine-grained attitudes. The model was pieced together over decades by many people and it goes by many names. In what follows we'll use two of them interchangeably: sometimes we'll speak of *the Bayesian model*, other times we'll speak of *Probabilism*.[1] The first label is drawn from the last name of the Reverend Thomas Bayes, who first emphasized a consequence of the model's mathematics (now known as Bayes' Theorem). The second label is drawn from the mathematical functions used by the model to measure strength of rational commitment to a claim. All key aspects of the approach will be explained from scratch. The next chapter takes up critical discussion of the model.

Like any full-dress theory of rationality, the Bayesian model has three moving parts: a theory of states, a theory of transitions between states, and a story about how the two fit together. Intuitively, the first bit of theory describes how fully rational attitudes hang together in a moment, the second describes how such attitudes change in the face of new input, and the third explains the extent (if any) to which moving parts in either of the first two components of theory can be explicated by appeal to those in the other. We shall explain each of these elements from scratch. Toward the end of this chapter we'll place particular emphasis on the internal relationship the model sees between conditional commitment and rational shift-in-view. Chapter 7 then explains why this idea leads to big trouble.

## 2.2 The Bayesian Theory of States

Every full-dress epistemic model contains a bit of formalism which functions as an empirical hostage to fortune in the model. Once that bit of formalism has been psychologically interpreted, it is possible for the model to go wrong in at least two different ways. The model might thereby represent psychological states which are completely alien to human cognition, i.e. states which humans never do or can get into. Or the model might fail to explicitly represent states which are crucial to human cognition, passing them over in its formalism completely. In the first case the model makes use of an over-developed psychology. In the second case it makes use of an

---

[1] There are actually several distinct models that go under these labels in the literature. We'll focus on one of them, a model which distills the classic insights which animate the approach.

under-developed psychology. The next chapter argues that the Bayesian theory of states commits both of these sins. Here we lay out the theory explicitly so that we can make the charge stick in the next chapter.

The starting point of the story is a simple observation of human psychology: we can be more or less confident in a claim's truth. For instance, we might place high confidence in the view that Lincoln was a great president, while placing low confidence in the view that phlogiston is the key to combustion. It is within our psychological gift to invest many types (or levels) of confidence, and by doing so our psychological states become subject to epistemic appraisal. We may ask whether a given level of confidence is reasonable to invest on current evidence, whether our confidence in a given claim is based aptly on our evidence, and so on. A full-dress approach to rationality should explain how confidence is to be configured when fully rational. That is what the Bayesian theory of states aims to do.

It begins by measuring the *strength* of confidence lent to a claim. For every type of confidence found in the Bayesian model—or every level of *credence*, as we'll put it—the model pairs that type of credence with a real number in the unit interval, i.e. a real number not lower than zero and not higher than one. Intuitively, larger numbers signify epistemic commitments which function more strongly in favour of a content than do commitments marked by smaller numbers. If the number assigned to credence lent to claim Φ is itself larger than the number assigned to credence lent to claim Ψ, therefore, the attitudinal commitment to Φ is stronger than the attitudinal commitment to Ψ.

This is a sensible beginning, but it is not a neutral one. Numbers used in the Bayesian model amount to a highly non-trivial set of assumptions about the workings of the human mind. Chief among them is the view that credal types come in strengths which relate to one another as real numbers do in the unit interval. This assumption requires detailed explanation. Picture it as in

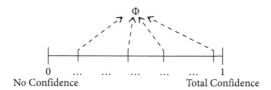

Figure 2.1

Think of Φ as any claim in which you invest credence. The line stretching from zero to one is meant to be continuous, built from a huge collection of points which shows no gaps. Each of the points represents a distinct types of credence you might lend to Φ.

The picture involves the idea that there is a maximally strong level of credence, something usefully called 'absolute certainty' (or 'certainty' for short). Think of this as the last full measure of epistemic devotion, the strongest type of attitudinal commitment. The Bayesian model then understands *other* types of credence by appeal to the notion of certainty. It measures their strength as a function of the strength of certainty. In effect, certainty is used by the model as a yardstick in relation to which other types of credence are compared. It is our grip on certainty, then, which provides the key to our understanding of all types of credence recognized by the model. When you lend 80% credence to Φ, for instance, the Bayesian model construes your take on Φ as one the strength of which is 80% that of certainty. This is what it means to describe you as '80% sure of Φ'. When you lend 25% credence to Φ, the Bayesian model construes your take on Φ as one the strength of which is 25% that of certainty. This is what it means to describe you as '25% sure of Φ'. And so on.

We can flesh out this story by posing and answering three further questions:

1. How many types of credence are recognized by the Bayesian model?
2. How do those types of credence relate to one another?
3. How is each of them conceived intrinsically?

To see how the Bayesian model answers these questions, note we can condense its approach with a single equation:

$$\text{cr}(\Phi) = \underline{n}, \text{ where } \underline{n} \text{ is in the unit interval } [0,1].$$

When a type of credence is assigned the number 0, that represents an attitude like total rejection, something with none of the pro-content functional force of certainty. When a type of credence is assigned the number 1, that represents an attitude like total acceptance, something with all the pro-content functional force of certainty. Between the extremes are cases in which a given type of credence is assigned a real number larger than 0 but smaller than 1. This represents a 'non-degenerate' case of credence, something with some-but-not-all of the pro-content functional force of certainty. We shall call these types of credence *in-between credence* in what follows. Eventually we'll see that they play a key role in several aspects of the Bayesian model.

The resulting take on our psychology makes for clear answers to the three questions posed above. Here are the answers (we'll explain them in a moment):

(Ai)   There are uncountably many types of credence.
(Aii)  They are linearly ordered by strength.
(Aiii) They are infinitely precise in intrinsic detail.

Let us spend a moment fleshing out what these answers come to. Once we have done that we will understand better the psychological assumptions built into the fabric of Probabilism.

(Ai) *Number*: Consider the set of natural numbers N. Intuitively this set begins with 0 and then has 1 and then has 2 and then has 3 and then continues on in that way without stopping. We might put this as follows:

$$\mathbf{N} = \{0, 1, 2 \ldots\}$$

But ask yourself this: how many numbers are inside this set, i.e. how many natural numbers are there? To answer this question we must say something about when two sets have the same number of elements.

The relevant thought about this—discovered by the mathematician Georg Cantor—is that two sets $S_1$ and $S_2$ have the same number of elements when those elements can be paired-up without remainder. In this technical and stipulated sense of 'same number', however, it turns out that many sets have the same number which intuitively fail to do so. The set of natural numbers, for instance, has the same number of elements—in the technical sense of 'same number'—as the set built solely from the even numbers! After all, members of each set can be paired-up without remainder. Here is one way to do so:

$$N = \{0, 1, 2, 3, 4, \ldots \underline{n}, \ldots\}$$
$$E = \{0, 2, 4, 6, 8, \ldots 2\underline{n}, \ldots\}.$$

The mathematical theory of *cardinal numbers* is based on Cantor's stipulated sense of same number.

We can use it to ask whether the number of types of Bayesian credence is the same as the same number of natural numbers. And the answer turns out to be Yes if, but only if, the unit reals can be paired- up without remainder with the natural numbers. But the unit reals cannot be so paired-up with the natural numbers; so in Cantor's sense of same number it turns out that there are *more* real numbers from 0 to 1 than there are natural numbers. When U is the set of unit reals, Cantor showed that U's members cannot be paired with the natural numbers without remainder; any such pairing will always leave out some of the real numbers. Intuitively: Cantor showed that we will always run out of natural numbers before matching each real number, and, for this reason, the sets U and N do not have the same number of members. U has more members than does N, in Cantor's stipulated sense of 'more'.[2]

This implies that there are more types of credence on the Bayesian story than there are natural numbers! After all, Bayesians pair-up types of credence and real numbers in the unit interval. It follows that in Cantor's sense there are an equal number of real numbers in the unit interval and types of credence according to the Bayesian model. In turn this means that there are more types of credence than there are natural numbers.

For any natural number $\underline{n}$, however, there will be no way to fully pair-up members of the set of natural numbers which stops at $\underline{n}$—i.e. no way to pair-up $\{0, 1, 2, \ldots, \underline{n}\}$—with members of N itself. But it follows from this that there are more members of N than there are in any such set, which means that there are more members of N than there are for any natural number $\underline{n}$. In turn this means that there must be an *infinity* of natural numbers. Yet we have seen that there are more real numbers in the unit interval than there are natural numbers. Hence we must conclude, with Cantor, that the number of real numbers is an infinite number which is larger (in Cantor's stipulated sense) than the infinite number of natural numbers! There are at least two kinds of infinite number, with the larger of the two giving the number of types of credence recognized by the Bayesian model.

This is a very large number indeed. It is known as an 'uncountable' infinity, since any set which has it as the number of its members cannot be pair-up without remainder with the counting numbers (i.e. the natural numbers). Since the Bayesian model presupposes that the number of types of credence is the same as the number of real numbers in the unit interval, and since there are uncountably many real

---

[2] See any set theory textbook for Cantor's 'diagonal' proof that the number of cardinal numbers is strictly greater than the number of natural numbers: e.g. (Enderton, 1977).

numbers in that interval, the Bayesian model presupposes that there are uncountably many types of credence. This is a very large number of types of credence to presuppose!

(Aii) *Linearity*: The Bayesian model presupposes that its huge infinity of types of credence can be linearly ordered by strength-of-credence. Let us get clear on what this come to. Intuitively: things can be linearly ordered when something about them makes for a way to put them into a line. Types of Bayesian credence can be linearly ordered when something about them makes for a way to put them into a line. Just as the age of each member of a group of direct descendants can be used quite literally to line them up, youngest-to-oldest say, the Bayesian model maintains that *strength of credal types* can be used to form them into a line too: weakest-to-strongest. But what is the structural cash value of the claim that a group of things can be formed into a line? And what is it about types of credence which makes it natural for Bayesians to claim that they can be so formed?

Well, we say that a relation between two things **R** linearly orders a group of objects when **R** has four properties:

**R** is *transitive*. For any things $x$, $y$, and $z$: if $x$ stands in **R** to $y$, and $y$ stands in **R** to $z$, then $x$ stands in **R** to $z$.

**R** is *reflexive*. For anything $x$ within **R**'s domain: $x$ stands in **R** to itself.

**R** is *antisymmetric*. For any things $x$ and $y$ within **R**'s domain: if $x$ stands in **R** to $y$, and $x$ is not equal to $y$, then $y$ does *not* stand in **R** to $x$.

**R** is *connected*. For any things $x$ and $y$ within **R**'s domain: either $x$ stands in **R** to $y$, or $y$ stands in **R** to $x$.

Consider the natural numbers and the greater-than-or-equal-to relation. That relation places those numbers in a line from zero:

$$0 \leq 1 \leq 2 \leq 3 \leq 4 \leq \ldots$$

It is trivial to verify that the greater-than-or-equal-to relation is transitive, reflexive, antisymmetric and connected; so it is trivial to verify that the ordering above is linear.

The Bayesian model sees types of credence in exactly the same way. It lines them up from weakest to strongest by their strength. The presupposition involved is that there is a relation which acts on types of credence as the greater-than-or-equal-to relation acts on numbers. This would be something like the being-as-strong-or-stronger-than relation holding between states of credence. We might label this relation with the **bold-face** symbol '$\boldsymbol{\leq}$'. Then the Bayesian picture would be

$$cr_0 \boldsymbol{\leq} \ldots cr_r \boldsymbol{\leq} \ldots cr_1,$$

where **r** can be any real number in the unit interval [0,1] (i.e. the interval stretching from 0 to 1).

On this way of thinking about types of credence, they line up according to strength. Some relation like the is-no-weaker-than relation slots between types of credence, and that relation turns out to be transitive, reflexive, antisymmetric, and connected. Specifically:

| | |
|---|---|
| The *transitivity* of credal strength: | For any $cr_x$, $cr_y$, and $cr_z$: if $cr_x$ is no weaker than $cr_y$, and $cr_y$ is no weaker than $cr_z$, then $cr_x$ is no weaker than $cr_z$. |
| The *reflexivity* of credal strength. For any credence **cr**: | For any credence **cr**: **cr** is no weaker than itself. |
| The *antisymmetry* of credal strength. | For any $cr_x$ and $cr_y$: if $cr_x$ is no weaker than $cr_y$, and $cr_y$ is not equal to $cr_x$, then $cr_y$ is weaker than $cr_x$. |
| The *connectedness* of credence. | For any $cr_x$ and $cr_y$: either $cr_x$ is no weaker than $cr_y$ or $cr_y$ is no weaker than $cr_x$. |

This is what it means—both structurally and conceptually—for the huge infinity of types of credence recognized by the Bayesian model to be linearly ordered. Those types of credence line up by their strength from the weakest to the strongest.

(Aiii) *Precision*: Intuitively: a group of things are precise if they have exact boundaries, if they do not shade into one another. Put the other way around we might say that a group of things are fuzzy if they do *not* have exact boundaries, if they do shade into one another. This way of putting the point can be applied to types of credence just like any other types. We say that types of credence are precise if they do not shade into one another, fuzzy or vague if they do.

To better understand what this comes to, suppose you are faced with a long line of people. Suppose the first person in line is a single day old, the next person in line is two days old, and so on. Suppose there are a huge number of people in the line. Specifically, suppose there are 36,500 people in the line. Setting leap years aside, it follows that the people stretch from a one-day-old newborn to someone who is one hundred years old. But ask yourself this: which of the people in line, exactly, are old?

There is no clear-cut answer to this question. The centurion is old for sure, that much is obvious, and the newborn is certainly not old. But the old folks in line fade into the not-old-folks in line, somehow and somewhere, between these extremes. As we move from centurion to newborn we find no ready-to-spot line between old folks and not-old folks; and this will be so no matter how carefully we examine the folks, no matter how much we learn about their age, and so on. It will be obvious that the centurion is old, that the newborn is not old, but the old/not-old categories will shade into one another murkily between the extremes. The division between old and not-old is ineluctably imprecise. Or as the point is put in the metaphysics classroom: the division between old and not-old is *vague*.

The Bayesian model construes types of credence as entirely un-vague. It sees them as sharp categories which line up from weakest to strongest in an un-blurred fashion. The Bayesian model sees distinct types of credence as manifesting hyper-precise differences in strength. Just as real numbers in the unit interval stand out from one another as punctate entities, always differing precisely in their size, so the Bayesian maintains that types of credence stand out from one another as punctate psychological types, always differing precisely in their strength. On the Bayesian perspective, types of credence do not fade into one another. They manifest levels of strength which are infinitely detailed, and, as a result, they are always sharply differentiated from one another.

For instance, consider the decimal expansion of π. It is known that this expansion involves an infinitely long non-recurring sequence of numbers after its decimal place, something of the form 3.14159... The Bayesian model recognizes a unique credence type the strength of which is exactly measured by what follows the decimal in such an expansion of π. The nature of this type of credence is not only incredibly precise, it is infinitely complex. And all other Bayesian types of credence involve that level of detail. Even being 50% sure manifests this level of complexity, for its strength is measured by an equally never-ending decimal expansion of .50000... Not only does the Bayesian model make use of a huge infinity of types of credence, then, it also views each type of credence as carrying an infinitely detailed functional nature.

In sum: the Bayesian model makes use of an uncountable infinity of types of credence; it sees those types as linearly ordered by strength; and it views that strength, in each case, as infinitely detailed in character. This means the Bayesian model views investment of credence as rather like the investment of infinitely divisible money: just as such money can be stashed in several banks at once, with real numbers measuring its overall configuration, so credence can be lent to several claims at once, with real numbers measuring its overall configuration.

We shall critically investigate this conception of credence in the next chapter. Here we work with a tinker-toy version of the approach on which the underlying psychology can be compressed into a simple equation:

$$(\Psi) \quad \text{con}(\Phi) = \underline{n}, \quad \text{where } 0 \leq \underline{n} \leq 100, \quad \text{with } \underline{n} \text{ a natural number.}$$

On this view, there are exactly one-hundred-and-one levels of confidence: 0% credence, 1% credence, 2% credence, etc. up to 100% credence (i.e. absolutely certainty). This is a far cry from the huge infinity of psychological kinds used in the full-dress version of the Bayesian model. It is nevertheless very much finer-grained than a single-attitude approach like the Belief Model we'll look at in Chapter 5.

## 2.3 The Partition Principle and the Ball Game

Every version of the Bayesian model involves constraints on the configuration of rational credence. Those constraints flow from a single idea. Since that idea looks very close to a conceptual truth, or a truth of logic, Bayesian constraints on the configuration of credence have struck many as a priori. To work up to them consider a claim A and its negation ¬A. Suppose the actual world @ is rolling down a forked path toward these two claims:

Figure 2.2

Either the actual world rolls along to make A true, or it rolls along to make ¬A true. Put another way: the actual world turns out to be either an A-world or a ¬A-world. These look to be logical facts about the actual world, facts which logic alone ensures are the case.

Suppose you've gathered enough evidence to be 90% sure of A. We can thus fill out our picture as in

Figure 2.3

In light of your evidence you are 90% sure that the actual world will go down the left-hand path and make A true. So you are not *certain* that the actual world will go down the left-hand path: your take on A is weaker than certainty. How sure should you be, in this situation, that the actual world will go down the right path instead of the left one? Put another way: how sure should you be in light of your evidence that ¬A is true?

You should be 10% certain of ¬A, of course. Our picture should be fleshed out as in

Figure 2.4

After all, logic ensures that exactly one of the set {A,¬A} is true; and we are supposing that you have gathered evidence which warrants 90% credence in A. This leaves something like a '10% epistemic gap'. Since the left-over uncertainty should attach to A's negation, we have

$$[\mathbf{cr}(A) + \mathbf{cr}(\neg A)] = 100\%.$$

Now consider a different set of claims, not the two-member set {A,¬A} but instead the three-member set {A&C, A&¬C, ¬A}.[3] Logic ensures that exactly one claim in the three-membered set is true as well. We have the following as a logical truth: either A is true together with C, A is true without C, or A is not true at all. The actual world faces a three-way fork in the logical road

---

[3] I use 'C' here rather than 'B' because doing so will help mnemonically in the next section, when we discuss conditional credence. In general I use 'A' and 'C' whenever I need two (names for) exemplar claims (but any two letters would do).

THE PARTITION PRINCIPLE AND THE BALL GAME    27

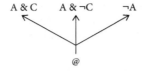

Figure 2.5

Suppose you've gathered enough evidence to be 10% sure that A and C are jointly true and 50% sure that A is false. The picture is then as shown in Figure 2.6.

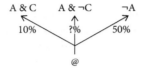

Figure 2.6

In these circumstances, how confident should you be that A is true while C is false, i.e. how sure should you be in (A&¬C)?

You should be 40% sure of the conjunction, of course. The full picture of your situation is shown in

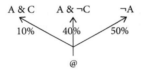

Figure 2.7

Once again your levels of credence should add up to 100%. In the vernacular of probability theory, those levels of credence should 'sum to unity':

$$[\text{cr}(A\&C) + \text{cr}(A\&\neg C) + \text{cr}(\neg A)] = 100\%.$$

Notice that the two-membered set {A,¬A} and the three-membered set {A&C, A&¬C, ¬A} have something in common. In both cases logic ensures that exactly one member of them is true. Sets which have this feature are known as *logical partitions*. Since they are the backbone of the Bayesian theory of states, we pause to explain how they work more fully.

In general, a partition is a division of something into exclusive and exhaustive sub-regions or bits. The spatial region R in Figure 2.8 is partitioned into sub-regions (a) thru (d).

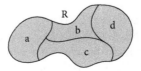

Figure 2.8

The undivided sub-regions are called 'cells' of the drawn partition. For our purposes they have two salient properties. First, they are *exclusive* in the sense that none overlap with one another: (a) is fully distinct from (b), (c) and (d); (b) is fully distinct from (a), (c) and (d); and so on. For this reason being inside one of the cells precludes being inside any of the others. Second, the cells are *exhaustive* in the sense that they add up to the original region out of which they are built. No bit of R fails to land in one of the partitioning cells. Putting them back together yields the original region with which we began.

A logical partition divides logical space into exclusive and exhaustive cells. The set {A, ¬A} is a simple example. It breaks logical space into the region in which A is true and the region in which ¬A is true. There is no overlap between these regions and no bit of logical space is left out. Similarly, the set {A&C, A&¬C, ¬A} is a logical partition in our sense: it breaks logical space into the region in which (A&C) is true, the region in which (A&¬C) is true, and the region in which ¬A is true. There is no overlap between these regions and likewise no bit of logical space left out.

As we have seen, rational credence adds up to 100% across logical partitions. This is an important *pattern* of rational thought which reflects the basic Bayesian constraint in the theory of states. I call it the Credence Partition Principle:

(CPP)  When $\{\Phi_1, \Phi_2, \ldots, \Phi_n\}$ are a logical partition: $[\mathbf{cr}(\Phi_1) + \mathbf{cr}(\Phi_2) + \ldots + \mathbf{cr}(\Phi_n)] = 100\%.$

This is a simple and compelling idea: when claims $\Phi_1$-$\Phi_n$ divide logical space into exclusive and exhaustive regions, fully rational credence adds up to 100% across $\Phi_1$-$\Phi_n$.

Think of the actual world as aimed at ways it could be. Let $\Phi_1$–$\Phi_n$ describe a partitioning of those ways. Then logic ensures that no two of them can be true, and also that at least one of them is true. Let $\mathbf{cr}_1$–$\mathbf{cr}_n$ be credence lent to $\Phi_1$–$\Phi_n$ respectively. We may picture the situation

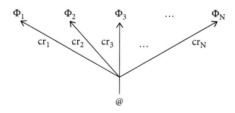

Figure 2.9

The Credence Partition Principle insists

$$[\mathbf{cr}_1 + \mathbf{cr}_2 + \ldots + \mathbf{cr}_n] = 100\%.$$

And in straightforward cases, at least, that seems right. Logic ensures that exactly one of the claims in play is true. No matter how the world turns out, therefore, a fully rational agent will know from logic that exactly one of the $\Phi_i$ is accurate.

Although intuitively plausible, the Credence Partition Principle is highly non-trivial. It entails that fully rational credence is structured like a certain kind of probability function.[4] This is why it is natural to describe the Bayesian model as a theory of *subjective probability*: the phenomenon it describes is subjective in the sense that it concerns our perspectival take on the world; and the phenomenon the model describes is probabilistic in that probability functions can be used to measure grades-of-certainty manifested by fully rational credence.

To understand this properly takes some work. One must develop a feel for the theory of probability as well as the Credence Partition Principle. Then one can see why the latter ensures that credence behaves like a probability measure. In my experience those coming to the area often have difficulty at just this point. They fail to develop an understanding of probability theory and/or the Credence Partition Principle before going on to think critically of the Bayesian model. But this is no good. To assess the model properly one must develop a modicum of insight into how it really works.

We shall introduce the relevant ideas via a game. Specifically, we shall work up to everything relevant here by appeal to the *Ball Game*. We'll see that there are easy-to-spot patterns in the game which echo salient patterns found in the Bayesian model's use of probability theory. Since that use is meant directly to echo the structure of fully rational credence, mastery of the Ball Game induces a feel both for probability theory and, thereby, the Bayesian model's take on full rationality.

The process takes three steps in total. First I explain the Ball Game, then I interpret the game to yield probability theory, then I *re*-interpret the game to yield the Bayesian theory of states.

## 2.4 The Ball Game

Suppose you have a box with two circles in it:

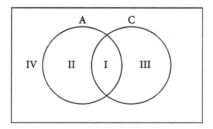

**Figure 2.10**

The circles partition the box, creating four undivided sub-regions I–IV. Suppose you toss 100 balls in the box. The result will be a distribution of balls across its sub-regions. Perhaps it looks as follows:

---

[4] Known as a 'finitely additive' probability function. See (Edgington, 1995) for a gentle introduction to some details.

## 30 THE BAYESIAN MODEL (PROBABILISM)

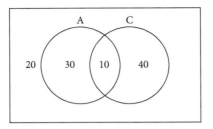

**Figure 2.11**

In the event, your toss of the balls generates a number assignment to sub-regions I–IV of the box; and that number assignment directly echoes the Partition Principle:

$$[10 + 30 + 40 + 20] = 100.$$

Let us use the hash-mark '#' to describe the number of balls in a relevant region. We read '#(X)' to mean 'the number of balls in regions X'. We may then symbolize the distribution of balls laid down by your toss in the following way:

$$[\#(A\&C) + \#(A\&\neg C) + \#(\neg A\&C) + \#(\neg A\&\neg C)] = 100.$$

Since we started with 100 balls and all of them went into the box, numbers associated with your toss add up to the overall number with which we began (100).

There are many ways the balls might land in the box. This means that there are many distributions of balls across sub-regions carved out by circles A and C. Figure 2.11 above shows one of the distributions. A more symmetrical distribution is

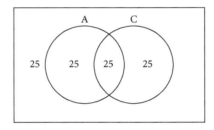

**Figure 2.12**

Here the same number of balls appears in each of the sub-regions above. And again we have

$$[25 + 25 + 25 + 25] = 100,$$

so again we have

$$[\#(A\&C) + \#(A\&\neg C) + \#(\neg A\&C) + \#(\neg A\&\neg C)] = 100.$$

By this stage a pattern in the Ball Game should begin to jump out at you. Let regions $R_1$–$R_n$ partition a box

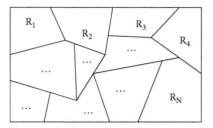

**Figure 2.13**

Now toss 100 balls in the box. This generates a distribution of balls in the box so that

$$[\#(R_1) + \#(R_2) + \ldots + \#(R_n)] = 100.$$

The distribution produced by your toss yields a number associated with each cell $R_i$ of the box's overall internal space. Since we start with 100 balls in play, numbers in that distribution sum back to 100:

$$\sum_{1 \leq i \leq 100} \#(R_i) = 100.$$

This is an instance of the Box Partition Principle:

(BoxPP)  When $R_1, \ldots, R_n$ partition a box:

$$[\#(R_1) + \ldots + \#(R_n)] = 100.$$

This Principle codifies a general pattern in the Ball Game.

There are other general patterns which are easy to see. Just consider the following diagram

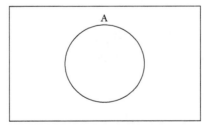

**Figure 2.14**

Circle A splits the box into two sub-regions: inside and outside the circle. For this reason, whenever you toss 100 balls in the box they will always land so that

(a) $\#(A) = [100 - \#(\neg A)]$.

The number of balls which land in the A-circle will be 100 minus the number of balls which land outside the A-circle, exactly in line with the Box Partition Principle. The pattern holds no matter how balls land in the box, no matter what distribution ends up happening. Principle (a) marks a basic pattern in the Ball Game.

## 32 THE BAYESIAN MODEL (PROBABILISM)

Other patterns result from a wrinkle we now add to the Game. Let regions in a box be *shaded* and stipulate that shaded regions are off limits to the balls. This generates further patterns of play in the Ball Game. Consider the following diagram

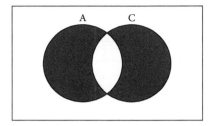

**Figure 2.15**

No matter how you toss 100 balls in the box it is clear that they land so that

(b) #(A) = #(C).

After all, by stipulation balls cannot land in the shaded areas. The (A&¬C) bit of the diagram is shaded like the (C&¬A) bit of the diagram. For this reason, balls can only go into A- or C-circle by landing in both circles at once. Hence pattern (b) holds true no matter how balls land in the box. Once regions II and III are shaded, pattern (b) holds true of all distributions of balls in the box.

Now consider this diagram

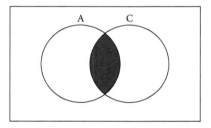

**Figure 2.16**

When you toss 100 balls in the box they will always land so that

(c) #(AvC) = [#(A) + #(C)].

The number of balls in the A- or C-circle will always be identical to the number got by adding the number in the A-circle to the number in the C-circle. After all, the intersection of A and C is shaded: balls cannot go there at all. Those in the A-circle must therefore be outside the C-circle, and those in C-circle must likewise be outside the A-circle. This is why the number of balls in either circle will be the sum of the numbers in regions II and III. Once region I is shaded, pattern (c) will emerge no matter how balls land in the box.

Now consider this diagram

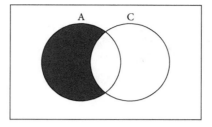

Figure 2.17

No matter how you toss 100 balls in the box they will land so that

(d) #(A)≤#(C).

The number of balls in the A-circle will not exceed the number of balls in the C-circle, since balls cannot go in shaded regions. For this reason balls in the A-circle must be in the C-circle too, hence the number in the former cannot exceed that in the latter. Pattern (d) will hold true in all distributions of balls in the box.

To sum up, then, we have a partition rule and four distribution-of-ball patterns in the Ball Game:

(BoxPP)   When regions $R_1, R_2, \ldots, R_n$ partition the box:

$$\sum_{1 \leq i \leq 100} \#(R_i) = 100\%.$$

(a) #(A) = [100−#(¬A)].
(b) #(A) = #(C),           when (A&¬C) and (C&¬A) are shaded.
(c) #(AvC) = [#(A) + #(C)], when (A&C) is shaded.
(d) #(A) ≤ #(C),           when (A&¬C) is shaded.

Since patterns (a) thru (d) are a consequence of the Box Partition Principle, moreover, we can think of that principle itself as the basic rule of the Ball Game.

*The Ball Game and Probability Theory*

Various patterns in the Ball Game echo laws to be found in probability theory. This is one reason why the Ball Game is useful in depicting how distributions of probability work. The key is to interpret the Ball Game in the correct way. Here is one way to do so.

Think of the box as *logical space* rather than physical space; and think of points in the box as logically possible worlds rather than physical points in a box (or on a page). In other words: think of points in the box as complete ways that the world might turn out to be. Each point in the box then represents a different way the world might turn out to be, a different possible world. Since the box represents logical space as a whole, no logical possibility will be ignored or left out: every full way that things might be, from a logical point of view, will correspond to exactly one point in the box.

Once we think of the box in this manner, we can think of regions in the box as *claims* rather than physical regions in a box (or on a page). We can think of the A-circle, for instance, as the claim that A is true—i.e. as a thing built from logical points or worlds at which A is true; and the same goes for the C-circle or any other sub-region of the Box. After all, the Box itself now represents a logical tautology: we are guaranteed by logic alone that the actual world is one of the points in the box, for it is a truth of logic that the full way things are is a full way they can be.

On this way of looking at the box regions, regions I–IV turn out to be conjunctions built from claims A, C, and their negations. As follows:

$$\begin{aligned} \text{I} &= A\&C \\ \text{II} &= A\&\neg C \\ \text{III} &= \neg A\&C \\ \text{IV} &= \neg A\&\neg C. \end{aligned}$$

In turn these correspond directly to lines in a standard truth-table:

|     | A | C | A&C | A&¬C | ¬A&C | ¬A&¬C |
|-----|---|---|-----|------|------|-------|
| I   | T | T | T   | f    | f    | f     |
| II  | T | f | f   | T    | f    | f     |
| III | f | T | f   | f    | T    | f     |
| IV  | f | f | f   | f    | f    | T     |

In this way such lines partition logical space into four cells; and regions I–IV of the diagram above do exactly the same thing once we think of points in them as full ways the actual world might be. Each of these depictions of a logical partition—the one associated with the box diagram, the one associated with the truth-table—involves a single set of claims: {A&C, A&¬C, ¬A&C, ¬A&¬C}.

This means we may think of balls in the Game as representing something like *percentages of probability*—in particular, we may think of a given ball as representing a single per cent of probability; and we may think of this per cent as landing on the claim represented by the region into which the ball has fallen. Since there are 100 balls in the Game, there are 100 'percentage bits' of probability to play with. By tossing balls in the box we find an interpretation of the Ball Game on which you create a probability distribution across logical space.[5]

For instance, such a distribution might be something like

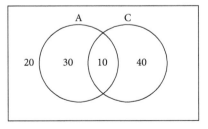

Figure 2.18

Since we are now thinking of the box as logical space, and circles within it as claims about that space, partitioning of the box represents partitioning of logical space by

---

[5] A more accurate representation of the maths here would involve a bucket of infinitely divisible mud being dumped into the box rather than 100 balls, and talk of proportions of the bucket landing in regions of a box rather than number of balls. But we leave these niceties aside for ease of learning.

the claims A and C. For this reason, your distribution makes for a number assignment to cells of a logical partition:

$$[10 + 30 + 40 + 20] = 100.$$

As we might put it:

$$[10\% + 30\% + 40\% + 20\%] = 100\%$$

This is our first probability distribution: $p_1$. We may write it up this way:

$$[p_1(A\&C) + p_1(A\&\neg C) + p_1(\neg A\&C) + p_1(\neg A\&\neg C)] = 100\%.$$

Since tossing balls in the box yields something which represents a probability distribution across cells of a logical partition, and since collections of balls in that representation add up to 100 in number, we have created a representation of the fact that probabilities across cells of a logical partition add up to 100%.

In this representation each way that balls can land in the box represents a way that probability can be spread across logical space. Each distribution of balls represents a probability distribution across that space. Figure 2.18 shows one of them and Figure 2.19 shows the symmetrical one from before.

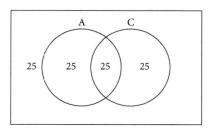

**Figure 2.19**

Now we have 25% probability assigned to each conjunction built from A, C and their negations:

$$[25 + 25 + 25 + 25] = 100.$$

This is our second probability distribution $p_2$. So we have

$$[p_2(A\&C) + p_2(A\&\neg C) + p_2(\neg A\&C) + p_2(\neg A\&\neg C)] = 100\%.$$

Both of these probability distributions—$p_1$ and $p_2$—sum to unity across the partition in play (i.e. they both add up to 100%). We can easily show this with the two rightmost columns of a truth table

|     | A C | A&C | A&¬C | ¬A&C | ¬A&¬C | $p_1$ | $p_2$ |
|-----|-----|-----|------|------|-------|-------|-------|
| I   | T T | T   | f    | f    | f     | 10    | 25    |
| II  | T f | f   | T    | f    | f     | 30    | 25    |
| III | f T | f   | f    | T    | f     | 40    | 25    |
| IV  | f f | f   | f    | f    | T     | 20    | 25    |
|     |     |     |      |      |       | 100%  | 100%. |

## 36  THE BAYESIAN MODEL (PROBABILISM)

The relevant pattern in probability theory should now come into focus.

To see it explicitly let $\Phi_1$-$\Phi_n$ partition logical space. This can be shown with a box partitioned into **n** regions

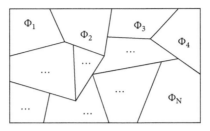

Figure 2.20

or a truth-table having **n** lines:

       R₁   R₂   ...   ...   Rₙ   p

L₁
L₂
*
*
*
*
Lₙ

Distributing probability across cells of the box is equivalent to distributing it down lines of the table. Both stories amount to a spreading of probability across cells of a logical partition. Both depict why the following equations hold

$$[p(R_1) + p(R_2) + \ldots + p(R_n)] = 100\%.$$
$$[p(L_1) + p(L_2) + \ldots + p(L_n)] = 100\%.$$

These equations correspond to the basic law of probability theory. This is the Probability Partition Principle:

(PPP)   When $\Phi_1,\ldots,\Phi_n$ partition logical space: $\Sigma_{1\leq i\leq 100} p(\Phi_i) = 100\%$.

Further laws of probability theory are now easy to spot: we need only interpret shading of regions as impossible combinations of claims, i.e. we need only think of shading as a representation of logical exclusion relations between claims.

For instance, suppose A logically implies C. Then it is impossible for A to be true while C is false. In these circumstances the conjunction A and ¬C is impossible, for the truth of A rules-out the truth of ¬C. The standard diagram for A and C does not reflect that sort of case (Figure 2.21).

With points in the box interpreted as possibilities, region II is composed of (A&¬C)-possibilities. When A entails C, though, there are no such possibilities, no (A&¬C)-worlds. The diagram misses that fact, being insensitive to the entailment from A to C.

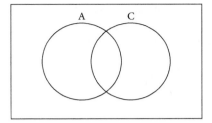

**Figure 2.21**

This is what shading is all about. To show that A entails C we simply shade region II

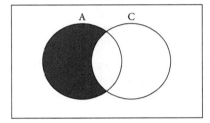

**Figure 2.22**

We stipulate that shaded points are *logically impossible* ways for the world to be. In turn this means that probability is not allowed to go in them. After all, anything impossible as a matter of logic has no chance of being true a priori. Since A entails C, it is a priori that there are no (A&¬C)-possibilities, no (A&¬C)-worlds represented as points in our diagram. Shading is designed to capture this logical fact. By darkening (A&¬C)-bits of the diagram, and disallowing balls from dropping into darkened areas, the Ball Game echoes the fact that positive probability never attaches to the logically impossible.

Now suppose that claims A and C are logically equivalent. Then it is impossible for either to be true without the other being true, and likewise impossible for either to be false without the other being false. The diagram will then look as follows

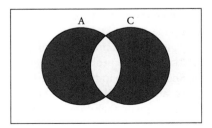

**Figure 2.23**

Since we stipulate that A entails C and vice versa, we stipulate that (A&¬C) is impossible and that (C&¬A) is too. Regions II and III are thus shaded: points in them represent bogus possibilities, for we've stipulated that it is impossible for A to be true without C and vice versa.

Or suppose that A and C are logically incompatible. Then it is impossible for both of them to be true. The diagram of the situation will then be

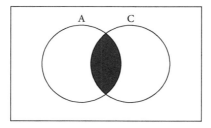

Figure 2.24

Here points in the (A&C)-bit of the diagram represent bogus possibilities; for this reason those points are shaded. And so on.

But now think back to probability theory and consider

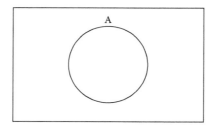

Figure 2.25

The circle partitions the box into two regions. Those regions represent the logical partition {A, ¬A}. No matter how you distribute probability across the diagram we have

(a)  $p(A) = [100\% - p(\neg A)]$.

The probability of A will be 100% minus the probability of ¬A. This is a pattern in all distributions of probability no matter how they turn out. In that sense principle (a) is a *law* of probability theory: for any claim A and probability distribution p, the probability of A equals 100% minus the probability of ¬A.

Or consider Figure 2.26. Shading here indicates that A and C are logically equivalent: across all of logical space, at any possible world, they are either both true or both false. Distribute probability as you will, therefore, it will turn out that

(b)  $p(A) = p(C)$.

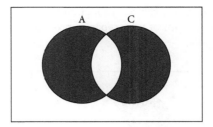

Figure 2.26

When A and C are logically equivalent, then, in every probability distribution, the probability of A equals the probability of C. Since (A&¬C) and (C&¬A) are both shaded, any putative situation in which A is true without C or C is true without A is in fact a bogus possibility. Probability must either be lent to A and C together or to neither at all. Put another way: if probability attaches to A in the first place, it does so by attaching to (A&C); and if probability attaches to C in the first place, it does so by doing the same. Since this will be so no matter how probability distributes, we have before us a pattern in all probability distributions. Principle (b) is a law of probability theory too: logically equivalent claims have the same probability.

Or consider

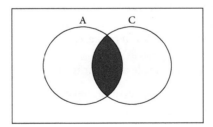

Figure 2.27

The shaded region means A and C are logically incompatible: across all logical possibility they oppose one another in truth-value. As a matter of logic: if A is true, C is false; and if C is true, A is false. No matter how you distribute probability, therefore, the following will be true

(c)  $p(A \vee C) = [p(A) + p(C)]$.

The probability of the disjunction (AvC) will itself equal the probability of A plus the probability of C. After all, probability cannot be lent to shaded areas; and the conjunction (A&C) is itself shaded. So probability lent to A must avoid C and probability lent to C must avoid A. Put another way: if probability attaches to A in the first place, it does so by attaching to (A&¬C); and if probability attaches to C in the first place, it does so by attaching to (C&¬A). Since this will be true no matter how probability distributes, once more we have a pattern in all distributions. Principle (c) is also a law of probability theory: when two claims are logically incompatible, the probability of their disjunction equals the sum of their separate probabilities.

Or consider

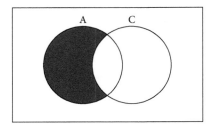

**Figure 2.28**

Here the shaded region means that A logically entails C: across all of logical possibility A is true only if C is as well. No matter how you distribute probability across the diagram, then, the following will be true

(d)  $p(A) \leq p(C)$.

The probability of A will not exceed that of C. After all, probability cannot attach to bogus possibilities, and in this case the conjunction (A&¬C) is such a possibility. Hence probability lent to A must also go to C. Or put another way: if probability attaches to A in the first place, it does so by attaching to (A&C). Since this will be true no matter how probability distributes, we have another pattern in probability distributions. Principle (d) is likewise a law of probability theory: the probability of a claim cannot exceed that of its consequences.

To sum up: we have a partition rule and four lawful patterns in probability theory:

(PPP)  When claims $C_1, \ldots, C_n$ partition logical space:
$\Sigma_{1 \leq i \leq 100} p(C_i) = 100\%$.

(a) $p(A) = [100\% - p(\neg A)]$     for any claims A and C.
(b) $p(A) = p(C)$,     when A and C are equivalent.
(c) $p(A \vee C) = [p(A) + p(C)]$,     when A and C are incompatible.
(d) $p(A) \leq p(C)$,     when A entails C.

Since patterns (a) thru (d) are a consequence of the Probability Partition Principle, moreover, we can think of the principle itself as the basic rule of the probability theory.

## The Ball Game and Bayesian Credence

Lawful patterns in the Ball Game directly echo lawful patterns in probability theory. They also echo Bayesian rules for fully rational credence. Once more the key is to interpret the Ball Game in the right way. This time we begin with an interpretation of the box as logical space and its points as total ways that a world could turn out to be. In line with this we think of regions in the box as representing claims or propositions, and the shading of regions as representing the impossibility of combinations of claims. So far everything is just as before.

But now we think of balls in the game as *fully rational degrees of credence*. On this interpretation tossing balls into the box creates a representation of a credal distribution across logical space. Such a spread of credence might be something like

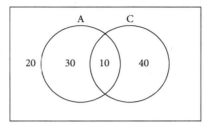

**Figure 2.29**

Once more we have numbers assigned to cells of a logical partition with

$$[10\% + 30\% + 40\% + 20\%] = 100\%.$$

This is our first credence distribution $cr_1$. It makes for a summation to unity in the normal way:

$$[cr_1(A\&C) + cr_1(A\&\neg C) + cr_1(\neg A\&C) + cr_1(\neg A\&\neg C)] = 100\%.$$

On this reading of the game, tossing 100 balls in the box makes for a representation of credence distributed across cells of a logical partition. Since we start with 100 balls, our representation underwrites the idea that rational credence should add up to 100%.

Think of each way that balls can land in the box as a way that credence can spread across logical space. Each distribution of balls depicts a credence distribution across a partition. Figure 2.29 shows one of them, and Figure 2.30 shows the symmetrical distribution from before.

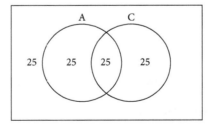

**Figure 2.30**

Now we have 25% credence assigned to each conjunction built from A, C, and their negations. Once more we have

$$[25\% + 25\% + 25\% + 25\%] = 100\%.$$

This is our second credence distribution $cr_2$. On it we have

$$[cr_2(A\&C) + cr_2(A\&\neg C) + cr_2(\neg A\&C) + cr_2(\neg A\&\neg C)] = 100\%.$$

Both our first and our second credence distributions sum to unity across the partition before us. This too can be depicted with a standard truth table

|     | A C | A&C | A&¬C | ¬A&C | ¬A&¬C | $cr_1$ | $cr_2$ |
|-----|-----|-----|------|------|-------|--------|--------|
| I   | T T | [T] | f    | f    | f     | 10     | 25     |
| II  | T f | f   | [T]  | f    | f     | 30     | 25     |
| III | f T | f   | f    | [T]  | f     | 40     | 25     |
| IV  | f f | f   | f    | f    | [T]   | 20     | 25     |
|     |     |     |      |      |       | 100%   | 100%.  |

So the relevant pattern comes into focus once more. Let claims $C_1$–$C_n$ partition logical space; then we can depict this with a box broken into **n** regions

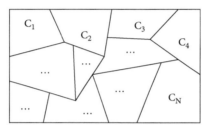

**Figure 2.31**

And we can also depict it with an n-line truth-table:

$$\begin{array}{cccccc} & R_1 & R_2 & \ldots & \ldots & R_n & cr \\ L_1 & & & & & \\ L_2 & & & & & \\ * & & & & & \\ * & & & & & \\ * & & & & & \\ * & & & & & \\ L_n & & & & & \end{array}$$

Distributing balls across cells of the box is equivalent to distributing them down lines of the table. In each case the result can be used to represent a spread of credence across cells of a logical partition. Both of these equations hold

$$[cr(R_1) + cr(R_2) + \ldots + cr(R_n)] = 100\%.$$
$$[cr(L_1) + cr(L_2) + \ldots + cr(L_n)] = 100\%.$$

Thus we arrive at the fundamental law in the Bayesian theory of states, the Credence Partition Principle:

(CrPP) When $C_1, \ldots, C_n$ partition logical space: $\Sigma_{1 \leq i \leq 100} cr(C_i) = 100\%$.

With this principle in place many further patterns of Bayesian credence are easy to spot.

Consider

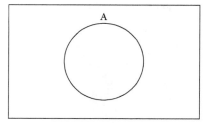

**Figure 2.32**

No matter how you distribute credence

(a)  $cr(A) = [100\% - cr(\neg A)]$.

Credence in A will be identical to 100% minus such credence in ¬A, and this will be true no matter how credence is distributed. The Bayesian theory of states insists that all rational agents invest credence in line with this thought. This is a structural requirement of the theory.

We have stipulated, though, that balls do not go into shaded regions (since points in those regions represent logically bogus possibilities). Since balls represent bits of rational credence, on the Bayesian Model, it follows by the Model's lights that such credence is never lent to such impossibilities. This means still further Bayesian patterns are easy to spot. Consider

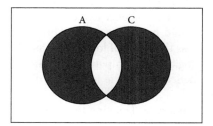

**Figure 2.33**

Under the intended interpretation A and C are logically equivalent: as a matter of logic either both true or both false. The Credence Partition Principle thus entails that no matter how you distribute credence

(b)  $cr(A) = cr(C)$.

When A and C are logically equivalent, the Bayesian theory of states insists that credence in A equals credence in C. Since A being true without C is logically impossible, as well as C being true without A, and since the Bayesian approach insists that credence only be lent to logical possibilities, the Bayesian theory of states requires that credence be lent to A and C in exactly similar fashion. The theory requires that rational agents lend equal credence to logically equivalent claims. This is a structural requirement of the theory.

Or consider this familiar diagram in which A and C logically oppose one another

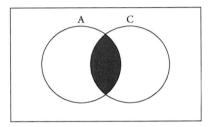

Figure 2.34

The Bayesian model insists that no matter how you distribute your credence

(c)  $cr(AvC) = [cr(A) + cr(C)]$.

Like probability theory itself, the Bayesian theory of states insists that when A and C are logically incompatible credence lent to their disjunction be equal to the sum of credence lent to each disjunct. When A and C are is logically incompatible—when there is no logically possibility that they are both true—the Bayesian theory of states requires that credence lent to (AvC) is equal to the sum of credence lent to A plus credence lent to C. After all, the theory forbids lending credence to bogus possibilities, and we are supposing that the joint truth of A and C is such a possibility. Hence the Bayesian approach insists that credence lent to A must avoid being lent to C, and credence lent to C must avoid being lent to A. This will be true no matter how credence is distributed across the space of logical possibilities. The theory maintains that when A and C are logically incompatible credence lent to their disjunction should be the sum of credence lent to the individual disjuncts. This is a structural requirement of the theory.

Or consider the familiar diagram depicting that A logically entails C

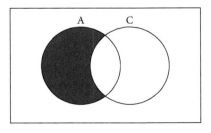

Figure 2.35

In this case there is no possibility of A being true without C being true. Hence the Bayesian theory of states requires that no matter how you distribute credence:

(d) $cr(A) \leq cr(C)$.

The strength of credence lent to A cannot exceed the strength of credence lent to C. When A entails C, the approach insists that pattern (d) lawfully holds in all rational distributions of credence. Bayesians insists that credence lent to a claim should not exceed credence lent to any of its consequences.

To sum up: we have a credence partition rule and four lawful patterns in the Bayesian theory of states:

(CrPP) When claims $C_1,\ldots,C_n$ partition logical space:
$$\sum_{1\leq i\leq 100} cr(C_i) = 100\%.$$

(a) $cr(A) = [100\% - cr(\neg A)]$.
(b) $cr(A) = cr(C)$,              when A and C are equivalent.
(c) $cr(A \vee C) = [cr(A) + cr(C)]$    when A and C are incompatible.
(d) $cr(A) \leq cr(C)$               when A entails C.

These patterns are meant to hold in all rational distributions of credence; and once again they are consequences of a partition rule in play. This is why the Credence Partition Principle is the backbone of the Bayesian theory of states.

## 2.5 Conditional Credence

In addition to working with the notion of credence, the Bayesian theory of states makes heavy use of a derivative notion called 'conditional credence'. The easiest way to understand this idea is to begin with an example and work through some details. So suppose you belong to a crack team of parachute commandos. Your 100-strong team is to be dropped into battle, and, naturally, the Drop Zone looks like a four-celled partition of logical space (Figure 2.36).

After being briefed on the mission by the Commanding Oracle, you are rationally certain that section C of the Drop Zone leads to Certain death. You know the A-section of the Drop Zone overlaps with the C-section, of course, and this leads you initially to suspect that the A-section is also dangerous. But the Oracle insists that the non-C bit of the A-section is fully safe. She tells you as well that areas outside the

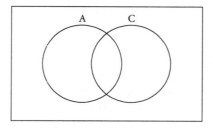

Figure 2.36

46   THE BAYESIAN MODEL (PROBABILISM)

A- and C-sections are also safe. Suppose you know that your team is to be distributed randomly this way

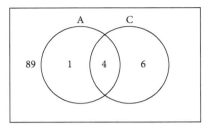

**Figure 2.37**

Should you be worried for your life?

Well, you should be 10% sure that you will land in the certain-death section of the Drop Zone, since you know that 10 random members of your team will land there. This means there is a non-trivial chance you are headed to your death. As we might put it

$$\mathbf{cr}(C) = 10\%.$$

On the other hand, you should start out 90% sure that you are *not* one of those who will land in the certain-death section of the Drop Zone. You should be 90% sure that you will come out of the mission just fine:

$$\mathbf{cr}(\neg C) = 90\%.$$

By your lights, then, things are bad but not completely hopeless: some of your team will die, the majority will live, you will very likely survive.

Suppose the Oracle then leans over and whispers in your ear: 'Good news soldier! You're on the A-team! You will land in the A-bit of the Drop Zone.' This is very bad news. After all, you know that 4 out of 100 commandos will land in the certain-death C-section of the Drop Zone, and you know they will do so *by* landing in its A-section. This is why you start out 4% sure that you will land in the intersection of the A- and C-bits of the Drop Zone:

$$\mathbf{cr}(A\&C) = 4\%.$$

But you also know that 5 out of 100 commandos will land in the A-bit of the Drop Zone. This is why you start out 5% sure that you will land in the A-bit of the Drop Zone:

$$\mathbf{cr}(A) = 5\%.$$

Intuitively, these two things together amount to your initial conviction that there is a 4 in 5 chance of you landing in the certain-death C-bit of the Drop Zone, *if* you land in the A-bit of that Zone. Put another way: your initial credences for (A&C) and A jointly lead to an 80% conviction that you will land in the C-section of the Drop Zone *given* (or on the supposition or assumption that) you land in the A-bit of that Zone. After all:

CONDITIONAL CREDENCE 47

$$80\% = 4\%/5\%.$$

The Bayesian theory of states shortens this ratio fact about credence with a definition:

$$80\% = 4\%/5\% = cr(A\&C)/cr(A) =_{df.} cr(C/A).$$

This is an instance of the theory's Conditional Credence Rule.

Putting things back-to-front, and a bit more generally, the rule says that for any claims A and C:

(cr/)  $cr(C/A) =_{df.} cr(A\&C)/cr(A)$,  when $cr(A)$ is non-zero.

This rule creates a definitional tie between credence and the Bayesian notion of conditional credence. The latter is defined as a ratio of the former. When non-zero credence is lent to a claim A, the strength of conditional credence lent to a claim C is defined as the strength got by taking the strength of credence lent to the conjunction of A and C and dividing that by the strength of credence lent to claim A.

The Conditional Credence Rule mimics the standard definition of conditional probability in orthodox mathematics. According to that definition:

(p/)  $p(C/A) =_{df.} p(A\&C)/p(A)$,  when $p(A)$ is non-zero.

To make sense of the relevant idea, let $n_1$–$n_4$ be numbers between 0 and 100. Suppose you toss 100 balls in a box with $n_1$ of them landing in region I, $n_2$ of them landing in region in II, $n_3$ of them landing in region in III, and so on. Pictorially this means

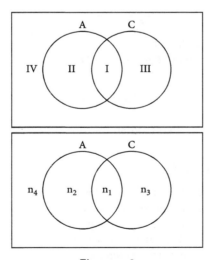

Figure 2.38

Then we can see straightaway that

$$\#(C/A) =_{df.} \#(A\&C)/\#(A).$$

48   THE BAYESIAN MODEL (PROBABILISM)

On the left-hand side of this equation we have something intuitively like the proportion of A-balls which are C-balls too. That is precisely what we find on the right-hand side of the equation. When p(A) is greater than zero, we thus have

$$p(C/A) =_{df.} p(A\&C)/p(A).$$

To see why the proviso is needed—the one requiring that p(A) be positive—suppose you pick up balls and toss them again, but this time none happen to land inside A. Then there will be no such thing as the proportion of A-balls which are C-balls too, for there will be no such thing as A-balls to begin with. The number of C-balls conditional on them being A-balls makes no sense, it's literally undefined. This is why a proviso is needed in the definition of Conditional Probability.[6]

The full Bayesian theory of states is now easy to make explicit. The model says that fully rational credence sums to unity across logical partitions, and it defines conditional credence via a ratio of fully rational credence. The approach has one basic rule and one stipulation:

(CrPP)   When $\{P_1, \ldots, P_n\}$ are a logical partition:
         $[cr(P_1) + cr(P_2) + \ldots + cr(P_n)] = 100\%$,

(cr/)    $cr(C/A) =_{df.} cr(A\&C)/cr(A)$,   when $cr(A)$ is non-zero.

So we may picture the Bayesian theory of states as in Figure 2.39.

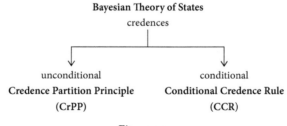

Figure 2.39

Our next task is to spell out the Bayesian transition theory.

## 2.6 The Marble Game

Although the Bayesian transition theory can look formally daunting, it is quite simple at bottom. And just as reflection on a child-like game—the Ball Game presented earlier in this chapter—can be used to develop a solid feel for the Bayesian theory of states, so reflection on a similar game can be used to develop a feel for the Bayesian transition theory. This is the *Marble Game*.

---

[6] By this stage the initiate will be chomping at the bit. Definitions are true by stipulation, after all, and there are strong reasons to worry about the definitional status of ratio formulae like those just rehearsed. These will be examined in the next chapter.

# THE MARBLE GAME 49

To see how it works, suppose the top of a table slopes gently from a point marked 'Start' to a region marked 'Finish'. Suppose a forking pattern of grooves is carved into the table which runs from its Start point to its Finish region. Imagine the table looks something like this

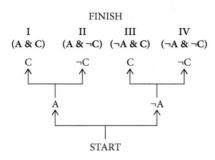

Figure 2.40

When the Marble Game is played, marbles are placed at the Start point and left to roll through the forking paths to the Finish region. When doing so the marbles must negotiate a pair of forks in the road: first they must go either left down the A-path or right down the ¬A-path, and then—no matter how that fork is negotiated—marbles must go either left down a C-path or right down a ¬C-path.

Suppose there is a machine inside the table which fixes objective chances of negotiating a given fork in the road. Those chances determine how objectively likely it is that a marble will go left or go right at a given fork in the road. Suppose further that the machine's original set-up looks as in Figure 2.41.

We may then define overall paths thru the tree-like structure as follows: path I is the route taken when a marble goes left and then left again through the overall tree; path II is the route taken when a marble goes left and then right through the overall tree; path III is the route taken when a marble goes right and then left through the overall tree; and path IV is the route taken when a marble goes right and then right through the overall tree.

What are the chances that a given marble will go down each of these paths in the Marble Game. Well, Figure 2.41 depicts explicitly that there is an 80% chance a

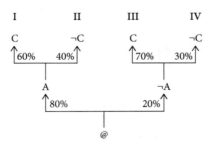

Figure 2.41

marble will take the A-path when faced with the initial fork in the road, as well as a 20% chance that it will not take that path (because it takes the ¬A-path instead). The Figure also depicts that there is a 60% chance that a marble will take a C-path after taking the A-path, as well as a 40% chance that it will not do so (because it takes the ¬C-path instead). The Figure depicts that there is a 70% chance a marble will take a C-path after taking the ¬A-path, as well as a 30% chance that it will not do so (because it takes a ¬C-path instead). Hence we can think of Figure 2.41 as depicting two sorts of things: unconditional chance of left/right at the initial fork in the structure, and conditional chance of left-right further down in the grooves.

Recall a machine inside the table sets initial probabilities for the Marble Game. Eventually we'll let them shift across time, so we'll call the initial one the 'old' probabilities. The machine inside the table fixes it so that there is initially a 60% chance of an 80% chance that a marble will take path I through the tree structure:

$$\mathbf{P}_{old}(I) = 60\% \times 80\% = 48\%.$$

We may think of this as the old-probability that (A&C) is true. The machine fixes the fact that there is a 40% chance of an 80% chance that a marble will take path II through the tree:

$$\mathbf{P}_{old}(II) = 40\% \times 80\% = 32\%.$$

We may think of this as the old-probability that (A&¬C) is true. And so on. Thus it is that we have

$$\mathbf{P}_{old}(III) = 70\% \times 20\% = 14\%,$$

and

$$\mathbf{P}_{old}(IV) = 30\% \times 20\% = 6\%.$$

Let us place these facts in a diagram of the Game's initial set-up (Figure 2.42).

### Original Probability Distribution Pold

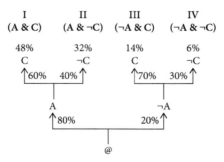

Figure 2.42

There is an easy-to-spot pattern manifested four times in this figure. The pattern links the chance of a conjunction with that of one conjunct together with the chance of the other conjunct given the first. Here are the four instances of the pattern:

$$p_{old}(I) = p_{old}(A\&C) = p_{old}(A) \times p_{old}(C/A),$$
$$p_{old}(II) = p_{old}(A\&\neg C) = p_{old}(A) \times p_{old}(\neg C/A),$$
$$p_{old}(III) = p_{old}(\neg A\&C) = p_{old}(\neg A) \times p_{old}(C/\neg A)$$
$$p_{old}(IV) = p_{old}(\neg A\&\neg C) = p_{old}(\neg A) \times p_o(\neg C/\neg A)$$

This pattern corresponds to what we'll call the *Conjunction Rule for Probability*. According to that rule, for any claims A and C:

(p&)   $p(A\&C) = p(A) \times p(C/A)$,   when $p(A)$ is non-zero.

The identity holds in all probability distributions and the Marble Game dramatizes why that is so.

Now have a look back at Figure 2.42: many chances appear explicitly in the Figure. The chances of A and of ¬A can be spotted straight off, as can the following conditional chances: C given A, ¬C given A, C given ¬A, and ¬C given ¬A. But the chance of C itself is *not* given explicitly in Figure 2.42. So ask yourself this: when the machine in the table fixes objective probabilities in line with the Figure, what does the resulting original probability set-up make of the claim that a marble will go down some C-path or other? As we might put it: what is the initial value for $p_{old}(C)$?

Well, there are two C-paths in the game: one involving the initial A-branch in the tree structure, the other involving the initial ¬A-branch in that structure. Marbles take a C-path in the Game by taking either path I through the tree or path III through the tree. There is no other way to take a C-path. The initial probability that a marble will take a C-path is thus the chance that it will take path I together with the chance that it will take path III:

(p*)   $p_{old}(C) = [p_{old}(A\&C) + p_{old}(\neg A\&C)] = 62\%$.

Our initial probability distribution lends a 62% chance to the claim that a marble will take a C-path, for it lends a 48% chance to the claim that it will do so by first going down the A-path, and it lends a 14% chance to the claim that it will do so by first going down the ¬A-path. Put another way: our initial probability distribution lends a 48% chance to (A&C) and a 14% chance to (¬A&C), with those incompatible conjunctions corresponding to the only two ways that a C-path can be taken in the Marble Game. Hence the chance of a C-path is the sum of the respective chances for the incompatible conjunctions.

But notice: the Conjunction Rule lets us *rewrite* (p*), since (p*) builds a chance for C by adding chances for each of a pair of conjunctions. The Conjunction Rule builds up those very chances by appeal to a pair of products of still further chances (found at lines ($p_{old}$-i) and ($p_{old}$-iii) above). So we can rewrite (p*) by substituting the products which pin down the chance of each conjunction in question. This yields:

(p**)   $p_{old}(C) = [p_{old}(A\&C) + p_{old}(\neg A\&C)] = 62\%$.

*This equation is central to the Bayesian transition theory.*

52  THE BAYESIAN MODEL (PROBABILISM)

Think of it this way. In the Marble Game the chance that a marble will take a C-path is itself identical to the chance that the marble goes down path I plus the chance that it goes down path III. In turn this is because the (A&C)-path and the (¬A&C)-path are the only C-paths in the Game. Line ($p_{old}$-i) makes it clear that the chance of path I is itself identical to the chance that the marble takes the A-path times the chance that it takes the C-path given it takes the A-path, while line ($p_{old}$-iii) makes it clear that the chance of path III is itself identical to the chance that the marble takes the ¬A-path times the chance that it takes the C-path given it takes the ¬A-path. The equation at ($p^{**}$) simply puts these pieces together. It calculates the chance of C by adding the chance of path I to the chance of path III, and by using the products which pin down these very path-chances.

Now suppose the chance-fixing machine in the table *changes* probabilities at the A/¬A-fork. Suppose it raises the chance that a marble will take the A-path from 80% to 90%, and thus lowers the chance that a marble will take the ¬A-path from 20% to 10%. This will create a new set-up on the table, a new version of the Marble Game. That new version will be built from old chances left untouched on the table together with new ones re-set by the machine

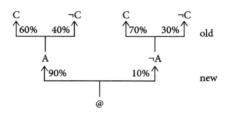

Figure 2.43

The A/¬A-fork is now governed by a new pair of chances while the C/¬C-forks are governed by old pairs of chance fixed in the initial round by the machine. Overall paths through the tree, in the new set-up, thus receive chances pinned down by old conditional chances together with new chances for the A/¬A-fork in the road. As follows:

$$p_{new}(I) = p_{new}(A\&C) = p_{new}(A) \times p_{old}(C/A) = 90\% \times 60\% = 54\%$$
$$p_{new}(II) = p_{new}(A\&\neg C) = p_{new}(A) \times p_{old}(\neg C/A) = 90\% \times 40\% = 36\%$$
$$p_{new}(III) = p_{new}(\neg A\&C) = p_{new}(\neg A) \times p_{old}(C/\neg A) = 10\% \times 70\% = 7\%$$
$$p_{new}(IV) = p_{new}(\neg A\&\neg C) = p_{new}(\neg A) \times p_{old}(\neg C/\neg A) = 10\% \times 30\% = 3\%.$$

These equations all display a pattern in the Marble Game. That pattern leads to our first rule-of-change for the Game:

> (Change-1)  When the original probability distribution lends A some chance, and the machine then *changes that chance*, the new chance of a

conjunction (X&Y), built from A/¬A and C/¬C respectively, will be the new chance of X times the old chance of Y given X. Or in other words: $p_{new}(X\&Y) = p_{new}(X) \times p_{old}(Y/X)$.

Instances of this rule-of-change occur at lines ($p_{new}$-i)-($p_{new}$-iv) above. Once the machine changes chance at the A/¬A-fork in the Game, however, what happens to the chance that a marble will take a C-path in the tree?

Well, since paths I and III are the only C-paths in the game, the new chance for C is fixed by new chances for these paths. Our rule (Change-1) shows how the new path-chances are themselves fixed by old conditional chances together with new chances for the A/¬A-fork in the road. Specifically:

$$p_{new}(I) = p_{new}(A\&C) = p_{new}(A) \times p_{old}(C/A),$$

and

$$p_{new}(III) = p_{new}(\neg A\&C) = p_{new}(\neg A) \times p_{old}(C/\neg A).$$

Once the machine has changed the chances at the A/¬A-fork in the road, therefore, the new chance that a C-path is taken is then a sum of new path-chances for path I and path III (i.e. it is a sum of the only C-paths available in the Game). This leads to our second rule-of-change in the Game:

(Change-2)   When the original probability distribution lends A some chance, and the machine then *changes that chance*, the new chance of C will be the new chance of path (I) plus the new chance of path (III). In other words:
$$p_{new}(C) = \{[p_{new}(A) \times p_{old}(C/A)] + [p_{new}(\neg A) \times p_{old}(C/\neg A)]\}.$$

Compare this with principle (p**) above. That principle calculates a chance for C by adding a chance for path I to a chance for path III. Those path-chances are in turn calculated by appeal to products of chances found on the way of each path. That is exactly what happens in our second rule-of-change (Change-2). It calculates a new chance for C by adding a new chance for path I to a new chance for path III, and products are used fix chances for each path. Those products use still further chances, of course, with some of them being recently fixed by the machine, and others being residue from our initial set-up in the Game. So new path-chances for paths I and III are a function of old and new chances. After the chance of A has been shifted, the chance of C is fixed by old and new chances in the Game. This represents the Bayesian transition theory for rational credence. Showing this is our next task.

## 2.7 The Bayesian Transition Theory: Jeffrey's Rule

The Bayesian approach to rational shift in view echoes the Marble Game. Rational credence is said to react to new evidence as C-chances react to a shift in A-chances in the Game. This is why the Game can be used to develop a feel for Bayesian transitions.

To see this, suppose you are a rational agent with the following initial credence distribution: you are 80% sure of A, 20% sure of ¬A, 60% sure of C given A, and 70%

54 THE BAYESIAN MODEL (PROBABILISM)

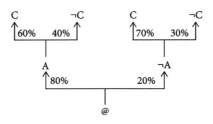

Figure 2.44

sure of C given ¬A. In the event, you will be 40% sure of ¬C given A and 30% sure of ¬C given ¬A. Your take on things may be pictured as in Figure 2.44.

Think of your take on things as involving a 'logical tree'. Each branch-point in the tree consists in a two-way logical partition. The Bayesian model insists—via its Credence Partition Principle—that your credence spread across such a two-way partition so that it sums to 100%. That is how your initial take on things works out.

In a sense you see the world as facing a four-way partition of its future: it can work out so that A and C are true together, work out so that A and C are false together, work out so that A is true while C is false, or work out so that A is false while C is true. (Of course these are just the four lines of the A/C truth-table.) Since you are 80% sure that the world ends-up making A is true, you are 20% sure that it ends-up making ¬A is true. Since you are 60% sure that the world ends-up making C true given it makes A true, you are only 40% sure that the world ends-up making ¬C true given it makes A true. And since you are 70% sure that the world ends-up making C true given it makes ¬A true, you are only 30% sure that the world ends-up making ¬C true given it makes ¬A true. These are the relevant details of your original rational distribution of credence. Since it is about to be replaced with a new distribution, let us call the original one '$cr_{old}$'.

Consider your take on paths through the A/C logical tree. How confident are you in your original distribution that the world travels down paths I–IV respectively? Well, things go here exactly as they did in the Marble Game, only now we are dealing in fully rational credence rather than objective chance. Specifically

$$cr_{old}(I) = cr_{old}(A\&C) = 80\% \times 60\% = 48\%.$$

$$cr_{old}(II) = cr_{old}(A\&\neg C) = 80\% \times 40\% = 32\%.$$

$$cr_{old}(III) = cr_{old}(\neg A\&C) = 20\% \times 70\% = 14\%,$$

$$cr_{old}(IV) = cr_{old}(\neg A\&\neg C) = 20\% \times 30\% = 6\%.$$

Let us put these facts about your initial credence distribution into a diagram (See Figure 2.45).

The same pattern manifests itself that we saw before, only now it plays out for rational credence rather than chance. There is a link between credence lent to a conjunction, credence lent to one of its conjunct, and credence lent to the other conjunct given the first conjunct is true:

## THE BAYESIAN TRANSITION THEORY: JEFFREY'S RULE 55

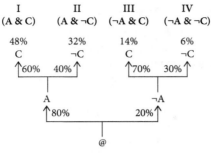

Figure 2.45

$(cr_{old}-i)\ cr_{old}(I) = cr_{old}(A\&C) = cr_{old}(A) \times cr_{old}(C/A),$

$(cr_{old}-ii)\ cr_{old}(II) = cr_{old}(A\&\neg C) = cr_{old}(A) \times cr_{old}(\neg C/A),$

$(cr_{old}-iii)\ cr_{old}(III) = cr_{old}(\neg A\&C) = cr_{old}(\neg A) \times cr_{old}(C/\neg A)$

$(cr_{old}-iv)\ cr_{old}(IV) = cr_{old}(\neg A\&\neg C) = cr_{old}(\neg A) \times cr_{old}(\neg C/\neg A)$

The Bayesian theory of states insists that fully rational credence acts like probability. So the theory endorses the *Conjunction Rule for credence*:

$(cr\&)\quad cr(A\&C) = cr(A) \times cr(C/A),\quad$ when $cr(A)$ is non-zero.

Now look back at Figure 2.45: many credences appear explicitly in the Figure. Credence lent to A and to ¬A can be spotted straight off, as can various conditional credences. But Figure 2.45 contains no explicit number for credence lent to C. So ask yourself this: when credence is lent to other things in line with the explicit numbers in Figure 2.45, what credence should also be lent to claim C? What is the appropriate value for $cr_{old}(C)$?

Well, logic guarantees that there are exactly two ways in which the world might make C true: either with A or without A (i.e. with A or with ¬A). The first way of making C true involves path I in Figure 2.45, the second involves path III. Since the paths are exclusive and exhaustive options, the Credence Partition Principle entails that fully rational credence in C should add-up from them. We have

$(cr^*)\quad cr_{old}(C) = [cr_{old}(A\&C) + cr_{old}(\neg A\&C)] = 62\%.$

You are 62% sure of C, lending 48% credence to C being true with A and 14% credence to C being true with ¬A.

The Conjunction Rule allows us to rewrite principle (cr*). Since credence lent to C is a function of credence lent to a pair of conjunctions—as in (cr*)—and credence lent to those conjunctions is itself a product of further credence—as in ($cr_{old}$-i) and ($cr_{old}$-iii)—we can rewrite (cr*) by substituting products which fix credence for each conjunction involved. Then we have

## 56 THE BAYESIAN MODEL (PROBABILISM)

(**cr\*\***) $\mathrm{cr_{old}}(C) = \{[\mathrm{cr_{old}}(A) \times \mathrm{cr_{old}}(C/A)] + [\mathrm{cr_{old}}(\neg A) \times \mathrm{cr_{old}}(C/\neg A)]\} = 62\%$.

*This principle is central to the Bayesian transition theory.*

Think of it this way. The world has exactly two ways to make C true: either with A or with ¬A. Those ways of making C true correspond to paths I and III of the A/C logical tree. Credence in C should add up from the options for C in that tree. Line ($\mathrm{cr_{old}}$-i) details how that works for the first option. Line ($\mathrm{cr_{old}}$-iii) details how it works for the second. Principle (**cr\*\***) puts these pieces together and calculates a level of credence for C by adding one for path I to another for path III. In doing so the principle uses products which fix credence for each path in the case to hand.

Now, suppose you get new information which rationally *shifts* your take on A from 80% certainty to 90% certainty. The new information leads you rationally to be more confident in A. How should this shift in your take on A—this upping of your credence for A—percolate through the rest of your credence distribution? How should your new take on other things be shifted in light of your new take on A?

The Bayesian model answers this question with a simple thought. When your take on A has been rationally shifted, but nothing else in your worldview has being perturbed, your new take on a claim C should build from the A/C-tree in the usual way; but that tree should itself involve your new take on A plus your *old* take on C/¬C given A, since by stipulation conditional credence has not been perturbed—since by stipulation, in other words, it is only your take on A which has changed by new evidence. So we have

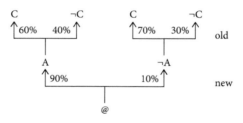

**Figure 2.46**

In this distribution some kind of input has led to new credence at the A/¬A-fork in the tree. It has not led to any shift in the forks downstream in the structure. Input has had no impact on conditional credence at all, and that's why we find old values sitting on top of new ones above. But this means that *paths* through the logical tree receive credence fixed by values drawn from your old and your new take on things. As follows:

($\mathrm{cr_{new}}$ – i)  $\mathrm{cr_{new}}(I) = \mathrm{cr_{new}}(A\&C) = \mathrm{cr_{new}}(A) \times \mathrm{cr_{old}}(C/A) = 90\% \times 60\% = 54\%$

($\mathrm{cr_{new}}$ – ii)  $\mathrm{cr_{new}}(II) = \mathrm{cr_{new}}(A\&\neg C) = \mathrm{cr_{new}}(A) \times \mathrm{cr_{old}}(\neg C/A) = 90\% \times 40\% = 36\%$

($\mathrm{cr_{new}}$ – iii)  $\mathrm{cr_{new}}(III) = \mathrm{cr_{new}}(\neg A \& C) = \mathrm{cr_{new}}(\neg A) \times \mathrm{cr_{old}}(C/\neg A) = 10\% \times 70\% = 7\%$

($\mathrm{cr_{new}}$ – iv)  $\mathrm{cr_{new}}(IV) = \mathrm{cr_{new}}(\neg A \& \neg C) = \mathrm{cr_{new}}(\neg A) \times \mathrm{cr_{old}}(\neg C/\neg A) = 10\% \times 30\% = 3\%$.

These equations display a transition pattern in the Bayesian model. It is captured in our first Bayesian Transition Rule:

(BT1) When an original distribution lends A some credence, and new input then rationally *changes that credence*, then, in those circumstances, new credence lent to a conjunction (X&Y)—built from A/¬A and C/¬C respectively—will be the new credence of X times the old credence of Y on the assumption that X is true. In other words: $p_{new}(X\&Y) = p_{new}(X) \times p_{old}(Y/X)$.

Instances of (BT1) occur at lines ($cr_{new}$−i) − ($cr_{new}$−iv). But what should happen to your take on C, after input has changed your take on A? Well, recall the logical tree built from A and C. There are only two ways in the tree that C can be made true: either with A or without A. Paths I and III in the tree correspond to the two ways in which C can be true. Your new take on C should add up from your take on whether C turns out to be true along with A, plus your take on whether C turns out to be true along with ¬A. Rule (BT1) shows how your take on these conjunctive questions are fixed by old conditional credence together with new credence for A. Specifically:

$$cr_{new}(I) = cr_{new}(A\&C) = cr_{new}(A) \times cr_{old}(C/A),$$

and

$$cr_{new}(III) = cr_{new}(\neg A\&C) = cr_{new}(\neg A) \times cr_{old}(C/\neg A).$$

Your new credence for C should add-up from your take on the two ways that C might be true: with A or with ¬A. In turn your new take on each of these ways that C might be true should itself be the product of your new take on A and your old take on C given A/¬A.

This leads directly to the fundamental Bayesian transition rule—first proposed by the philosopher Richard Jeffrey—which has come to be known as *Jeffrey Conditionalization*:

(J-Cond) When your original credence distribution lends A in-between credence, but new input rationally shifts your view to a new in-between credence, then, in those circumstances, your new take on any claim C should line up with your new take on A together with your old take on C given A/¬A. Specifically: $cr_{new}(C) = \{[cr_{new}(A) \times cr_{old}(C/A)] + [cr_{new}(\neg A) \times cr_{old}(C/\neg A)]\}$.[7]

Compare this with principle (cr\*\*) above. The latter calculates a credence for C by adding together a credence for path I in the A/C-tree and a credence for path III in that tree. In turn those credences are calculated by appeal to products of credences found along the way of each path. In effect Jeffrey Conditionalization calculates a new credence for C by adding a new credence for (A&C) to a new credence for (¬A&C), with products being used to fix credence for each of those conjunctions. The products involve credence recently fixed by new input as well as conditional credence left

---

[7] For a different but likewise intuitive explanation of Jeffrey's rule, see the last section of Chapter 4, where that rule is generalized to cover shift of conditional credence too.

unchanged by that input. Hence Jeffrey Conditionalization sees your new take on C as fixed by your old take on C given A, your old take on C given ¬A, and your new take on A/¬A fork in the road.

## 2.8 A Matching Psychology: Creda

In Chapter 1 we noted that any full-dress theory of rationality will have three major moving parts: a theory of states, a transition theory, and linking theory (i.e. a story about how the first two things fit together). The theoretical template is this

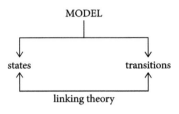

**Figure 2.47**

In this chapter we've seen how the Bayesian model fills out the template

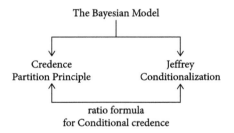

**Figure 2.48**

In Chapter 1 we also noted that it's helpful for three things to be true of a formal model:

1. basic facts in its target domain are explicitly marked by basic elements in the model;
2. derivative facts in its target domain are explicitly marked by derivative elements in the model;
3. derivative facts in the target domain are grounded in target basic targets so that grounding relations are mirrored between markers and what's being marked.

When all of these things happen a model *metaphysically matches* its target domain; and when a model so matches its target domain one can read off from the surface of the model how derivative and basic facts in the target domain fit together. Question: what would it take for a target psychology to be so matched by the Bayesian model?

Well, it would have to consist in basic states of mind marked explicitly by basic elements of the model; it would have to consist in derivative states of mind marked by derivative elements of the model; and these two aspects of the target domain would have to fit together grounding-wise as their markers do in the model. When thinking about a target domain matched by the Bayesian model, therefore, it helps to start with this question: what is the fundamental moving part of the model?

It is the probability function. The Bayesian theory of states characterizes an overall configuration of credence with such a function; and its outputs are meant to mark strength-of-credence lent to claims in the function's domain. The basic kind of mental state meant to be marked by the approach is thus credence. Jeffrey Conditionalization is then meant to characterize how an overall configuration of credence should change when perturbed by new input. And the ratio definition of conditional credence hooks up the model's approach to states with its approach to state-transitions.

To see how this might match the workings of a hypothetical creature, suppose we are faced with an unusual individual: Creda.[8] She invests credence in whatever functional sense we do, and her states of credence are psychologically basic. Creda thinks in a language-like system of inner representations—a language-of-thought, so to say—and she has a gigantic transparent head. Within that head there are one hundred and one smaller transparent boxes, marked '0', '1', '2', etc. These are the credence boxes of Creda's psychology. She lends $n$% credence to a claim C by placing a C-meaning sentence of her language-of-thought in the '$n$-box', i.e. the credal box marked '$n$'. We stipulate that whenever a C-meaning sentence is in Credas's $n$-box she thereby manifests the signature function of $n$% credence lent to C (whatever that turns out to be). But this is just a fancy way of saying that Creda's boxes have a functional cash-value identical to that of credence in humans. We stipulate further that sentences in Creda's boxes satisfy the Credence Partition principle, and they shift en masse in line with Jeffrey Conditionalization.

In the event, the Bayesian model metaphysically matches Creda's psychology. We have reverse engineered her to ensure this is so. The fundamental marking element in the Bayesian theory of states is the probability value. This corresponds to the basic mental element in Creda's psychology: credence. Various derivative elements of Creda's psychology are likewise marked by derivative elements of the Bayesian model—chief among them will be conditional probability and comparative probability—so let us consider them in turn.

When a credence function in the Bayesian theory of states lends 80% probability to claim A, for instance, and also lends 60% probability to the conjunction A&C, the ratio of the latter probability to the former is automatically 75%. This ratio fact exists the moment the two more fundamental facts about probability are in place. The Bayesian credence function thus generates a derivative conditional probability for C given A. This exactly mimics how conditional credence gets off the ground in Creda's psychology. When she has an A-meaning sentence of her

---

[8] Creda is based on a highly influential thought-experiment by Stephen Schiffer, first put forward in his 'Truth and Theory of Content' (1981). In §5.8 we cook-up a similar creature to match the Belief Model: Bella.

language-of-thought in a credal-box the strength of which is 80% that of certainty, and she has an (A&C)-meaning sentence of her language-of-thought in a credal-box the strength of which is 60% that of certainty, the ratio of the latter's strength to the former's is automatically 75%. This ratio fact is likewise there the moment the two states of credence are in place. Creda's psychology thus generates a derivative state of credence for C given A. The Bayesian theory of states metaphysically matches conditional credence in Creda's mind.

Similarly, when a credence function in the Bayesian theory of states lend 80% probability to A, and 60% probability to C, the comparative probability relation between these two claims will automatically be fixed. Once the probability values are in place, it will thereby be the case that cr(A) is greater than cr(C). It is automatic that .8 is greater than .6, after all, and these are the values for cr(A) and cr(C) respectively. This is exactly how comparative confidence gets off the ground in Creda's psychology. When she has an A-meaning sentence of her language-of-thought in a credal-box the strength of which is 80% that of certainty, and a C-meaning sentence of her language-of-thought in a credal-box the strength of which is 60% that of certainty, comparative confidence for these two claims will be automatically fixed. Once her two states of credence are in place, it will thereby be the case that she is more confident of A than C, for that's all there is to Creda being more confident of one claim than the other.

By design, then, the Bayesian model matches Creda's psychology. It marks fundamental aspects of her mind with basic elements of its machinery, derivative aspects of her mind with derivative elements of its machinery, and the model ensures that fundamental and derivative facts in its target domain fit together like their markers do in the model. In the next chapter we'll explore whether this is a sensible picture of our rational architecture.

# 3
# The Bayesian Theory of States
## Critical Discussion

## 3.1 Preview

The Bayesian model is the best-known model of rational fine-grained attitudes. Its mathematical properties are elegant, extensively investigated, and of permanent use in many areas of theoretical concern (e.g. in the history and philosophy of science). The model has proved to be of intrinsic interest as well as practical worth. Unfortunately is not a fully satisfying formalism of our rational fine-grained attitudes.

This chapter canvasses some of the difficulties faced by the Bayesian theory of states. It argues in the next section that there are more types of rational confidence than credence, i.e. more types of such confidence than point-valued subjective probability. It argues in §3.3 that the ratio-based conception of conditional credence is mistaken. In §3.4 the chapter explores generalizing the Bayesian model by appeal to interval-valued probability functions. §3.5 critiques that generalization by appeal to so-called 'tertiary propositional attitudes' such as comparative confidence. §3.6 explores a further attempt to generalize the Bayesian model by appeal to multiple probability functions rather than a single function, but we'll see that there are serious interpretive difficulties with this approach. By the end of the chapter we'll have a much firmer grip on what a formal model of rational states must do.

## 3.2 Contra Bayesian States: One Type of Fine-grained Attitude?

There is a curious symmetry in the epistemology of coarse- and fine-grained attitudes. A common thought in the former—as we'll see in Chapter 5—is that there is really only one basic kind of coarse attitude: belief. A common thought in the latter—as the Bayesian Model reflects—is that there is really only one basic kind of fine attitude: credence. We'll find the commitment to a sparse set of coarse-attitudes wanting in Chapter 5. We put forward an analogue worry about the Bayesian theory of states here.

The case shall be made in a style similar to the one shaped by David Lewis in his famous discussion of credence and chance. To a rough first approximation, Lewis argued that whenever an agent is rationally certain about the chance of a future outcome, she should set her credence in that outcome equal to that chance. Lewis defended this 'principal principle' by vigorous appeal to intuition concerning rational credence in thought-experiment scenarios. He implored his reader to share his

*The Rational Mind.* Scott Sturgeon, Oxford University Press (2020). © Scott Sturgeon.
DOI: 10.1093/oso/9780198845799.001.0001

intuitions about cases constructed, to re-think intuition if it did not agree with his, and to reflect carefully on the overall power of the approach he could build by appeal to intuition about cases.[1]

Similarly, I defend a thesis about the character of the attitude rationally lent to a claim and the character of evidence used in the attitude's formation. I introduce my thesis—the *Fitting Character Thesis*—with a series of thought experiments; and I defend it by appeal to intuitions from which powerful theory will eventually follow (in Chapter 8). The thought-experiments used here are not much like real life in their physical set-up, but they are *very* like real life in how evidence makes for rational confidence. My hope is that you will share my intuitions about these cases, you will re-think intuition when you do not, and you will reflect on the power and scope of the final theory of confidence generated by them. That theory does a great deal more than underwrite pre-theoretic intuition about cases.

Here is our first thought-experiment:

### POINT-BOX

You are faced with a black box while rationally certain of this much: the box is filled with a huge number of balls; the balls have been thoroughly mixed; exactly 85% of the balls are red; touching a ball does not shift its colour. You reach in the box, grab a ball, and wonder about its colour. You have no view about anything else relevant to that issue. Question-1: how sure should you be that you hold a red ball?

Point-Answer: you should be 85% sure, of course.

It is a basic assumption of the Bayesian model—as well as a datum of everyday life—that there are states as credence.[2] Once that is recognized, however, it's clear that your evidence in POINT-BOX rules-in exactly one attitude: 85% credence. Intuitively put, when all you know in a black-box scenario is that 85% of the balls are red, and being 85% confident is an attitude in your attitudinal repertoire, then, in those circumstance, you should be 85% sure that a randomly-grabbed ball from the box is red. In situations like POINT-BOX, therefore, you should adopt a point in the Bayesian space of attitudes. Your take on R should be pictured as follows

**Figure 3.1**

But things are not always so simple. Consider:

---

[1] (Lewis, 1980).

[2] Of course using hyper-precise real numbers to represent states of credence is an idealization in the ordinary sense found in science, just like using such numbers to model the length of a table. See (Cook, 2002) or (Edgington, 1997).

INTERVAL-BOX
You are faced with a black box while rationally certain of this much: the box is filled with a huge number of balls; the balls have been thoroughly mixed; exactly 80-to-90% of the balls are red; touching a ball does not shift its colour. You reach in the box, grab a ball, and wonder about its colour. You have no view about anything else relevant to that issue. Question-2: how sure should you be that you hold a red ball?

Interval-Answer: you should be exactly 80-to-90% sure, of course.

This answer is every bit as obvious as the answer we have in POINT BOX. Yet Interval-Answer does not rely in any obvious way on a psychological state found in the Bayesian model. If we're to stick with this second answer, therefore, and take it at face value, we'll need to enrich the Bayesian theory of states. We begin with three points about the proposed enrichment.[3]

First, evidence in INTERVAL-BOX clearly rules out certain types of credence as too weak. Any credence of strength less than 80% is too weak an attitudinal stance in light of the evidence in play. Intuitively put: when all you know in a black-box scenario is that 80-to-90% of the balls are red, it is obvious that you should be at least 80% sure that you have grabbed a red ball. The evidence makes weaker-than-80% credence too weak concerning whether you've grabbed a red ball.

Second, evidence in the case clearly rules out certain types of credence as too strong. Any credence of strength more than 90% certainty is too strong an attitudinal stance in light of the evidence in play. Intuitively put: when all you know in a black-box scenario is that 80-to-90% of the balls are red, it is obvious that you should be no more than 90% sure that you have grabbed a red ball. The evidence makes stronger-than-90% credence too strong concerning whether you've grabbed a red ball.

Third, evidence in INTERVAL-BOX does not oblige any credence which fails to be too weak or too strong. That is to say, evidence in the case does not rule-in one of the credences uncovered by the previous two paragraphs. Were you to adopt one of those credences, therefore—say by becoming 85% sure that you hold a red ball—your attitudinal stance would not be recommended by particulars of the evidence in play. It might be defended by appeal to consideration of symmetry, or simplicity, or something like that; but those sorts of consideration are in play in every case whatsoever. They are not part of the evidential particulars in INTERVAL-BOX. Moreover, it is hotly disputed whether considerations of those sorts can rationalizes a particular credence in such a case. This is an issue about which there is no agreement in the literature.[4] Hence credence in the 80-to-90% range is not *clearly* recommended in INTERVAL-BOX, it not *clearly* motivated by evidential particulars in play.

In light of Interval-Answer's strong intuitive appeal, therefore, and points in the previous three paragraphs, we shall take Interval-Answer at face value. This will involve admitting that there is such a thing as being 80-to-90% sure that you hold a red ball, and generalizing the thought in two directions. First, we'll admit that the 'spread out' attitude acknowledged here—being 80-to-90% confident—can be lent to

---

[3] This is the fine-grained analogue of the enrichment of the Belief Model's theory of states put forward in Chapter 5.
[4] See especially debates about *permissivism*, e.g. (White, 2005) or (Schoenfield, 2013).

**Figure 3.2**

any claim whatsoever. There is nothing special about the claim to which confidence is lent in Interval-Answer. The relevant spread-out attitude can attach to any claim entertain-able by one of us. Second, we'll admit that confidence can be 'spread out' in myriad different ways (not just from 80-to-90%). This second admission will be spelled out more fully as we go along. The full category of confidence brought into view by these two admissions involves what I call *thick confidence*.[5] One of the major goals of this chapter is to show that such confidence is no creature of darkness, that it is found at the heart of common sense, and that one can make perfectly good philosophical sense of the idea.

To see how thick confidence works, note that the evidential particulars of INTERVAL-BOX seem to demand—as we might put it—a region of credal space. This is to say that those particulars seem to demand an attitudinal stance spread out from 80% to 90% (Figure 3.2).

Talk of thick confidence is rather metaphorical, of course, and talk of confidence spread through regions of credal space is definitely so. But sometimes a well-chosen metaphor is the right tool for the job. It is my view that this is one of those times, and there are at least four reasons why this is so. Here they are in reverse order of importance:

- Talk of thick confidence connects humorously and mnemonically with the important fact that evidence in INTERVAL-BOX is meagre, that it rationally makes for an attitude of relative stupidity. Intuitively put: when all you know is that 80-to-90% of balls in the box are red, and you care whether the grabbed ball is red, then, in a parody British sense, at least, you are 'thick' about relevant details of your situation. Your evidence warrants thick confidence that you hold a red ball.
- Talk of thick confidence captures the palpable spread-out feel of the attitude introduced by INTERVAL-BOX. In a recognizable sense that attitude is coarser than any real-valued subjective probability. And intuitively, at least, the relevant attitude is warranted in INTERVAL-BOX precisely *because* evidence in the case is too rough for credence, too meagre to rule-in point-valued subjective

---

[5] This sort of confidence goes by many names in the literature: 'mushy credence', 'imprecise probability', 'interval-valued probability', and so on. Some of these labels suggest that thick confidence is always somehow vague or imprecise—or at least that such confidence is always somehow less precise than is credence—but that is definitely not the case. Some kinds of thick confidence are every bit as precise as credence, so labels which suggest otherwise are thereby inapt. Conversely, other common labels for thick confidence suggest that it is always precise like a unit-valued interval. But that is also not the case. As we'll see some kinds of thick confidence are vague or imprecise—they enjoy fuzzy boundaries, so to say—so labels which suggest otherwise are thereby inapt. What it is that all types of thick confidence have in common is being coarser in nature than credence. Sometimes that coarseness comes with all the precision found in a credence. Other times it does not.

probability. Talk of thick confidence is apt in the case not only because it captures the spread out feel of the relevant attitude, but also because it echoes something about evidence warranting that attitude.
- Talk of thick confidence links directly with the orthodox formal model of the phenomenon. As we'll see more fully below, that model associates types of thick confidence with *sets* of probability functions rather than a single probability function. When a rational agent responds to her evidence by lending 80-to-90% confidence, say, orthodoxy sees her take via a set of probability functions which contains, for every number in the interval [.8, .9], a probability function assigning that number to the claim in which she lends confidence. Hence orthodoxy associates thick confidence with a region of the unit interval rather than with one of its points, a region pinned down by output-probabilities found in its sets. This sort of approach is meant to put 'a human face' on the Bayesian model—in Richard Jeffrey's memorable phrase[6]—precisely because it uses something mathematically juicier than a single probability function. Yet the approach builds its juicier gizmo directly from its model of credence. Talk of confidence spreading across regions of credal space thus directly echoes the orthodox formal approach to thick confidence.
- That approach models the rational shift of thick confidence with a procedure for changing probability functions found in its sets. Yet the resulting transition theory yields counter-intuitive results (as we'll see in the next chapter). At this stage of our theorizing, therefore, we have no well-functioning *non*-metaphorical model of thick confidence to hand.

These points make it clear that talk of thick confidence—like talk of confidence spreading through regions of credal space—is well motivated. We should be mindful that such talk is in certain ways metaphorical. We should not let that aspect of its nature stop us from being guided by the talk in our work.

In this respect it is important to note that there was a time in philosophy when talk of ordinary thick confidence was considered perfectly fine, yet talk of point-valued subjective probability was viewed with great suspicion. Exactly this combination of ease-and-suspicion was rather common, in fact, right after it became clear that probability theory could be used to shed a great deal of light on a number of topics: epistemic rationality, scientific confirmation, rational decision, more. It's as if the hyper-precise approach was so successful that many came to question its psychological presuppositions, as if they'd been surreptitiously reverse-engineered from the beginning for success. The worry was simple: while ordinary rough confidence was a familiar bit of common-sense psychology, real-valued subjective probability was no more than a theorist's fiction.[7]

---

[6] (Jeffrey, 1965).

[7] Classic discussion can be found (Keynes, 1921), (Ramsey, 1925/1990) and (Kolmogorov, 1933). More recent philosophical discussion can be found in (Hacking, 1995), (Jeffrey, 1983), (Joyce, 2005), (Kaplan, 1983), (Levi, 1974), and (Maher, 2008). Van Fraassen first presented his 'representor' approach in (van Fraassen, 1985) and followed it up in (van Fraassen, 1990). In a nutshell, thick confidence is basically Ramsey's subjectivism stripped of its real-valued mathematics and overly precise metaphysics. For recent technical discussion of the area see (Walley, 1991) and (Halpern, 2003).

Oh how times change.

Most philosophers today are of the opposite view to the one just described. They are happy to make use of point-valued subjective probability without comment on its psychological bona fides. They are deeply hostile to the very idea of thick confidence, and normally require for its use some kind of apologia or theoretical *cri de coeur*. Here is Cian Dorr vocalizing the recent perspective with characteristic vigor:

> There is no adequate account of the way thick confidence should be manifested in decision-making... the only viable strategies which would allow for someone in a state of thick confidence to maintain a reasonable pattern of behavioural dispositions over time involve, in effect, choosing [a particular credence function] as the one that will guide their actions.... [But] if this is all we have to say about the decision theory, we lack an acceptable account of what it is to be in a given state of thick confidence—we cannot explain what would constitute the difference between someone with [a credence] and someone with a thick confidence [where the thickness involved intuitively covers the credal value]. Thick confidences seem to have simply been postulated as states that get us out of tricky epistemological dilemmas, without an adequate theory of their underlying nature. It is rather as if some ethicist were to respond to some tricky ethical dilemma—say, whether you should join the Resistance or take care of your ailing mother—by simply postulating a new kind of action that is stipulated to be a special new kind of combination of joining the Resistance and taking care of your mother which lacks the objectionable features of obvious compromises (like doing both on a part-time basis or letting the outcome be determined by the roll of a dice). It would be epistemologically very convenient if there was a psychological state we could rationally be in in which we neither regarded a claim Φ as less likely than another Ψ, regarded Ψ as less likely than Φ, nor regarded them as equally likely. But we should be wary of positing psychological states for the sake of epistemological convenience.[8]

When it comes to credence and thick confidence, this passage captures a great deal of the present-day zeitgeist. In my view nearly every claim made in Dorr's passage is mistaken. I do think, though, that it ends with an important truth, so let me start with the good news.

It is a fundamental tenet of this book—emphasized in Chapter 1—that mental kinds are not to be postulated purely for normative purposes. This is primarily because such kinds are viewed in this work as natural kinds. They are part of an agent's empirical endowment. This means that mental kinds help to constitute an agent's causal capacities, and that they should be individuated physically or functionally rather than by appeal to normative facts. In a catch-phrase, the perspective assumed here is that nothing in nature is by nature fraught with ought. When natural phenomena are attended by ought-facts of some kind, therefore—and our discussion of epistemic rationality presupposes that they are for mental kinds—those ought-facts follow

---

[8] (Dorr 2010: 201). I have changed his terminology to fit with our discussion.

on from natural phenomena. They are not part of the nature or essence of the phenomena themselves.

It's a good thing, then, that our use of thick confidence does not amount to a postulation of mental kinds for epistemic convenience. After all, our use of thick confidence does not amount to a postulation of mental kinds at all, for thick confidence is a central plank of the manifest (or ordinary or everyday) image of mind. We are simply locating an aspect of that image and placing a label on it. By adding thick confidence to our named stock of attitudes, then, we are merely adding left-out bits of common sense to the Bayesian model, insisting that our epistemology of confidence recognize all types of confidence found in the manifest image.

To work up to this point from a different perspective, consider the view that humans invest confidence only if they lend credence. If that view is correct, humans invest high-, low-, or middling-strength confidence only if they invest high-, low-, or middling-strength credence. The perspective entails the following three principles:

(High)     high-con($\Phi$) $\rightarrow$ There is a relatively large unit-real $r$ so that cr($\Phi$) = $r$,
(Low)     low-con($\Phi$) $\rightarrow$ There is a relatively small unit-real $r$ so that cr($\Phi$) = $r$,
(Medium)   mid-con($\Phi$) $\rightarrow$ There is a middling unit-real $r$ so that cr($\Phi$) = $r$.

It is a datum of everyday life that each of these principles is false.

After all, credence is point-valued subjective probability. To invest credence is to adopt a hyper-precise attitude, to configure an exact spread of confidence across every niche of epistemic possibility (so to say). We do seem to manage it from time to time, if common sense is to be taken at face value, anyway, and idealized in scientific ways. That is why Bayesian psychology is not philosophical fiction from the start. But there are plenty of circumstances in which we manifest confidence *without* lending point-valued subjective probability. Indeed this looks to be more the norm than the exception in everyday life.

Think of a numerical case. Suppose you are holding a coin which you know to be objectively biased to heads—a 95% bias, let's say. Perhaps the coin was built by someone who spent years perfecting the creation of such coins. Since you know all of that you begin rationally certain that the coin has a 95% objective bias to heads. Then you decide to flip the coin and wonder if it will land heads on the toss. In the event, it is a plain fact of common sense that you will be 95% sure that the coin will land heads. And it is a plain fact of common sense that this mental aspect of you will play out a certain way in your behaviour. You will be empirically discriminable from someone who is 94%- or 96%- (or any other per cent)-certain that the coin will land heads. Common sense recognizes your occupation—as we might say—of a position in the Bayesian space of attitudes. It is not any sort of stretch of the truth or philosophical fiction to say that humans lend credence. Bayesian psychology is a recognized bit of common sense.[9]

---

[9] As we mentioned in Chapter 2, though, it also seems quite clear that humans do not—indeed cannot—occupy every position in the Bayesian space of attitudes. But this is an ordinary type of idealization of a sort which should not bother epistemologists. The point of the main text is just that humans do, quite obviously, occupy some of the positions in the Bayesian space of attitudes. See (Cook, 2002) or (Edgington, 1997).

But ordinary cases do not normally involve explicit numerical values. Consider whether it will be sunny in Tucson tomorrow. If you are like me, you know that Tucson is located in the Sonoran Desert and is almost always sunny. But you will have no precise statistics about how often it is sunny in Tucson, and nor will you have evidence about the objective chance of sun there tomorrow. All you will have is qualitative evidence to the effect that it is extremely likely to be sunny in Tucson tomorrow. It is a manifest fact about such evidence, though, that it does not pin down a real number for how likely it is that it will be sunny in Tucson tomorrow. Although your evidence does strongly support the view that it will be sunny in Tucson tomorrow, it does not do so to any real-number-theoretic degree.

For this reason, common sense underwrites the idea that you should be confident that it will be sunny in Tucson tomorrow, given your evidence; but it does not insist that you should lend a specific credence to that hypothesis. And nor does common sense see you as picking one just to get on with things rationally. No. The ordinary description of a case like this involves high confidence without credence. To insist otherwise is to demand precision in psychology beyond what is recognized by common sense. In effect it's to demand precision in functionality beyond what common sense admits. Were you to display firm commitment to point-valued betting odds to do with sun in Tucson tomorrow, for instance, common sense would be startled at your stable and seemingly over-precise functionality, and it would wonder why *those* were your particular betting odds rather than others exquisitely like them, odds which were equally copacetic in light of your evidence.

To put an edge on the point: in a case like the one we're considering, common sense maintains that you will be highly confident that it will be sunny in Tucson tomorrow, despite there being no $r$ such that the strength of your high confidence is identical to $r$% of certainty's strength. Since you invest credence in sun for Tucson only if there is such an $r$, it follows that common sense maintains, in a case like this one, that you do not invest credence in sun for Tucson tomorrow. Your high confidence is no state of credence at all. So common sense recognizes the possibility of high confidence without credence, and thereby rejects principle (**High**).

A similar point holds for (**Low**). Since common sense sees you with high confidence for the claim that it will be sunny in Tucson tomorrow, it also sees you with low confidence for the claim that it will not be sunny in Tucson tomorrow. Since common sense insists that there is no $r$ such that the strength of your high confidence for sun is identical to $r$% of certainty's strength, common sense insists that there is no $r$ such that the strength of your low confidence for no-sun is identical to $r$% of certainty's strength. But you invest low credence only if there is such an $r$. It follows that common sense maintains, in a case like this, that you do not invest low credence in the claim that it will not be sunny in Tucson tomorrow. Your low confidence is no state of credence at all. Common sense recognizes the possibility of low confidence without credence and thereby rejects principle (**Low**).

A similar point holds for (**Medium**). Just think of a claim about which you have very little information—say the claim that there is a smelly vinegar factory in Slough. If you are like me, you have no clue about whether that's true. Once the issue has been raised, though, and you've considered it for a good while, common sense sees you as lending some kind of middling-strength confidence to the view that there is a smelly vinegar factory in Slough. But it will definitely not see you as investing credence. To insist otherwise is again to locate a level of precision that goes well beyond what is seen by common sense. Here too were you to display firm and stable point-valued betting odds, for instance, on there being a smelly vinegar factory in Slough, common sense would be startled. It would wonder why those were your odds rather than others very like them which were equally copacetic in light of your evidence. Just as common sense recognizes the possibility of lending high or low confidence without lending credence, it also recognizes the possibility of lending middling-strength confidence in the absence of credence. This is why it rejects principle (**Medium**) too.

Principles (**High**), (**Low**), and (**Medium**) entail—contrary to obvious psychological fact—that high-, low-, and middling-strength confidence requires high-, low, and medium-strength credence. This is simply not true, and the manifest image of mind recognizes that it's not true. But this is just a fancy way of saying that common sense admits the routine investment of thick confidence. By using such confidence, then, we are not postulating some sort of creature of darkness or made-up psychology. We are using an ordinary bit of common sense psychology by appeal to an extra-ordinary label we've made-up ourselves.

Thick confidence is the bread and butter of everyday life. To see how it works functionally, recall the attitude recommended in INTERVAL-BOX: 80-to-90% certainty. We'll call this sort of thick confidence 'sharp' in what follows, since it has fully-precise edges or end-points. Once our story about the functionality of this attitude has been glossed—and extended to other forms of sharp thick confidence—the story will be extended still further to fuzzier types of confidence, types which do not have fully-precise edges or end-points. These types of confidence will be called 'fuzzy' in what follows.

Suppose, then, that a fully rational agent lends some kind of confidence to claim R (the claim that you hold a red ball in INTERVAL-BOX). It turns out there are five salient ways in which her take on R might relate to a given unit-real $r$:

(i) $con(R) = a$, where $a$ is no smaller than $r$;
(ii) $con(R) = a$, where $a$ is smaller than $r$;
(iii) $con(R) = [a, b]$, where $a$ is no smaller than $r$;
(iv) $con(R) = [a, b]$, where $b$ is smaller than $r$;
(v) $con(R) = [a, b]$, where $r$ falls within $(a, b]$ (i.e. where $r$ is bigger than $a$ but no larger than $b$).

The first two scenarios involve credence, the last three involve sharp thick confidence.

When asked if R is at least $r$-likely to be true, moreover, for illustrative purposes we may think of the rational agent as firmly disposed to answer *Yes* when she falls into category (i) or (iii), firmly disposed to answer *No* when she falls into category (ii) or (iv), and firmly disposed to *remain silent* when she falls into category (v). And we can use this functional profile as a tinker-toy model of what the agent's thick confidence amounts to, as a tinker-toy model of its signature function. There is an intuitive distinction between the functionality of thick confidence and credence. Our tinker-toy model will echo it clearly.

70   THE BAYESIAN THEORY OF STATES: CRITICAL DISCUSSION

Suppose we are faced with two fully rational agents: one with 85% credence lent to R, the other with 80-to-90% thick confidence lent to R. Suppose each of them is asked, for every unit-real $r$, whether R is at least $r$-likely to be true. The first agent's dispositional response profile will appear like this

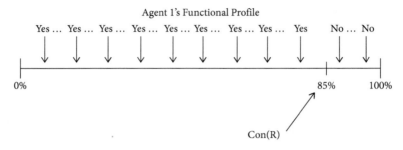

**Figure 3.3**

The second agent's dispositional response profile will appear as follows

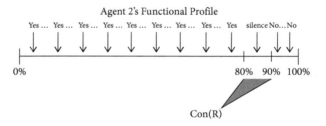

**Figure 3.4**

The first agent will be disposed to answer every question with a firm 'Yes' or 'No'. This complex verbal disposition is our tinker-toy theory of the underlying nature of 85% credence. The second rational agent will not manifest the same complex verbal disposition. When asked whether R is at least $r$-likely to be true, for every unit-real $r$, she will be firmly disposed to respond like the first agent when, but only when, $r$ is *outside* the interval [.8,.9] (i.e. exactly when $r$ is less than .8 or greater than .9). Otherwise the second agent will be disposed to remain silent. This second complex verbal disposition is our tinker-toy theory of the underlying nature of 80-to-90% confidence.

Sharp thick confidence is recognizably coarser than credence. One of the functional profiles before us—the one for 85% credence in R—involves a firm disposition to respond with 'Yes' or 'No' to the full range of $r$-likelihood questions about R. The other functional profile before us—the one for sharp thick confidence in R—involves a firm disposition to respond only to a partial range of those questions (together with a firm disposition to remain silent the rest of the time). Credence thus draws finer-grained yes/no discriminations in modal reality than sharp thick confidence.

Here's another way to think about the functional relationship between credence and sharp thick confidence. Sometimes action is tantamount to the endorsement of a particular claim's truth. When that happens an action presupposes—which is to say it makes situational sense—only if the claim is true. If you take an umbrella to keep dry, for instance, the action you perform is tantamount to the endorsement of rain (or its likelihood or some-such). And more generally, for any claim $\Phi$, there is a three-way chunking of action to be made: acts are either pro-$\Phi$, con-$\Phi$, or $\Phi$-irrelevant. In the first case action is tantamount to the endorsement of $\Phi$'s truth. In the second case action is tantamount to the endorsement of $\Phi$'s falsity. In the third case action is neither of these first two sorts of endorsement.

This fact makes it is easy to compare the functional thrust of credence and sharp thick confidence. We may say this: credence in $\Phi$ is something like a firm disposition to presuppose in action—across the *full* range of live possibilities—$\Phi$'s truth or its falsity; and sharp thick confidence in $\Phi$ is something like a firm disposition to presuppose in action—across a *partial* range of the live possibilities—$\Phi$'s truth or its falsity, together with a firm disposition to refrain from action in remaining live possibilities.

In a way the functional nature of credence and sharp thick confidence mirrors the mathematical relationship between points in the unit interval and units in that interval. Just as points can be thought of as limit-case intervals—namely, intervals with identical lower and upper bounds—states of credence can be thought of as limit-case states of sharp confidence—namely, sharp confidence with identical lower and upper bounds. Units with non-identical bounds are intuitively coarser than those with identical bounds. States of sharp thick confidence are intuitively coarser than states of credence.

One more point should be made at this junction. Although it is true that for any real numbers $a$ and $b$ we have

$$(a > b) \text{ or } (b > a) \text{ or } (a = b),$$

it is <u>not</u> the case that for any unit intervals $[a,b]$ and $[c,d]$ we have

$$([a,b] > [c,d]) \text{ or } ([c,d] > [a,b]) \text{ or } ([a,b] = [c,d]).$$

There is no most-natural generalization of the greater-than relation to apply to intervals. For instance, consider the intervals $[.42, .48]$ and $[.4, .5]$. The latter stretches further up the unit interval than does the former, and it also stretches further down the unit interval. The two intervals involve distinct end-points, of course, so they are not strictly identical (i.e. they are not the same interval). So which is: is $[.4, .5]$ greater than $[.42, .48]$, is $[.42, .48]$ greater than $[.4, .5]$, is neither the case?

In a clear sense there is a first and last interval in the unit interval: namely, $[0,0]$ and $[1,1]$ respectively. Other than that we have no clear pre-theoretic ordering of intervals. They simply don't organize themselves in any straightforward way, which means questions of the form '$[a,b] > [c,d]$?' don't make straightforward sense.[10] We can force them into sensible form if we choose, by legislating a new meaning for '>'. But there is no most-natural legislation to be used here. Although the following is definitely true

---

[10] Intervals in the unit interval are not linearly ordered, for instance. See §2.4.

$$\neg ([.4, .5] = [.42, .48]),$$

it is *not* a consequence of this definite truth that

$$([.4, .5] > [.42, .48]) \quad \text{or} \quad ([.42, .4.8] > [.4, .5]).$$

Something similar plays out for credence and sharp thick confidence.

To see this, let '≫' stand for the stronger-than relation which holds between types of confidence, and '≡' stand for the equally-strong relation. Then for any states of credence $cr_1$ and $cr_2$ we'll have this obviously true:

$$(cr_1 \gg cr_2) \text{ or } (cr_2 \gg cr_1) \text{ or } (cr_1 \equiv cr_2).$$

Either $cr_1$ is a stronger state of credence than $cr_2$, $cr_2$ is a stronger state of credence than $cr_1$, or these states of credence are equally strong. But nothing like that is straightforwardly true of sharp thick confidence, for there is no most-natural way to generalize the notion of being stronger-than to apply to sharp thick confidence in full generality.

Consider being 42-to-48% certain and being 40-to-50% certain. The latter seems stronger than the former toward its top but weaker towards its bottom. The two states of sharp thick confidence are clearly not of exactly the same strength. So which is it: is being 40-to-50% sure a stronger take on a claim's truth than being 42-to-48% sure? Is it the other way around? Is there no fact of the matter about this?

Well, in a clear sense certainty is the strongest type of confidence and no-confidence is the weakest type of confidence. Other than that there is no obvious way to organize-by-strength the full range of confidence-theoretic states. Since they don't line themselves up by strength—i.e. since their strength does not put them in a linear order—questions of the form 'is this state of confidence stronger than that one?' don't make straightforward sense. We can legislate the situation into sensible form, to be sure; but there is no most-natural legislation to be done by appeal solely to the nature of the states. Being 40-to-50% sure is not the same thing as being 42-to-48% sure—the states must differ in strength somehow—but it is simply not the case that the former state of confidence is straightforwardly stronger than the latter, nor is it the case that the latter state of confidence is straightforwardly stronger than the former.

To sum up, the greater-than relation has no most-natural generalization from numbers to intervals. There are many equally good ways to generalize the notion. On some of them there will be intervals such that it is neither the case that one of those intervals is greater than the other—in the relevant generalized sense—nor is it the case that the intervals are identical. And the same thing is true of sharp thick confidence. The more-confident-than relation has no most-natural generalization from states of credence to states of sharp thick confidence. There are multiple good ways to generalize it. On some of them there will be states of sharp thick confidence such that it is neither the case that being in one of them is being more confident than being in the other—in the relevant generalized sense—nor is it the case that being in either is being in an equally strong state of confidence.[11]

---

[11] For 'interval arithmetic' see (Moore, 1966), and for an interesting philosophical discussion of the phenomena in play see the discussion of 'parity' in (Chang, 2015).

We have seen, then, that the following main points are true:

1. When making use of sharp thick confidence in epistemic theory, we are not postulating a mental kind for epistemic convenience. We are using a component of common-sense psychology, and we are doing so because that component seems like the best tool for the job to hand. The same thing is true when we use credence in epistemic theory. The psychological bona fides of sharp thick confidence and credence are exactly like one another: they stand or fall together. Moreover if common sense is taken at face value, they both definitely stand.
2. In outline, at least, we have a good grip on the functional relationship between sharp thick confidence and credence. The former involves pro- or con-functionality across the full range of live possibilities. The latter involves pro- or con-functionality across a sub-part of that range, together with stable sloth across the rest of it.
3. States of sharp thick confidence do not relate to one another (or to states of credence) the way that numbers do so. When faced with two states of sharp this confidence, it is not always the case that one of them stronger than one another or they are equal in strength.

We are thus free to admit what seemed obvious from the start, namely, that in INTERVAL-BOX a rational agent will adopt a sharp thick confidence. In particular she will be 80-to-90% sure that she holds a red ball. We'll now see that there are cases which call for less precise thick confidence too.

## INTERVALISH-BOX

You are faced with a black box while rationally certain of this much: the box is filled with a huge number of balls; the balls have been thoroughly mixed; *roughly* 80-to-90% of the balls are red; touching a ball does not shift its colour. You reach in the box, grab a ball, and wonder about its colour. You have no view about anything else relevant to that issue. Question-3: how sure should you be that you hold a red ball?

Interval-ish-Answer: you should be roughly 80-to-90% sure, of course.

In POINT-BOX you began rationally certain that the box before you contained exactly 85% red balls. This led to a fully rational credence of 85%. In INTERVAL-BOX you began rationally certain that the box before you contained exactly 80-to-90%. This led to a fully rational sharp thick confidence of 80-to-90%. In INTERVAL-ISH BOX you begin rationally certain that the box before you contains roughly 80-to-90% red balls. This leads to fully rational thick confidence the strength of which is roughly 80-to-90% that of certainty.

Just as rational confidence in POINT-BOX can be naturally represented with the precise real number .85, and rational confidence in INTERVAL-BOX can be so represented with the sharp interval [.8,.9], rational confidence in INTERVAL-ISH BOX can be naturally represented with a vague interval v[.8,.9]. We may think of this is the region—or perhaps $\underline{a}$ region—which vaguely begins at .8, extends along the unit interval, and then vaguely ends at .9. Since evidence in INTERVAL-ISH BOX is essentially fuzzy, it warrants an attitude the strength of which is likewise fuzzy.

We may picture this fuzzy thick confidence as follows

**Figure 3.5**

And when asked for any unit-real *r* whether R is at least *r*-likely to be true, we may picture the dispositional response profile in INTERVAL-ISH BOX as in Figure 3.6.

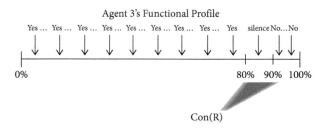

**Figure 3.6**

From 0 to roughly .8 you are firmly disposed to say 'Yes'. From roughly .9 to 1 you are firmly disposed to say 'No'. In between those vague boundaries you are firmly disposed to remain silent. Can we tell exactly where your disposition to respond with 'Yes' drops off and your disposition to remain silent begins? No, we can't tell when that happens, for the transition in question is vague. Can we tell exactly where your disposition to remain silent drops off and the disposition to respond with 'No' begins? No, we can't tell when that happens either, for that transition is likewise vague. So long as the vagueness of your functional profile lines up with that of your thick confidence, however, everything is fine; for the functional nature of that confidence is *meant* to be fuzzy through and through.

Somewhat ironically, though, situations like INTERVAL-ISH BOX involve semi-precise boundaries, i.e. boundaries which are vague but nevertheless indexed to precise quantities. That too is often not the case in ordinary life. This leads to our next scenario.

### FUZZ-ONLY BOX

You are faced with a black box while rationally certain of this much: the box is filled with a huge number of balls; the balls have been thoroughly mixed; touching a ball does not shift its colour; and one more thing... (five versions):

1. A slim majority of balls in the box are red.
2. A solid-but-not-total majority of balls in the box are red.
3. A very-solid-but-not-total majority of balls in the box are red.
4. A very-very-solid-but-not-total majority of balls in the box are red.
5. Every ball in the box is red.

In each version of FUZZ-ONLY-BOX you reach in a box, grab a ball, and wonder about its colour; and in each version you have no view about anything else relevant to the issue about which you wonder. In each version of FUZZ-ONLY-BOX, then, how confident should you be that you hold a red ball?

Well, it is obvious in each version of the case that you should be more than 50% sure you hold a red ball. It is also obvious that your confidence should be weaker in the first version of the case than it is in the second, weaker in the second version of the case than it is in the third, weaker in the third version of the case than it is in the fourth, and weaker in the fourth version of the case than it is in the fifth. And it is obvious that your confidence in the claim that you hold a red ball should be maximal in the fifth version of the case. Putting all this together we have

$$50\% < \text{con}_{(i)}(R) < \text{con}_{(ii)}(R) < \text{con}_{(iii)}(R) < \text{con}_{(iv)}(R) < \text{con}_{(v)}(R) = 100\%.$$

You should be mildly confident that you hold a red ball in version (i) of the case, fairly confident that you do so in version (ii), very confident but not certain that you hold a red ball in version (iii) of the case, extremely confident but not certain that you do so in version (iv), and you should be sure that you hold a red ball in version (v).

These facts about confidence do not hold because you are less than fully rational with evidence. They hold because fuzzy thick confidence is all that can be *got* from evidence in each version of the case. Fully rational thinkers can do no better. Since the evidence is vague through and through in each version of FUZZ-ONLY-BOX, fuzzy thick confidence is all that can be got from the evidence in them. And thus we arrive at a perspective on which rational confidence is many-splendored: sometimes it is maximally precise as well as maximally thin—as we find in the Bayesian model—and sometimes it is thicker than that—as we find with both sharp and fuzzy thick confidence.

## 3.3 Contra Bayesian Conditional Credence

The Bayesian model uses probability functions to represent fully rational states of credence. Such functions are like input-output machines which take propositions as input and yield unit-real numbers as output. Those numbers represent how probable it is that an input proposition is true.

There are uncountably many real numbers used in the Bayesian model. They are linearly ordered and have no finite upper bound on their complexity.[12] This leads many to think that the model is committed to three claims about fully rational credence:

- There are uncountably many types of such credence.
- They are linearly ordered by strength.
- Those strengths manifest no finite upper bound on their precision.

This line of thought involves a certain kind of projection. Specifically, it projects bullet-pointed aspects of the Bayesian model onto psychological phenomena being

[12] See §4.2 for an explanation of these notions.

modelled by it. When this happens we should always ask if the projection is truly legitimate.

It is clear that a Bayesian projection will be appropriate in some-but-not-all cases. Suppose you are rationally 50% certain of Φ. Then the Bayesian model will represent your take on Φ with the unit-real number .5, the number is the *mark* of your confidence in the model. So the marker for your mental state is a mathematical object: it is divisible by 2, seemingly outside of space, seemingly outside of time, and so on. Your take on Φ is itself a psychological phenomenon, a propositional attitude. It is not divisible by 2 (or any other number), it is seemingly located within space and time, etc. It would be entirely inappropriate to project mathematical aspects of the number .5 onto the psychological state marked by that number in the Bayesian model.

In general: when a model's marker $\underline{m}$ stands for an element of a domain ε, and $\underline{m}$ has a feature F, it does not follow that ε has F too. It may be the case that ε has F in line with its marker—that is certainly possible—but it does not *follow* from the fact that a marker has F that the thing it marks does so as well. We must take care, then, when claiming that an aspect of a model's mark for a thing ends-up being projected onto that thing as well. Sometimes the projection will be sensible, other times it will not be.

This is relevant to conditional credence for the following reason. The Bayesian model uses orthodox conditional probabilities to mark such credence. Those probabilities enjoy a decidedly second-class status in probability theory (to be explained in a moment). We must decide if that second-class status legitimately projects onto conditional credence. If it does, then such credence enjoys a decidedly second-class status in our psychology. If it does not, conditional credence has a mental life of its own. The former situation would entail that the Bayesian model metaphysically matched conditional credence. The latter would entail that it failed to do so. Our task will be to decide which of these notional possibilities is actual.

The story begins with a fact about probability theory as such, namely, it is a branch of pure mathematics. Probability theorists study abstract functions which take elements of algebras as input and map them onto real numbers as output; and like all areas of pure mathematics, probability theory has a number of differing approaches to its subject matter. The Bayesian model uses the orthodox approach to probability. On this approach the subject matter is put forward in axiomatic form, with rules or laws being presented initially and taken to pin down the topic of discussion. As it happens those rules always concern *un*conditional probability. They are rules like:

For any claims A and B: whenever A entails B, **p**(A) is no greater than **p**(B).

It is only after axioms like this have been introduced that conditional probability makes an appearance. And then it shows up only as *shorthand* for something already present:

$$(\mathbf{p}/_{df.}) \quad \mathbf{p}(C/A) =_{df.} \mathbf{p}(A\&C)/\mathbf{p}(A), \quad \text{when } \mathbf{p}(A) \text{ is non-zero.}$$

It is important to realise what '$=_{df.}$' means here. The symbol's meaning can be captured by phrases like 'is true by stipulation' or 'is true by definition'.

On this approach, conditional probability is introduced solely as a device of abbreviation. It is stipulated that the formula '**p**(C/A)' is nothing but short-hand for the ratio formula '$p(A\&C)/p(A)$'. In turn this has non-trivial consequences for what conditional probabilities *are* within orthodox probability theory, for it entails that they are nothing more than ratios of unconditional probabilities. On the standard approach, then, formula like

$$p(C/A)$$

are nothing but shorthand for formula like

$$p(A\&C)/p(A).$$

Conditional probability turns out to be entirely derivative, a metaphysical free-rider, something which comes for free once facts about unconditional probability are in place.[13]

Consider a close analogy: for any person $P_i$ let $H_i$ be her height. Then for any three people $P_1$, $P_2$, and $P_3$ there will be a quantity we might invent—call it 'the snazzy feature'—which is got in two steps: first, multiply $H_1$ and $H_2$ together, and second, divide the result by $H_3$. Suppose we are interested in the snazzy feature. Then we can easily introduce short-hand for it:

$$(\mathbf{h}/_{df.}) \quad \mathbf{h}(H_1, H_2, H_3) =_{df.} [\mathbf{h}(H_1) \times \mathbf{h}(H_2)]/\mathbf{h}(H_3).$$

Once we have done this our notation will abbreviate something which manifests the mathematical properties of height. If snazzy feature $\mathbf{h_1}$ is larger than snazzy feature $\mathbf{h_2}$, for instance, and snazzy feature $\mathbf{h_2}$ is larger than snazzy feature $\mathbf{h_3}$, then, it follows that snazzy feature $\mathbf{h_1}$ is larger than snazzy feature $\mathbf{h_3}$. And so on. Snazzy features are perfectly real. Their structural properties are easy to work out via their mathematical definition. But snazzy features are entirely derivative. Facts about them are no more than facts about ratios of ordinary heights and their products. Snazzy facts are genuine free-riders: they come for free once ordinary height is in place. It is only by virtue of facts about ordinary height that there are snazzy facts at all. The latter are nothing over and above the former.

The orthodox approach to probability sees conditional probability as snazzy-like. The approach entails that facts about conditional probability are free-riders: they come for free once facts about unconditional probability are in place. It is not our job to pronounce on this way of thinking about conditional probability—that's for mathematicians to do[14]—but it *is* our job to note that the orthodox approach to conditional probability views it as utterly derivative. Since that approach is used by the Bayesian model, we face a pointed interpretive question: should we project the second-class status of orthodox conditional probability onto conditional credence? Or should we see such credence as psychologically non-derivative?

We'll now argue for the view that conditional credence does not have second-class status. The view to be defended is that conditional credence has a psychological life of its own, that it's an explanatorily fundamental moving part in our rational

---

[13] In the vernacular: orthodoxy entails that conditional probability is 'grounded' in unconditional probability. See (Correia & Schnieder, 2012).

[14] See discussion and references in (Fine, 1973).

psychology.[15] On this view, facts about conditional credence are not free-riders. They do not come for free once ratio facts about unconditional credence are in place. Instead facts about conditional credence and ratio facts are two-way dissociable: it is possible to have either of them without the other.

We argue for this by appeal to three thought-experiments. The first two involve cases in which rational conditional credence exists without the unconditional elements needed to ground it via the ratio formula. The third case shows that unconditional credence can exist in the absence of conditional credence thought classically to be grounded by it via that formula.

### RED-SPOTTED BALL

You are faced with a black box about which you are rationally certain of this much: the box is filled with coloured balls; some of them have red spots; the balls are thoroughly mixed; touching a ball does not shift its colour; there are exactly three blue balls in the box, one of which has a red spot. That is all you know relevant to the case. You reach in and grab a ball. Before pulling it out how confident should you be, on the assumption that you have grabbed one of the blue balls, that you have also grabbed one with a red spot?

The answer is entirely clear: your conditional credence should be 1/3rd. When

R = the claim you hold a red-spotted ball

and

B = the claim you hold a blue ball,

your rational credence for R given B will and should be:

$$cr(R/B) = 1/3.$$

But think back to the Conditional Credence Rule. Applied to the case it yields

$$cr(R/B) = cr(B\&R)/cr(B), \quad \text{when } cr(B) \text{ is non-zero.}$$

So ask yourself this: how confident should you be in RED-SPOTTED-BALL that you are holding a red-spotted blue ball? And how confident should you be that you are holding a blue ball full stop? In other words: what are the values for the numerator and denominator in the ratio formula above?

This much seems clear: you should have no fixed credence in either of these claims. There is just not enough evidence in the case to make for rational credence. In RED-SPOTTED-BALL neither your take on the conjunction (B&R) nor your take on the

---

[15] Suppose it turns out, as we shall now argue, that conditional credence is psychologically non-derivative. Would it then follow from the fact that we manifest conditional credence that the Binary Attitudes Assumption is false? No; for it is consistent with the psychologically basic nature of conditional credence that such credence is really *un*conditional deep down. Both things would happen if for any two claims A and C there was a conditional claim built from them, con(A,C), such that what it was to have conditional credence of C given A equal to *x* was to have credence of *x* lent to con(A,C). This notional possibility will be explored in Chapter 7.

claim B itself should end-up as any kind of credence. The standard ratio formula does not apply: neither its numerator nor its denominator is defined.

This indicates that it is rationally possible to have well-defined conditional credence without unconditional credence found in the associated ratio formula. If that is so, however, conditional credence has a psychological life which is more robust than the metaphysical life conditional probability enjoys within orthodox probability theory; for conditional credence does not reduce to unconditional credence via the ratio formula. Conditional credence is a self-standing psychological phenomenon, a paid-up member of the epistemic mix, its own component of our psychological life. That is the position defended here.

### CHOICE OF RESTAURANT

You are faced with a choice between two restaurants for the evening meal: Fish-Dish and Noodle-Doodle. The former is your favourite seafood restaurant, the latter is your favourite noodle bar. You know each of the restaurants well, and you're familiar with chefs on duty this evening. Let

F = the claim that you go to Fish-Dish,
N = the claim that you go to Noodle-Doodle,
S = the claim that you are satisfied by your meal.

Suppose you are sure to go either to Fish-Dish or Noodle-Doodle:

$$cr(FvN) = 100\%.$$

Assume also that you are rationally close to sure that you will be satisfied with each restaurant if you go there:

$$cr(S/F) = 99\%,$$

$$cr(S/N) = 99\%.$$

The situation is designed to ensure that you face a tough choice. Intuitively, you know you'll enjoy whichever restaurant you choose, so the choice turns on whether you're in the mood for fish or in the mood for noodles. But suppose that aspect of the situation is murky: it is unclear to you, when you turn your attention to the matter, whether you are in the mood for fish or in the mood for noodles.

Now think back to the Conditional Credence Rule. Applied to the case it yields

$$cr(S/F) = cr(S\&F)/cr(F), \quad \text{when } cr(F) \text{ is non-zero,}$$

and

$$cr(S/N) = cr(S\&N)/cr(N), \quad \text{when } cr(N) \text{ is non-zero.}$$

So ask yourself this: how sure should you be that you will go to Fish-Dish and be satisfied? And how sure should you be that you will go to Noodle-Doodle and be satisfied? These questions ask after the credal values of numerators found above. Similarly, ask yourself this: how sure should you be that you will go to Fish-Dish

80  THE BAYESIAN THEORY OF STATES: CRITICAL DISCUSSION

tonight? And how sure should you be that you will go to Noodle-Doodle? These questions ask after the credal values of denominators found above.

In both cases the answer is clear: you should have no fixed credence at all, for you have yet to decide what to do. Intuitively put: since you are deliberating precisely about where to go for supper, but have yet to make up your mind, and since you know that whether you end-up at Fish-Dish or Noodle-Doodle turns precisely on your decision, you should be of no fixed credence about where you will end-up this evening.[16] But this entails that you should likewise be of no fixed credence in whether you will end-up being satisfied at Fish-Dish or at Noodle-Doodle. In these circumstances—perfectly realistic circumstances, in fact—the ratio formula doesn't apply. Neither its numerator nor its denominator is well defined.

This indicates that it is rationally possible to have well-defined conditional credence without the unconditional credence said by the Bayesian model to ground it. If that is so, however, conditional credence has a psychological life which is more robust than the metaphysical life of conditional probability within orthodox probability theory, for conditional credence does not reduce to unconditional credence via the ratio formula. Instead it is a self-standing psychological phenomenon, its own component of our psychological life.

DROP-ZONE (AGAIN, SEE CHAPTER 2)

You're on a team of 100 commandos about to be dropped into battle. The drop zone looks like a four-celled partition of logical space (naturally)

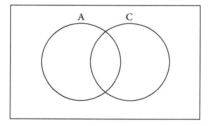

Figure 3.7

You're briefed on the mission by Commanding Officer, in whom you rationally place full trust. She tells you that section C of the drop zone leads to Certain death, that everywhere else in the drop zone is perfectly safe, and that commandos will be distributed at random as in Figure 3.8.

You set your credences accordingly. But then you are asked a question by your partner after the briefing: 'how likely is it that you will die on the mission if you land in A-section?'

---

[16] Which is not to say that you should be of no fixed opinion on the subject. The relevant point is that practical decision-making about whether to Φ is itself incompatible with rational credence about anything Ψ which is such that one is rationally sure that the truth-value of Ψ turns directly on whether one Φ's.

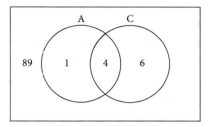

**Figure 3.8**

Well, Commanding Officer has given you enough information to answer your partner's question. But to do so you'll first need to work out the answer. In working out the answer, however, there will be a period during when the following three things will be true:

1. you will lend rational credence to the claim that you land in the C-bit of the A-section,;
2. you will lend rational credence to the claim that you land in the A-section; but
3. you will not yet lend rational credence to the claim that you land in the C-section on condition that you land in the A-section.

After all: when working out an answer to the question put to you by your partner, the very thing you are doing is calculating the correct conditional credence for landing in the C-section given you land in the A-section; and the tools used to make this calculation are states of credence set on the basis of the Oracle's brief (found at 1 and 2). More specifically, in working out an answer to your partner's question, there will be a stage of calculation when

$$cr(A\&C) = 4\%$$

and

$$cr(A) = 5\%,$$

but there is not yet a value for

$$cr(C/A).$$

It will be on the basis of the former two values that the following becomes true, once you are finished with your calculation:

$$cr(C/A) = 80\%.$$

There is a stage in the process, then, when the relevant ratio of credences exists, since the credences themselves exist, but the conditional credence meant to be grounded in that ratio does not yet exist. Of course your psychology is sub-optimal at that point, from an epistemic point of view, since it's not yet got everything worked out and lined up properly. But the possibility of such a sub-optimal scenario indicates that conditional credence does not derive from ratio facts in the way presupposed by the Bayesian model.

Since the model marks conditional credence with orthodox conditional probability, and since orthodox conditional probability is entirely derivative upon ratio facts, the Bayesian model matches its target only if conditional credence is utterly derivative in likewise fashion. But conditional credence is no such thing: it has a psychological life of its own. This means the Bayesian model does not match its target phenomenon, for it passes off conditional credence as derivative upon ratio facts when it's is not derivative upon such facts. To build a matching model, therefore, we'll need a new type of fundamental ingredient in our notation. This will be explored in the next section and also in Chapter 7.

## 3.4 Generalizing Bayesian States I: Intervals and Midpoints

To this point we've seen that the rational mind is more substantive than the Bayesian model makes out. §3.2 showed that it involves states of thick confidence as well as states of credence. §3.3 showed that that the rational mind involves non-ratio states of conditional credence. Yet the functional thickness of a state is one thing, and the non-ratio nature of conditionality is another. Hence the two lessons just mentioned are orthogonal to one another. A creature might be subject to either of them without being subject to the other. As it happens we are subject to both lessons at once. For this reason, any matching model of our rational mind will make room on its surface for at least four things: credence, conditional credence, thick confidence, conditional thick confidence. The key question to be asked is how best to model these building-blocks of our rationality.

The most obvious strategy would be to generalize the Bayesian theory of states. Recall that it makes use of two basic laws: the Credence Partition Principle and the Conditional Credence Rule:

(CrPP)  When $\{P_1, \ldots, P_n\}$ are a logical partition: $[\text{cr}(P_1) + \ldots + \text{cr}(P_n)] = 1$,

(cr/)  $\text{cr}(C/A) =_{dr.} \text{cr}(A\&C)/\text{cr}(A)$,  when $\text{cr}(A)$ is non-zero.

We might try extending these principles so that they cover all four ingredients mentioned before. In turn this would involve two crucial moves. First, we'd need to modify the Conditional Credence rule so that our new rule is not simply a device of abbreviation. Second, we'd need to generalize the Credence Partition Principle—along with our new rule for conditional credence—so that our new rules subsume thick states of confidence and conditional confidence as well as maximally thin ones. The resulting position would see states of conditional confidence as psychologically robust, and it would recognize both conditional and unconditional confidence in all levels of functional grain.

The first of these two steps is easy to take. We just replace the true-by-definition sign in the conditional-credence rule with a sign for strict identity:

(cr/=) $\text{cr}(C/A) = \text{cr}(A\&C)/\text{cr}(A)$,  when $\text{cr}(A)$ is non-zero.

The thought here is that rationality requires the measure of strength of conditional credence to be identical to the ratio of the relevant measures of strength for unconditional credence. Nothing in this idea is meant to be true by stipulation. Rather, the rule codifies a structural demand on rationality, obliging that conditional credence and its unconditional counterpart line-up with one another as specified in the ratio. This is a sensible major demand on structural aspects of the rational mind. We'll take it as read in what follows.

The second step is not so easily taken. Once we move from a conception of agency which presupposes only credence and conditional credence, to a conception of agency which uses thick confidence and conditional thick confidence, we'll need to expand our partition principle as well as our revised rule for conditional credence. But how should we do so?

Well, to this point we've used intervals to represent states of thick confidence. But everything we've said applies with equal felicity to states of conditional thick confidence. If our aim is to cover conditional and unconditional states of thick confidence, therefore, as well as conditional and unconditional credence, a natural suggestion is this: construe points in the unit interval as limit-case intervals—i.e. intervals with lower- and upper bounds identical to one another—and then generalize the additive spirit of the Credence Partition Principle, as well as the ratio-based spirit of the conditional-credence rule, so that they cover intervals broadly construed. This will be the initial strategy discussed for generalizing the Bayesian model.

The first step is to think of unit-real numbers as limit-case intervals. This means we see the unit real number .7, for instance, as the interval [.7, .7], the unit real number .37 as the interval [.37, .37], and so on. The opening move requires thinking of limit-case intervals as something like the result of 'shrinking down' multi-point intervals to a single point. As mentioned before, though, the idea involves really no more than thinking of limit-case intervals as intervals with lower- and upper-bounds identical to one another.

Next we generalize the additive spirit of the Credence Partition Principle so that it applies to the new more-inclusive conception of an interval. Since this idea is best understood by appeal to example we start with three of them.

*EXAMPLE 1*

You are faced with a two-cell partition: $\{\Phi, \neg\Phi\}$. Suppose you start out fully rational in lending 30-to-40% confidence to $\Phi$. Then you wonder how sure you should be that $\neg\Phi$. The intuitive answer is this: since you are at least 30% sure that $\Phi$ is true, you should be at most 70% sure that $\neg\Phi$ is true; and since you are at most 40% sure that $\Phi$ is true, you should be at least 60% sure that $\neg\Phi$ is true. When you start out rationally 30-to-40% sure that $\Phi$ is true, therefore, you should also be 60-to-70% sure that $\neg\Phi$ is true.

Now have a look at the lower- and upper-bounds for confidence in this example. In each case the lower-bound for one claim adds together with the upper-bound for the other claim to yield unity (i.e. 100%). This is an interval-based echo of the sum-to-unity idea in the Credal Partition Principle. A natural thought is to generalize this phenomenon and demand, of all lower- and upper-bounds in an interval distribution—i.e. to demand of all intervals assigned to cells in a finite partition—that lower bounds sum-to-unity when put together with upper bounds found in other intervals of the assignment, and vice versa. This yields:

## NAÏVE PRINCIPLE

When (i) $P_1, \ldots, P_n$ are a logical partition, and
(ii) each $P_i$ is assigned a confidence interval $[l_i, u_i]$, then,
(iii) for every such interval $[l_j, u_j]$
(a) $[l_j + \Sigma u_{k, \text{ for } k \neq j}] = 1$

and

(b) $[u_j + \Sigma l_{k, \text{ for } k \neq j}] = 1.$

In other words: when $P_1$ thru $P_n$ are a logical partition, and confidence intervals are assigned to its members, each lower bound should sum to unity with upper bounds drawn from other intervals in the assignment, and each upper bound should sum to unity with lower bounds drawn from other intervals in the assignment. That's how things work in the two-cell partition case above. The Naïve Principle demands that things always work out that way.

The demand is no good. Consider:

## EXAMPLE 2

You are faced with a three-cell partition: {A, B, C}. Suppose you rationally lend 20-to-30% confidence to A and 30-to-40% confidence to B. Then you wonder how confident you should be of C. The intuitive answer is this: since you are at least 20% sure of A, and at least 30% sure of B, you should be most 50% sure of C. And since you are at most 30% sure of A, and at most 40% sure of B, you should be at least 30% sure that of C. When you rationally lend 20-to-30% confidence to A and 30-to-40% confidence to B, therefore, you should lend 30-to-50% confidence to C.

Numbers in this example are internally coherent. Only some of them satisfy the Naïve Principle. Here are the relevant sums for each cell in the partition:

A
[up(A) + low(B) + low(C)] = .9
[low(A) + up(B) + up(C)] = 1.1
B
[up(B) + low(A) + low(C)] = .9
[low(B) + up(A) + up(C)] = 1.1
C
[up(C) + low(A) + low(B)] = 1
[low(C) + up(A) + up(B)] = 1.

The Naïve Principle holds only for the last cell in the partition. It is striking, though, how numbers work out in the other three cells. There's a pattern there which might hold-up in other cases. Consider another example:

## EXAMPLE 3

You are faced with a four-cell partition: {A, B, C, D}. Suppose you rationally spread confidence intervals in the following way: you're 5-to-10% sure of A, 10-20% sure of B, 10-to-15% sure of C, and 55-to-75% sure of D. The numbers are internally coherent here too, but once again they do not satisfy the Naïve Principle. Here are the relevant sums:

$$A$$
$$[up(A) + low(B) + low(C) + low(D)] = .85$$
$$[low(A) + up(B) + up(C) + up(D)] = 1.15$$
$$B$$
$$[up(B) + low(A) + low(C) + low(D)] = .9$$
$$[low(B) + up(A) + up(C) + up(D)] = 1.1$$
$$C$$
$$[up(C) + low(A) + low(B) + low(D)] = .85$$
$$[low(C) + up(A) + up(B) + up(D)] = 1.15$$
$$D$$
$$[up(D) + low(A) + low(C) + low(C)] = 1$$
$$[low(D) + up(A) + up(B) + up(C)] = 1.$$

A pattern most definitely shines through these examples. Let's see what we can do with it.

We begin with a finite partition and assign intervals to its cells. Each upper and lower bound in an interval of our assignment has a 'partition total' (in the assignment, of course, which caveat we henceforth leave silent). When the bound in question is an upper bound, its partition total is the result of summing it with lower bounds in other intervals in the assignment. When the bound in question is a lower bound, its partition total is the result of summing it with upper bounds in other intervals in the assignment. The Naïve Principle demands that partition totals in an assignment sum to unity. The prescription reduces to the Credal Partition Principle when intervals in play are all limit-case intervals. The prescription is satisfied in sensible interval assignments to two-cell partitions. Yet the Naïve Principle falters when larger partitions get off the ground.

In every interval assignment used above, however, partition totals within an interval sum to 2. The partition total of an interval's lower-bound adds to the partition total of its upper-bound to yield 2 every time, without exception. This reflects an important fact about the distribution of fully rational thick confidence: on average its strength works in a recognizably Bayesian way. When fully rational confidence is lent to the cells of a partition, and we represent that confidence with intervals, those intervals will have midpoints which behave like Bayesian states of credence. We might generalize the Bayesian model, therefore, by demanding that midpoints of intervals in a confidence assignment act in a Bayesian way. With '$mid[l_{Pi}, u_{Pi}]$' denoting the midpoint of the interval assigned to the $i^{th}$ member of a finite partition $P_i$, the relevant additivity idea will be this:

*MIDPOINT PARTITION PRINCIPLE*
When $P_1, \ldots, P_n$ are a logical partition: $\Sigma(mid[l_{Pi}, u_{Pi}]) = 1$.

The basic thought here is that confidence should be spread in a way which respects exclusion relations between cells of a partition, and which also respects the logical necessity of the partition as such. When $P_1, \ldots, P_n$ are a logical partition, after all, the truth of any $P_i$ logically precludes the truth of any other $P_j$—so, intuitively, confidence lent to a given $P_i$ should be taken away from other $P_j$'s—and the extent to which confidence is spread across cells of the partition should acknowledge that their disjunction is an unavoidable fact of logic. When dealing with limit-case-only distributions of confidence—i.e. distributions which use only limit-case intervals—the Midpoint Partition Principle reduces to the Credal Partition Principle. When thick confidence enters the picture the Midpoint Partition Principle generalizes the additive spirit of the Bayesian model, insisting that intervals relate to one another on average like Bayesian credence.

This move in generalizing the Bayesian model extends in an obvious way to conditional confidence. With 'mid$[l_{C/A}, u_{C/A}]$' standing for the midpoint of the interval assigned to C given A, the extension is the

### MIDPOINT CONDITIONAL CONFIDENCE RULE
$$\text{mid}[l_{C/A}, u_{C/A}] = \text{mid}[l_{A\&C}, u_{A\&C}]/\text{mid}[l_A, u_A]$$

This principle demands that conditional thick confidence act on average like conditional credence. When conditional thick confidence is rational, its average strength is identical to the average strength of the corresponding ratio formula. When dealing with limit-case-only distributions of confidence—i.e. distributions with only limit-case intervals—the Midpoint Conditional Confidence Rule reduces to the Conditional Credence Rule. When thick confidence enters the picture the Midpoint Conditional Confidence Rule generalizes the Bayesian perspective, insisting that on average conditional confidence relate to unconditional confidence like conditional credence relates to unconditional credence.

The Midpoint Partition Principle and the Midpoint Conditional Confidence Rule generalize the Bayesian model to an interval-based conception of rational states. The resulting perspective is both intuitive and mathematically tractable.[17] It involves an easy-to-make change in our model and a harder-to-make change. The former has to do with the shift from '$=_{df.}$' to '$=$' in the ratio-based conception of conditional attitudes. The latter has to do with the move from a point-based conception of fine-grained attitudes to an interval-based conception of them.

The philosophical significance of these changes is inversely proportional to the difficulty with which they are made. It's a trivial matter to shift from '$=_{df.}$' to '$=$' in a ratio-based formulae for conditional states. Yet the notational shift indicates a significant re-conception of conditionality. On the old conception—the one echoed by '$=_{df.}$'—conditional confidence is an ontic free-rider on ratio facts, something which springs automatically from them like circles spring from points arranged just so. On the new conception—the one echoed by '$=$'—conditional confidence is not something which springs automatically from ratio facts but rather a fundamental moving part of well-developed epistemic theory. Hence the notational move from identity-by-definition to strict-identity reflects a significant shift in the basics of the rational mind.

---

[17] See (Kyburg, 1998).

The move from a point-valued conception of confidence to an interval-valued one is not like this. It does not represent a fundamental shift in our conception of the basics of rationality. Instead it merely marks the addition of further binary attitudes to those we already have on the table. These new attitudes are functionally-coarser-than-credence types of confidence. The notational move from points to intervals, then, reflects no more than a coarsening of the rational machinery already in use.

## 3.5 Generalizing Bayesian States II: Intervals and Tertiary Attitudes

The interval-based generalization of the Bayesian model involves two main ideas. One is the view that conditional confidence is not a ratio-based derivative phenomenon. Another is the view that fully rational confidence can be thick as well as maximally thin. The new perspective makes use of a richer conception of fine-grained rationality than the one which prompts the Bayesian model.

Many formal epistemologists think the new perspective is not rich enough. To see why, consider a puzzle surrounding either of two thought experiments:[18]

### STRANGE ORACLE

You are rationally certain to draw a ball from each of two boxes: left-box and right-box. You've no clue what's in either box—save for balls, of course—so you ask a Strange Oracle passing by. You place full rational trust in the Oracle when she replies: 'The objective chance of drawing a blue ball from left-box is somewhere strictly between 20-and-30%. The objective chance of drawing a blue ball from right-box is in that range as well. The objective chance of drawing a blue ball from left-box is greater than the objective chance of drawing a blue ball from right-box.' The Strange Oracle then disapparates.

Once you have digested her reply, how sure should you be that you'll draw a blue ball from left-box? How sure should you be that you'll draw a blue ball from right-box? What should your confidence be, for short, in left-box and in right-box?

Defenders of thick confidence—for instance those who favor an interval-based generalization of the Bayesian model—face a puzzle about this case. That puzzle is generated by two points which seem true of the case.

First: your evidence in it for left-box as well as your evidence in it for right-box has a three-fold nature:

- It obliges an attitude stronger than 20% that of certainty.
- It obliges an attitude weaker than 30% that of certainty.
- It fails to oblige credence between these extremes.

---

[18] I used to think further resources were needed too, and in that vein I offered the first of these thought-experiments in a grad-seminar at Harvard in 2002 (and variants of it in Michigan in 2005, Oxford in 2008, and Brown in 2010). The second thought-experiment is based (via memory) on unpublished work by Jim Joyce (although Branden Fitelson [and his pal Mathematica] helped with its quadratic equation, since I couldn't remember exactly how Joyce had things). Since cooking it up I discover that the intended moral of each thought-experiment is endorsed in (Rinard, 2017).

It would be less than fully rational in STRANGE-ORACLE, for instance, to end-up 20% sure of left-box (or less); for your evidence in the case makes it plain that there is a greater-than-20% chance that you will draw a blue ball from the left box. Similarly, it would be less than fully rational in the case to end-up 30% sure of right-box (or more); for your evidence makes it plain that there is a less-than-30% chance that you will draw a blue ball from the right box. Were you to adopt any particular credence between 20% and 30%, however—say by ending up 23% sure of left-box, or 27% sure of right-box—you would thereby function as if you had more specific evidence than you actually possess. You would be attitudinally outrunning your evidential headlights.

Second: after fully digesting the Strange Oracle's evidence, you will be more confident of left-box than of right-box, and this fact about your comparative confidence will be perfectly rational. Given your evidence in the case, after all, it is fully rational to be more confident of left-box than of right-box. That is what the evidence indicates.

These two points make for a puzzle together.

The first one—the point laid out three paragraphs back—suggests that in STRANGE ORACLE a *single* attitude should be lent both to left-box and to right-box. In particular it suggests that a thick confidence running strictly between 20% and 30% of certainty should be lent to each claim in the case. But the second point in play—the one laid out two paragraphs back—seems to conflict with that suggestion; for it is natural to think that states of comparative confidence flow metaphysically from binary attitudes lent to the claims involved. When someone is 50% sure of $\Phi$, say, while being 40% sure of $\Psi$, the natural thought is that all there is to their being more confident of $\Phi$ than of $\Psi$ is the credal states just mentioned. In the vernacular: their state of comparative confidence—the fact that they are more confident of $\Phi$ than of $\Psi$—is fully grounded in the credence they lend to $\Phi$ and to $\Psi$. The two credal states make it the case that they are more confident of $\Phi$ than of $\Psi$. Their being more confident of $\Phi$ than of $\Psi$ is nothing over and above their being 50% sure of $\Phi$ while being 40% sure of $\Psi$.

If we let the expression '$(\Phi \gg \Psi)$' stand for the state of being more confident of $\Phi$ than of $\Psi$, and we use the odd symbol '⤳' to sit between two conditions when the one above it is nothing over and above the one below it, then, the natural thought about comparative confidence can be put this way:

$$(\Phi \gg \Psi)$$
$$⤳$$
$$[(\text{cr}(\Phi) = 50\%) \,\&\, (\text{cr}(\Psi) = 40\%)].$$

And more generally: if we let '$\text{att}(X)$' stand for the binary attitude lent to claim X—for any type of confidence in the human repertoire, say, and for any claim X—and we let the funny expression '$??(\Phi \gg \Psi)??$' stand for *whether or not* one is more confident of $\Phi$ than of $\Psi$, then, a natural thought about comparative confidence is this:

$$??(\Phi \gg \Psi)??$$
$$⤳$$
$$[\text{att}(\Phi) \,\&\, \text{att}(\Psi)].$$

On this view, whether or not someone is more confident of Φ than of Ψ turns precisely on the binary attitudes they lend to Φ and to Ψ. States of comparative confidence flow automatically from states of non-comparative confidence lent to the claims involved. This is how it seems to work when credence is in play. The natural first thought is that this is how it always works, even when thick confidence is in play.

Suppose that is so and that you are rational in STRANGE-ORACLE to lend the same attitude to left-box and to right-box. Then it is not true that you are rational to be more confident in the case of left-box than of right-box, for it is not true that you <u>are</u> more confident of left-box than of right-box! The puzzle generated by STRANGE-ORACLE, then, is simple: we must decide which of the following three claims is false in the case:

- You lend the same thick confidence to left-box and to right-box, namely, the one marked by the open interval (.2,.3).
- You are more confident of left-box than of right-box.
- Comparative confidence is fully grounded in binary attitudes lent to the claims involved.

Since there is much to say in favour of each of these claims, the puzzle is to reckon which is least painful to give up.

The same puzzle is generated by a similar case:

### RANDOM SUPPER

You are rationally certain of the following.

You face a pair of decisions about what to eat for supper. Each of them is to be made by coin flip. You have a main-dish coin **M** and a pudding-coin **P**. The former has 'fish' written on one side and 'fowl' written on the other. The latter has 'cake' written on one side and 'custard' written on the other. You are to flip the coins and eat accordingly. M's bias to 'fish' is somewhere in the open interval (.4, .6), though you have no idea where in that interval it is. P's bias to 'cake' is a quadratic function of M's bias to 'fish', namely:

$$p = [2m - m^2 - 6/25].$$

Once you have digested these details, so to say, how confident should you be that you will have fish for supper? And how confident should you be that you will have cake?

Well, it is clear from the details that you should lend a thick confidence to the claim that you will have fish for supper. After all, your evidence ensures that you should be more than 40% certain that you will have fish for supper, less than 60% certain that you will do so, but nothing in your evidence plumps for a particular credence between these extremes. Yet the exact same thing is true when it comes to the claim that you will have cake for supper. Your evidence ensure that you should be more than 40% certain of this claim, less than 60% certain of it, but nothing in your evidence plumps for a particular credence between these extremes. In both cases, therefore, it is natural to think that you should lend a thick confidence marked by the open interval (.4,.6).

On the other hand, consider the graph of the quadratic equation

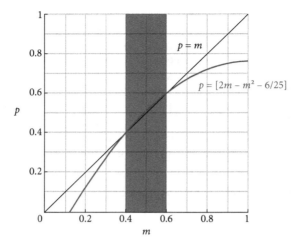

Figure 3.9

We've marked the unit interval along the x- and the y-axes and put the .4-to-.6-bit of the x-axis in **bold**. Note the diagonal line consists in points <x, y> such that x is identical to y; and the curve represents P's bias for 'cake' as a function of M's bias for 'fish'. The crucial thing about that relationship is this: outputs for the P-function are greater than inputs throughout the open interval (.4, .6). That's why the graph of the quadratic function arcs above the diagonal (x=y)-line at every point where an x-coordinate is in the open interval. This reflects something important and known to an agent in the case, namely, that in every possibility consistent with its set-up P-bias for 'cake' is _stronger_ than M-bias for 'fish'. No matter what the latter turns out to be—consistent with the set-up, of course—the former is stronger. This is why it seems intuitive that a fully rational agent in the case will end up being more confident that she will have cake than that she will have fish.

So we face the same kind of puzzle as before. At least one of these thoughts is wrong in RANDOM SUPPER:

- A rational agent will lend the same thick confidence to fish and to cake, namely, the thick confidence marked by the open interval (.4,.6).
- A rational agent will be more confident of cake than of fish.
- States of comparative confidence are fully grounded in the binary attitudes lent to the claims involved.

Since there is much to say in favour of each of these claims, the puzzle is to decide which is least painful to give up.

After reflecting on situations like STRANGE-ORACLE and RANDOM-SUPPER, formal epistemologists sometimes conclude that the interval-based generalization of the Bayesian model is insufficient to mark the workings of the rational mind. They conclude that thick confidence is insufficient on its own to capture states of comparative confidence, for instance; and for similar reasons they maintain that a richer formalism is needed to capture the rational mind.[19] Such epistemologists do not much agree with one another on exactly what's left out of the interval-based conception, but they do tend to agree on the formalism that should replace the interval-based generalization. Our last major task in this chapter is to consider how best to understand that formalism.

## 3.6 Generalizing Bayesian States III: Representors

The Bayesian story begins with the thought that full rationality is well modelled with a single probability function. It does not take long for this idea to come under pressure. Primarily the pressure is due to the myriad ways in which evidence and attitude can fit together. When faced with this fact there are two main reactions to be explored. We might hold on to the idea that a single function be used when modelling an agent's full rationality, but give up on the thought that only points in the unit-interval are that function's output. Or we might hold on to the thought that only such points are the output of any function we use when modelling an agent's full rationality, but give up on the idea that a single function be used when doing so.

The previous section explored the former strategy. In this one we explore the latter strategy. It does not attempt to enrich output-values for a single function when modelling full rationality, but rather makes use of multiple classic probability functions to get the job done. Rich *sets* of classic probability functions—often called 'representors'—are used to capture all aspects of an agent's full rationality.[20]

To see how this works, suppose agent Smith is rational and his overall state of opinion is modelled by a particular representor $R$ (that is to say a particular set of probability functions). Suppose five things are true of Smiths' representor:

(1) probability values given to A by members of $R$ cover precisely the interval [.2,.3]. This means two things: for every real number $r$ in [.2,.3], some probability function in $R$ is such that **prob**(A) = $r$; and a probability function is in $R$ only if there is a real number $r$ in [.2,.3] such that **prob**(A) = $r$.

(2) $R$-values for B are always .6. This means that every probability function in $R$ is such that **prob**(B) = .6.

(3) $R$-values for C and for D cover precisely the open interval (.4,.6) even though $R$-values for C are always greater than those for D (i.e. each function in $R$ is such that **prob**(C) > **prob**(D)).

---

[19] And many other states as well: see the list mentioned in (Joyce, 2005), for instance.
[20] In the next chapter we'll consider how those sets are used to model rational state transitions. We'll also not fuss much over the details of representors, prescinding from whether they should be the set-theoretically smallest sets which satisfy certain natural properties, for instance, or whether they should only contain classical probability functions, or whether their members should always give non-degenerate value to epistemic contingencies, and so on. Van Fraassen first presented his supervaluation-styled version of the representor approach in (van Fraassen, 1985) (later developed in (van Fraassen, 1989)). (Halpern, 2003), (Jeffrey, 1983), (Joyce, 2005), (Kaplan, 1983), (Levi, 1974), (Walley, 1991) all present versions of the approach. In my view, the best technical expression of it also happens to be its most full-throated philosophical defence: (Joyce, 2005) and (Joyce, 2010).

(4) *R*-values for E given F cover precisely the interval [.7,.8].
(5) every function in *R* is such that **prob**(G/H) = **prob**(G).

The key issue is what to make of the formal machinery. In particular how do we recover Smith's rational states from mathematical facts like (1)-thru-(5)? Put more colloquially: how do we read off his epistemic states from the guts of his representor?

Sadly there is no agreement about this among defenders of the representor approach. Of course this leaves us in an unsatisfying position. After all, leading figures in formal epistemology—pioneers such as Richard Jeffrey or Isaac Levi, second-generation leaders such as Mark Kaplan or James Joyce, and so on—all agree that quotidian evidence calls for thick confidence. And they all agree that this is a common-sense fact about us. This leads them to insist that rational thick confidence is well modelled by richly membered sets of probability functions. But they do not say in any detail how to interpret those sets when they are at work. This makes it more than a bit obscure how they are thinking of the mind being modelled by those sets.

Fortunately, there is a Goldilocks story to be told about this, and like all such stories it involves three major elements. Each of them is a view about how to read off an agent's epistemic states from a representor. One of the views is 'too hot' in the sense that it over-generates mental states, one of them is 'too cold' in that it under-generates mental states, and one of the views does about as well as any could when it comes to reading off epistemic states from a representor. Consider the answers in turn:

1. *The face-value strategy: too hot.* We might maintain that a representor metaphysically matches its target domain. If that is so, key basic elements of a representor mark basic elements of the rational mind and key derivative elements of a representor mark derivative elements of that mind. Since the fundamental element of a representor is a classic probability function, and since that sort of function is a measure of Bayesian rationality, the face-value answer leads to the idea that agents like Smith are literally composed of self-coherent-but-potentially-disagreeing mini-agents—or, at least, that agents like Smith are composed of self-coherent-but-potentially conflicting credence distributions.

This is to treat Smith as a corporate agent.[21] When asked about his take on claims A thru H, for instance, the face-value approach looks at Smith's representor *R* and sees each of those stances as literally built from countless sub-agential credence distributions. With the symbol '☺' standing for face-value, the approach sees representor facts like (1)-thru-(5) in the following way:

☺-(1) Smith's sub-agential credence distributions lend A precisely the values in the interval [.2,.3]; this grounds the agential fact that Smith lends 20-to-30% thick confidence to A.

☺-(2) each of Smith's sub-agential credence distributions lends 60% credence to B; this grounds the agential fact that Smith lends 60% credence to B.

---

[21] See (List & Pettit, 2011).

☺-(3)  Smith's sub-agential credence distributions lend C and lend D precisely the values in the (open) interval (.4,.6); and each of them involves more credence for C than for D; this grounds the agential fact that Smith is more confident of C than of D.

☺-(4)  Smith's sub-agential credence distributions lend E conditional on F precisely the values in interval [.7,.8]; this grounds the agential fact that Smith lends a thick conditional confidence of 70-to-80% to E given F.

☺-(5)  Smith's sub-agential credence distributions take G to be independent of H; this grounds the agential fact that Smith's confidence for G conditional on H is identical to his confidence for G.

At this point, however, the face-value approach faces an obvious difficulty: sub-agential credence is a creature of darkness. What is this mental phenomenon? Why does it deserve the honorific 'credence'? What on Earth are we talking about here?

There are two ways forward at this point. One—most naturally aligned with the spirit of the face-value approach—says that sub-agential credence is credence in exactly the same sense as agential credence, that there is one phenomenon found on differing agential levels (so to say). This is to take consequences of the face-value approach at face value! The other way forward—still basically in the spirit of the face-value approach, though more sensitive to its difficulties—says that sub-agential credence is not credence in *exactly* the same sense as agential credence. Instead it says that sub-agential credence is some kind of credence-like phenomenon which shows up at the sub-agential level. On this version of the face-value interpretation of a representor, sub-agential credence is not precisely like credence lent by Smith, but it is enough like it to deserve the honorific 'credence'.

The first of these answers is functionally incoherent. If sub-agential credence is credence in exactly the way that Smith lends credence, the very idea of one agent housing countless sub-agential credence distributions is functionally impossible. Just as it is functionally impossible for one agent to lend 30% *and* 33% credence to a given claim Φ (at the same time)—since the signature functions of these states preclude one another—it is functionally impossible for one agent to house countless conflicting credences for Φ. Moreover, it is functionally impossible for a range of conflicting credal-states to ground a thick confidence, for both individually and jointly the putative grounding states are incompatible with the signature profile of thick confidence. If sub-agential credence is exactly like agential credence, therefore, the face-value answer is functionally impossible.

The second answer does not suffer this indignity. If sub-agential credence is not credence in exactly the same sense as agential credence, if it is some kind of credence-like phenomenon showing-up only at the sub-agential level, say, then it is notionally possible that the signature functional profile of sub-agential credence can be made out so that multiple sub-agential credence profiles can be housed in the same agent; and it is notionally possible that a range of sub-agential credences can ground an agential state of thick confidence.

But we have yet to be given any reason to take the position seriously. We've not been told how the functional profiles of sub-agential credence work out. Nor have we been told what evidence there is for the existence of these heretofore unknown mental states. Although the second reading of the face-value answer does not immediately lead to functional impossibility, it does lead to a view on which agent's like Smith are corporate entities with minds built out of sub-agent mental states. We do not have a clear grip (or indeed any sort of grip) on what those new mental states do for a living. We do not have serious reason to suppose they exist.

The face-value answer over-generates mental states. When asked to detail the confidence-theoretic states of Smith, for instance, by appeal to his representor, the face-value view ends-up recognizing countless credence-like states we did not recognize before. Those states occur at a sub-agential level. There is little reason to think they make sense, and no reason in this ballpark to think they exist (even if they do make sense). Hence we should reject the face-value approach to representors. When asked to detail the epistemic states of Smith by appeal to his representor $R$, for instance, we should not see $R$ as metaphysically matching its target. Whatever is going on in Smith when he's well-modelled by $R$, we should reject the idea that his mind involves countless sub-agential distributions of credence-like mental states.

2. *The agreement strategy: too cold.* We might say that a representor marks something real in a target mind exactly when there is agreement between members of the representor. On this view: whenever members agree about something—say by giving a particular claim the same probability-value, or always giving one claim a higher probability-value than another—there is an aspect of the targeted mind which corresponds to the point of agreement; conversely, there is an epistemically-salient aspect of the targeted mind only if it corresponds to a point of agreement in the agent's representor. The view is basically this:

(*)   A rational agent manifests feature F if and only if there is agreement about something F-like between members of the agent's representor.[22]

Consider how this approach views Smith's mind in light of his representor. When '&' stands for agreement we have this reading of (1)-thru-(5):

&-(1)   Since $R$-values for A cover the interval [.2,.3], there is no $R$-agreement about the value of A. This marks the fact that Smith takes no particular attitude to A.

&-(2)   Since $R$-values for B are always equal to .6, there is $R$-agreement about B. This marks the fact that Smith lends 60% credence to B.

&-(3)   Since $R$-values for C cover the open interval (.4,.6), and $R$-values for D do the same, there is no $R$-agreement about C or about D. This marks the fact that Smith takes no stand on C and no stand on D. But $R$-values for C are always greater than $R$-values for D, so there is $R$-agreement that C is more probable than D. This marks the fact that Smith is more confident of C than of D.

---

[22] This view is defended in (Joyce, 2005) and (Joyce, 2010). Were I to defend the agreement approach, though, I'd relax the need for full agreement—plumping for the view instead, as Lewis would put it, on which 'near enough is good enough' (See (Lewis, 1994)). Suppose an agent's representor gives Φ and gives Ψ exactly the values in the interval [*l,u*], but gives a higher probability for Φ everywhere but at point *l*. It seems plausible that the agent is more confident of Φ than of Ψ, even though the left-to-right direction of (*) is false. Of course it will be a vague matter whether there is enough agreement in a representor for a given factor to be considered presented in the target mind. For the approach to work, therefore, that vagueness should align with vagueness in that mind's manifestation of a target feature.

♣-(4)  Since *R*-values for E given F cover the interval [.7,.8], there is no *R*-agreement about the conditional probability of E given F. This marks the fact that Smith takes no stand on E given F.

♣-(5)  Since every member of *R* entails that **prob**(G/H) = **prob**(G), there is *R*-agreement that G is probabilistically independent of H. This marks the fact that Smith's confidence for G given H is equal in strength to his confidence for G.

There is good news and bad news for this approach.

The good news is that it does not over-generate mental states. Since the approach marks real elements of mind only with agreement within a representor, it does not use individual probability functions to mark anything on their own. Hence the approach avoids the pitfall which felled the face-value theory. It fails to entail that there are countless conflicting sub-agential credence-like distributions in an agent like Smith. Since there are in fact no such credence-like distributions, that failure is good news.

The bad news is that the agreement approach strikingly under-generates mental states, for the raison d'être of the representor machinery is to make room in our modelling for thick confidence. Yet the agreement approach to representors treats that confidence as a disappearing act! Instead of seeing Smith as lending sharp thick confidence of 20-to-30% to A, for instance—as you would expect on the basis of the evidential facts which generate aspect (1) of his representor—the approach sees Smith as lending no particular attitude to A at all. That is plainly at odds with the foundational motivations of the representor approach. After all, there is nothing indeterminate or non-factual or less-than-real about sharp thick confidence: it is simply confidence which is functionally coarser than credence. The agreement approach to representors treats sharp thick confidence as if it weren't real, turning a blind eye to the very phenomena which motivate the mathematical framework in the first place. In a real sense, then, the agreement approach to representors is 'too cold'. Since it only recognizes classic Bayesian states as really there in an agent, the approach leaves out mental states central to the rational mind.

3. *The Either-Or Strategy: just right?* We might say that a representor marks something real in a mind exactly when one of two things occurs: members of a representor jointly make for a significant coarse-grained output (such as an interval), or they agree on something significant (like comparative probability). This is the either/or approach to a representor. It attempts to graft together the best features of the previous two approaches but avoids their pitfalls. With 'V' standing for either/or consider its take on (1)-thru-(5):

V-(1)  *R*-values for A cover the interval [.2,.3]. This marks the fact that Smith lends 20-to-30% confidence to A.

V-(2)  *R*-values for B are always equal to .6. This marks the fact that Smith lends 60% credence to B.

V-(3)  *R*-values for C and for D exactly cover the open interval (.4,.6). This marks the fact that Smith lends to each claim an open thick confidence of strictly between 40-and-60% certainty. Further, *R*-values for C are always greater than those for D. This marks the fact that Smith is more confident of C than of D.

V-(4)   *R*-values for E given F exactly cover the interval [.7,.8]. This marks the fact that Smith is 70-to-80% confident of E given F.

V-(5)   *R*-values for G given H are always equal to *R*-values for G. This marks the fact that Smith's confidence for G given H is equal in strength to his confidence for G.

There are two bits of good news and one bit of bad news for this approach.

The first bit of good news is simple: the either/or approach avoids the pitfall which plagued the face-value interpretation of representors. Since the approach—like its agreement-based cousin—only marks elements of a targeted mind with multiple probability functions, it does not over-generate mental states by attempting to mark them with individual functions. The approach fails to entail that there are sub-agential distributions of credence. This is a good thing, of course, since there are no such distributions underneath our states of confidence.

The second bit of good news is equally simple: the either/or approach avoids the pitfall which fell the agreement-based interpretation of representors. Since the either/or approach—like its face-value-based cousin—says that the upshot of disagreeing probability functions can jointly mark elements of a targeted mind, it has no difficulty in recognizing the reality or bona fides of thick confidence. This is a good thing, of course, since it means the approach can tackle the phenomena which motivates its mathematics. And it means that the approach avoids the under-generation worry which plagues the agreement-based interpretation of representors.

In a way, then, the either/or approach can have its cake and eat it too. Since it lets intervals generated by multiple probability functions stand for targeted elements of mind, the approach gracefully models thick confidence and credence (with limit-case intervals, of course). Since it says agreement between probability functions stands for targeted elements of mind, the approach gracefully models comparative probability and other tertiary attitudes. There is something to worry about, though, when it comes to such tertiary relations; and this worry surfaces when we focus on the kind of case normally used to motivate representors. Consider one from before:

### STRANGE ORACLE

You are rationally certain to draw a ball from each of two boxes: left-box and right-box. You've no clue what's in either box—save for balls, of course—so you ask a Strange Oracle passing by. You place full rational trust in the Oracle. She replies: 'The objective chance of drawing a blue ball from left-box is somewhere strictly between 20-and-30%. The objective chance of drawing a blue ball from right-box is in that exact range as well. The objective chance of drawing a blue ball from left-box is greater than the objective chance of drawing a blue ball from right-box.' The Strange Oracle then disapparates.

Once you have digested her reply, how sure should you be that you'll draw a blue ball from left-box? How sure should you be that you'll draw a blue ball from right-box? What should your confidence be, for short, in left-box and in right-box?

It is natural to think that the following two claims are true in this case:

(A) You lend an open thick confidence of 20-to-30% to left-box and to right-box.
(B) You are more confident of left-box than of right-box.

But it is also natural to think that comparative confidence is grounded in binary attitudes in a particularly simple way. In STRANGE-ORACLE the thought would be

(C) Your being more confident of left-box than right-box is grounded in the confidence you lend to left-box and the confidence you lend to right-box.

Point (A) insists that in STRANGE-ORACLE you lend the very same attitude to left-box and to right-box. Point (B) insists that you end-up more confident in the case of one claim than the other. And point (C) rules out both of the previous two points being true at once. In this way (A), (B), and (C) are jointly inconsistent.

When faced with that inconsistency the either/or approach must reject (C). The representor model is motivated precisely by a desire to say things like (A) and (B) in cases like STRANGE-ORACLE. Yet the rejection of (C) calls for serious comment. Note that claims like (C) are basically undeniable in credence-only scenarios. When you lend 80% credence to Φ, for instance, while lending 70% credence Ψ, it follows that you are more confident of the first claim than of the second. And the best explanation for *why* this follows—for why it must be that in cases like this you are more confident of Φ than of Ψ—is that comparative confidence in them is nothing over and above the two binary states of credence in play. More generally it seems hard to deny that whenever credence is lent to a pair of claims a fact about comparative confidence is thereby generated: either you are more confident of one claim than you are of the other, or, failing that, you are equally confident of the two claims. Facts about comparative confidence seem fully derivative upon states of credence, whenever such states exist to generate them.

If (C) is false, therefore, one of two things must be true in STRANGE-ORACLE. Either

(☹-1)   comparative confidence is fully grounded in binary attitudes lent to more claims than left-box and right-box,

or

(☹-2)   comparative confidence is not fully grounded in binary attitudes.

We'll now see that the first option undercuts the need for representors, and the second leads to a pair of serious worries. Consider the options in turn.

First, suppose (A), (B) and (☹-1) are true. Then in STRANGE-ORACLE you lend an open thick confidence of 20-to-30% to left-box and to right-box, you are more confident of left-box than of right-box, but this state of comparative confidence is fully grounded in binary attitudes lent to contents. Since you lend the same binary attitude to left-box and to right-box in the case, it follows that grounding contents for comparative confidence involve more than those two claims.

It is not hard to see what further claim should be involved. STRANGE-ORACLE is described to ensure that left-box has a higher chance of being true than right-box. This is why every member of a representor in the case lends more probability to left-box than to right-box. Presumably agents are meant to be certain of the set-up of the case which generates their representor. So every member of that representor will give full probability to the claim that left-box has a higher chance of being true than does right-box.

We might propose that an agent's state of comparative confidence, then—at least when it comes to left-box and right-box in STRANGE-ORACLE—is grounded in her take on left-box, together with her take on right-box, together with her certainty about their relative chances. In the event, the situation would be this:

left-box » right-box

⇹

tc(left-box) & tc(right-box) & cert[chance(left-box) > chance(right-box)]

Put another way: being more confident of left-box than of right-box is grounded in the same thick confidence being lent to each claim plus certainty being lent to the claim that left-box has a greater chance of being true than does right-box.

This perspective maintains that credence is enough on its own to get comparative confidence off the ground, so to speak, when credence is around to do the job. But it also maintains that thick confidence is not always capable of getting that job done; and when it's not thick confidence must join forces with credence if comparative confidence is to be gotten off the ground.[23] More specifically, in cases like STRANGE-ORACLE the thought is that certainty is lent to claims about particulars of the set-up and that this credence joins forces with thick confidence to make for whatever tertiary attitudes are present in the case.

If this story is right, however, we should be able to capture rationality as well with an interval-valued probability function as we can with a representor. We must only bear in mind that tertiary states do not always flow from binary attitudes in a super-simple way. When there are enough credal states around, tertiary states flow that way from a credal base. When there are not states of thick confidence enter the scene and things get more complicated. Extra binary attitudes are then needed to get derivative tertiary states off the ground. So in a sense tertiary states are multiply realized: they flow from simple combinations of credence when that sort of attitude is around to get the job done, and they flow from more complex states of credence otherwise. The either/or interpretation of representors does not sit happily with the view that tertiary states are always grounded in binary attitudes. That view contains the seeds of a story which undermines the representor approach to rationality.

Suppose, then, that a defender of the either/or approach says that (A), (B), and (⊗-2) are true. Their view will then be that in STRANGE-ORACLE you lend an open thick confidence of 20-to-30% to left-box and to right-box, you are more confident of left-box than of right-box, and this state of comparative confidence is

---

[23] Some states of thick confidence will be capable of grounding comparative confidence on their own. When you are 60-to-70% confident of Φ, for example, and 20-to-30% confident of Ψ, you are thereby more confident of Φ than of Ψ. Since states of thick confidence are not linearly ordered by strength, though, it won't always be the case that thick confidence on its own grounds comparative confidence. The line presently being sketched says that in some of those cases further binary attitudes fill the gap.

not fully grounded in binary attitudes of any sort. In the event—and even if we grant that you're sure in the case that left-box has a higher chance of being true than right-box—your state of comparative confidence will be thought to involve a new kind of mental element. More than binary attitudes will be involved in anchoring your comparative confidence. Perhaps that confidence turns out to be basic—i.e. a fundamental element of rationality—perhaps a new mental gizmo helps to ground it.[24] Either ways something non-binary plays an ineliminable role in grounding comparative confidence.

In the event, defenders of the either/or approach face a new over-generation worry. Recall the old one involved the idea (near enough) that familiar mental kinds crop up in unhappy places: e.g. sub-agential distributions of credence. The new over-generation worry can but need not take this form. That will depend on what story is told about *why* tertiary attitudes (such as comparative confidence) fail to be fully grounded in binary states. And there are two stories to be told about that. Defenders of the either/or strategy might say that tertiary attitudes fail to be fully grounded in binary states because tertiary attitudes are ungrounded, because they are basic elements of the rational mind. Or defenders of the either/or strategy might say tertiary attitudes (such as comparative confidence) fail to be fully grounded in binary states because tertiary attitudes are grounded in some other non-binary gizmo.

If defenders of the approach take the first option—if they say that tertiary attitudes fail to be fully grounded in binary states because tertiary attitudes are basic elements of rationality—the new over-generation worry will be similar to the old one we have discussed. After all, the story being told now entails that states we already recognize—comparative confidence, commitment to probabilistic independence, and so forth—surprisingly show up at the fundamental level of our psychology. That's a coherent idea, of course, though it's difficult to believe; for none of these tertiary attitudes were thought fundamental before the representor model was put under the microscope. Shifting our take on them now requires serious rethinking of our rational architecture. Among other things it requires dropping the Binary Attitudes Assumption at the heart of our project. This is the view that in creatures like us basic epistemic architecture always involves lending an attitude to a content. The perspective does not deny that there are tertiary attitudes in rationality; but it does deny that those attitudes are psychologically basic. If the present defence of the either/or approach is accepted, the Binary Attitudes Assumption is false, there are familiar tertiary attitudes at the base of our rational architecture. States like comparative confidence, commitment to independence, and so on turn out to be on all fours with states of thick confidence, but *only* when states of credence are not around to ground them. We thought those states were derivative in their nature—and they *are* derivative when enough credence is around—but it turns out that these tertiary attitudes are fundamental aspects of the rational mind when there is not enough credence in play to get them off the ground.

This rejigging of our take on rational architecture seems a high price to pay, since all we get for it is a push-back to an objection to a model which misleads

---

[24] This assumes that conditional credence is not used to spell out comparative confidence.

about the metaphysics of rationality! If tertiary attitudes fail to be fully grounded in binary attitudes, after all—say because some-but-not-all of their instances are fundamental—then the surface of the representor model fails to echo the metaphysics of tertiary attitudes; for it always marks them with multitudes of probability functions, as if they were derivative phenomena, even though many of their instances are psychologically basic. A better approach would be to drop representors and build a model which both can and should be taken at face value. This would put us in a better position to understand the rational mind than we are afforded by any model which misleads about the phenomena it's meant to mark.

On the other hand, if defenders of the either/or approach say that tertiary attitudes fail to be fully grounded in binary cousins because tertiary attitudes are grounded in some other sort of non-binary gizmo, then, the new generation worry for the either/or approach will be even worse than the old one. The story being told now entails the existence of a new non-binary mental kind about which we know nothing positive, save that it plays some kind of grounding role in the production of tertiary attitudes. We do know negative things about this new gizmo—it's not a binary attitude like credence, it's not a familiar tertiary attitude like comparative confidence—but what it is in itself we have no clue. We only know that it sits at the foundation of our mental architecture and somehow helps to ground tertiary attitudes.

This view amounts to little more than a bet that there is something non-binary at the foundation of our mind which grounds familiar tertiary states such as comparative confidence. That may be true, of course, but we have no substantive reason to believe it. This version of the either/or approach involves mental resources about which we know next to nothing. Those resources are doing serious work in the metaphysics of mind. Since we know next to nothing about them, however, we cannot see if they are suited to that work. We have no sense of how they are in themselves, and, for this reason, no sense of how or why they are suited to play the role given them by defenders of the representor approach to rational states. We are simply told that these states exist and do their work. This is a believe-it-if-you-can theory if ever there were one.

# 4
# The Bayesian Transition Theory
## Critical Discussion

### 4.1 Preview

The Bayesian transition theory consists in a single update rule: Jeffrey Conditionalization. There is a great deal of confusion about what this rule amounts to, so one of the main goals of this chapter is to clarify its purpose or point. To that end, §4.2 introduces the distinction between a theory's dynamics and its kinematics, and it argues that a theory of inference belongs to the former while update rules like Jeffrey's belong to the latter. §4.3 discusses the distinction between conditional credence and credence lent to an indicative conditional; then it introduces the difference between a binary and tertiary approach to conditional commitment. §4.4 explains two worries for Bayesian kinematics: one to do with the 'rigidity' of conditional credence in the model (in a sense to be glossed), and the other to do with the model never permitting (or even speaking of) contact-point shift in conditional credence. §4.5 defends a natural conception of conditional commitment—the restricted-vision conception of conditionality—and spells out various properties of conditional commitment which follow from it. §4.6 uses those properties to show that the most straightforward strategy for dealing with the two worries is hopeless. §4.7 then argues that *modus-ponens* style arguments are unlike other valid formal syllogisms in corresponding to obligatory pathways forward in thought, and this point is used to support the tertiary approach to conditional commitment. §4.8 then spells out that approach in detail: it is shown that the tertiary approach leads naturally to the rigidity of conditional commitment and motivates its own update rule for contact-point shift in such commitment.[1]

### 4.2 Bayesian Transition: Inference or What?

When the Bayesian model targets an epistemic agent it aims to capture her fully rational states. The model lays down laws for how states should relate to one another

---

[1] Well-known worries for a generalized Bayesian kinematics of confidence—based on the *dilation* of representors—as well as new worries for that approach—based on undercutting defeat and the incommensurability of evidential force—will be discussed in Chapter 12, after a theory of confidence has been developed which helps make sense of those worries.

*The Rational Mind.* Scott Sturgeon, Oxford University Press (2020). © Scott Sturgeon.
DOI: 10.1093/oso/9780198845799.001.0001

at any given time, and it presupposes that states undergo rational transition or shift across time. The rule for the latter is Jeffrey Conditionalization (J-Cond).

When someone shifts opinion, it is notionally possible that they do so by changing their mind about everything at once. But that's not how humans shift opinion, of course, and nor is it how the Bayesian model sees them as doing so.[2] In essence, the model speaks of what happens after a fully rational agent changes an in-between credence for a particular claim A and no more. Jeffrey's rule says that once this has happened, then, for any claim C, the agent's new take on C should be identical in strength to the sum of two specific products. In Chapter 4 we codified the prescription in the following way:

(J-Cond)  $cr_{new}(C) = \{[cr_{new}(A) \times cr_{old}(C/A)] + [cr_{new}(\neg A) \times cr_{old}(C/\neg A)]\}$.

Let's unpack what this comes to.

Suppose a credal agent begins in a fully rational position—an epistemic equilibrium so to say. Each of their attitudes fits together perfectly. We may suppose that they've surveyed their evidence fully and apportioned credence accordingly. Suppose also that the agent lends in-between credence to a particular claim A: her take on A is stronger than zero-strength credence but weaker than certainty. Then suppose—and this is the crucial bit—that the agent shifts her take on A, moving intellectually *from* an in-between credence *to* some other credence (which may or may not be in-between).

In the event—and before anything else happens—the agent's epistemic attitudes are sub-optimal. They have gone from an equilibrium position to a state of probabilistic incoherence. Since the agent's new set of views places a new credence for A alongside old credence for everything else, probabilistic incoherence is the result. After all, her new credence for A doesn't fit with her old take on things: only her *old* take on A will do that! Once a new take on A is adopted, therefore, the agent's attitudes no longer fit together coherently. They are in disequilibrium.

Jeffrey's rule describes what should be the overall upshot of the shift responsible for that disequilibrium. It answers the following question: how should the agent change her mind *further* to regain equilibrium, once disequilibrium has been brought on by the absorption of new input? When rational attitudes are perturbed by a shift-in-view at some contact-point—i.e. by a shift to do solely with a particular claim—less-than-full rationality is thereby introduced into the agent's attitudes. Jeffrey's rule recommends a specific way to shift attitudes further so that full equilibrium is regained. In effect, it specifies which equilibrium position should be the attitudinal upshot of the initial contact-point perturbance.

Jeffrey Conditionalization takes the form of an equation, of course. When you look at the equation you'll see the name of a number on its left-hand side, and a simple sum on its right-hand side. The left-hand number is meant to measure strength of new credence for C—credence adopted after incoherence has been introduced via perturbance of an equilibrium state—and the right-hand sum is meant to pin down the strength of that new credence for C. Moreover, each summand in the right-hand

---

[2] This is a matter of stipulation, of course, something we've cooked into the model from the start.

sum is a product of three things: the new take on A, the old take on C given A, and the old take on C given ¬A.[3]

This generates the appearance that Jeffrey's rule is some kind of inference procedure. And that's certainly how it is taken by many in formal epistemology, decision theory, and other Bayesian areas of inquiry.[4] Mental-state transitions which adhere to Jeffrey's rule are routinely referred to as episodes of 'Bayesian inference'. The thought seems to be that the rule is an inference procedure to be used in inferential efforts to regain equilibrium, or at least that it describes what should happen inferentially when someone attempts to regain coherence. But this is a deep confusion, for taken at face value Jeffrey's rule is no inference procedure at all; and nor is it something to be used in inference-based efforts to regain full rationality. Instead, Jeffrey Conditionalization is something deeply removed from the topic of inference.

To understand why this is so, we must first consider the fundamentals of inference as such. And the first thing to say about inference is this: not every systematic mental-state transition is inferential in character. The shift from normal to starry-eyed consciousness, for instance, brought on by a punch—or the shift from thought-of-salt to thought-of-pepper brought on by association, or the shift from cessation of pain to onset of relief—all of these can be systematic. But none of them are inferential in character. None involve conclusions being drawn from prior epistemic commitment, much less being rationally so drawn.

Consider a bog-standard case of inference. Suppose you are fully rational in believing that Sascha is either in Paris or in Barcelona (though you've no idea which city it is). You get new input and come rationally to believe that Sascha is not in Paris. If that is the only shift in your view, and you are thinking carefully, and you are not too tired, etc., then, your belief about Paris-or-Barcelona will join forces with your belief about not-Paris, and together they will generate a new belief that Sascha is in Barcelona. Moreover, they will do so precisely because the input-beliefs to the mental-state transition support the output-belief. This is how inference works in bog-standard cases. What can we say about episodes like it if we aim to characterize their central features?

Well, the key mental-state transition involves a couple of input states: your belief that Sascha is either in Paris or Barcelona, and your belief that she is not in Paris. The transition itself involves a single output state—the belief that Sascha is in Barcelona—and the latter is based on the two input states. Moreover, the process of basing somehow reflects a sensitivity to the fact that input contents *evidentially support* the output content. Bog-standard cases of inference are like this too. They involve a small clutch of input states of a certain kind producing an output state of that kind, and the process of generation looks to be somehow content-driven in that it is sensitive to how input-contents support the output content.

---

[3] Of course the new take on ¬A is directly a function of the new take on A, and the old take on C given ¬A is directly a function of C given A; so Jeffrey's rule really makes the new take on C a direct function of two things: the new take on A, and the old take on C given A.

[4] For instance in work on the Bayesian Brain. See various pieces of work in (Trommershauser, Kording, & Landy, 2011).

This leads to the *Core Inference Principle*:

(CIP) A mental-state transition is a bog-standard inference if[5]

1. Its input is a small number of instances of an attitude taken to contents.
2. Its output is a new instance of that attitude taken to a content.
3. The output is formed on the basis of the input.
4. The shift from input to output reflects sensitivity to the fact that input-contents evidentially support output-content.

Taken at face value each clause of (CIP) captures something essential to ordinary cases of inference. This makes for a mismatch, however, between those cases of inference and mental-state transitions in line with Jeffrey's rule; for *no* clause of the Core Inference Principle need be satisfied for a mental-state transition to be in line with Jeffrey Conditionalization. Consider the clauses in turn:

1. Standard cases of inference involve a transition *from* a small number of mental states. Jeffrey Conditionalization involves a transition from an entire epistemic position. When an agent is accurately described by Jeffrey's rule, exactly two things make that the case: she begins in an overall epistemic state of disequilibrium, brought on by contact-point shift of in-between rational credence; and she ends-up in an overall epistemic state of equilibrium described—for any claim C—by the right-hand sum in Jeffrey's equation. The input to the transition is built from an infinite number of credal states which happen not to fit together optimally. This is hardly the stuff of inference! The input condition typically involves countless attitude-types: one for each type of credence in play. So there are two ways in which Jeffrey transition conflicts with clause 1 of the Core Inference Principle: its input is global rather than local, and its input is typically built from a huge number of attitude types.

2. Standard cases of inference involve transition *to* a single propositional attitude. Jeffrey Conditionalization involves transition to an entire epistemic position, a new overall state of equilibrium. The output of a Jeffrey transition is thus built from an infinite number of credal states. This too is not the stuff of inference, involving as it does a global output condition rather than a local one, and typically involving countless attitude-types in the output (one for each type of credence on show in the new equilibrium). So there are two ways in which a Jeffrey transition conflicts with clause 2 of the Core Inference Principle: its output is global rather than local, and its output typically involves a huge number of attitude types.

3. All cases of inference involve a transition in which the output is formed on the basis of the input. This key aspect of inference has to do with the *basing relation*.[6] No mental-state transition could be inferential if its output was not based on its input.

---

[5] I do not say 'only if' because there are worries about whether all inference-like mental-state transitions satisfy (CIP). Think of reckoning involved in a case of *reductio ad absurdum*. Once a contradiction has been proved, the exact opposite of what is initially supposed is endorsed. That transition looks inferential, but it does not satisfy condition (ii) of (CIP), and it may not satisfy condition (iv) either. Having said that standard cases of inference—like those which take place within a *reductio* bit of reckoning—do satisfy (CIP). That's all we need for the arguments of this chapter. See Chapter 12 for further discussion.

[6] See (Korcz, 1996), (Sturgeon, 1987), or (Sturgeon, 1994). See also Chapter 13.

Yet basing is not required for a transition to satisfy Jeffrey's rule. All that must happen is that the agent begins in an epistemic state of disequilibrium brought on in a certain way, and that she end-up in an epistemic state of equilibrium described—for any claim C—by the right-hand sum in the equation promoted by Jeffrey. This can happen without the overall output being based on the overall input (either in part or in whole). Since basing is a key ingredient of inference, satisfying Jeffrey's rule is insufficient for inference.

4. Inference is mental-state transition sensitive to evidential relations. Consider template examples described colloquially:

- when someone infers *B* from their take on *(A or B)* and *Not-A*, they form an output state with *B* as its content, they do so on the basis of input states with *(A or B)* and *Not-A* as their contents (respectively), and they do so because input-contents jointly entail *B*.
- when someone infers *(o is F)* from their take on *(The vast majority of As are F)* and *(o is A)*, they form an output state with *(o is F)* as its content, they do so on the basis of input states with *(The vast majority of As are F)* and *(o is A)* as their contents (respectively), and they do so because input-contents make *(o is F)* sufficiently likely.
- And so on.

A major aspect of these template examples can be captured in slogan form: inference is driven by evidential relations between contents.

When taken at face value, this is not how Jeffrey Conditionalization works, for Jeffrey's rule turns on how attitudes fit together rather than how their contents support one another. In slogan form: with inference the action takes place at the level of content but with Jeffrey Conditionalization it takes place at the level of attitude. With rational inference it is essential that the content of the input-state(s) should have something to do support-wise with the content of the output state. Nothing like that happens with Jeffrey Conditionalization at all. With Jeffrey's rule the action takes place in structuring how attitudes hang together as a function of their strength.[7]

We can draw our discussion together in the following way. Jeffrey's rule has to do with structural properties of an overall epistemic position. These properties are meant to be constitutive of epistemic equilibrium. Rules of inference have to do with local properties of a small clutch of attitudes. These properties are meant to explain why local bits of cognition push forward in an evidentially-sensitive way. The mismatch indicates that Jeffrey's rule and inference rules belong to different bits of epistemic theory. Specifically, they indicate that the former belongs to *rational kinematics* and the latter belong to *rational dynamics*.[8]

---

[7] Caveat is needed, of course, for the way that logical aspects of content play out in the structure of probability functions. See Chapter 2 for teaching-level discussion of this point, and (Christensen, 2004) for state-of-the art discussion of its philosophical significance.

[8] Presumably this is why Jeffrey called his approach 'probability kinematics'. The difference between rational kinematics and dynamics is the transition-theory analogue of the distinction between propositional and doxastic justification. See Chapters 9 and 12 for further discussion.

These distinct elements of a transition theory are not always separated as they should be. As we'll see in Chapter 10, however, differences between them are crucial to the notion of idealization at work in epistemic theory; and we'll see now that they are crucial to the proper critique of the Bayesian transition theory. For this reason, we'll take a moment to clarify the distinction between kinematics and dynamics in general, as well as how it plays out in epistemology.

For our purposes—and in full generality—a kinematics for a system involves the description of general structures or forms manifested across time. The description is meant to pick out a systematic pattern, and, crucially, to abstract from forces and/or boundary conditions which generate the pattern described. The aim of kinematic theory is to capture structural regularities manifested in a system as it changes over time. The so-called 'golden ratio', for instance, plays a central role in a stunning number of systems: pinecones, seashells, space–time topology, galaxies, and much more.[9] Systematic treatment of cross-temporal structure will make central appeal to the golden ratio in all of these systems. The ratio itself will be central to their kinematics. In each case, though, nothing will be said about forces or boundary conditions which generate the golden-ratio structure in a given type of thing. The focus in kinematic theory is solely on the structure itself across time.

By contrast—and again in full generality—a dynamics for a system involves description of forces and/or boundary conditions which account for the manner in which it changes over time. Since the shape or structure of a system is but one way in which it changes over time, a system's full-dress dynamics will entail its kinematics. But the reverse entailment fails, for a system's dynamics essentially relies on the interaction of forces and/or boundary conditions which play no role in its kinematics.

A rational dynamics—i.e. the dynamical component of an epistemic transition theory—aims to explain how an agent's epistemic states should impact one another over time, how they should push one another along (so to say). And it aims to do so by appeal to the situation-specific aspects of an agent's mind—i.e. which epistemic commitments she has—together with general facts about how evidential forces play out between epistemic commitments. These two things are jointly meant to account for which particular path(s) forward is/are the rational one(s).[10] And for creatures like us, at least, this is where inference enters the picture, for it is with inference that humans chase down consequences and conflicts in their epistemic situation.[11]

A rational kinematics describes recurring patterns in the shift from one rational overall epistemic position to another. The theory makes no appeal to epistemic forces which account for those patterns, much less to situation-specific details about the epistemic commitments which contribute to their manifestation on a given occasion.

---

[9] The golden ratio is about 1.618. For many of its remarkable properties, see https://www.goldennumber.net/category/math/

[10] The caveats are needed because there is a hotly-contested question—not relevant here—about whether at any given moment an ideal agent has only one way forward intellectually. See (White, 2005) or (Schoenfield, 2013).

[11] For more on inference and dynamics, see the discussion of coordinated epistemic reasons in Chapter 13.

The theory is simply not in the business of appealing to epistemic particulars when dealing with equilibria. It is only concerned with recurring structural patterns in the equilibria.

This is where Jeffrey Conditionalization enters the picture, for it recommends a structural pattern in credence across time. More specifically, it recommends a particular pattern in all shifts from a certain type of disequilibrium—brought on by contact-point perturbance of rational in-between-credence—to full coherence. Rules of inference don't do anything like that, for they turn on content-theoretic features meant to explain why local bits of cognition push forward rationally. Since these are different theoretical tasks, Jeffrey's rule and rules of inference belong to differing parts of a transition theory. The former is located in rational kinematics, the latter is located in rational dynamics.

For this reason, effective critique of Jeffrey Conditionalization must properly conceive of it as a kinematical rule, as something meant solely to describe patterns in the rational flux of fine-grained attitudes across time. This means that effective critiques of Jeffrey Conditionalization must aim at the recommended pattern. They must deny that a certain pattern or structure is always rationally present. This will be our strategy.

## 4.3 Conditional and Indicative Credence

Conditional credence is the key to the Bayesian update rule. When rational credence is perturbed—when in-between credence for a given claim A is shifted (and no more)—Jeffrey's rule prescribes that for any claim C, one's new take on C should be a particular function of one's new take on A together with one's old take on C given A.[12] Conditional credence is a lynchpin of the update. In effect Bayesians insist that equilibrium is regained by appeal to conditional credence.

We've seen that conditional credence should itself align where possible with a ratio of unconditional credence:

$$cr(C/A) = cr(A\&C)/cr(A).$$

Let us call this *the ratio norm*. We'll now see that this norm interacts in interesting ways with another emphasized by the great philosopher F. P. Ramsey. In the most fecund remark on conditionality put forward by a philosopher, Ramsey said this in a footnote:

When two people are arguing 'If P, will Q?' and are both in [some] doubt as to P, they are adding P hypothetically to their stock of knowledge and arguing on that basis about Q; so that in a sense 'If P, Q' and 'If P, ¬Q' are contradictories. We can say they are fixing their degree of belief in Q given P. If P turns out false, these degrees of belief are rendered *void*. If either party believes ¬P for certain, the question ceases to mean anything to him except as a question about what follows from certain laws or hypotheses.[13]

---

[12] Since her old take on C given ¬A is itself 1 minus her old take on C given A.
[13] (Ramsey 1990: 143).

Many important ideas appear in this passage. At this stage we'll focus on one of them, an idea we'll call *Ramsey's norm*:

(R =)   cr(A→C) = cr(C/A).

This prescription maintains that strength of credence for a certain type of conditional should be identical to the strength of a certain conditional credence. To understand the idea properly, we must clarify what sort of conditional is at work in Ramsey's prescription. So consider fact-stating claims like these:

1. It's snowing.
2. Caesar crossed the Rubicon.
3. The UK will not leave the EU.

Each of these fact-stating claims can be restricted by an if-clause. For instance each of them can be restricted by a clause like 'If fortune favours the wise' or 'If the coin landed heads' or 'If tomorrow is Friday'. Were that to happen the result would be an *indicative conditional*:[14]

(1a) If fortune favours the wise, it's snowing.
(1b) If the coin landed heads, it's snowing.
(1c) If tomorrow is Friday, it's snowing.
(2a) If fortune favours the wise, Caesar crossed the Rubicon.
(2b) If the coin landed heads, Caesar crossed the Rubicon.
(2c) If tomorrow is Friday, Caesar crossed the Rubicon.
(3a) If fortune favours the wise, the UK will not leave the EU.
(3b) If the coin landed heads, the UK will not leave the EU.
(3c) If tomorrow is Friday, the UK will not leave the EU.

If-sentences like these are perfectly meaningful, and they look to state facts like other sentences which end in a period. Indeed indicatives like (1a)–(3c) look to be fact-stating claims *built* from other fact-stating claims. And in philosophy, at least, it is common to refer to those other fact-stating claims as a conditional's 'antecedent' and its 'consequent'. Specifically, a conditional's antecedent is the fact-stating claim located within its if-clause, and its consequent is the fact-stating claim restricted by that if-clause (i.e. located in the conditional but outside the if-clause). This is why the letters 'A' and 'C' are often used when discussing conditional credence and conditional sentences. The letters are meant to be mnemonic devices helpful in tracking Antecedents and Consequents respectively. In these terms, indicatives like (1a)–(3c) look to be fact-stating claims built from fact-stating antecedents and fact-stating consequents.[15]

---

[14] So-called because the conditionals are supposedly in the indicative mood. There are also subjunctive conditionals—sometimes known as 'counterfactuals'—which are supposedly in the subjunctive mood. But we leave them aside since they play no role in our discussion. When conditionals are mentioned in the text, it is indicatives like (1a)-thru-(3c) under discussion. See (Bennett, 2003) or (Edgington, 1995) for details.

[15] There are other sorts of conditionals too: conditional commands and conditional questions, for instance. And in my view is it a serious constraint on our approach to conditionals that it dovetails gracefully with our approach to these other sorts of conditional constructions. In (Sturgeon, 2000) I call this the 'force constraint'. See (Edgington, 1997) and (Woods, 1997) for further discussion.

Over the remainder of this chapter (and in the next) we'll see that conditionals behave in puzzling ways. Often those ways suggest that conditionals are *not* fact-stating claims after all, a view eventually to be defended. Before doing so, however, we'll focus on ways in which the ratio and Ramsey norms together generate pressure for the view that epistemic states are binary propositional attitudes. And we begin with a simple observation.

We can lend credence to a conditional just as we can lend credence to its antecedent or its consequent. Since we are restricting discussion to indicatives, let us call credence lent to a conditional 'indicative credence'. Ramsey's norm then insists that the following is true: indicative credence is identical in strength to conditional credence lent to the indicative's consequent given its antecedent. There are actually *two* identity-based norms, then, anchoring our discussion of conditional credence: one is the ratio norm of the Bayesian model, the other is Ramsey's norm for conditionals. Side-by-side they make for a discussion-structuring double equation:

$$(2 =) \quad cr(A \rightarrow C) = cr(C/A) = cr(A\&C)/cr(A).$$

If this double equation is true, then, for any rational credence distribution, indicative credence is identical in strength to credence lent to an indicative's consequent given its antecedent; and credence lent to an indicative's consequent given its antecedent is measured by the number got by dividing (intuitively put) the strength of credence lent to the conditional's antecedent conjoined with its consequent by the strength of credence lent to the conditional's antecedent.

Note that the far-left and far-right of our double equation speak to different kinds of phenomena. The Binary Attitude Assumption entails that $cr(A \rightarrow C)$ is a fine-grained binary attitude which holds between an agent and a claim to which credence is lent. The ratio mentioned on the far-right of (2=) is something altogether different. It is not a relation between a thinker and a thing thought, but, instead, a relation between a thinker and two things thought (so to say): (A&C) and A. This tertiary relation occurs exactly when a thinker's take on the relevant pair of claims lines up in the ratio way. Hence the far-left and far-right of (2=) stand for different kinds of phenomena: a binary attitude and a tertiary ratio-based relation respectively. The key issue before us is what to make of the *middle* term in (2=): how should we think of conditional credence?

In §3.3 we saw that conditional credence does not reduce to ratio facts like those on the far-right of the double equation. This is consistent with conditional credence reducing to unconditional credence like that seemingly found on the far-left of (2=). But it is also consistent with conditional credence being a *sui generis* phenomenon: neither ratio-like nor credence-in-fact-stating-claim-like deep down. And if that turns out to be so—if conditional credence turns out to be *sui generis*—it could also turn out that indicative credence reduces to conditional credence. In other words: it could also turn out that *sui generis* conditional credence *masquerades* as normal credence lent to a conditional. But if that were the case it would not really be true that normal credence is lent to a conditional. Instead we have merely the appearance of normal credence being lent to a fact-stating conditional. Deep down we have *sui generis* conditional credence masquerading as unconditional credence. Eventually we'll make a suggestion about what *sui generis* conditional credence might be, at bottom, and we'll defend the view that credence lent to a conditional is really the *sui generis* psychological phenomenon suggested. Before getting to that, however, we'll need to be clear on the logical geography of the area.

Here's one way to think of it.

When faced with the left-hand identity in (2=), first ask whether the same type of psychological phenomenon appears on its left- and right-hand sides. If the answer to that question is Yes, then ask whether the psychological phenomenon in question is binary or tertiary in nature. The dialectic then plays out as follows

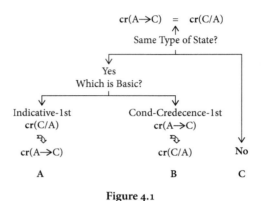

**Figure 4.1**

When it comes to conditional credence, position [A] is similar to the Bayesian Model in one respect: it claims that conditional credence is reductively spelled out by appeal to its unconditional cousin. The Bayesian model insists that conditional credence is grounded in ratio facts to do with regular credence (those found in the ratio formula). Position [A]—which we'll call *the binary view of conditionality* (or *binary view*, for short)—insists that conditional credence is simply regular credence lent to a conditional fact-stating claim. On both views conditional credence is nothing over and above its unconditional cousin. The binary view says also that conditional credence is a binary attitude lent to a fact-stating conditional.

Position [B] insists that conditional credence is *sui generis* and that indicative credence is really conditional credence deep down. Not only is it the case that conditional credence is something over and above unconditional credence, on this view—indeed something *sui generis*—it's also the case that indicative credence is that *sui generis* something. If that's right, however—if the view we'll call *the tertiary view of conditionality* (or *tertiary view*, for short) is true—the Binary Attitude Assumption is wrong. Certain epistemic states are not binary attitudes taken to contents. Conditional credence and indicative credence are really tertiary attitudes lent to a pair of contents (so to say).

When it comes to conditional credence and indicative credence, the binary and tertiary views are mirror-image *monist* positions, while position [C]—which we'll call *dualism about conditionality*, for obvious reasons—is a rejection of monism. The former views recognize a single kind of psychological phenomenon when it comes to conditionality. They just disagree about what that phenomenon is. The binary view says it's a binary attitude taken to a proposition. The tertiary view says it's a tertiary attitude taken to a pair of propositions. The dualist view rejects both types of monism, maintaining (in line with the tertiary view) that conditional credence is a *sui generis* tertiary attitude, and (in line with the binary view) that indicative credence is a binary attitude lent to a fact-stating conditional.

Now, the ratio norm and Ramsey's norm jointly entail that strength of rational indicative credence is measured by the relevant ratio. Not only does this claim fit well with intuition about basic cases, as we'll see, but it also generates a logic of conditionality which entails surprising-yet-confirmed results.[16] Of course this is a happy circumstance: the fact that identities in (2=) jointly make for flourishing theory strongly indicates that something is right about each of them. Their coordinated goodness reflects well in both their directions.

Moreover, notice that Ramsey's norm was *presupposed* when the Bayesian model was laid out in Chapter 2. This was done on purpose precisely so that the presupposition could be flagged here along with its ready consumption. The fact that no alarm bells rang at the time, that not even a whiff of magic or sleight of hand permeated our discussion then—despite its ready movement from indicative credence to conditional credence, and vice versa—is clear evidence of two things: something is deeply right about Ramsey's norm, some kind of monism about conditionality is likely to be true. The fungibility of talk about credence lent to C *if* A and talk of credence lent to C *given* A—at least when C and A are clear fact-stating claims—strongly indicates one of two things: either conditional credence reduces to unconditional credence lent to a conditional, or the reverse is true and credence lent to a conditional reduces to essentially conditional credence.

As we'll now see, though, once the ratio norm is put with Ramsey's norm all hell breaks loose. There are conflicts and contradictions all over the place: between the Bayesian theory of states, the Bayesian transition theory, other things we'd like to say about the rational role of the indicative... oh my! Before showing this, though, we should first specify the role of conditional credence in the Bayesian model. Then we can lay out the bother in light of Ramsey's norm and decide what to make of it. The story begins with the Bayesian transition theory and conditional credence.

## 4.4 Rigidity and Conditionality in the Bayesian Model

The Bayesian model treats conditional credence in peculiar ways. For instance it entails that credence conditional on A should never be revised after contact-point shift of in-between credence for A. And the model implies that conditional credence is never itself the contact-point of rational shift-in-view. So in a sense the model

---

[16] For instance, it seems natural to think that whenever you lend rational credence to (A→¬C) you should also lend such credence to (C→¬A)—in the vernacular, it is natural to think that indicative conditionals *contrapose*. But that turns out to be false. One may easily lend high credence to the claim that it won't rain ten inches tomorrow if it rains without lending such credence to the claim that it won't rain tomorrow if it rains tens inches! For a nice introduction to this sort of thing see (Adams, 1998) or (Bennett, 2003); and for canonical statement of the logic which flows from Ramsey's norm see (Adams, 1996).

treats conditional credence as *sacrosanct*: never to be shifted when attempting to regain coherence after a change of opinion in a conditioning event, and never to be shifted directly on the basis of new input.

Why should that be so? Why should conditional credence play such an unusual role in our rational lives? Given the correlation between conditional credence and indicative credence, moreover—as required by Ramsey's norm—both of these striking features carry over to indicative credence; and this is more than a bit puzzling (to put it mildly). At a minimum we need a story about conditional and indicative credence which makes sense of why it is that they are sacrosanct in these ways.

Recall Jeffrey's rule: whenever in-between credence for A is shifted exogenously—in a manner that is to be rationally preserved—an agent's new take on any claim C should be identical to products combining old and new credence. Here's the prescription in our canonical notation:

(J-Cond) $\quad cr_{new}(C) = \{[cr_{new}(A) \times cr_{old}(C/A)] + [cr_{new}(\neg A) \times cr_{old}(C/\neg A)]\}.$

Of course the Bayesian model insists that credence manifests the structure of a probability function. In §3.3 we saw that the following equation holds of any such function which lends in-between probability to A:

$$p(C) = \{[p(A) \times p(C/A)] + [p(\neg A) \times p(C/\neg A)]\}.$$

So the Bayesian model entails that for any credence function which lends in-between credence to A:

(*) $\quad cr(C) = \{[cr(A) \times cr(C/A)] + [cr(\neg A) \times cr(C/\neg A)]\}.$

In essence this equation holds because Bayesians insist that rational credence always displays the structure of a probability function.

If (*) is true of every rational credence function, though, it's true of every one of them got by Jeffrey's rule after in-between credence in A has been shifted. In those circumstances the Bayesian model entails:

($cr_{new}$) $\quad cr_{new}(C) = \{[cr_{new}(A) \times cr_{new}(C/A)] + [cr_{new}(\neg A) \times cr_{new}(C/\neg A)]\}.$

Note the left-hand sides of (J-Cond) and ($cr_{new}$) are identical. This means their right-hand sides are identical as well. In other words, the following bit of (J-Cond)

$$\{[cr_{new}(A) \times cr_{old}(C/A)] + [cr_{new}(\neg A) \times cr_{old}(C/\neg A)]\}$$

must be equal to the following bit of ($cr_{new}$)

$$\{[cr_{new}(A) \times cr_{new}(C/A)] + [cr_{new}(\neg A) \times cr_{new}(C/\neg A)]\}.$$

The only way *that* can happen, however, is for two further things to be true:

$$cr_{old}(C/A) = cr_{new}(C/A)$$

and

$$cr_{old}(C/\neg A) = cr_{new}(C/\neg A).$$

Thus we arrive at a stark implication of the Bayesian model: when rational in-between credence for A is shifted by new input, credence lent to any claim C on condition that A, like credence lent to any claim C on condition that ¬A, remains unchanged. The model entails that conditional credence is constant—or *rigid*, in the vernacular—across rational shift concerning conditioning claim.

Ramsey's norm then ensures that two further things are true:

$$cr_{old}(A \to C) = cr_{new}(A \to C)$$

and

$$cr_{old}(\neg A \to C) = cr_{new}(\neg A \to C).$$

Thus we arrive at a further stark implication brought on by the addition of Ramsey's norm to the model: when rational in-between credence for A is shifted by new input, credence lent to any conditional of the form 'If A, then....', like credence lent to any conditional of the form 'if ¬A, then....' remains unchanged. Corresponding indicative credence is likewise rigid.

Let us call this the *updating assumption*:

(UA) When a rational agent starts with in-between credence for A, and new input leads to a rational shift in that credence, then, for every claim C:

1. new credence for C given A is identical to old credence for C given A;
2. new credence for C if A is identical to old credence for C if A;
3. new credence for C given ¬A is identical to old credence for C given ¬A;
4. new credence for C if ¬A is identical to old credence for C if ¬A.

When in-between credence for A is perturbed, the Bayesian model insists that one's take on anything conditional on A or on ¬A remains constant; and Ramsey's norm parlays that aspect of the model into something exactly similar for A-restricted conditionals.

This makes for two problems.

To see them clearly, suppose you lend in-between credence to A. Then a logical tree can be used to represent your take on A's relation to any claim C

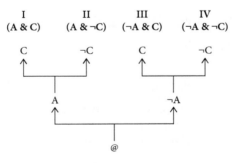

**Figure 4.2**

Since you rationally lend in-between credence to A, it follows by the Credal Partition Principle that you lend in-between credence to ¬A. Credence conditional on A and credence conditional on ¬A are both well-defined. This means that credence lent to any claim C will itself be a function of conditional credence. With $cr_{old}$ as your initial distribution:

($cr_{old}$) $\quad cr_{old}(C) = \{[cr_{old}(A) \times cr_{old}(C/A)] + [cr_{old}(\neg A) \times cr_{old}(C/\neg A)]\}.$[17]

In terms of our logical tree, credence for C adds up from credence for the tree's path I plus credence for the three's path III.

Ramsey's norm allows principle ($cr_{old}$) to be rewritten with the arrow of a conditional replacing the backstroke of conditional credence:

($cr_{old}\rightarrow$) $\quad cr_{old}(C) = \{[cr_{old}(A) \times cr_{old}(A\rightarrow C)] + [cr_{old}(\neg A) \times cr_{old}(\neg A\rightarrow C)]\}.$

This equation codifies your take on a pair of *arguments*. In essence, you start with a spread of credence across premises corresponding to paths I and III of the logical tree:

| Path I | Path III |
|---|---|
| $cr_{old}(A)$ | $cr_{old}(\neg A)$ |
| $cr_{old}(A\rightarrow C)$ | $cr_{old}(\neg A\rightarrow C)$ |
| ∴ $cr_{old}(C)$ | ∴ $cr_{old}(C)$ |

The first premises of these arguments make for a two-member logical partition. The second premises speak to C on condition that one or the other of those partition-members is true. Your take on the arguments is a look from top to bottom down paths I and III of the logical tree built from A and C, with the strength of your take on C summing from products of credence lent to premises along the paths. Intuitively this is why principle ($cr_{old} \rightarrow$) is true.

But notice: when your credence shifts merely in the unconditional premises of the arguments above—the arguments corresponding to paths I and III of the A/C logical tree—the Bayesian model insists that your take on C should be recalculated with minimal fuss, without shifting your take on other commitments involved. This can be symbolized with the backstroke of conditional credence as in Jeffrey's rule:

(J-Cond) $\quad cr_{new}(C) = \{[cr_{new}(A) \times cr_{old}(C/A)] + [cr_{new}(\neg A) \times cr_{old}(C/\neg A)]\}.$

But the minimal-fuss prescription can also be symbolized with the arrow of conditionality via Ramsey's norm:

(J-Cond$\rightarrow$) $\quad cr_{new}(C) = \{[cr_{new}(A) \times cr_{old}(A\rightarrow C)] + [cr_{new}(\neg A) \times cr_{old}(\neg A\rightarrow C)]\}.$

It is natural to see the Bayesian transition theory as based on a minimal-fuss prescription for the recovery of coherence. When you start in a coherent position, but change your take on the unconditional premises of the arguments above—thereby bringing on

---

[17] See §2.3 for a full explanation of this and surrounding issues.

disequilibrium—the root recommendation is that coherence be recovered by holding fast to your take on the second premises of those arguments and recalculating a view for C in light of your new take on the first premises.

This is not implausible. Once it is expressed with conditionals, however—and path-arguments to which they correspond—a pair of worries intellectually pops out:

(a$_\rightarrow$) When in-between credence for A shifts, why *must* one's new take on (A→C) and one's new take on (¬A→C) be identical to one's old take on the conditionals? Why <u>can't</u> such an initial shift in credence lead rationally to a shift concerning (A→C) or (¬A→C)?

(b$_\rightarrow$) What should happen when one's initial shift-in-view concerns a conditional like (A→C) rather than an unconditional claim like A? How should update proceed then?

There is no need, of course, to use Ramsey's norm to get the fundamental issues on the table here, for there are direct analogues of (a$_\rightarrow$) and (b$_\rightarrow$) which can be put to the Bayesian model in its own terms (having to do with conditional credence rather than credence lent to conditionals). But appeal to Ramsey's norm brings the relevant issues to life. It helps to vivify the issues and make it obvious that they are in need of immediate attention.[18]

Here are the issues put in terms of conditional credence rather than indicative credence:

(a$_/$) When in-between credence for A shifts, why *must* one's new take on C given A and one's new take on C given ¬A be identical to one's old take on C given A and one's old take on C given ¬A? Why *can't* such an initial shift lead to a shift concerning C given A or C given ¬A?

(b$_/$) What should happen when one's initial shift-in-view concerns conditional credence? How should update proceed then?

The queries at (a$_/$) and (b$_/$) are direct analogues of those at (a$_\rightarrow$) and (b$_\rightarrow$). In the latter case relevant issues have to do with indicative credence. In the former case they have to do with conditional credence. Ramsey's norm builds a bridge between the worries.

In both cases we have the following. A self-standing epistemic commitment of some kind involves a particular claim A. The theory before us entails that this self-standing epistemic commitment can never be rationally changed by way of reaction to a rational shift in one's take on A. The theory also entails that this self-standing epistemic commitment can never itself be the contact-point of rational shift-in-view. Given the epistemic commitment in question is self-standing, each of these claims is exceedingly puzzling. Since that commitment is not anything like a ratio of other commitments, one wonders why it *can't* rationally shift in reaction to a rational change in one's take one of its components? and one wonders why it *can't* rationally be the contact-point of shift-in-view?

---

[18] I have found this is especially so with those who presuppose the sort of ratio-based reductive conception of conditional credence rejected in Chapter 3.

The suggestion behind ($a_/$) and ($a_\rightarrow$) is that the Bayesian model harbors a faulty update rule. The suspicion is that a certain kind of sensitivity in rational updating—downstream from the contact-point of rational movement—is precluded by the model when it should not be. Since the idea is that the model rules out a kind of rational revision it should leave as rationally possible—due to the rigidity of conditional credence and indicative credence within Bayesian transition theory—let us call this *the rigidity worry*.

The suggestion behind ($b_/$) and ($b_\rightarrow$) is that the Bayesian model lacks an account of certain kinds of rational transition. The suspicion is that the model fails to cover cases in which conditional commitment is itself the contact-point of rational movement. Since the worry is that the model fails to speak to cases in which coherence should be regained, let us call this *the incompleteness worry*.[19]

The most straightforward approach to these problems comes in two steps: first, treat the indicative—and thereby conditional credence via Ramsey's norm—as if it gloms onto facts; and second, apply Jeffrey Conditionalization to indicatives in the hope that rigidity falls out of the model. In other words, plump for the binary view of conditionality and then apply the model straightforwardly. Were this to work out, the rigidity worry and the incompleteness worry would be dealt with, for it would turn out that indicative credence and conditional credence could be the contact-point of rational shift-in-view, and it would turn out that their values happened to be rigid when that contact-point involved shift in one's take on a conditioning claim. Let us see if the most straightforward approach to our problems can be made to work.

## 4.5 Conditionality and Restricted Vision

When theorizing about rationality it is quite useful to begin with the idea of an epistemically possible world. We think of an epistemic agent as having at her cognitive command a collection of maximally detailed situations. None have been ruled out by the agent as her own situation, and, for this reason, each of them counts as epistemically possible. Each of them is sufficiently detailed to ensure that adding further detail only generates conflict or redundancy, and, for this reason, each of them counts as maximally fine-grained.

Once we think of an agent as working with a collection of maximally fine-grained epistemic possibilities, we can use them to understand her 'epistemic space'. Intuitively, this is the region of thought that the agent can draw from when conceiving her own situation. And thinking of it as built from epistemically possible worlds is a helpful way to sharpen our grip on the Binary Attitudes Assumption. This is the view, recall, that epistemic states are in fact binary relations which agents stand in to contents or propositions or some such. Epistemic space built from possible worlds can be used to anchor our grip both on the contents which figure into epistemic states, and the strength of the binary relations which do so as well.

---

[19] These issues relevant to the incompleteness worry are tricky and contention. In the final section of this chapter they will be discussed in full. Examples of contact-point shift of conditional credence will be given, and a rule for updating when that happens will be proposed.

For instance, we can think of the contents as collections of epistemically possible worlds. When an agent is 99% sure that it rains in Rio, on this view, we can see the claim to which she lends that credence as itself a set of maximally detailed situations. These are the epistemically possible worlds at which it rains in Rio. Or when an agents is 50% sure that the coin will land heads on its next toss, we can see the claim to which this credence is lent as itself the set of epistemically possible worlds at which the coin lands heads, etc. And once we've construed propositions as sets of epistemically possible worlds, we can go on to see logical relations between contents as echoed in set-theoretic relations between sets which are those contents. What it is for one claim to entail another, on this view, is for the entailer to be a subset of the entailed. What it is for two claims to be logically incompatible, on this view, is for them to have an empty intersection. And so on. Epistemically possible worlds prove useful in understanding the contents to which credence is lent.

Further still: once we think of rational agents as having a collection of epistemic possibilities at their cognitive command, and we construe contents to which credence is lent as sets of epistemically possible worlds, we can use the epistemic space thereby developed to sharpen our grip on strength of credence. And there are a number of ways we could do so. For instance, strength of credence can be echoed by the internal geometry of epistemic space. We think of epistemically possible worlds as points in a two-dimensional epistemic box; then in line with our worlds-based conception of contents we think of claims to which credence is lent as regions in that two-dimensional box. Strength of credence is then pictured by area of content-representing region.

On this way of proceeding, epistemic space is 'rubbery' in the sense that it can flex back and forth. Shifting areas of regions within it then represent shifting credal strengths. When rubbery epistemic space is flexed one way, for instance, the region of epistemic space consisting of worlds at which Φ is true amounts to 90% of the overall space

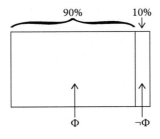

Figure 4.3

This represents that 90% credence is lent to Φ. When epistemic space is flexed another way, the region consisting of worlds at which Φ is true amounts to 10% of the overall space (Figure 4.4). This represents that 10% credence is lent to Φ. And so on. On this approach the strength of credence lent to a content is intuitively echoed by the proportion of epistemic space taken up by the worlds at which that content is true.

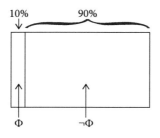

Figure 4.4

It is by no means obligatory to think of agents as equipped with a set of epistemically possible worlds. But it is definitely useful to do so. The practice helps to elicit and regiment intuition about strength of credence, logical relations between contents, connections between these two topics, and more. The possible-worlds machinery is simply too helpful not to use.

But now recall the ratio norm for conditional credence:

$$(\text{Ratio}) \quad \mathbf{cr}(C/A) = \frac{\mathbf{cr}(A\&C)}{\mathbf{cr}(A)}, \quad \text{where } \mathbf{cr}(A) > 0.$$

The Bayesian model says this identity holds in all rational credence distributions. If that is so, then rational conditional credence is a strict function of what's going on in the *A-portion* of an agent's epistemic space. The value on the right side of (Ratio), after all, turns solely on the relation between C- and ¬C-worlds *inside* the A-portion of that space. In effect, the ratio norm prescribes that strength of conditional credence for C given A is measured by the proportion of A-worlds which are also C-worlds.

This means the ratio norm ensures that conditional credence behaves like a *restricted-vision credence-like distribution of opinion*. We've seen how the norm prescribes that conditional credence take values which are a function of what's happening in a restricted portion of an agent's epistemic space. It is in this sense that conditional credence is meant to behave like a restricted-vision opinion.[20] But the ratio norm also entails that strength of conditional credence sums to unity across cells partitioning the restricted portion of epistemic space. Divide that portion into exclusive and exhaustive sub-bits, then assign conditional-credence values to the sub-bits in line with the ratio norm, and those values will add-up across cells of the partition to 100%. It is in this sense that conditional credence is meant to behave like a credence-like opinion: it is meant to satisfy a partition principle within its restricted range of vision. The ratio norm thus requires that conditional credence function like a distribution of fine-grained opinion which happens to be restricted in scope or

---

[20] The portion might actually be the agent's entire epistemic space, when the restricting claim is recognized by the agent to be true throughout her epistemic space. Credence for C conditional on everything being self-identical, for instance, is probably so restricted for you. In what follows we set this sort of thing aside, along with the opposite scenario in which a restricting claim isn't recognized to be true anywhere in an agent's epistemic space. For relevant discussion see (Edgington, 1995) and (McGee, 1994).

vision. In this sense the norm requires that conditional credence behave like a blinkered distribution of credence.[21]

Ramsey's norm parlays this fact about conditional credence into something similar for indicative credence. Since conditional credence for C given A is solely a function of the A-portion of epistemic space, the following must hold

$$[cr(C/A) + cr(\neg C/A)] = 1,$$

since every A-world is such that C is true there or it's not true there. Ramsey's norm then entails

$$[cr(A \to C) + cr(A \to \neg C)] = 1$$

by the substitution of indicative credence for conditional credence. By the Partition Principle we know

$$\{cr(A \to C) + cr[\neg(A \to C)]\} = 1,$$

since every well-formed formula and its negation function in theory as a two-cell partition. So the previous pair of equations jointly entail that negation *distributes* across the conditional:

$$(\neg\text{Dist}\to) \quad cr[\neg(A \to C)] = cr(A \to \neg C).$$

Think about what this means. In effect, it guarantees that the proportion of an agent's modal space in which the conditional (A→C) fails is identical to the proportion of her A-worlds at which C fails. The negation principle forces the failure of a conditional to be attitudinally indistinguishable from the failure of its consequent given its antecedent.

This idea is not flatly inconceivable—though we'll see in the next chapter that it cannot hold in non-trivial settings—but it does mean that the failure of a conditional is equi-credible with the failure of its consequent restricted to worlds at which its antecedent is true. Since Ramsey's norm guarantees the success of a conditional is equi-credible with the success of its consequent restricted to the worlds at which its antecedent is true, it follows that the ratio norm and Ramsey's norm jointly ensure that indicative credence likewise functions as if it is a restricted-vision distribution of fine-grained opinion.

This is relevant to the debate between binary and tertiary approaches to conditionality. On the binary view, after all: conditionals are fact-stating discourse, credence lent to a conditional is ordinary credence, and conditional credence is ordinary credence deep down. This means the binary view together with the ratio norm ensures that for rational agents, at least, conditionals partition epistemic space in a striking way; for the two views together entail that the proportion of epistemic space in which a conditional holds exactly matches the proportion of antecedent worlds at which the consequent holds. Put another way: the two views together entail that in all

---

[21] Dorothy Edgington has done more than anyone else to emphasize the importance of this fact for the semantics of conditionals. See her (Edgington, 1986), (Edgington, 1995), (Edgington, 1996) and (Edgington, 2014).

rational distributions of credence, the proportion of epistemic space in which (A→C) is identical to the proportion of A-worlds which are C-worlds. In the next chapter we'll see that this striking correlation can only hold in trivial epistemic spaces.

On the tertiary view of conditionality: conditionals are not fact-stating discourse, credence lent to a conditional is really conditional credence deep down, and conditional credence is itself a *sui generis* tertiary attitude. This means the tertiary view together with the ratio norm ensures that for rational agents, at least, conditionals do no more than mark the proportion of antecedent-worlds at which consequents hold. Conditionals do not partition epistemic space as such, into regions where the conditional is either true or false.

On both approaches to conditionality, of course, the ratio norm entails that indicative and conditional credence function as a restricted-vision distribution of fine-grained opinion. We'll now see, however, that this functional role by itself undermines the straightforward attempt the answer the incompleteness and rigidity worries. Recall that that attempt aims to address the incompleteness worry by using Jeffrey's rule with the conditional as input; and it aims to address the rigidity worry by showing that indicative credence—and thus conditional credence via Ramsey's norm—is rigid when the update rule is applied to a conditional after shift of opinion with respect to its antecedent.

Unfortunately, once the implications of the restricted-vision aspect of conditionality are spelled out it is easy to show that the straightforward strategy for dealing with our worries is hopeless. We'll use three principles along the way in showing this, together with the distribution-of-negation norm mentioned above. Here are the three principles:

1. First we have a credal-based version of what's known in the conditionals literature as the *Import/Export Law*:

(I/E)   A→(B→C)   iff   (A&B)→C.[22]

When taken from left-to-right the idea behind this law is that the antecedent of a right-nested conditional 'exports' into conjunct position in the antecedent of an un-nested conditional. When taken from right-to-left the idea is that any claim which plays such a conjunct role 'imports' into an antecedent within a consequent of a right-nested conditional.

If commitment to a conditional is understood in the restricted-vision way—e.g. if the ratio and Ramsey norms are both true—then Import/Export is exactly what you'd expect of the conditional. After all, restricting your epistemic vision to A-worlds and then restricting it further to B-worlds should land you in exactly the same portion of your original epistemic space as restricting your vision in one go to the (A&B)-worlds; and vice versa.[23] The restricted-vision conception of conditional commitment strongly supports the import-export behaviour of a conditional.

---

[22] See (Fitelson, 2013), (Gibbard, 1981), (McGee, 1989), or (Sturgeon, 2002). In my paper the credal version of Import/Export is discussed as a consequence of Ramsey's norm, and in that paper and Fitelson's it is fingered as responsible for triviality.

[23] See §7.4 for further discussion.

This is exactly what we find in a Bayesian setting with the Ramsey norm in place. Then we have the *Credal-Import/Export* norm:

(cr-I/E)   $cr[A \to (B \to C)] = cr[(A\&B) \to C]$.

### Proof

Suppose $cr_A$ is got from $cr$ by Conditioning on A (i.e by Jeffrey's rule when $cr_A(A) = 1$). Then we have:

$$\begin{aligned}
cr[A \to (B \to C)] &= cr_A(B \to C) & \text{by definition.} \\
&= cr_A(C/B) & \text{by (R=)} \\
&= cr_A(B\&C) \div cr_A(B) & \text{by CCR} \\
&= cr[(B\&C)/A] \div cr(B/A) & \text{by definition} \\
&= [cr(A\&B\&C) \div cr(A)] \div [cr(A\&B) \div cr(A)] & \text{by definition} \\
&= cr(A\&B\&C) \div cr(A\&B) & \text{by algebra} \\
&\phantom{=} cr[C/(A\&B)] & \text{by CCR} \\
&= cr[(A\&B) \to C] & \text{by (R=).}
\end{aligned}$$

Top-to-bottom we have the Credal Import/Export Law:

$cr[A \to (B \to C)] = cr[(A\&B) \to C]$.

In all distributions of rational credence, then, Ramsey's norm joins with the Bayesian model to entail that credence lent to a right-nested conditional is identical in strength to an un-nested conditional with an appropriate conjunctive antecedent.

2. The next principle supported by the restricted-vision conception of conditionality is the *Presumption of Non-contradiction* norm:

(Pres-NC)   $cr(A \to C)$ presumes A is not an explicit contradiction.

To see how it works, consider a contradiction of the form $(A\&\neg A)$. Two things stand out about it right away: the claim cannot be true, and nor can a rational agent lend positive credence to it. After all, $(A\&\neg A)$ is ruled out by logic in the most straightforward of ways. Anyone who misses that fact thereby fails to be rational. For this reason, a rational agent will rule-out an explicit contradiction in all corners of her epistemic space. Any claim of the form $(A\&\neg A)$ will count as straightforwardly impossibility, true at no epistemically possible world.

This suggests that a rational agent will have no ordinary use for thoughts of the form

If $(A\&\neg A)$, then ...

Since she gives no cognitive hearing to an explicit contradiction—since none of her epistemic space is given over $(A\&\neg A)$-worlds—she has no everyday use for thoughts querying what will occur *if* $(A\&\neg A)$. Conditionals of the form

If $(A\&\neg A)$, then ...

are for her decidedly screwy. This raises a delicate issue: how does an agent relate to claims of that form when she considers them? Does she find the claim involved incoherent or genuinely intelligible but literally incredible?

We might say that she finds them incoherent. Then on our view it would be a precondition for the intelligibility of a conditional that its antecedent is not explicitly contradictory. Thoughts of the form

If (A&¬A), then...

would be literally gibberish, on a par with putative thoughts like

If (is A true?), then...

At first blush this seems too harsh a judgement on conditionals with explicitly contradictory antecedents. Even if we have no ordinary use for them in day-to-day life, they don't initially seem to be non-sense. But let us keep every option on the table at this point just in case.

We might say that conditionals with explicitly contradictory antecedents are intelligible but literally incredible. On this view it would be a precondition for the usefulness of a conditional that its antecedent is not an explicit contradiction. Although thoughts of the form

If (A&¬A), then...

count as intelligible, they turn out to be entirely pointless, infected by the surface-level illogicality of their antecedent.

When it comes to conditionals with explicitly contradictory antecedents, then, choosing between these theoretical options is not easy. So it's a good thing that we don't have to make the choice, that we can get by with the thought that serious use a conditional—the sort of use we see in everyday life—presumes that a conditional's antecedent is not an explicit contradiction. For our purposes, we can assume merely that everyday use of a conditional is either pointless or worse when that presupposition fails.

Ramsey's norm and the ratio norm jointly explain why this should be so. After all, the former says

$$cr(A \to C) = cr(C/A)$$

while the latter says

$$cr(C/A) = cr(A\&C)/cr(A), \quad \text{when } cr(A) \text{ is non-zero.}$$

Together they make for a bridge from indicative credence to a ratio of everyday credence. The bridge is in place, however, only when positive credence is lent to the antecedent of the conditional. This explains why the Presumption of Non-contradiction Thesis is true. The very raison d'être of indicative credence is to align with ordinary credence in the ratio way. That way is ill-defined when the antecedent of a conditional receives no positive credence—as it would if the antecedent were a flat-out contradiction—so indicative credence presumes that the antecedent is not such a contradiction. Conditionals with explicitly contradictory antecedents are pointless or worse: either they codify no thoughts at all or thoughts not worth having.

3. The final principle supported by the restricted-vision conception of conditionality turns on conditionals of this form:

$$[(x \rightarrow y) \rightarrow z].$$

In English such left-nested conditionals make no sense. Consider three of them:

- (iv) If if apples are edible, then oranges are edible, then bananas are too.
- (v) If if Trump is President, then Corbyn is Prime Minister, then Labour are happy.
- (vi) If if Jefferson was a grandfather, then Washington was grandfather, then both were married.

These claims are so ungrammatical that they are literally incoherent. Rearranging helps out a bit:

- (iv)* If oranges are edible if apples are, then bananas are too.
- (v)* If Corbyn is Prime Minister if Trump is President, then Labour are happy.
- (vi)* If Washington was a grandfather if Jefferson was a grandfather, then both were married.

But even here coherence is not really on show. The following make good sense:

- (iv)** If apples and oranges are edible, then bananas are too.
- (v)** If Trump is President and Corbyn is Prime Minister, then Labour are happy.
- (vi)** If Jefferson and Washington were grandfathers, then both were married.

But they are not left-nested conditionals of the form

$$[(x \rightarrow y) \rightarrow z].$$

They are ordinary conditionals of the form

$$[(x \& y) \rightarrow z].$$

We already know ordinary conditionals of this form make sense, they figure in the Credal Import/Export norm. Left-nested conditionals do not really make sense: they are quite literally unintelligible. Thus we arrive at the Unconditional Antecedents Assumption:

(UAA)    cr(A→C) assumes that A is not a conditional.

This is exactly what you'd expect of a conditional with the ratio and Ramsey norms in place. Since they lead to the restricted-vision conception of conditionality, a left-nested conditional will be seen as tantamount to an instruction to restrict one's epistemic vision to the upshot of an act of restricting one's epistemic vision, which makes no sense. If anything it amounts to an instruction to restrict one's epistemic vision to a raw proportion value: good luck with that! Such an 'instruction' seems more like a category mistake than anything else. Hence the restricted-vision conception of conditionality underwrites the Unconditional Antecedents Assumption.

124  THE BAYESIAN TRANSITION THEORY: CRITICAL DISCUSSION

In sum: we'll make use of six norms to do with conditionality. The fundamental among them are the ratio norm and Ramsey's norm. Together these two enjoin the Reduction-of-Negation norm, the Credal Import/Export norm, the Presumption-of-Non-Contradiction norm, and the Unconditional Antecedents Assumption. In symbols:

(Ratio) $\quad cr(C/A) = \dfrac{cr(A\&C)}{cr(A)}$, where $cr(A) > 0$.
(Ramsey) $\quad cr(A\to C) = cr(C/A)$.
($\neg$Dist$\to$) $\quad cr[\neg(A\to C)] = cr(A\to \neg C)$.
(cr-I/E) $\quad cr[A\to(B\to C)] = cr[(A\&B)\to C]$.
(Pres-NC) $\quad cr(A\to C)$ presumes A is not an explicit contradiction
(UAA) $\quad cr(A\to C)$ assumes that A is not a conditional.

With these norms in place it is easy to make mischief for Bayesian transition theory. We need only ask four questions:

(I) How should $cr(A\to C)$ change when $cr(A)$ changes?
(II) How should $cr(A\to C)$ change when $cr(C)$ changes?
(III) How should $cr(A)$ change when $cr(A\to C)$ changes?
(IV) How should $cr(C)$ change when $cr(A\to C)$ changes?

Sometimes the Bayesian model yields a coherent-but-wrong answer to one of these questions, other times it yields flat-out incoherence. The model never produces a plausible view; and that means the direct strategy for answering the incompleteness and rigidity worries is hopeless. In the next section we'll see why this is so.

## 4.6 Conditionality and Bayesian Kinematics

We can now make explicit how the Bayesian model mishandles restricted-vision conditionality. To do so we'll consider each of the four questions with which the last section ended:

*Question (I): How should $cr(A\to C)$ change when $cr(A)$ changes?*
Suppose you lend 80% credence to A and then input causes you to shift it to 90% (and nothing else happens). How should this affect your credence for $(A\to C)$? Well, the Bayesian model has one rule for updating credence, Jeffrey's, but Ramsey's norm entails Jeffrey's rule yields incoherence or contradiction when applied to the case.

To see this, think how the rule would apply: let the conditional itself be the claim in need of new credence after credence in A has been bumped up. Substituting $(A\to C)$ for C in Jeffrey's rule we have

(i) $\quad cr_{new}(A\to C) = \{[cr_{new}(A) \times cr_{old}[(A\to C)/A]] + [cr_{new}(\neg A) \times cr_{old}[(A\to C)/\neg A]]\}$.

So by Ramsey's norm

$= \{[cr_{new}(A) \times cr_{old}[A\to(A\to C)]] + [cr_{new}(\neg A) \times cr_{old}[\neg A\to(A\to C)]]\}$.

So by the Credal Import/Export norm

$= \{[cr_{new}(A) \times cr_{old}[(A\&A)\to C)]] + [cr_{new}(\neg A) \times cr_{old}[(\neg A\&A)\to C)]]\}$.

But (A&A) is trivially equivalent to A, so we can simplify the left-most conditional

$$= \{[cr_{new}(A) \times cr_{old}(A \to C)] + [cr_{new}(\neg A) \times cr_{old}[(\neg A\&A) \to C)]]\}.$$

Rewriting from top-to-bottom gives the Bayesian answer to question (I) under present assumptions:

(IA) $cr_{new}(A \to C) = \{[cr_{new}(A) \times cr_{old}(A \to C)] + [cr_{new}(\neg A) \times cr_{old}[(\neg A\&A) \to C)]]\}.$

As we have seen, however, Bayesians are committed to the rigidity of conditional credence. This means we have the following in the case to hand:

$$cr_{old}(C/A) = cr_{new}(C/A).$$

So by Ramsey's norm

$$cr_{old}(A \to C) = cr_{new}(A \to C).$$

When we put this last equation with (Ia), though, we have

$$cr_{old}(A \to C) = \{[cr_{new}(A) \times cr_{old}(A \to C)] + [cr_{new}(\neg A) \times cr_{old}[(\neg A\&A) \to C)]]\}.$$

The Presumption-of-Non-Contradiction thesis entails the right-most conditional here is pointless or worse: either incredible or gibberish. If the latter, Bayesians cannot answer question (I) coherently; so assume the relevant conditional is merely incredible. Then the right-hand product above vanishes and we have

$$cr_{old}(A \to C) = [cr_{new}(A) \times cr_{old}(A \to C)].$$

For this to be true, however, it must also be the case that

$$cr_{new}(A) = 100\%.$$

But we stipulated that new credence for A is 90% in the case. Hence we have found conflict between the Bayesian model and Ramsey's norm. Since the norm fits nicely with base-case practice, and it generates fecund theory, this is bad news for the Bayesian model.

*Question (II): How should cr(A→C) change when cr(C) changes?*
Suppose you lend in-between credence to C and then input causes you to shift it (and does no more). How should this affect your credence for (A→C)? The Jeffrey rule yields an incorrect answer this question under current assumptions. To see this, apply the rule by doing two things: let the conditional play the C-role in the rule itself, and let C play the A-role in the rule. In other words, put (A→C) in for C in Jeffrey's equation and put C in for A. This yields

$$cr_{new}(A \to C) = \{[cr_{new}(C) \times cr_{old}[(A \to C)/C]] + [cr_{new}(\neg C) \times cr_{old}[(A \to C)/\neg C]]\}.$$

So by Ramsey's norm

$$= \{[cr_{new}(C) \times cr_{old}[C \to (A \to C)]] + [cr_{new}(\neg C) \times cr_{old}[\neg C \to (A \to C)]]\}.$$

So by the Credal Import/Export norm

$$= \{[cr_{new}(C) \times cr_{old}[(C\&A) \to C)]] + [cr_{new}(\neg C) \times cr_{old}[(\neg C\&A) \to C)]]\}.$$

Yet by Ramsey's norm

$$= \{[\text{cr}_{\text{new}}(C) \times \text{cr}_{\text{old}}[C/(C\&A)]] + [\text{cr}_{\text{new}}(\neg C) \times \text{cr}_{\text{old}}[C/(\neg C\&A)]]\}.$$

It is trivial that the first conditional credence is 100%; and it is trivial that the second conditional credence is zero. So we have

$$= \text{cr}_{\text{new}}(C).$$

Rewriting from top-to-bottom gives the Bayesian answer to question (II) under present assumptions:

(IIA)  $\text{cr}_{\text{new}}(A \to C) = \text{cr}_{\text{new}}(C).$

The Bayesian says that whenever your in-between credence in C is shifted, your new credence for (A→C) should align with your new view of C.

This is a coherent answer, of course, but it is not a good answer; for it is not generally true that one's credence for a conditional should align with one's take on its consequent after a shift in one's take on that consequent. Here is a clear counter-instance to (IIA). Let A be the claim that Elizabeth Warren has recently become known to her political opponents to be a Russian spy. Let C be the claim that Warren wins the 2020 election. Initially, you are close to certain that A is false, and (suppose) middling in confidence about the election. For definiteness, suppose your initial take on A and C is this:

$$\text{cr}_{\text{old}}(A) = 1\%$$

$$\text{cr}_{\text{old}}(C) = 50\%.$$

But you realize that *if* Warren has recently become known to her political opponents to be a Russian spy, then she will *not* win the 2020 election. Of that you are basically certain, so your initial take on the conditional running from A to C is almost nil:

$$\text{cr}_{\text{old}}(A \to C) = 1\%.$$

This is to say that you lend almost no credence to the thought that if Warren has become known as a spy to her opponents then she will win in 2020. Suppose new input then raises your credence in C: an authority you trust says that Warren will win the election. This input makes you more sure that Warren will be elected in 2020:

$$\text{cr}_{\text{new}}(C) = 75\%.$$

The Bayesian model entails that your new credence for the conditional should align:

$$\text{cr}_{\text{new}}(A \to C) = 75\%.$$

That is obviously wrong. Your new credence for the conditional should *not* go up in a case like this, it should not be shifted at all. You should remain almost sure that if Warren has become known as a Russian spy she will not win the 2020 election. You should continue to lend almost no credence to (A→C).

Intuitively, one's take on a conditional should not *automatically* shift in response to a shift in one's take on its consequent. The appropriate reaction will depend on details of the case (as we'll see in the next chapter). An approach to the issue based on

Ramsey's norm explains this nicely, of course, but *if* that equation is assumed—as it intuitively should be—Bayesians must say that one's take on a conditional should always align with one's new take on its consequent. But that seems plainly wrong. Once again we can see that the Bayesian model together with Ramsey's norm lead to counter-intuitive prescription for the rational shift of opinion.

*Question (III): How should cr(A) change when cr(A→C) changes?*
Suppose you lend in-between credence to (A→C) and then new input causes you to shift it (and no more). How should this affect your credence in A? Jeffrey's rule leads to difficulty because it requires there to be left-nested conditional thoughts, which conflicts with the Unconditional Antecedents Assumption.

To see this, apply Jeffrey's rule to the case by putting (A→C) in for A and A in for C in the rule. This yields

$$cr_{new}(A) = \{[cr_{new}(A\to C) \times cr_{old}A/(A\to C)]] \\ + [cr_{new}[\neg(A\to C)] \times cr_{old}[A/\neg(A\to C)]]\}.$$

By the distribution of negation norm

$$= \{[cr_{new}(A\to C) \times cr_{old}[A/(A\to C)]] + [cr_{new}[(A\to \neg C)] \\ \times cr_{old}[A/(A\to \neg C)]]\}.$$

By Ramsey's norm

$$= \{[cr_{new}(A\to C) \times cr_{old}[(A\to C)\to A]] + [cr_{new}[(A\to \neg C)] \\ \times cr_{old}[(A\to \neg C)\to A]]\}.$$

Rewriting from top-to-bottom gives the Bayesian answer to question (III) under present assumptions:

(IIIA) $\quad cr_{new}(A) = \{[cr_{new}(A\to C) \times cr_{old}[(A\to C)\to A]] + [cr_{new}[(A\to \neg C)] \\ \times cr_{old}[(A\to \neg C)\to A]]\}.$

This is no good: there are multiple left-nested conditionals on the right side of this answer, i.e. conditionals with conditionals as their antecedents. We have seen, though, that conditionals of the form

$$[(x\to y)\to z]$$

make no sense. That is what led us to the Unconditional Antecedents Assumption. With the restricted-vision conception of conditionality in place, the Bayesian model conflicts with that assumption.

*Question (IV): How should cr(C) change when cr(A→C) changes?*
Suppose you lend in-between credence to (A→C) and then new input causes it to shift but does no more. How should this affect your credence in C? Jeffrey's rule leads to difficulty here too by leading to thoughts which supposedly query something on condition that a conditional is so. This makes no sense with the restricted-vision conception of conditionality in place, for that conception leads directly to the Unconditional Antecedents Assumption.

To see this consider Jeffrey's prescription with (A→C) for A in the rule. This yields

$$cr_{new}(C) = \{[cr_{new}(A\to C) \times cr_{old}[C/(A\to C)]] + [cr_{new}[\neg(A\to C)]$$
$$\times cr_{old}[C/\neg(A\to C)]]\}.$$

By the distribution of negation norm we have

$$= \{[cr_{new}(A\to C) \times cr_{old}[C/(A\to C)]] + [cr_{new}[(A\to\neg C)]$$
$$\times cr_{old}[C/(A\to\neg C)]]\}.$$

So by Ramsey's norm

$$= \{[cr_{new}(A\to C) \times cr_{old}[(A\to C)\to C]] + [cr_{new}[(A\to\neg C)]$$
$$\times cr_{old}[(A\to\neg C)\to C]]\}.$$

Rewriting from top-to-bottom gives the Bayesian answer to question (IV) under present assumptions:

(IVA) $\quad b_{new}(A) = \{[cr_{new}(A\to C) \times cr_{old}[(A\to C)\to A]] + [cr_{new}[(A\to\neg C)]$
$$\times cr_{old}[(A\to\neg C)\to A]]\}.$$

This is also no good, for there are left-nested conditionals in each product here as well. Those conditionals conflict with the Unconditional Antecedents Assumption brought on by the restricted-vision conception of conditionality.

Drawing this all together, then, the Bayesian model generates rigidity and incompleteness worries about the role of conditional credence in rational state transition. When focused on base-case instances of indicative and conditional credence, though, the two types of credence seem to line up perfectly in strength. This prompts a very direct strategy for dealing with both rigidity and incompleteness: accept the Ramsey norm with natural piety, feed indicative credence into Jeffrey's rule, treat the result via Ramsey as a solution to the incompleteness worry, and hope that the result joins issue gracefully with the fact that conditional credence is rigid in the Bayesian model. But we've seen that the straightforward strategy is hopeless. It leads to mistaken prediction, contradiction, even incoherence.

It's not hard to see why. Ramsey's norm ensures that conditional commitment functions as a *restricted*-vision distribution of fine-grained opinion. This is true no matter what conditional commitment turns out to be—binary commitment, tertiary commitment, something else yet again—so long as Ramsey's norm is in place. Feeding conditional commitment into Jeffrey's rule treats it as if such commitment involves normal fact-stating discourse. But commitment like that traffics in *unrestricted*-vision distribution of fine-grained opinion. Putting the two moves together, then—subjecting conditional commitment to Ramsey's norm and to Jeffrey's rule—treats it as if it has systematic double-vision.

It is not the slightest bit surprising that this leads to trouble. After all, the approach requires in all rational credence distributions that an agent's take on C, when restricting her epistemic vision to A-worlds, is identical in strength to some kind of A- and C-involving conditional commitment which involves all of epistemic space. It's good work if you can get it, of course, but this chapter and the next each makes clear that it's work only to be had in trivial settings. For any normal epistemic space, no type of commitment can play both these roles.

## 4.7 The Nozick–Harman Point, *Modus Ponens*, and Supposition

One sensible conclusion to draw on the basis of the previous section is this: to the extent that conditional commitment is subject to the ratio norm, the binary approach to conditionality is wrong. For the binary approach treats conditional commitment as if it concerns all of epistemic space. Ramsey's norm forces conditional commitment to be a function of what occurs in a restricted portion of that space. This is much more in line with the tertiary approach to conditionality, and, for this reason, the ratio norm fits much better with that approach than it does to the binary view.

In this section we explore another reason to think that the tertiary approach to conditionality is correct. It comes from insights made initially by Robert Nozick, insights picked up and fully developed by Gilbert Harman.[24] In a nutshell, Nozick noticed that there is a fundamental difference between a rule of entailment and a rule of inference. The former has to do with what follows from what—semantically, proof-theoretically, conceptually—while the latter has to do with rational shift-in-view, i.e. the cognitive activity of updating opinion. These topics are not unrelated, but Nozick realized that they are not identical either; for it is always possible to be situated epistemically so that it more reasonable to *retract* commitment to a bit of some complex rule of entailment—the moment all of its pieces fall into place—rather than *go forward* inferentially in line with the rule.

For example, let M be the claim that there are Martians in the White House. Suppose you have overwhelming evidence that M is false, which leads you to have low credence for M. Let A be the claim that there are Apples in the fridge. Suppose you know me to be generally trustworthy about the fridge and I tell you that there are Apples in there. This leads you to lend high credence to A. You realize, of course, that A implies the disjunctive claim (A or M)—intuitively the fact that there are Apples in the fridge entails that either there are apples in the fridge or there are Martians in the White House—so you dutifully lend high credence to (A or M) too. But your epistemic stance is sensible: it reflects your grip on the fact that your take on the disjunction is fully dependent on your credence for its first disjunct. You lend high credence to the claim that either there are Apples in the fridge or Martians in the White House precisely because you lend high credence to the claim that there are Apples in the fridge.

Suppose you then look in the fridge and see clearly that there are no Apples there. How should you react to the news? Well, obviously, you should drop your credence

---

[24] See (Nozick, 1990). His insight was taken up by Harman in his 'Induction: a discussion of the relevance of the theory of knowledge to the theory of induction (with a digression to the effect that neither deductive logic nor the probability calculus has anything to do with inference)' (1970), and considerably developed in (Harman, 1986). In the first instance, the Nozick–Harman point has to do with rules of inference, as we'll see. But we've already seen that a full-dress dynamics for credence entails its kinematics, so the Nozick–Harman insight will be relevant to Jeffrey's rule as well.

in A; and since your commitment to (A or M) is dependent upon your commitment to A, you should drop your credence in (A or M) too. That much is clear. It would be madness in your situation to infer that there are Martians in the White House after seeing that there are no Apples in the fridge. But this indicates that there is a stage of your epistemic development at which you should *not* infer in line with Disjunctive Syllogism. After all, once you have looked in the fridge and dropped your credence in A, but done nothing further to update your take on things, both of Disjunctive Syllogism's premises will be in place. Yet it will not be rational to go forward with the entailment rule. The sensible thing to do is drop commitment to one of its parts.

Recall what Disjunctive Syllogism says:

$$\begin{array}{c} A \text{ or } M \\ \underline{\neg A} \\ \therefore \ M. \end{array}$$

This is a bona fide rule of entailment. As a matter of logic, whenever premises of its form are true, a conclusion of its form is true as well. At one stage in your epistemic journey you lend high credence to claims of the Disjunctive-Syllogism form. It is not sensible, though, in that situation, to go on and lend high credence to the related conclusion. The sensible move at that stage of your epistemic development is to drop commitment to one of Disjunctive Syllogism's moving parts. After you see for yourself that there are no Apples in the fridge, and come to have high credence in ¬A—but before your mind is changed further, so while you still lend high credence to (A or M)—it would be silly to go forward with high credence for the view that there are Martians in the White House. This is so despite the fact that at this stage of your epistemic journey you have strong commitment to premises manifesting the Disjunctive-Syllogism-form. Hence Disjunctive Syllogism is not a rule of inference. It is merely a rule of entailment.

Consider what happens in the Apple case. You begin with high credence for (A or M) which rests on high credence for A. But A is the logical opposite of Disjunctive Syllogism's second premise, so you start with a commitment to its first premise which rests on a take against its second premise. When strong evidence comes in to support that second premise, therefore, it cuts against the argument form's first premise. It would be irrational, for this reason, to stick with the (A or M)-claim once you've lent credence to A but not yet adjusted the rest of your view. This does not show that Disjunctive Syllogism fails as an entailment rule. It does show that Disjunctive Syllogism fails as a required route forward in the quest to better one's epistemic position. It shows that Disjunctive Syllogism is no rule of inference.

The same thing is true of other two-part rules of entailment. Consider the rule known as Conjunction Introduction:

$$\begin{array}{c} P \\ \underline{Q} \\ \therefore \ P\&Q. \end{array}$$

It is easy to cook-up an epistemic journey which relates to this rule like the Apple–Martian journey relates to Disjunctive Syllogism. For example, suppose you are painting the walls of a windowless room when a friend John walks by. He reports that it's begun to rain outside (claim R). You come to lend high credence to R in the usual way. A moment later John's partner drops by and reports that John has been pranking people all day about the weather. In reaction to this news you lend high credence to the claim that John has been pranking people all day about the weather (claim P). Before updating your view of things further you lend high credence to R and high credence to P. It would be silly, though, in your situation, to lend high credence to (R&P); for P *undercuts* the credence you've lent to R.[25] The sensible move *in situ* is to reduce credence in R rather than increase credence in (R&D). You should not update in line with Conjunction Introduction. This does not show that Conjunction Introduction fails as a rule of entailment. It does show that Conjunction Introduction fails as a rule of inference.

There's a pattern here. With both Disjunctive-Syllogism and Conjunction-Introduction we begin with a two-part entailment rule, something of the form:

(R)  $$\begin{array}{c} X \\ \underline{Y} \\ \therefore Z. \end{array}$$

We then describe an epistemic journey in three steps:

1. The agent comes to possess good reason to commit to X but not to Y.
2. The agent gets new evidence which supports Y in the first instance; but the evidence somehow attacks the agent's commitment to X. As a result:
3. It is unreasonable to form a commitment to Z in line with entailment rule (R). The reasonable move is to retract commitment to X.

We thereby show that (R) is no inference rule, it is merely a two-part rule of entailment.

A natural thought at this stage is that *any* two-part entailment rule is subject to this sort of treatment, and, for this reason, that no such rule is a genuine rule of inference, no such rule provides an obligatory path forward when it comes to rational shift of credence. This would be bad news for the Bayesian model, of course, since its update rule is basically the double-whammy application of *Modus Ponens*:

$$\begin{array}{c} A \to C \\ \underline{A} \\ \therefore C. \end{array}$$

The connection between Jeffrey Conditionalization and *Modus Ponens* is clearest in the limit-case application of the former, when an update is to occur after becoming certain of A. In such a case Jeffrey's rule says that one's new take on C should be equal in strength to one's old take on (A→C). In essence Jeffrey recommends that one move forward in thought with *Modus Ponens*. If that rule of entailment is subject to

---

[25] See (Pollock, 1986) for the classic view of undercutting defeat, and (Sturgeon, 2014) for an alternative view.

the Nozick phenomenon, however—if we can construct an epistemic journey with it on which (1)-thru-(3) hold—we'll have thereby located a counter-instance to the Bayesian model. Jeffrey Conditionalization will recommend a palpably irrational way forward in the case.

Formally, at least, there is no reason why such a story cannot be constructed for *Modus Ponens*, like it can for other two-part rules of entailment. The story would involve circumstances in which one began with a rational commitment to (A→C) but not to A, then one received new input in support of A, but somehow that input undermined—perhaps in light of one's other commitments—one's extant commitment to (A→C). If there are such circumstances it would be more sensible in them, after shifting one's take on A, to shift one's credence for (A→C) as well—and thereby take *Modus Ponens* off the table—rather than to hold fast in one's take on (A→C) and move forward in line with the entailment rule. Putting the point in terms of conditional credence rather than credence lent to a conditional: notionally at least it looks as if there ought to be circumstances in which one begins with rational high conditional credence for C given A, but low credence for A, then one receives new input in support of A, but somehow that input undermines—perhaps in light of other commitments—one's conditional credence for C given A. If there are circumstances like that, they provide a straightforward counter-example to the Bayesian model; for it is more sensible in them, after upping one's credence for A, to lower one's conditional credence for C given A rather than to hold fast and move forward in line with Jeffrey's rule.

If this sort of scenario is *not* possible, though, an explanation of that fact is sorely needed. We should have a story about why, for instance, the simplicity of one's worldview cannot be best served after shifting credence for A by shifting credence for (A→C) (or shifting conditional credence for C given A). We should have a story about why a rational agent's epistemic state cannot see a link between a conditional and its antecedent, so that shifting credence for the latter has rational knock-on effects when it comes to her credence for the former—or, put another way, we'll need a story about why your epistemic state cannot see a link between your conditional credence for C given A on the one hand and your credence for A on the other. If anything like this turns out to be rationally possible, after all, the Bayesian transition theory is wrong.

When I first began thinking about this (a long time ago) it seemed to me that a case could be built which manifested the Nozick–Harman point for *Modus Ponens*. But I was thinking about things in a bad way. Years of teaching the material have shown that this the bad way of thinking is popular not only with my earlier self but also with students, so I begin with a sketch of the mistaken line of thought. Then I explain in detail why it is a mistaken, and only then discuss whether it is possible to correct for the mistake. As we'll see—somewhat to my surprise still—it does not look possible to do so in any obvious or uncontentious way. This will be yet another reason to think that conditional commitment is not binary. If it were simply binary commitment to a conditional being the case across all of epistemic space, after all, surely it would be possible to concoct a scenario which stands to *Modus Ponens* as the Apple–Martian case stands to Disjunctive Syllogism.

We look at three attempts to construct such a case.

## Attempt 1: *THE MARBLE GAME*

The story begins with the Marble Game of Chapter 2. Recall it involves grooves cut in a table which form into a branching tree

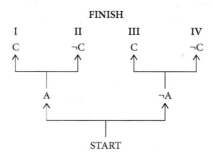

**Figure 4.5**

The table itself slopes from a Start Point to a Finish region, with marbles dropped at the former rolling to the latter. En route they must negotiate four possible choice- or branch-points in a tree-like structure of grooves. A machine inside the table fixes objective probabilities for each branch-point. From time to time the machine changes the objective probabilities associated with the branch-points in the Game.

Suppose there is a giant screen above the table which continuously displays what the chance at a moment is that a marble will branch left at the first branch-point in the Game; and suppose the chance-fixing machine inside the table ensures that the second-tier chance of C given A—i.e. the objective probability that a marble will follow a C-path, given it has already followed an A-path—is itself always identical to the chance that the marble was to go down A-path in the first place. In other worlds, suppose the chance-fixing machine in the table fixes a chance for C given A, at time t, equal to the chance of A at that time. Suppose finally that you are rationally certain of all this before you begin playing the Game.

You see on the screen above the table that the initial chance of A is 70%. So you lend 70% credence to A and 70% credence to C if/given A. Then you notice on the screen that the A-chance has shifted from 70% to 80%. So you dutifully shift your credence in A accordingly, and dutifully shift your take on C if/given A as well. Question: doesn't that cut against the Updating Assumption of the Bayesian model? After all, you start with in-between credence for A, rationally shift to a new credence for A, and then rationally shift downstream to a new commitment conditional on A. Doesn't that contradict the model's Updating Assumption about conditionality?

No. For the Assumption applies only when credence in A is the *sole* thing rationally shifted by input. That is not so in the case to hand. When you see the screen say that the A-chance is 70%, that fixes your initial take on A. But it does not do so directly: it leads you first to lend full credence to the claim that the A-chance is 70%, and reliance on that new full credence leads you to a 70% credence for A.

Your initial take on A is based on your initial take on A's chance; and your initial take on A's chance is itself based on a range of other background commitments plus your view of the screen. Similarly: when you see the screen come to say that the A-chance is 80%, that fixes a new take on A. But it likewise does not do so directly: it leads you first to lend full credence to the claim that the A-chance is 80%, and reliance on that new full credence leads you to lend 80% credence to A. Your revised take on A is based on your revised take on A's chance; and your revised take on A's chance is based on a range of background commitments plus your view of the screen.

In the case just sketched, then, new evidence does not shift your take on A and nothing but A. It shifts your take on A *by* shifting your take on a range of other things. It is easy to miss that when thinking about the case, and, as a result, to misclassify the case as a counter-instance to Jeffrey Conditionalization. But the thought experiment is no such thing. It refutes neither Jeffrey's rule nor the Updating Assumption; for that Assumption holds, on Jeffrey's rule, only in very special circumstances: only when new evidence makes for a rational shift in credence for A and no more.

It is important to keep these special circumstances in mind when deciding whether a given scenario is a counter-instance to the Updating Assumption; for it can often be unclear whether the special circumstances obtain. To see this consider three further attempts to create a counter-instance to the Updating Assumption.

## Attempt 2: THE HURT LOCKER

Suppose I'm a bomb-disposal guy in a war zone, like the protagonist of the movie *The Hurt Locker*. Suppose also that I have a mental condition which makes it the case that every so often I have what is known in my outfit as a 'bad day'. When I have such a day it turns out that I am terrible at my job, even though I take myself on the bad day to be great at my job, and I take myself to be responsible for all good things which happen around me, etc. Suppose that normally when I have a bad day I look slightly off in a way you can recognize, and you know all this to be so.

One day you walk up as I'm standing by an IED in the road. There are dozens of us bomb-disposal guys hanging out there, any one of whom could have dealt with the device. You look at me and ask: 'Did you take care of that?' I reply normally: 'Well, let me put it this way:

(1)   If I'm having a bad day, we're all in big trouble.'

Let A be the claim that I'm having a bad day, B be the claim that I took care of the IED (rather than one of the other bomb-disposal guys), and C be the claim that we're all in big trouble. After I produce (1), three things happen rationally:

—you lend low credence to A;
—you lend high credence to B; and
—you lend high credence to the indicative conditional produced by me: if I'm having a bad day, we're all in big trouble.

So you start in the case with high credence for the major premise of *Modus Ponens*:

$$(A \rightarrow C)$$
$$A$$
$$\text{so, } C.$$

But you have low credence for the minor premise of the argument: A.

Then I walk off down the road. A few minutes later a real expert on my bad days—perhaps my commanding officer—walks up and says:

(2)  Sturgeon's having a bad day.

In this situation it is clear that you should raise your credence in A. But it is not clear that you should hold fast to your high credence for (A→C), much less that you should put your old high credence for (A→C) together with your new high credence for A to produce even-newer high credence for C. Instead it looks as if you should decide that it wasn't me after all who took care of the IED, that it was likely one of the other bomb-disposal guys, that I was taking credit for something I didn't do, and that I was doing so because I'm having a bad day. This leads to the thought, of course, that you should lower credence in (A→C) after raising credence in A, which in turn seems to indicate that THE HURT LOCKER is an instance of the Nozick phenomenon for *Modus Ponens*.

From another perspective, though, the Nozick point does not apply to the case; for the new input created by the production of (2) is not simply that Sturgeon is having a bad day, but rather the claim

(3)  The expert says that Sturgeon is having a bad day.

If that is the right way to look at things, though, it is not the antecedent of (A→C) that is supported in the first instance by the expert's production of (2), in which case the Nozick point doesn't apply after all. So our view on whether the THE HURT LOCKER provides a *Modus-Ponens* style instance of the Nozick phenomenon will depend on how we see testimonial evidence in the case. If the analogue of dogmatism in the theory of perception is accepted, and we say that the expert's production of (2) yields the news precisely that Sturgeon is having a bad day, then, the Nozick point does seem to apply to the case.[26] Before the expert's testimony, after all, you lend high credence to (A→C) and low credence to A. The testimony leads simply to an upping of credence for A. The sensible thing to do, however—by way of reaction to that upping—is to lower your credence in the conditional, not raise your credence in C. This means the Nozick–Harman point applies to the case, and, therefore, that *Modus Ponens* is not an update rule but merely a rule of entailment.

If the analogue of dogmatism in the theory of perception is rejected, however, and we say (e.g.) that the expert's production of (2) yields the news precisely that the expert says that Sturgeon is having a bad day—i.e. if we say that the production of (2) yields exactly (3) as the news—then, Nozick's point does not apply to the case. Prior to the commander's testimony you lend high credence to (A→C) and low

---

[26] For discussion of dogmatism see (Pollock, 1986), Jim Pryor's (2000)—from which the label is taken—Pryor (2013), (Sturgeon, 1998) or (Sturgeon, 2008).

credence to A. The non-dogmatic view of testimony entails that it is not A but rather (3) that is news. But it has *never* been plausible in the vignette that if (3) is the case then so is (A→C). The following will never have been lent high credence in the story:

(4) If the expert says that Sturgeon is having a bad day, then, if Sturgeon is having a bad day, we're all in big trouble.

We know from our discussion of the Credal Import/Export Law, after all, that this complex conditional is equi-credible with

If the expert says that Sturgeon is having a bad day, and he is having a bad day, then we're all in big trouble,

which can be rephrased colloquially as

(5) If the expert says truly that Sturgeon is having a bad day, then we're all in big trouble.

But (5) is implausible throughout the vignette. If the dogmatic view of testimony is rejected, therefore, and testimonial news in the case is something like (4) or (5), then, we do not see an instance of the Nozick point in the story; for we do not see a case where one lowers credence in the consequent of a conditional by way of reaction solely to a shift in credence for the conditional's antecedent. Whether THE HURT LOCKER illustrates Nozick's point for *Modus Ponens* depends on the epistemology of testimony: a sorely-contested area. There is no uncontentious reading of the case on which it manifests the Nozick point.

*Attempt 3:* COPPER WIRE

Suppose you see an old piece of copper wire in a derelict house. As it happens you collect wire as a hobby and have a particular fondness for the copper variety. You bend down to pick up the piece of copper wire which you see. At that moment you have high credence that you will touch the wire, and you have low credence that you will be killed if you do so. Then someone calls out from behind: 'Hey!

(6) If you touch the wire, you'll die!'

You immediately stand up. At this point, your credence for (6) has gone up, and, as a result, your credence for its antecedent has gone down. You no longer lend high credence to the view that you'll touch the wire, since you now lend high credence to the view that you'll die if you touch the wire.

You have a special friend PATH, though, so-called because she has a long and fruitful history of Predicting Actions which lead to Tremendous Happiness. You take note when PATH says

(7) You will touch the wire.

After hearing this prediction, your credence for (7) goes back up—you become confident that you will touch the wire—but you don't end up confident that you're about to die, for your credence in the conditional (6)—the claim that you'll die if you touch the wire—goes back down. Doesn't that show the Nozick point applies to the case?

Once again the answer depends on our approach to testimonial evidence. And once again there are two major options to hand: we can treat the news in COPPER WIRE as if it is (7)—the claim that you will touch the wire, in line with a dogmatic approach to testimony—or we can treat it as

(8) PATH says that you will touch the wire

in line with a non-dogmatic approach to testimony. If we take a dogmatic approach to testimony, and treat news in the case as (7), it follows that there is a stage of the story at which you have high credence for (T→K) together with low credence for T, then, at the next stage, you raise your credence for T by way of reaction to evidence precisely for T, and then you lower your credence for the conditional rather than raise your credence for its consequent. This is exactly the Nozick phenomenon. If we take a dogmatic approach to testimony, therefore, the Nozick point applies to the case.

If we take a non-dogmatic approach to testimony, however, and treat news in COPPER WIRE as (something like) (8), then, Nozick's point fails to apply; for the relevant conditional in the case is

(9) If PATH says that you will touch the wire, then, if you touch the wire, you will die which can be colloquially rephrased as

(10) If PATH says that you will touch the wire and you do touch it, you will die or as

(11) If PATH says truly that you will touch the wire, you will die.

But neither (10) nor (11) has ever been credence-worthy in the vignette. At no stage in COPPER WIRE should you lend high credence to either of them. If we take a non-dogmatic approach to testimony, therefore, the Nozick point has no purchase on the case. Since the best approach to testimony is hugely contentious, COPPER WIRE is not a straightforward example of the Nozick point applying to *Modus Ponens*.

*Attempt 4: ALIEN THREAT*
Suppose we belong to a group of humans who are kidnapped by aliens. The aliens take us to their home world and leave armed ships surrounding Earth. They tell us that we'll be tested in various ways over months, and then in full view of everyone they take me aside for a private discussion. When I return I say this: 'The aliens seem very dangerous. Strangely they also seem to *hate* announcements—so much so, in fact, they told me that if I ever *begin* an announcement they will cremate the human race within the hour.' You listen carefully to the story and then lend high credence to

(12) If Scott begins an <u>A</u>nnouncement, humans will be <u>C</u>remated within the-hour. (A→C)

The abducted humans are then put through their paces. Toward the end of a perplexing day, after several months of testing, I say the following

(13) I hereby make an announcement...

This creates new evidential input. In reaction to that input you should raise your credence for A: the claim that I begin an announcement. But *in situ* it initially seems that you could rationally lower your credence for (12): the claim that if I begin an announcement, humans will be cremated within the hour. So have we finally found a case which manifests the Nozick phenomenon for *Modus Ponens*?

Well, there is no scope here for a debate like the one we had about testimony in the previous two cases. When I produce (13) I simply begin an announcement. I don't report anything to be the case. Beginning an announcement is precisely what's needed to make the antecedent of (12) true, and you realize that this is so. It is thus natural to think that new evidence in the case favours exactly that A is true. If you rationally react to the news by lowering your credence for (A→C), rather than raising it for C, then Nozick's point applies to the case.

This would not mean that your reaction to news in the vignette is inexplicable or anomalous. It would be clear what had happened, after all: since you thought me clever and extremely unlikely to do anything which would lead to the destruction of humanity, upon perceiving my initiation of an announcement, it struck you that I must have figured out that (12) is false, somehow, and that I produced (13) to illustrate the insight. Instead of leaning on (12) in light of (13), therefore, and coming to invest high credence in C, you end-up lowering credence for (12) after raising your credence for (12)'s antecedent.

If this is the right way to think about ALIEN THREAT, the case involves a 4-stage epistemic journey. In the first stage there is high credence for (A→C) and low credence for A. In the second stage there is receipt of news precisely that A is true. In the third stage there is the creation of high credence for A, by way of reaction to the second stage news. And in the fourth stage there is a shift to low credence for (A→C) by way of reaction to the upshot of stage-3.

If this is what happens in ALIEN THREAT, indicative credence is not always rigid when credence changes solely in its antecedent. Sometimes indicative credence can rationally shift after credence has changed solely for the antecedent of the relevant conditional. If Ramsey's norm holds in all rational credence distributions, though, it follows that conditional credence is likewise not rigid across certain rational shifts— like those found in ALIEN THREAT—where credence has changed solely in a conditioning claim. The Bayesian transition theory entails that conditional credence is rigid across shifts of view like that. Our current take on ALIEN THREAT, therefore, is incompatible with the Bayesian model garnished with Ramsey's norm.

Having said that, it's *not* really clear that Nozick's point actually applies to ALIEN THREAT; for it's unclear that you lend high credence to (A→C) at the relevant point in the vignette. This can be seen with a tool mentioned in our original quote from Ramsey. Recall its opening remarks:

When two people are arguing 'If A, will C?' and are both in [some] doubt as to A, they are adding A hypothetically to their stock of knowledge and arguing on that basis about C...we can say that they are fixing their degree of belief in C given A.[27]

---

[27] We've changed the variables once again to fit them into our discussion.

When Ramsey speaks of 'adding A hypothetically to [a] stock of knowledge', and then 'arguing about C', it is not fully clear what he's talking about. We'll interpret him to be talking about *suppositional reasoning*.

This is the sort of reasoning that occurs when someone explicitly supposes that something is true and then reasons their way to new conclusions while making that supposition. These new conclusions are reached 'within the scope' of the explicit supposition being made. More will be said about this kind of reasoning later on. Here we note merely that some sort of fine-grained opinion can shift within the scope of an explicit supposition. This sort of opinion is not itself genuine credence, of course, since it is dependent upon being lent within a context set up by an act of supposition. But the opinion can wax and wane nonetheless, strengthening and weakening as one thinks various things through within the scope of a supposition.

Call such supposition-dependent fine-grained opinion 'suppositional credit', or *sup-cred* for short. The attitude is credence-like in its grain and its norms, and it depends for its existence on the context of supposition. It is through suppositional credit that Ramsey forges a bridge between indicative credence and the reason-theoretic happenings which occur within the scope of a supposition. To see how this works, let us develop some notation for the suppositional credit lent to C under the supposition of A:

$$sup_A[\mathbf{cred}(C)].$$

With this notation in place we can condense Ramsey's thought in the following way: indicative credence should be identical in strength to analogue suppositional credit. In other words, credence lent to a conditional should be identical in strength to the fine-grained opinion lent to its consequent within a supposition that its antecedent as true.

We'll call this the *Suppositional Ramsey Norm*:

$$(\text{SRN}) \quad cr(A \rightarrow C) = sup_A[\mathbf{cred}(C)].$$

The idea is also known as the 'Ramsey's Test' for indicatives. Here's why: suppose you want to know the level of credence that should be lent in your circumstances to (A→C). The Suppositional Ramsey Norm yields an answer in four steps: first, suppose that A is true; then reason along within the scope of that supposition until your suppositional credit settles into a new equilibrium; then check the strength of your take on C in the suppositional equilibrium; finally, set the strength of credence for (A→C) equal to $sup_A[\mathbf{cred}(C)]$. This is precisely what the Suppositional Ramsey Norm maintains: indicative credence should line up with credit for C inside the scope of a supposition of A.

We can use the Suppositional Ramsey Norm to foreground the main reason why it does *not* seem that Nozick's point truly applies to ALIEN THREAT. The key move in the strategy involves posing a question which targets the moment *before* Stage-3 of the story occurs. Specifically, our question will target the moment just before you get news to the effect that A is true in ALIEN THREAT. Here is the question: do you or do you not regard me at that moment as someone who wouldn't freely and knowingly do something which led to humanity's destruction?

140 THE BAYESIAN TRANSITION THEORY: CRITICAL DISCUSSION

For simplicity, let us pretend there are only two answers to this question: yes and no. Assume that at the relevant moment you either fully accept or fully reject that I am the sort of person who wouldn't freely and knowingly do something which led to humanity's destruction. In the first case, we'll abbreviate this by saying that what you fully accept is that I'm a good person; and in the second we'll do so by saying that what you fully accept is that I am a bad person. OK, if the first answer is true, then just before Stage 3 in ALIEN THREAT—i.e. just before I create evidence precisely that I'm beginning an announcement—you fully accept that I'm a good person. Consider what happens in those circumstances when you suppose that I begin an announcement? How does reasoning proceed within the scope of that supposition?

We can vocalize it as follows:

Suppose that Sturgeon begins an announcement. Well, since he's a good person he'd never do that unless he's somehow realized that the aliens were bluffing (or at least wrong) about the annihilation of humanity. So he's using (13) to demonstrate this fact.

When you accept that I'm a good person, and then suppose that I begin an announcement, you end up reasoning suppositionally forward to a low-strength take on the claim that humanity is about to be destroyed. This means that $sup_A[\mathbf{cred}(C)]$ is low in these epistemic circumstances. By the Suppositional Ramsey Norm, credence for (A→C) should be low as well. If you find yourself accepting that I'm a good person, therefore, just before Stage-3 of ALIEN THREAT, and you are rational, you will have low credence in (A→C). This means that Nozick's point doesn't apply in the circumstances if you are rational, for you have low rather than high indicative credence when news arrives to the effect that the relevant antecedent is true.

In the second case you accept that I might well freely and knowingly do something which led to humanity's destruction. You think me precisely the sort of fellow who might risk humanity for personal glory, say. In those circumstances, with that low opinion of me in place, what happens when you suppose that I begin an announcement and then reason forward?

We can vocalize the upshot as follows:

Suppose that Sturgeon begins an announcement. Since he's precisely the sort of person who'd knowingly risk humanity, and the aliens have said they'll destroy us if someone begins an announcement, it looks like we're all in big trouble.

After supposing that I begin an announcement, when you take me to be a risky sort of fellow, reasoning suppositionally forward leads you to a high-strength take on the view that humanity is doomed. This means that $sup_A[\mathbf{cred}(C)]$ is high rather than low in these circumstances. The Suppositional Ramsey Norm then insists that credence for (A→C) should be high as well. If it is genuinely the case, therefore, just prior to Stage-3 of ALIEN THREAT, that you reject that I'm a good person, then, you'll have high credence in (A→C).

But it also seems that you should go forward *in situ* with the conditional, once news of my announcing comes in. Once you realize that I've started an announcement, you should come to think that humanity is doomed, since you accept that it's doomed if anyone starts an announcement. When you see me produce

(13) you ought to raise your credence for the view that humanity will be cremated within the hour; and you should do so precisely because you have high credence in (A→C) together with high credence for A. The Nozick point is inapplicable to the case.

In a nutshell, either you think me the sort of person who might risk humanity or you reject that idea. In the former case the Suppositional Ramsey Norm indicates that you should have high credence for (A→C) when news comes in precisely to the effect that A is true. This underwrites the thought that your high indicative credence should be used in the production of high credence for C upon receipt of the news. In the latter case the Suppositional Ramsey Norm indicates that you should have low indicative credence when the news comes in. Either way Nozick's point fails to apply in ALIEN THREAT. Either way you should go forward with *Modus Ponens*, or you don't have all of its pieces in place to begin with.

We have looked at four attempts to construct a case in which Nozick's point applies to *Modus Ponens*: THE MARBLE GAME, THE HURT LOCKER, COPPER WIRE, and ALIEN THREAT. We have seen that Nozick's point fails to apply straightforwardly to any of the cases. This does not show that Nozick's point never applies to *Modus Ponens*. But it does strongly suggest that it never applies. After all, it is strikingly *easy* to construct a case in which Nozick's point applies to other two-part rules of entailment. It is strikingly easy to see that they fail to specify obligatory patterns of inference, obligatory ways forward in thought. This is simply not so for *Modus Ponens*. It is nigh on impossible to construct a case in which a rational agent has high credence for (A→C), receives news precisely to the effect that A is true, but should intuitively react to the news by giving up (A→C) rather than going forward to endorse C. This suggests that *Modus Ponens* does specify an obligatory pattern of inference, unlike other two-part rules of entailment.[28]

This indicates that we occupy a particular spot in the logical geography of the area. Recall that geography

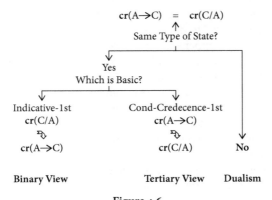

**Figure 4.6**

---

[28] For relevant discussion see Chalmers on the scrutability of truth in (Chalmers, 2012).

It is highly unlikely that indicative and conditional credence are two kinds of thing: dualism about conditionality is almost certainly wrong. Once it is granted, though, that monism about conditionality is correct, and hence that indicative and conditional credence are the same kind of thing, it is unclear which of them is explanatorily basic. If the binary view of conditionality is true, though, and binary indicative credence is the fundamental moving part in the area, it should be easy to concoct a case showing that *Modus Ponens* is merely a rule of entailment, that it is not a rule of inference. But it is not at all easy to do that—in fact we've been unable to do it so far. This indicates that conditional credence is the basic moving part in the area, that indicative credence reduces to conditional credence, that the tertiary view of conditionality is correct. In the next chapter we'll see more reason to endorse this perspective.

## 4.8 Restricted-Vision Conditionality and Bayesian Kinematics

We are left, then, with two worries for the Bayesian transition theory: the rigidity worry and the incompleteness worry. Both turn on the central ingredient found in Bayesian kinematics: conditional credence. The first problem turns on the puzzling fact that after a rational shift-of-view with respect to a particular claim, the Bayesian story entails that credence conditional on that claim never changes. The second problem turns on the failure of the Bayesian story to recognize that conditional credence can itself be the contact-point of rational shift-in-view.

In our discussion of these problems we saw that the ratio and Ramsey norms jointly lead to restricted-vision functioning of conditional commitment, for they entail that strength of commitment is always a function of what happens in a restricted portion of an agent's epistemic space.[29] This might be due to the fact that an unrestricted epistemic commitment just happens to match, in every rational distribution of credence, something going on in a restricted portion of an agent's epistemic space. Or it might be due to the fact that conditional commitment is literally restricted in vision. This latter idea is precisely what the tertiary approach to conditionality maintains. According to the tertiary view strength of conditional commitment is always a function of what happens in a restricted portion of epistemic space *because* such commitment concerns only what happens in that portion of epistemic space.

We'll now see that if a tertiary approach to conditionality is adopted, both the rigidity worry and the incompleteness worry can be gracefully handled. Before seeing that though, it helps to be clear about what it is, exactly, to adopt the tertiary approach to conditionality. So ask yourself this: what is it to maintain, for instance, that conditional credence is a tertiary relation which holds between a thinker and two claims figuring in thought?

There are a number of ways to spell out the idea. The simplest among them approaches conditional commitment with a resource we've already seen: *suppositional*

---

[29] Actually that portion might be the whole space, the 'restricting' claim involved is recognized as true throughout an agent's epistemic space. Credence for C conditional on everything being self-identical, for instance, is like conditional credence so restricted. We set this and its opposite (when the restricting claim isn't recognized as true anywhere in an agent's epistemic space) aside in what follows.

*credit*. In the first instance the view maintains that conditional credence reduces to such credit. So not only is it the case that the following identity-of-strength thesis holds in each rational distribution of commitment,

$$cr(C/A) = sup_A[cred(C)],$$

it is also true that the identity-of-strength thesis holds in all *ir*rational distributions, for the psychological kind mentioned on the left just above (conditional credence) is said to be the same psychological kind as the more basic one mentioned on the right (suppositional credit). This makes it automatic, of course, that strength of the former lines-up with strength of the latter—not only when commitment is rational but also when it is not—since conditional credence is literally suppositional credit deep down. There is only one kind of state there to begin with.

Suppose that is so and recall Ramsey's norm

$$(\text{Ramsey}) \quad cr(A \to C) = cr(C/A).$$

There is a very strong case not only for the view that this norm holds because indicative and conditional credence are one and the same thing, but also for the view that conditional credence is the basic ingredient in the area, in which case the tertiary approach to conditionality is correct. With that approach in hand, as well as the identity-of-kind thesis for conditional credence and suppositional credit, we have resources sufficient to explain the Suppositional Ramsey Norm:

$$(\text{SRN}) \quad cr(A \to C) = sup_A[cred(C)].$$

After all, indicative credence has been unmasked as conditional credence, and the identity-of-kind thesis maintains that conditional credence is suppositional credit deep down. It follows that indicative credence is such credit as well, which means that the Suppositional Ramsey Norm holds automatically. If $cr(A \to C)$ and $sup_A[cred(C)]$ are psychologically one and the same thing, it is trivial that strength of $cr(A \to C)$ lines-up with strength of $sup_A[cred(C)]$. This is true independently of whether epistemic commitment is rational, for there is only one kind of state there to begin with.

For decades this sort of view has been defended by Dorothy Edgington. For most of that time I rejected her view when we spoke of it, even though I've always endorsed the major conclusion of her work on conditionality, namely, that the tertiary approach to conditionality is correct. To see the source of my resistance consider an ordinary-but-clever girl named 'Sascha'. Being ordinary she knows full well what her name is, and she does so in the usual sorts of ways. Being clever she realizes that there is an outside epistemic chance—a teentsy bit of her epistemic space, so to say—in which she is not named 'Sascha' after all. In the ordinary run of things, of course, Sascha doesn't think about this outlier possibility. She's a normal kid, after all; but she does recognize the outlier possibility and lend non-zero credence to the view that she's not really named 'Sascha'. This is precisely why Sascha has high conditional credence that she's been misled about her name, given it turns out that she's not named 'Sascha' after all.

This high conditional credence rarely appears on the surface of Sascha's mind. Only when she's in a particularly philosophical frame of mind—say after speaking with her philosopher parents!—does Sascha ever explicitly consider the subject. Whenever she does, though, she's virtually certain that she's been misled about her name if it's not really 'Sascha'. In fact, Sascha *always* has this high conditional credence—whether she thinks about it or not—but it's only on the surface of her mind when she's in a particularly philosophical frame of mind.

This means there can be such a thing as non-occurrent conditional credence, i.e. conditional credence that's psychologically real but not part of surface-level or conscious thought. In this respect conditional credence is exactly like ordinary credence or even belief. Just as there are states of regular credence and states of regular belief which are psychologically real but not part of conscious thought, so there are states of conditional credence 'below the surface', so to say, states that are psychologically real but not part of conscious thought. Sascha's high credence for being misled about her name if it's not actually 'Sascha' is almost always a sub-surface conditional credence.

However: if indicative/conditional credence is really suppositional credit deep down—as Edgington maintains—and it is not possible to have a state of suppositional credit without a state of supposition—as I maintain—then, it is not possible to have indicative/conditional credence without a state of supposition. We've just seen, though, that it is possible to have conditional commitment below the conscious surface of thought. This means the suppositional approach to conditionality entails that there is such a thing as sub-surface supposition.[30]

It is natural to worry about this. After all, our grip on supposition looks to come via reflection on cases in which it is a voluntary psychological phenomenon, something done on purpose, say in the context of suppositional reasoning or conditional proof. In turn this suggests that it makes little sense to postulate sub-surface states of supposition. The very idea of such supposition might seem oxymoronic, like voluntary action done sub-personally by the brain. Once it is granted, though, that purposeful cognitive action cannot be found below the surface of conscious thought, and also granted that supposition is perforce such action, it follows there cannot be such a thing as sub-surface supposition. The suppositional view of conditionality joins with this conclusion to entail that there cannot be sub-surface states of conditional credence. Since the case of Sascha makes clear that there can be sub-surface states of conditional credence, the suppositional view of conditionality must be wrong.

Even if one goes this far, though, one need not reject the restricted-vision take on conditionality. One need only deny that conditional commitment reduces to suppositional credit. It is perfectly compatible with such a denial that there are *two* kinds of restricted-vision opinion, one found with indicative/conditional credence, and the other with credit lent within the scope of surface-level voluntary supposition.[31]

---

[30] I presuppose that Sascha's non-occurrent state of indicative/conditional credence does not involve an occurent supposition.

[31] Naively this was my view of the matter from about 1993—when I first began talking to Edgington about conditionality—to Michaelmas 2010, when I began to think differently about agency and norms. Some of the upshot of that shift can be found in my Brown-Blackwell Lectures: http://certaindoubts.com/sturgeons-brownblackwell-lectures-available/

But this line of thought is too quick.

Let it be granted for argument's sake that our grip on supposition comes by appeal to cases in which supposition is a voluntary cognitive act. And let it be so granted that there can be no such act (cognitive or otherwise) below the surface of conscious thought. Even if we further admit that suppositional credit requires supposition, it *still* doesn't follow that there can be no such thing as sub-surface suppositional credit. For supposition may canonically present one way yet essentially be another. Everything granted at the outset of this paragraph, in other words, may turn out to be true even though supposition occurs all the time below the surface of conscious thought.

To see this just think of breathing. This is an activity we often go in for in an entirely voluntary way. When a doctor tells us to take a deep breath and hold it, for instance, our breathing is done entirely on the surface of agency. And in ordinary circumstances we can always take control of our breathing and make it unfold as we see fit, quite voluntarily, quite on purpose. There is no question but that breathing is a part of our voluntary agency. But that doesn't mean breathing doesn't go on below the surface of that agency most of the time. We already know that most of the time our breathing goes on without any sort of thought about it at all, without any sort of purposeful control. In those sub-surface cases of breathing, however, it is not as if the phenomenon is done by sub-agential systems. No, it is we who breathe all the time, even when we don't think about it. Sometimes our doing so is on the surface of purposeful agency, most of the time it is not.

It is conceptually possible, therefore, that supposing is like breathing. And if this turns out to be true, supposing is something we do all the time below the surface. Of course this is perfectly consistent with it also being true that supposing is something we often do voluntarily on the surface of cognitive agency; and it's consistent with our grip on supposition coming by reflection on surface-level instances of the phenomenon, from situations in which supposition figures in voluntary cognitive agency. This might lull us into thinking that it was essential to supposition that it occur on the surface of purposeful agency, but that would not really be true. It is at least conceptually possible that the anti-supposition set-up of the previous paragraph is correct, even though the supposition theory turns out also to be correct. If supposing were relevantly like breathing this is precisely what would be the case.

At all events, there are two main ways to react to the large-scale dialectic playing out about conditionality at this stage of discussion. The simplest reaction locates a single category of restricted-vision attitude, suppositional credit, and reduces other conditional commitment to that category. The resulting view is psychologically parsimonious but requires a surprising amount of sub-surface suppositional phenomena. The other main reaction is to endorse two kinds of restricted-vision attitude—suppositional credit and conditional credence—to see the former as perforce part of surface-level cognitive agency, and to see the latter as located both upon and below the surface of conscious thought.

Both reactions involve the tertiary view of conditionality, since each sees conditional commitment as a three-place relation between a thinker and two contents which figure in thought. We'll now see that this view can be used to assuage both the rigidity worry and the incompleteness worry for Bayesian kinematics. Consider each worry in turn:

1. Rigidity.
The main ingredient needed to help with this is the ratio norm:

$$\text{(Ratio)} \quad \text{cr}(C/A) = \frac{\text{cr}(A\&C)}{\text{cr}(A)}, \quad \text{where cr}(A) > 0.$$

As we've seen this norm forces conditional credence to function in a restricted-vision way. It turns out that so functioning accounts for the rigidity of conditional credence. Here's how:

*Rigidity*

Since the ratio norm is correct, conditional credence functions like a restricted-vision distribution of credence, i.e. like a mini-distribution of opinion within a restricted range of possibilities. The details of any such mini-distribution—how the relevant opinion is spread in its restricted domain—have nothing to do with how dominant the restricting claim's truth is in epistemic space. In other words: how mini-opinion plays out within its restricted domain has nothing to do with how much of epistemic space is taken up by that domain. The details of the mini-distribution have solely to do with how mini-opinion is spread across the restricted domain. In geometrical terms, those details have only to do with how much of the restricted domain is taken up by a particular claim. Strength of mini-opinion is measured by the relevant proportion, i.e. by the proportion of the restricted domain taken up by the claim to which mini-opinion is lent. When news comes in about the restricting claim itself, therefore, *solely* to the effect that it takes up a revised proportion of absolute epistemic space, well, the news simply has nothing to do with how mini-opinion is spread within its proprietary domain. By stipulation the news has only to do with how much of total epistemic space is taken up by the restricted domain. It has nothing to do with what happens mini-distribution-wise within that domain. Fully absorbing the news, therefore, has only to do with adjusting epistemic space with respect to the bifurcation made in *it* by the restricting claim. It has nothing to do with how mini-opinion is distributed across worlds where that bifurcating claim is true. This is why conditional credence remains constant thru the absorption of such news. Conditional credence is a mini-opinion which has nothing to do with such news.

This explanation is echoed, of course, by the Credal Import/Export Law

$$\text{(cr-I/E)} \quad \text{cr}[A \rightarrow (B \rightarrow C)] = \text{cr}[(A\&B) \rightarrow C].$$

On the restricted-vision approach to conditionality, conditional commitment is marked by conditional and indicative credence. In a sense, then, $\text{cr}[A \rightarrow (A \rightarrow C)]$ is a mark within $\text{cr}(\text{-})$ of how $\text{cr}(C/A)$ turns out when it's learned that A takes up all of one's epistemic space. By the Credal Import/Export Law

$$\text{cr}[A \rightarrow (A \rightarrow C)] = \text{cr}[(A\&A) \rightarrow C)],$$

which by Ramsey's norm (and probability theory) yields

$$\text{cr}[(A\&A) \rightarrow C)] = \text{cr}(A \rightarrow C) = \text{cr}(C/A).$$

In this way we have marked in our notation already that $\text{cr}(C/A)$ remains constant after A has been given full credence. This is a limit-case instance of the rigidity phenomenon.

The restricted-vision approach to conditionality makes sense of why conditional commitment should be constant across shift-in-view concerning a conditioning claim. Since conditional commitment is restricted in vision, it functions like a mini-distribution of opinion within a restricted portion of epistemic space. How that distribution plays out has nothing to do with the dominance of a restricting claim in one's full epistemic space. For this reason, news solely to do with that dominance has no impact on mini-distribution of opinion, which is to say that it has no impact on conditional credence. Thus we find that conditional credence is rigid in transitions described by Jeffrey rule. These are shifts of opinion brought on by news solely to do with the dominance of a particular claim in full epistemic space. Opinion conditional on that claim should remain constant in light of the news. It should be rigid exactly as described in our Bayesian kinematics.

2. INCOMPLETENESS.

The Bayesian transition theory does not cover cases in which there is contact-point shift in conditional credence. The model's transition rule, Jeffrey Conditionalization, applies only when there is such shift in unconditional credence. The restricted-vision take on conditionality allows us to cook-up a similarly-motivated rule for when conditional credence is the contact point of shift-in-view. And the best way to explain the new rule is first to locate the rationale behind Jeffrey Conditionalization, then to apply that rationale to the contact-point shift of conditional credence. We'll see that it is in this second step that the restricted-vision conception of conditionality comes into its own.

To begin, note that the rationale behind Jeffrey Conditionalization is easy to locate. Once equilibrium has been lost—say after shift of in-between credence for A but before anything else has changed—there should be minimal fuss in the recovery of equilibrium. Basically the thought is that as much of one's old view should be retained consistent with the new credence for A. This is spelled out via the recommendation of a new equilibrium most structurally like the old one but with the new credence for A in place.

We can picture this process using boxes for epistemic space. As before we think of points in a box as epistemic possible worlds, and regions in a box as contents or claims to which credence is lent. Unlike in previous chapters, though, we now let the proportion of an epistemic box taken up by a claim represent credence lent to it, so that credence is easy to see in our diagrams. When you are certain that $\Phi$ is true, for instance, every point in your epistemic space is a world at which $\Phi$ is true, and, for this reason, $\Phi$ should occupy the entire box representing your epistemic space. When you are certain that $\Phi$ is false, likewise, no point in your epistemic space is a world at which $\Phi$ is true, so, for a similar reason, $\Phi$ should occupy no point in the box representing that space. When you are 50% sure that $\Phi$ is true, fully half of your epistemically possible worlds make $\Phi$ true, so, $\Phi$ should occupy half of the box representing your epistemic space. And so on.

With these conventions in place, consider a hyper-focused agent. Suppose Smith is someone who wonders only if $\Phi$ is true; and he ends-up lending $\Phi$ a credence of 20%. Then we may picture his epistemic space

148   THE BAYESIAN TRANSITION THEORY: CRITICAL DISCUSSION

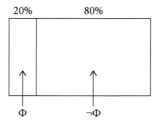

Figure 4.7

Next suppose Smith receives new evidence to which he rationally reacts; and suppose his reaction involves a contact-point shift of credence from 20% to 60% for Φ. We can depict the minimal change in view consistent with this by simply blowing up the Φ-portion of Smith's epistemic space

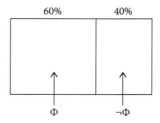

Figure 4.8

This shift of opinion involves a certain *change factor*. Specifically, the number 3 yields the new take on Φ when multiplied with the old take on Φ:[32]

$$\mathbf{new}(\Phi) = [\mathit{cf}_\Phi \times \mathbf{old}(\Phi)].$$

In general when an agent starts with in-between credence for a particular claim Φ, then shifts her opinion about Φ, there will be a change-factor in play (like the number 3 is here). That factor will be the number which, when multiplied with an agent's old take on Φ, yields her new take on Φ. Hence the change factor may be recovered by solving the equation above. This yields

$$\mathit{cf}_\Phi = \frac{\mathbf{new}(\Phi)}{\mathbf{old}(\Phi)}.$$

Moreover, once we have the change factor relevant to a region of epistemic space, we can use it to make sense of the rationale behind Jeffrey's rule. Then we can combine

---

[32] Actually this is a sloppy way of putting the point, since you can't really multiply a number and an a psychological state. The relevant point is really this: the number 3 yields a measure of Smith's new take on Φ when it is multiplied with an appropriate measure of his old take on Φ. I will continue to use the sloppy way of putting things, though, since it is easier and unlikely to lead to confusion.

that rationale with the restricted-vision take on conditionality to motivate an update rule for the contact-point shift of conditional credence. This will be our strategy.

To begin, consider a more complicated agent Jones. She wonders mainly if $\Phi$ is true, but she recognizes four disjoint ways that it might be. Suppose Jones gives each of them an equal share of her 1/3rd credence in $\Phi$. Then her epistemic space will look something like this

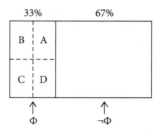

Figure 4.9

Next suppose Jones receives new input and reacts rationally to it, shifting from 1/3rd to 2/3rds credence for $\Phi$. The relevant change-factor is then equal to 2, for this is the number which yields (intuitively put) the proportion of $\Phi$-space in her new way of looking at things when multiplied with the proportion of $\Phi$-space in her old way of looking at things.

The no-fuss revision of her worldview simply blows up the $\Phi$-portion of her original epistemic space—by a factor of 2, of course—while keeping everything else the same

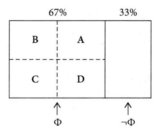

Figure 4.10

But notice: *four* things have happened in this shift of view:

1. $\Phi$-space has increased by a factor of 2;
2. The internal structure of $\Phi$-space has been preserved;
3. $\neg\Phi$-space has shrunk commensurately; and
4. the internal structure of $\neg\Phi$-space has been preserved.

Whenever you change the proportion of epistemic space taken up by a claim $\Phi$, therefore—to reflect a shift of in-between credence for $\Phi$—the proportion of

150  THE BAYESIAN TRANSITION THEORY: CRITICAL DISCUSSION

epistemic space not taken up by Φ must also change (in line with the Partition Principle). And if the overall shift of opinion is to be minimal—if it's to preserve as much as possible of one's old way of looking at things consistent with the new view of Φ—the internal structure both within and without Φ-space must be left alone.

A clean way to describe this sort of shift-in-view makes appeal to change factors within and without Φ-space. After shifting in-between credence for Φ, the idea is that minimal-fuss revision shifts everything within Φ-space by a change-factor relevant to Φ, and it shifts everything without Φ-space by a change-factor relevant to ¬Φ. This way of thinking about things generates a rather clean understanding of Jeffrey Conditionalization. Just consider the logical fact that for any claims Φ and A, exactly one of three things must be the case: either Φ is true with A, Φ is true without A, or Φ is not true at all. It is a truth of logic, after all, that

$$\Phi \Leftrightarrow [(\Phi \& A) \vee (\Phi \& \neg A)].$$

But the Bayesian model insists that credence play out like probability. Since disjuncts in the displayed formula just above are disjoint—the truth of either precludes that of the other—the Bayesian model insists that credence for Φ builds from credence for the disjuncts. In all rational distributions the following will hold

$$\mathbf{cr}(\Phi) = [\mathbf{cr}(\Phi \& A) + \mathbf{cr}(\Phi \& \neg A)].$$

Suppose, then, that rational distribution **new**(-) created by a no-fuss revision of the disequilibrium state brought on by a contact-point shift of credence for A in an old rational distribution **old**(-). Then for any claim Φ

$$\mathbf{new}(\Phi) = [\mathbf{new}(\Phi \& A) + \mathbf{new}(\Phi \& \neg A)].$$

But we've seen that after a no-fuss shift of credence for A truths which occupy A-space will take old credal values multiplied by the change factor for A-space, and truths which occupy ¬A-space will take old credal values multiplied by the change factor for ¬A-space. After a no-fuss revision brought on by a contact-point shift of opinion for A, therefore, for any claim Φ, new credence for (Φ&A) will be identical to old credence for (Φ&A) multiplied by the change factor for A, and new credence for (Φ&¬A) will be identical old credence for (Φ&¬A) multiplied by the change factor for ¬A. In other words

$$\mathbf{new}(\Phi) = \{[\underline{\mathit{cf}}_{(A)} \times \mathbf{old}(\Phi \& A)] + [\underline{\mathit{cf}}_{(\neg A)} \times \mathbf{old}(\Phi \& \neg A)].$$

By substituting change factors into the equation, though, we arrive at a familiar idea:

$$\mathbf{new}(\Phi) = \left[\frac{\mathbf{new}(A)}{\mathbf{old}(A)} \times \mathbf{old}(\Phi \& A)\right] + \left[\frac{\mathbf{new}(\neg A)}{\mathbf{old}(\neg A)} \times \mathbf{old}(\Phi \& \neg A)\right]$$

This is really Jeffrey Conditionalization in disguise. Hence the no-fuss change-factor approach entails that for any claim Φ:

(J-Cond)  $\mathbf{new}(\Phi) = \mathbf{new}(\Phi) \times \mathbf{old}(\Phi/A) + \mathbf{new}(\neg A) \times \mathbf{old}(\Phi/\neg A).$

Put slightly differently: after contact-point shift of in-between credence for A, then for any claim Φ, one's new take on (Φ&A) should be identical to one's old take modified by the change factor for A, and one's new take on (Φ&¬A) should be identical to one's old take modified by the change factor for ¬A.

The new view of Φ should thus build up from suitably modified views about Φ being true with A and Φ being true without A. This is basically what Jeffrey Conditionalization comes to. In effect, the recommendation is that after a shift of in-between credence for A, epistemic space both within and without A should be modified by respective change factors, and everything else should basically stay put (i.e. interrelations strictly within cells of the A/¬A cut in epistemic space should be left intact).

Once the restricted vision take on conditionality is in place, it is easy to apply the very same no-fuss strategy to an update brought on by contact-point shift in conditional credence; for the restricted-vision conception suggests exactly how to implement the no-fuss strategy. To see this consider a standard A/C epistemic space

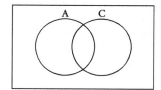

Figure 4.11

The restricted-vision take on conditionality insists that conditional credence for C given A concerns no more and no less than how C-truth plays out in A-worlds. More specifically, the restricted-vision take insists that conditional credence for C given A concerns precisely the proportion of A-space that's also C-space, exactly the proportion of A-worlds that are also C-worlds.

If that is right, however, minimal revision after a contact-point shift of conditional credence for C given A should involve a changed take on the A-restricted relation between C and ¬C, and it should keep everything else as much like it was as possible consistent with that changed take. This sort of shift of opinion will have nothing to do with the internal workings of

* ¬A-space,
* (A&C)-space, or
* (A&¬C)-space.

It will *only* concern how C and ¬C relate to one another within A-space.

For this reason the minimal revision of a worldview after contact-point shift of conditional credence for C given A should do four things:

1. Preserve the new conditional credence for C given A.
2. Leave everything internal to ¬A-space alone, thereby respecting that conditional credence for C given A has nothing to do with ¬A-space.
3. Modify everything internal to (A&C)-space by the change factor relevant to (A&C)-space.

152  THE BAYESIAN TRANSITION THEORY: CRITICAL DISCUSSION

4. Modify everything internal to (A&¬C)-space by the change factor relevant to (A&¬C)-space.

Since the relevant suggestion here is important, let me pause to rephrase its basic rationale one more time.

Here's how it goes.

The restricted-vision nature of conditional credence motivates four ideas about the recovery of equilibrium. After conditional credence for C given A has been shifted: new conditional credence for C given A is to be respected (of course); happenings solely within ¬A-space are to be left alone, since perturbed conditional credence has nothing to do with them (and we're shooting for minimal revision); happenings solely within (A&C)-space are to be modified by a change factor brought on by the contact-point shift of conditional credence; and happenings solely within (A&¬C)-space are to be modified by a related change factor brought on by that shift.

Intuitively, after a contact-point shift of conditional credence for C given A: we want the proportion of A-space taken up by C-space to be in line with the new conditional credence, and we want everything else left alone as much as possible. Minimal-fuss recovery of equilibrium after such a contact-point shift should satisfy four desiderata:

(D1) It should respect the new conditional credence for C given A.

(D2) It should leave intact whatever happens solely within ¬A-space.

(D3) It should modify whatever happens solely within (A&C)-space by the change factor for that space.

(D4) It should modify whatever happens solely within (A&¬C)-space is by the change factor for that space.

These desiderata correspond to (1)-thru-(iv) above.

OK, consider a trivial fact about logic: every troika of claims Φ, A, and C are such that

$$\Phi \Leftrightarrow [(\Phi \& A \& C) \lor (\Phi \& A \& \neg C) \lor (\Phi \& \neg A)].$$

Whenever Φ is true at all, it is a matter of logic that it is true either with A and C, with A but not C, or without A. Since the Bayesian model insists that credence distributes like probability, and since disjuncts in the tautology above are disjoint, the Bayesian model entails that credence for Φ sums from credence lent to disjuncts. In all rational distributions the following will hold:

$$\mathbf{cr}(\Phi) = [\mathbf{cr}(\Phi \& A \& C) + \mathbf{cr}(\Phi \& A \& \neg C) + \mathbf{cr}(\Phi \& \neg A)].$$

Since this equation is meant to hold in all sensible distributions of credence, however, it must hold for sensible distributions got via update after contact-point shift of conditional credence; and a fortiori it must hold when such update occurs in line with an update rule.

Suppose, then, that rational distribution **new**(-) is created by a no-fuss revision of the disequilibrium state brought on when distribution **old**(-) is perturbed by a contact-point shift of conditional credence for C given A. Then for any claims Φ, A, and C

(*)   **new**(Φ) = [**new**(Φ&A&C) + **new**(Φ&A&¬C) + **new**(Φ&¬A)].

And now we can appeal to our four desiderata to cook-up change factors for each of the summands on the right-hand-side of this equation. For instance, (D2) ensures that the A/¬A-cut in epistemic space remains constant in a no-fuss move from **old**(-) to **new**(-); so the change factor relevant to the right-most summand will be

$$cf_{(\neg A)} = \frac{\mathbf{new}(C/A)}{\mathbf{old}(C/A)} = 1, \quad \text{since numerator and denominator are in fact identical.}$$

In turn (D3) and (D4) jointly ensure that the change factor relevant to (A&C)-space has only to do with the shift from old to new conditional credence for C given A

$$cf_{(A\&C)} = \frac{\mathbf{new}(C/A)}{\mathbf{old}(C/A)}.$$

And they likewise ensure that the change factor relevant to (A&¬C)-space has only to do with the shift from old to new conditional credence for ¬C given A

$$cf_{(A\&\neg C)} = \frac{\mathbf{new}(\neg C/A)}{\mathbf{old}(\neg C/A)}.\ [33]$$

But we can use these change factors and **old**(-) to reformulate (*):

$$\mathbf{new}(\Phi) = \{[\ cf_{(A\&C)} \times \mathbf{old}(\Phi\&A\&C)] + [\ cf_{(A\&\neg C)} \times \mathbf{old}(\Phi\&A\&\neg C)] \\ + [\ cf_{(\neg A)} \times \mathbf{old}(\Phi\&\neg A)]\}.$$

And by putting the change factors in explicitly we can produce a rule for the no fuss **R**ecovery of **E**quilibrium **A**fter **C**onditional-credence **T**ransfer:

(REACT)

When a rational agent starts with **old**(-) and then undergoes contact-point shift of conditional credence for C given A, the Jeffrey-like no-fuss reaction requires that for any claim Φ:

$$\mathbf{new}(\Phi) = \{\frac{[\mathbf{new}(C/A) \times \mathbf{old}(\Phi\&A\&C)]}{\mathbf{old}(C/A)} + \frac{[\mathbf{new}(\neg C/A) \times \mathbf{old}(\Phi\&A\&\neg C)]}{\mathbf{old}(\neg C/A)} + \mathbf{old}(F\&\neg A)\}.$$

The basic no-fuss idea for the recovery of equilibrium is simple. When equilibrium is lost due to contact-point shift in an epistemic commitment, the new equilibrium

---

[33] Since **old**(A) equals **new**(A), of course—in line with (D2)—the last two ratios in the main text can be simplified to **new**(A&C)/**old**(A&C) and **new**(A&¬C)/**old**(A&¬C) respectively. Given we're dealing with contact-point shift of conditional credence, though, and working with a non-reductive view of such credence, it makes good sense to leave the ratios in the main text as they are.

position should hold onto that new epistemic commitment and change everything else as little as possible. When the perturbed commitment is credence, the most natural no-fuss update rule is Jeffrey's. When the perturbed commitment is conditional credence, and the restricted-vision take on conditionality is in place, the most natural no-fuss update rule is (REACT). The restricted-vision take on conditionality thus proves central to extending the Bayesian model so that it covers contact-point shift in conditional credence.

# 5
# The Belief Model
(AGM)

## 5.1 Preview

In this chapter we lay out one of the best-known formal models of coarse-grained epistemic attitudes. The model was invented by Carlos Alchourrón, Peter Gärdenfors, and David Makinson in a series of letters they sent to one another in the 1970s. Eventually they realized that their independently developed thoughts about rationality were converging. The resulting formalism is the Belief Model (also known as the AGM Model).

Like other models of rationality, the Belief Model has three moving parts: a theory of states, a transition theory, and a linking theory. The model uses a particular formalism to represent rational attitudes at a time, builds on that formalism to represent rational shifts between attitudes across time, and locates a kind of epistemic commitment which forges an internal link between the two stories. First we'll look at its theory of states, then we'll unpack the transition theory, and then we'll clarify how the model sees the two things fitting together.

## 5.2 The Belief Model's Theory of States

The Belief Model recognizes no matter of degree when it comes to epistemic attitudes. Basically the thought is that one either believes something or one does not. On this kind of view, epistemic attitudes can be usefully indexed in a couple of different ways. On the one hand, we might index a configuration of rational beliefs, say, by appeal to *what* is believed in the configuration; and were we to do so it would be natural to index a configuration of beliefs with a set of propositions (i.e. a set of things believed). On the other hand, we might index a configuration of beliefs by appeal to sentences used to express what is believed, in which case a configuration of beliefs would be naturally indexed by the collection of sentences. The Belief Model takes the latter approach.

Think of it this way. Suppose you are asked to say something which you believe, and in reply you sincerely utter sentence S. Next you are asked to say something else you believe, so you sincerely reply with sentence S*. Let the process continue until you have nothing left to say. At that point gather up all the sentences you've used and put them into a set $\underline{B}$. Then everything you believe is expressed by a member of $\underline{B}$, and every member of $\underline{B}$ expresses something you believe. Intuitively, for any proposition $p$: you believe $p$ exactly when there is a sentence S such that (i) S expresses $p$, and

*The Rational Mind*. Scott Sturgeon, Oxford University Press (2020). © Scott Sturgeon.
DOI: 10.1093/oso/9780198845799.001.0001

(ii) S is a member of B̲. In a good sense, then, B̲ captures your configuration of beliefs at the time in question.

Yet B̲ isn't a belief set in the technical sense of the Belief Model, for it is insufficiently ideal. Like the Bayesian model of chapter 2, the Belief Model of this chapter makes idealizing assumptions when choosing its formalism. This amounts to ignoring certain aspects of real-world cognition (about which we'll have more to say in Chapter 13). In the present case, the Belief Model idealizes away from two aspects of real-world cognition. It refuses to allow a belief set to contain logical conflict between its members—even tacit conflict—and it refuses to allow a belief set to be logically incomplete in a certain way. Consider these idealizations in turn.

First, the Belief Model idealizes away from logical conflicts which plague ordinary thought. When such problems infect a thinker's beliefs, those beliefs cannot all be true: logic ensures at least one of them is mistaken. Such conflict may be deep and/or difficult to see but it is there as a matter of logic (i.e. logic alone is sufficient to ensure the conflict is present); and when that happens, a given thinker cannot have correct beliefs through and through, for she is bound (by logic) to have made a mistake. The Belief Model idealizes away from such bother, presuming that rational sets of belief logically hang together. The model requires that such sets be logically consistent:

(Con)   Belief sets are logically consistent.

Second, the Belief Model precludes a certain kind of logical incompleteness in its belief sets. The model idealizes away from a certain sort of open-endedness of ordinary thought. To see the point clearly recall your belief set B̲. As it happens you do not accept everything logically entailed by things you believe, for like everyone else you have not had time (or inclination) to work everything out. This means that your belief set B̲ is in a certain sense not fully logical—or perhaps better put: it is not fully informed by logic. Your belief set does not contain all that is logically entailed by its members. From a logical point of view that set would be improved were it to contain everything logically entailed by things you believe. After all, your beliefs would then be logically complete.

The Belief Model ignores such incompleteness and presumes that rational agents have chased down all logical implications of things they believe. The model presumes that their belief sets are logically complete:

(Entail)   For any belief set **B** and sentence S: if the members of **B** logically entail S, then S belongs to **B**.

This principle guarantees that belief sets are fully logical in the following sense: there is no way to break out of them by chasing down the logical consequences of their members. Everything entailed by a given belief set is already in that set. The technical way to express this is to say that belief sets are 'closed' by logical consequence. But all that means is that belief sets satisfy the requirement (Entail). The model insists that everything entailed by members of a given belief set is also a member of that set.

Principles (Con) and (Entail) are idealizing constraints in the Belief Model. They directly echo powerful ideas emphasized over a century ago by William James. In particular, James emphasized that at least two goals seem to be deeply connected with our cognitive practice. In some sense we aim in thought to

(T)  Believe truth.

But we also aim in thought to

(F)  Avoid error.[1]

James pointed out that these are different goals. The acquisition-of-truth goal (T) is maximally satisfied by believing everything, after all—and so everything true—while the avoidance-of-error goal (F) is maximally satisfied by suspending judgement in everything, i.e. by never believing or rejecting anything at all. These two cognitive goals, then—(T) and (F)—pull us in opposite directions. They tug against one another in our practice.

Intuitively: the value of cottoning onto truth encourages epistemic risk, while the disvalue of stumbling into error counsels epistemic caution. Our cognitive practice pulls us in opposite directions, then, in the sense that one of its aims motivates risk-taking while another of its aims motivates intellectual caution. Epistemic rationality seeks a good mix of risk and caution, one which well reflects the value of truth and the disvalue of error.

The demands of logical consistency and closure—(Con) and (Entail) above—fall out of these twin goals. One way to take (F) to a logical extreme, after all, is to hear it as saying that we should not accept a claim if it is guaranteed by logic to be false. But an even stronger reading hears it as saying that we should not accept a collection of claims if logic ensures that they jointly contain an error. The first reading counsels one never to accept a logical contradiction, the second never to accept a collection of claims which harbours logical conflict in its members. This latter thought is exactly the content of (Con), so the consistency requirement can be seen as the demand to avoid error taken to a logical limit.

Similarly, one way to take the truth goal (T) is to hear it as saying that we should accept anything which is guaranteed by logic to be true. But an even stronger reading would hear it as saying that we should accept anything logically implied by things we accept. The first reading counsels one to accept logical truths, so to say; the second reading counsels one to accept logical consequences of things accepted. This latter thought is exactly the content of (Entail). Hence the model's closure requirement can be seen as the demand to believe truth taken to a certain kind of logical limit.

Yet one thing is clear: neither the consistency requirement (Con) nor the closure requirement (Entail) is satisfied by any real person. Indeed neither of these requirements *can* be satisfied by any real person. Our cognitive limits preclude our doing so: any being with a rich and changing set of beliefs like ours, who also satisfies the consistency requirement (Con), or the closure requirement (Entail), thereby fails to be recognizably human in her cognition. Any such being is recognizably a super-human thinker, someone whose cognition goes far beyond the reach of ordinary folk.

This prompts an obvious question: how could it be a necessary condition on human rationality—even full human rationality—that our epistemic attitudes satisfy the consistency requirement (Con) or the closure requirement (Entail)? After all, it is

---

[1] For an argument that these goals underpin the accuracy-based epistemology of credence, see my 'Epistemology, Pettigrew Style' (*Mind*, 2018).

not humanly possible to satisfy either of these requirements. The attendant thought here—once the question has been posed explicitly—is that it is *not* a necessary condition on human rationality—even full human rationality—that our epistemic attitudes satisfy requirements like (Con) or (Entail). The thought is that it is not possible for humans to satisfy such conditions, and, for this reason, doing so cannot be a requirement on rationality, even full rationality.

This line of thought is grounded in a Kantian idea:

(Kant)  One ought rationally to satisfy condition C *only if* one can satisfy condition C.

Approaches to rationality which aim to respect this Kantian principle insist that the bounds of human rationality—even full human rationality—do not outstrip the bounds of human possibility. On this way of thinking about things, a configuration of epistemic attitudes is rational only if it is a humanly-possible configuration of attitudes, i.e. only if it is possible for humans to manifest that configuration of attitudes.

The Belief Model resolutely rejects this Kantian perspective. It insists that full rationality places requirements on attitudes which human cannot satisfy. Hence the theory is meant to detail various constraints on epistemic attitudes which are not within our power to satisfy. Those constraints are constitutive of what we might think of as super-human rationality, a kind of rationality manifested only by super-human agents, a kind of rationality to which real-world agents can aspire, perhaps, but never properly manifest. Just as our actions in a lifetime can only aspire to be morally perfect, the thought would be—with no real human being capable of leading a morally perfect life—so it is with our epistemic lives: no human can adopt a configuration of attitudes in line with the Belief Model.[2]

With such preliminaries in place, then, it is easy to state the model's constraints on the configuration of epistemic states. At any given moment, the model insists that an agent's attitudes shouldbe consistent and closed by logic. Put another way: at any given time, a rational configuration of states should be modelled by a belief set in the technical sense.

## 5.3 The Belief Model's Transition Theory

The Belief Model's transition theory is not nearly so simple; but like its theory of states it's best to sneak up on the model's transition theory by appeal to the underlying psychology it presupposes. So recall that the model kicks off, like a great deal of everyday practice, by seeing coarse-grained epistemic attitudes as a three-part affair: either you believe something, disbelieve it, or suspend judgement. The Belief Model recognizes three attitudes you might take to a proposition P. In shifting your take on P, therefore, the model (and much of commonsense) requires that there be mental movement *from* one of these three attitudes *to* one of the others.

---

[2] Chapter 13 discusses a weakening of (Kant) which proves central to rationality.

The underlying psychology recognizes no other shift in view. Hence there are exactly six ways to adjust your take on P:

1. Shift from belief to disbelief
2. Shift from belief to suspended judgement
3. Shift from suspended judgement to belief
4. Shift from suspended judgement to disbelief
5. Shift from disbelief to belief
6. Shift from disbelief to suspended judgement.

Within the Belief Model framework a shift in one's take on P occurs only if one of these six changes takes place. But note they are incompatible: no two of them can happen at once. There can be a model-recognized shift in one's take on P, therefore, only if *exactly* one of the six changes takes place.[3]

This suggests the Belief Model transition theory will have six rules for changing one's mind: one for when belief shifts to disbelief, one for when belief shifts to suspended judgement, and so forth. But that is not how it goes. In fact the Belief Model endorses just *one* kind of non-trivial change: the model boils everything down to logical changes plus a single non-logical rule; and it does this by making a series of alignment assumptions. These are claims to the effect that the presence of one attitude lent to a content perforce aligns with a potentially different attitude lent to a potentially different content.

The model uses five such alignment assumptions. Three of them look initially plausible—at least as idealizations—and they permit the reduction of changes (a) thru (f) down to three types of shift in view. A pair of further alignment assumptions are then brought into play in order to line up the three remaining types of shift with one *uber*-rule. But neither of these further alignment assumptions looks at all obvious or commonsensical, even as idealizations. They do make for a highly simple

---

[3] More generally: suppose you can take a finite number of belief-like attitudes $A_1, \ldots, A_n$ to a proposition P. Then you have these possible shifts in view concerning P:

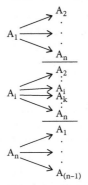

For each belief-like attitude $A_i$ that you might take to a proposition P, there are (n−1) other belief-like attitudes you might shift $A_i$ into. When we assume there are n belief-like attitudes at your disposal, therefore, there are n(n−1) possible shifts in view.

theoretical foundation, though, a view on which all rational shift of opinion is defined by logic plus a single non-logical rule.

This is good work if you can get it. In the next chapter it will argued that the work is not to be had, but in this chapter we merely lay out the manner in which the Belief Model bases its transition theory on a single non-logical rule.

*Alignment Assumption 1*
The Belief Model treats disbelief as if it is belief in negation, marking no difference between *dis*belief in P and belief in ¬P. In effect the model assumes that disbelief is definable by appeal to belief and negation, so its first alignment assumption is

(AA$_D$)     Disbelief in P always aligns with belief in ¬P.

For instance: disbelief in the claim that grass is green is treated by the model as if it is belief in the claim that grass is not green; disbelief in the claim that Oswald acted alone is treated by the model as if it is belief in the claim that Oswald did not act alone; and so forth. The Belief Model insists that disbelief and belief in negation stand or fall together.

This might be so for at least two reasons. Deep down it might turn out that disbelief is really nothing more than belief in negation. Or it might turn out that the notionally-distinct attitudes are psychologically distinct, deep down, but that rational agents disbelieve exactly when they believe a related negation. On this latter view, disbelief is a psychological attitude over and above belief in negation; but rationality requires that an agent invests disbelief exactly when she believes the relevant negation. We shall take no stand here on such a non-reductive endorsement of (AA$_D$). The next chapter resists the reduction of disbelief to belief in negation.

*Alignment Assumption 2*
The Belief Model treats belief in a doubly negated content as if it is belief in that which is doubly negated, marking no difference between belief in ¬¬P and belief in P. In essence the model assumes that belief in a double negation is definable by appeal to belief itself. Its second alignment assumption is

(AA$_{¬¬}$)     Belief in ¬¬P always aligns with belief in P.

For instance: belief in the claim that it is not the case that it is not the case that grass is green is treated by the model as if it is belief in the claim that grass is green; belief in the claim that it is not the case that it is not the case that Oswald acted alone is treated by the model as if it is belief in the claim that Oswald acted alone; and so forth. The Belief Model insists that belief in a double negation and belief in what is so negated stand or fall together.

Again this might be so for at least two reasons. Deep down it might turn out that belief in a double negation is really nothing more than belief in what is so negated. Or it might turn out that the notionally distinct states are psychologically distinct, deep down, but that rational agents believe a double negation exactly when they believe what is so negated. We shall take no stand here on either of these routes to (AA$_{¬¬}$). The next chapter presents prima facie worries for both lines of thought.

*Alignment Assumption 3*
The Belief Model treats suspended judgement as if it is the absence of belief and disbelief, marking no difference between suspending judgement in P and failing both to believe and to disbelieve P. In essence the model assumes that suspended judgement is definable by appeal to belief and negation. Its third alignment assumption is

(AA$_S$)  Suspended judgement in P always aligns with failure of both belief in P and disbelief in P.

For instance: suspended judgement in the claim that grass is green is treated by the model as if it is avoidance of belief and disbelief in the claim that grass is green; suspended judgement in the claim that Oswald acted alone is treated by the model as if it is avoidance of belief and disbelief in the claim that Oswald acted alone; and so forth. The Belief Model insists that suspended judgement and the absence of belief/disbelief stand or fall together.

This too might be so for at least two reasons. Deep down it might turn out that suspended judgement is really nothing more than the joint absence of belief and disbelief. Or it might turn out that suspended judgement is something more that such an absence, but, that rational agents suspend judgement exactly when they neither believe nor disbelieve. We shall take no stand here on such a non-reductive endorsement of (AA$_S$). The next chapter resists a reductive approach to suspended judgement.

Now, recall the six types of shift in view mentioned earlier:

1. Shift from belief to disbelief
2. Shift from belief to suspended judgement
3. Shift from suspended judgement to belief
4. Shift from suspended judgement to disbelief
5. Shift from disbelief to belief
6. Shift from disbelief to suspended judgement.

Alignment assumptions concerned with disbelief and suspended judgement permit (a) thru (f) to be rewritten solely in terms of belief and negation. As follows:

applying (AA$_D$) to (a) yields

(a)*   Shift belief in P to belief in ¬P;

applying (AA$_S$) to (b) and then (AA$_D$) to the result yields

(b)*   Shift belief in P to neither belief in P nor belief in ¬P;

applying (AA$_S$) to (c) and then (AA$_D$) to the result yields

(c)*   Shift neither believing P nor believing ¬P to belief in P;

applying (AA$_S$) to (d) and then (AA$_D$) twice to the result yields

(d)*   Shift neither believing P nor believing ¬P to belief in ¬P;

applying (AA$_D$) to (e) yields

(e)*   Shift belief in ¬P to belief in P;

and applying (R$_S$) to (f) and then (AA$_D$) twice to the result yields

(f)*   Shift belief in ¬P to neither belief in P nor belief in ¬P.

162  THE BELIEF MODEL (AGM)

In a nutshell: the alignment assumptions (AA$_D$) and (AA$_S$) reduce disbelief and suspended judgement to belief plus negation. This means (a)-(f) can be rewritten as (a)*-(f)*. Shift in disbelief and suspended judgement boils down to shift in belief plus negation. That is ensured by the model's alignment assumptions for disbelief and suspended judgement.

Further still: the placeholder in the starred rules above—namely P—can go for any proposition whatsoever. So the alignment rule (AA$_{\neg\neg}$) can be used to reduce the starred principles to *three* kinds of change. Specifically:

- (AA$_{\neg\neg}$) implies (a)* and (e)* are instances of a single kind of change: shift from belief to opposing belief. The Belief Model calls that *revision*.
- (AA$_{\neg\neg}$) implies (b)* and (f)* are instances of a single kind of change: shift from belief to suspended judgement. The model calls that **contraction**.
- (AA$_{\neg\neg}$) implies (c)* and (d)* are instances of a single kind of change: shift from suspended judgement to belief. The model calls that **expansion**.

In a nutshell: the Belief Model begins with the common-sense thought that one believes, disbelieves, or suspends judgement. This creates six ways to shift one's opinion. The model also accepts alignment assumptions for disbelief, double negation and suspended judgement. Those assumptions boil down the six types of shift-in-view to three: revision, contraction, and expansion. All of these transitions begin with a set of beliefs which is consistent and closed by logic. Revision is then shifts from belief to opposing belief, contraction is then shift from belief to suspended judgement, and expansion is then shift from such judgement to belief.

Let's formalize all this in the style of the model.

Suppose you are in an epistemic state characterized by belief set **B**. Let ¬P be a member of **B** (i.e. you believe ¬P). Then *the revision of **B** by P* is the shift from **B** to a new belief set containing P. The model names this sort of transition '(**B**\*P)', so we have

(**B**\*P) = the result of revising **B** by P.

Intuitively, revision of belief occurs when you are rationally turned entirely around on a claim: first you endorse it, then you come to endorse its logical opposite (and then you settle everything else accordingly).

But suppose you start out believing P rather than believing its negation. Then *the contraction of **B** by P* is the shift from **B** to a new belief set not containing P. The model names this sort of transition '(**B**-P)', so we have

(**B**-P) = the result of contracting **B** by P.

Intuitively, contraction of belief occurs when you rationally give up a commitment to a claim: first you endorse it, then you fail to endorse or to reject (and then you settle everything else accordingly).

Finally, suppose neither P nor ¬P starts out in **B**. By the model's lights you begin with suspended judgement in P, neither believing nor disbelieving. Then *the expansion of **B** by P* is the shift from **B** to a set containing P. The Belief Model names this sort of transition '(**B**+P)', so we have

(**B**+P) = the expansion of **B** by P.

Intuitively, expansion of belief occurs when you rational commit to a claim: first you have no such commitment, then you endorse the claim in question (and then you settle everything else accordingly).

The Belief Model takes revision, contraction and expansion as explanatorily fundamental. Once we get clear on the alignment claims $(AA_D)$, $(AA_{\neg\neg})$ and $(AA_S)$—once we get clear, that is to say, on the alignment of disbelief and suspended judgement to belief plus negation—it turns out there are three notionally basic shifts in view: revision, contraction, and expansion. It comes as a shock, then, to see that the Belief Model boils down these three types of transition to shifts defined by logic plus one non-logical rule. This further bit of the model is not the slightest bit obvious, so we'll need a good argument for it if we're to endorse the overall view. Our next task is to explain the rest of the model. In the next chapter we'll examine it critically.

## 5.4 Further Claims About Rational Transitions

At the end of the day the Belief Model endorses a single kind of non-logical belief change. The key to its simple transition theory comes via two further claims: one concerns expansion, the other concerns revision. We'll take them in order and then spend a good deal of time explaining the non-logical rule endorsed by the model.

The root idea behind the model's transition theory is *epistemic conservatism*. This principle has it, roughly, that a rational shift in view should be minimal, that it should be the least drastic change in belief called for by the required epistemic transition. Once such a principle is accepted—and it seems entirely natural to accept it, of course—it is also natural to say three further things: one about rational expansion, one about rational contraction, and one about rational revision. Namely:

- *Expansion* should be the minimal shift in belief brought on by adding something about which one had suspended judgement.
- *Contraction* should be the minimal shift in belief brought on by suspending judgement in something previously believed.
- *Revision* should be the minimal shift brought on by accepting something reviously rejected.

These principles capture the philosophical spirit of the Belief Model's transition theory, and they look entirely sensible on their face. As we saw in the previous chapter, moreover, a principle very like the three above captures the spirit of formal work on the rational shift of fine-grained epistemic attitudes. Epistemic conservatism underwrites most work on rational shift in view.

Now, in this conservative spirit the model puts forward the idea that expansion is defined by logic. The expansion of **B** by P is set equal to the set got by adding P to **B** and then simply tossing in all the new logical consequences. We have the following rule for expansion:

$$(+) \quad (\mathbf{B} + P) = \{\Phi : \{\mathbf{B} \cup \{P\}\} \Rightarrow \Phi\}.$$

More in English: the expansion of **B** by P is the set got by adding P to **B** and then closing the result by logic. This is the set of claims $\Phi$ such that $\Phi$ is entailed by **B**-members together with P.

This is a very simple idea. Recall that expansion is meant to be a minimal shift from suspended judgement to belief. Recall too that states of belief are assumed to be consistent and closed by logical implication. If such an idealized initial state involves suspended judgement in P, then, adding P will generate no conflict in the result. After all, the initial state is consistent and closed by implication, but contains neither P nor its negation. So the initial state does not contain claims which logically entail P or its negation. Adding P to that initial state thus yields no logical difficulty. Principle (+) then insists that the expansion of **B** by P should result in the set you get when you add P to **B** and then toss in all the resulting logical consequences.

The idea is motivated by epistemic conservatism: expansion is meant to be the minimal shift in view brought on by adding something about which one had previously suspended judgement. Since the Belief Model construes all rational configurations of belief as closed by logical implication—i.e. they all obey the closure rule (Entail)—the logical consequences of P plus one's initial beliefs must result from coming to accept P. But rock-ribbed epistemic conservatism then counsels adding no more than one logically must after that. When expanding by P, then, the model's rule (+) says that one should accept P along with everything one previously accepted, plus anything new which logically follows in light of coming to belief P, but no more than this. If that is right, however, then rational expansion may be defined by logic. It is simply the addition of new content plus whatever follows from the resulting enriched configuration of belief. This is the model's first claim about rational state transition which does not seem initially obvious. In the next chapter we'll see why that is so.

The second such claim concerns rational revision. Recall that this sort of transition involves the move from rejection to acceptance. Since the model's belief sets are logically consistent, revision will oblige *taking things out* of your belief set as well as putting things in. The model then appeals to epistemic conservatism to motivate a natural thought, namely, that the revision of belief set **B** by claim P is itself a two-step affair: first one removes the minimal from **B** so as to preclude a commitment to ¬P, then one inserts the minimal to the resulting impoverished set of commitment to ensure a commitment to P. But recall that the contraction of **B** by P is itself meant to be the first of these steps, while expansion of the result by P is itself meant to be the second of these steps. This leads the model to endorse what is known as the *Levi identity*:

$$(*) \quad (\mathbf{B}^*P) = ((\mathbf{B} - \neg P) + P).^4$$

This equation sets the revision of **B** by P equal to the upshot of a two-step process: first the contraction of **B** by ¬P, then the expansion of the result by P.

Now, recall that rational revision is meant to be the minimal shift from belief to opposing belief. Rational revision by P is thus meant to be the minimal shift from disbelief in P to belief in P. Rule (*) says that such a minimal shift can be got by contracting and then by expanding. On this view the shortest cognitive route *from* a belief set committed to ¬P *to* a belief set committed to P involves subtracting ¬P and then adding P. If this is right, revision boils down to contraction plus expansion.

---

[4] See (Levi, 1977), or (Gärdenfors, 1988).

That is the Belief Model's second claim about rational shift in view which does not seem initially obvious. In the next chapter we'll see why that is so.

In a nutshell, then, the model makes two unobvious claims about rational state transition. Rule (+) says that rational expansion boils down to logic. Rule (*) says that rational revision boils down to contraction and then expansion. Together these rules imply that rational revision boils down to contraction plus logic, which means that *every type of rational shift in view boils down, ultimately, to contraction plus logic*. In this way the Belief Model endorses an expansion function defined by logic, a non-trivial contraction function yet to be glossed, and their iteration in reverse order. In a good sense, then, the model's transition theory boils down to one non-logical bit of theory: contraction. That is our next topic.

## 5.5 Contraction

We have noted that there is really a single driving force behind the Belief Model's approach to rational shift in view: epistemic conservatism. Gärdenfors calls this 'the principle (or criterion) of informational economy'; and he makes a number of non-trivial claims about it. In particular, he puts forward the follow thoughts about epistemic conservatism:

> The key idea is that, when we change our beliefs, we want to retain as much as possible of our old beliefs—information is in general not gratuitous, and unnecessary losses of information are therefore to be avoided. (Gärdenfors 1988: 49)

> The criterion of informational economy demands that as few beliefs as possible be given up so that the change is in some sense a *minimal* change of **B** to accommodate P...there are in general several ways of fulfilling the minimality requirement. (ibid.: 53)

> When forming the contraction (**B**-P) of **B** with respect to proposition P, the principle of informational economy requires that (**B**-P) contain as much as possible from **B** without entailing P. (ibid.:75)

We can capture the vibe here with the principle of information economy:

   (Info-Econ)   Shift in view should avoid needless loss of belief.

Given the idealizing assumptions of the Belief Model, this principle can look quite compelling. After all, it is a presupposition of the model that one starts in a rational belief state. As Gärdenfors puts it: belief sets are immune to 'forces of internal criticism'; so whenever an external force induces a rational shift in view, it seems plausible that that shift should itself echo its cause but no more than its cause. In other words, the rational shifts in view should be exactly commensurate with their causes or prompts. They should not be over-reactions. They should involve only the minimal perturbance of an equilibrium position.

Who could argue with that?

Well, no one really. But it is natural to ask for clarification. In particular, it is natural to ask for clarification concerning the notion of minimality at work in the foregoing line of thought. Since the principle of informational economy is given a non-trivial role in the Belief Model, we need a clear specification of how minimal change is to be understood.

That specification is found in Gärdenfors's final quote above. Read literally, the idea is that the contraction of **B** by P should contain all of **B** it can while remaining a belief set and avoiding P. Or in other words: (**B**-P) should retain as much of **B** as possible while being consistent, closed by logic, yet failing to retain P. On this view, the contraction of **B** by P is the minimal perturbance of **B**-members brought on by the need to remove P yet preserve consistency and closure.

To formalize this it helps to use notions from set theory. So forget belief sets for a moment and think of sets more generally. We say that set S is a <u>*subset*</u> of S*—written S ⊆ S*–when everything in S is also in S*. Formally put

(⊆)  S ⊆ S* iff $(\forall x)[(x \in S) \supset (x \in S^*)]$.

And we say S is a *proper subset* of S*—written S ⊂ S*—when everything in S is also in S* but S* contains members not in S. In other words, S is a proper subset of S* when two things happen: S is a subset of S*; and S* is not a subset of S. The second condition obliges something to be in S* but not in S. Formally put

(⊂)  S ⊂ S* iff $\{(S \subseteq S^*) \,\&\, (\exists x)[(x \in S^*) \,\&\, (x \notin S)]\}$.

Of course belief sets are special kinds of sets: they have logically consistent members and they are closed by logical implication: belief sets harbor no conflict and anything implied by their members is itself a member.

This means the contraction of **B** by P must do more than remove P. It must also ensure that no **B**-claims which remain in the contraction jointly imply P. For belief sets are closed by logic: anything implied by their members is in them. So the Belief Model faces a general question about contraction: when contracting a belief set **B** by a claim P, what more than P should be removed from **B**?

This is one place where the principle of informational economy plays a crucial role. Think back to final quote from Gärdenfors:

When forming the contraction (**B**-P) of **B** with respect to proposition P, the principle of informational economy requires that (**B**-P) contain as much as possible from **B** without entailing P.

The idea is that the principle of informational economy should guide retraction. When contracting **B** by P, for instance, and deciding what must be taken out of **B** in addition to P, one should be maximally conservative when tossing things out. One should remove only what is obliged by the demands of consistency, closure, and the removal of a commitment to P. One should remove only what is demanded by logic in light of these needs. So the idea is basically this:

(**B**-P) =  The belief set **B**\* which is a subset of **B**, does not contain P, and is no proper subset of anything which also does both of these things.

More formally put, Gärdenfors's guiding thought is

(G)   (**B**-P) = The belief set **B**\* such that
  (1) **B**∗ ⊆ **B**
  (2) P ∉ **B**∗
  (3) ¬(∃**B**^)[(a) **B**∗ ⊂ **B**^
         (b) **B**^ ⊆ **B**
         (c) P ∉ **B**^].

It is important to realize that (G) is built from a certain take on what minimal shift in view amounts to, i.e. a certain understanding of informational economy. Two ideas ground clauses in principle (G):

1. Informational economy entails that contraction leads to a subset of what is contracted;
2. X is less radically shifted from Z than is Y iff X and Y are subsets of Z; but Y is a *proper* subset of X.

Clause (1) of principle (G) itself grows from 1 while clause (3) of that principle itself grows from 1 and 2 together. The net result is a view on which the rational contraction of B by P is the belief set which is a subset of B, removes P from B, yet is no proper subset of anything which manages also to do both those things.

To get a feel for what is going on here, we should test the guiding thought in the neighbourhood with some tinker-toy examples. To that end, let **Con**(S) be the set of logical consequences of S:

$$\underline{\text{Con}}(S) = \{\text{logical consequences of S}\}.$$

Assume all the sets we are now dealing with are consistent; and let **B** be the belief set consisting of P, Q and their logical consequences:

$$\mathbf{B} = \underline{\text{Con}}(P, Q).$$

**B** is a belief set in the technical sense of the Belief Model. It captures the configuration of belief which endorses P, Q, and all that follows logically from them.

Now consider the contraction of **B** by P. In our notation this is

$$[\underline{\text{Con}}(P, Q)] - P.$$

It seems pre-theoretically plausible that this contraction should be simply the consequences of Q by itself (i.e. **Con**({Q})). But it also looks as if the set of those consequences itself plays the **B***-role in the Gärdenfors principle (G), which in turn looks to confirm the guiding thought behind (G). More formally put, when **B** is **Con**({P,Q}) we have:

$$\underline{\text{Con}}(\{Q\}) = \text{The belief set } \mathbf{B^*} \text{ such that}$$
    (1) $\mathbf{B^*} \subseteq \mathbf{B}$
    (2) $P \notin \mathbf{B^*}$
    (3) $\neg(\exists \mathbf{B^{\wedge}})[$(a) $\mathbf{B^*} \subset \mathbf{B^{\wedge}}$
                  (b) $\mathbf{B^{\wedge}} \subseteq \mathbf{B}$
                  (c) $P \notin \mathbf{B^{\wedge}}$].

And this suggests that principle (G) captures the idea of minimal perturbance in a belief set brought on by the need to remove a given claim while retaining consistency and closure.

Having said that, take a second look at Gärdenfors's guiding thought about contraction:

(G)   (B-P) = The belief set **B*** such that
        (1) $\mathbf{B^*} \subseteq \mathbf{B}$
        (2) $P \notin \mathbf{B^*}$
        (3) $\neg(\exists \mathbf{B^{\wedge}})[$(a) $\mathbf{B^*} \subset \mathbf{B^{\wedge}}$
                      (b) $\mathbf{B^{\wedge}} \subseteq \mathbf{B}$
                      (c) $P \notin \mathbf{B^{\wedge}}$].

This principle assumes that there exists a unique belief set which plays the B*-role. That cannot be taken for granted. Although it is true in some cases, as we've just seen, it is not true in others. Indeed (G)'s existence and uniqueness assumptions can each fail: there may be no belief set to play the B*-role in (G), or there may be more than one set to play it. Everything depends on the details of the case.

1. For instance, take any belief set B and any truth of logic L. Consider the contraction of B by L. There is simply no way to remove L from B yet keep the result closed by logic, for L is a consequence of logic. This means that L is a member of every belief set and thus no such set satisfies (G2): no belief set fails to contain L. In this sort of case the existence assumption of (G) fails: when L is a truth of logic, there is no belief set to play the B*-role in (G).

2. Other cases involve a failure of (G)'s uniqueness assumption. Let B equal the consequences of X and Y:

$$B = \underline{Con}(\{X,Y\}).$$

Let P be the conjunction of X and Y:

$$P = X\&Y.$$

Then P is a member of B, of course, since it is a trivial consequence of X and Y together. But consider the contraction of B by P. Here there are *two* sets which play the B*-role in (G): one is $\underline{Con}\{X\}$, the other is $\underline{Con}\{Y\}$. We have

(1) $\underline{Con}\{X\} \subseteq B$
(2) $P \notin \underline{Con}\{X\}$
(3) $\neg(\exists B^\wedge)[$(a) $\underline{Con}\{X\} \subset B^\wedge$
    (b) $B^\wedge \subseteq B$
    (c) $P \notin B^\wedge].$

And we also have

(1) $\underline{Con}\{Y\} \subseteq B$
(2) $P \notin \underline{Con}\{Y\}$
(3) $\neg(\exists B^\wedge)[$(a) $\underline{Con}\{Y\} \subset B^\wedge$
    (b) $B^\wedge \subseteq B$
    (c) $P \notin B^\wedge].$

Nevertheless: $\underline{Con}\{X\}$ and $\underline{Con}\{Y\}$ are distinct sets. So in this case (G)'s uniqueness assumption fails: more than one set plays the B*-role in (G).

To sum up: for arbitrary B and P, the Belief Model wants the contraction of B by P to be the minimal perturbance of B brought on by the need to remove P while preserving consistency and closure. When smallness of change is measured set-theoretically—as in 1 and 2 above—a problem crops up: sometimes no such change exists (much less a minimal one), while other times multiple changes satisfy the criteria.

What to do?

Well, think back to the model's guiding thought:

(G)  (B-P) = The belief set B* such that
  (1) B* ⊆ B
  (2) P ∉ B*
  (3) ¬(∃B^)[(a) B* ⊂ B^
      (b) B^ ⊆ B
      (c) P ∉ B^].

When a set of claims plays the B*-role in (G), it is a belief set by hypothesis. So any set which plays the B*-role in (G) is itself consistent and closed by logic. But any such set is also a subset of B, since it satisfies condition (1) of principle (G); and any such set is a maximal subset of B too, since it satisfies conditional (3) of principle (G). So any set which plays the B*-role in (G) is a *maximal non-P belief subset of B*.

This is a mouthful we'd do well to shorten. When a set plays the B*-role in (G), then, let us say that it is a 'maximal subset of B', but always keep in mind that the set in question is a maximal non-P subset of B. OK, put all the maximal subsets of B together into a set:

$$(B\perp P) = \{\text{maximal subsets of } B\}.$$

This set is composed of other sets, of course, since its members are sets which play the B*-role in (G). And we have seen that there are exactly three cases to consider when it comes to members of (B⊥P): the case in which no sets play the B*-role in (G), the case in which precisely one set does so, and the case in which multiple sets play the B*-role in (G):

(A) (B⊥P) = the empty set Ø (i.e. the set with no members at all).
(B) (B⊥P) = a set with just one member.
(C) (B⊥P) = a set with more than one member.

Eventually we'll see that the model treats the first two cases here as special instances of the treatment it gives to the third case; but superficially, at least, the model defines contraction rather differently in each of these cases. So it is helpful to consider them in turn.

*Case (A)*. Here the set of maximal subsets of B is empty: there are no sets which are consistent, closed by logic, yet fail to entail P. But consider

$$L = \{\text{logical truths}\}.$$

L is consistent and closed by logic, we shall suppose; so L is the ideal pure logician's belief set, capturing exactly the dictates of logic. Now ask yourself this: is P a member of L?

There are two sub-cases to consider: when P is a member of L, and when it is not. Suppose we are in the first sub-case: P is a member of L. Then it is clear why there are no maximal subsets of **B**; for P is guaranteed by logic to be true, so no belief set can avoid a commitment to P. On the other hand, suppose we are in the second sub-case: P is not a member of **L**. Then intuitively we can add B-claims to **L** until logic demands that P be added as well. Just before reaching that point, however, our construction will be a maximal subset of **B**. But that contradicts the defining feature of Case (A), namely, that (**B**⊥P) is empty. So we may conclude:

$$[(\mathbf{B}\perp P) = \emptyset] \text{ iff } P \in \mathbf{L}.$$

In English: the set of maximal subsets of **B** is empty just when P is ensured by logic.

Suppose, then, that (**B**⊥P) is empty: there are no maximal sub-sets of **B**, i.e. no set plays the **B**\*-role in (G). When that happens the Belief Model says that contraction comes to nothing, as it were, for the model sets the contraction of **B** by P equal to the original set **B**. In effect the model says that in this particular Case—when there are no maximal subsets of **B**—the process of contraction puts one back into the very state that one started out in.

This aspect of the model could be viewed as its expression of the opinion that one cannot rationally retract something which is guaranteed by logic to be true. Or perhaps it is no more than a technical convenience. At this stage we needn't decide why the Belief Model treats retraction in this peculiar way; we need only note that when there are no maximal subsets of **B**, the model insists that the contraction of **B** by P is identical to **B** itself:

$$(\mathbf{B} - P) = \mathbf{B}.$$

*Case (B)*. Next suppose that the set of maximal subsets of **B** has exactly one member. There is a unique set **B**\* such that

(1) $\mathbf{B}* \subseteq \mathbf{B}$
(2) $P \notin \mathbf{B}*$
(3) $\neg(\exists \mathbf{B}^\wedge)[$(a) $\mathbf{B}* \subset \mathbf{B}^\wedge$
    (b) $\mathbf{B}^\wedge \subseteq \mathbf{B}$
    (c) $P \notin \mathbf{B}^\wedge]$.

In this case

$$(\mathbf{B}\perp P) = \{\mathbf{B}^*\},$$

so it's no surprise that the Belief Model sets the contraction of **B** by P equal to **B**\*:

$$(\mathbf{B}\text{-}P) = (\mathbf{B}\perp P)\text{'s one member} = \mathbf{B}^*.$$

This reflects the model's commitment to the principal of informational economy, with the idea being that minimal information should be lost in contraction. But recall that the Belief Model measures relative amounts of information across sets with the subset relation. Hence it sees minimal damage to information after P-removal as some kind of maximal non-P subset. When the set of maximal subsets of **B** has exactly one member, then, it is unsurprising that the model sets the contraction of **B** by P equal to **B** itself.

*Case (C).* Finally suppose that the set of maximal subsets of **B** has more than one member. There are multiple sets $\mathbf{B}^{1,2,3\cdots n}$ which play the **B**\*-role in (G). This means that for any such set $\mathbf{B}^i$:

(1) $\mathbf{B}i \subseteq \mathbf{B}$
(2) $P \notin \mathbf{B}i$
(3) $\neg(\exists \mathbf{B}^{\wedge})[$(a) $\mathbf{B}^i \subset \mathbf{B}^{\wedge}$
    (b) $\mathbf{B}^{\wedge} \subseteq \mathbf{B}$
    (c) $P \notin \mathbf{B}^{\wedge}]$.

Recall that the model measures loss of information with the subset relation. In this case there are several maximal subsets. Hence the model cannot use its standard take on informational economy to pin down how contraction should go. When there are several maximal subsets of **B**, and information is measured by the subset relation, the principle of informational economy does not pin down a unique solution to the contraction problem. It does not pin down a unique set to be the contraction of **B** by P.

What to do?

At this point the Belief Model makes appeal to a new resource. In effect it admits that not all belief sets are equal, that some are more *epistemically entrenched* than others. Gärdenfors has this to say about such entrenchment:

> This is a notion that [applies] to a single sentence... It is the epistemic entrenchment of a sentence in an epistemic state that determines the sentence's fate when the state is contracted... When a belief set **B** is contracted, the sentences in **B** that are given up are those with the *lowest* epistemic entrenchment... The fundamental criterion for determining the epistemic entrenchment of a sentence is how useful it is in inquiry and deliberation. Certain pieces of [information] are more important than others when planning future actions, conducting scientific investigations, or reasoning in general... The epistemic entrenchment of a sentence is tied to its explanatory power and its overall informational value within the belief set. (Gärdenfors 1988: 86–7)

The idea, then, is to use entrenchment to break ties between maximal subsets of **B**. When multiple sets satisfy the model's guiding thought (G)—that is to say, when multiple sets $\mathbf{B}^{1,2,3\cdots n}$ are such that for any of them $\mathbf{B}^i$:

(1) $\mathbf{B}^i \subseteq \mathbf{B}$
(2) $P \notin \mathbf{B}^i$
(3) $\neg(\exists \mathbf{B}^{\wedge})[$(a) $\mathbf{B}^i \subset \mathbf{B}^{\wedge}$
    (b) $\mathbf{B}^{\wedge} \subseteq \mathbf{B}$
    (c) $P \notin \mathbf{B}^{\wedge}]$,

entrenchment is used to break the tie. Epistemic entrenchment is used to build the contraction of **B** by P from the maximal subsets of **B**.

Here's how it goes. First one compares entrenchment of maximal subsets of **B**, with there being two sub-cases to consider: either one finds a maximal subset more entrenched than all others, or one does not. If there is a winner on the entrenchment front—i.e. a best-entrenched maximal subset of **B**—then, the Belief Model sets the contraction of **B** by P equal to that best-entrenched set. In this sub-case we have

## 172 THE BELIEF MODEL (AGM)

(B-P) = The belief set $B^e$ which is more entrenched than any other maximal subset of **B**.

If no maximal subset of **B** is uniquely best entrenched, however, there will be entrenchment ties amongst the maximal subsets of **B**. In this scenario there are multiple maximal subsets of **B** which are all equally well entrenched, and which are all more entrenched than other maximal subsets of **B**. In that case the Belief Model says the following about contraction:

(B-P) = {Φ: Φ belongs to *each* best-entrenched maximal subset of **B**}.

In other words: when there are multiple best-entrenched maximal subsets of **B**, the contraction of **B** by P is built from what they have in common.

So we can chase down the Belief Model's take on contraction with three questions. For any **B** and P

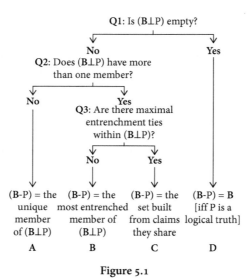

**Figure 5.1**

But notice that (A) is a special case of (B) and (B) is a special case of (C). This means that the model's treatment of contraction boils down to this thought:

(B-P) = **B**, when P is logical necessary
{what is common to the most entrenched otherwise.
members of (B⊥P)},

Once more set theory helps make this precise.

When S and S* are sets their *intersection* is the set containing members of both. This is written S ∩ S*:

(∩)   S ∩ S* = {x : x is a member of S and S*}.

When set S is composed of other sets $S^{1,2,3\cdots n}$, the *generalized intersection* of S—written ∩S—is the set of things common to all sets in S, i.e. common to all the $S^i$'s:

(∩S)   ∩S = {x : x is a member of $S^1$, and $S^2$, and ... and $S^n$}.

Now think back to the set of maximal belief subsets of **B**, (**B**⊥P). We know that for any **B** and P

(A)   (**B**⊥P) = the empty set ∅

or

(B)   (**B**⊥P) = a set with exactly one member

or

(C)   (**B**⊥P) = a set with more than one member.

And we have seen that in Case (A) the Belief Model sets the contraction of **B** by P equal to **B** itself, while in Case (B) the model sets the contraction of **B** by P equal to (**B**⊥P)'s sole member; but in Case (C), when more than one set satisfies the model's guiding thought (G), the model calls on the idea of epistemic entrenchment, collecting together the most-entrenched members of (**B**⊥P). The model then sets the contraction of **B** by P equal to the set of things those most-entrenched members of (**B**⊥P) have in common.

Let **max**-E[(**B**⊥P)] be the set of most entrenched maximal subsets of **B**. Note when it has just one member **B***:

$$\cap \mathbf{max}\text{-}E[(\mathbf{B}\perp P)] = \mathbf{B}^*.$$

This is why the Belief Model can treat Cases (B) and (C) in a single way, with the following contraction rule

(\*)    CONTRACTION
For any **B** and P:   (**B**-P) =   **B**,                    if (**B**⊥P) = ∅;
                                    ∩**max**-E[(**B**⊥P)],   if (**B**⊥P) ≠ ∅.

In effect the contraction rule lays down a function from pairs of things—a belief set and one of its members—to other belief sets. And there is a technical name for this sort of function—a *partial meet contraction function*—but don't worry about what that means. Gärdenfors canvasses the idea nicely:

> The intuitive idea is that the [entrenchment function **max**-E] picks out the maximal subsets of (**B**⊥P) that are epistemologically most entrenched. Thus a proposition P is in (**B**-P) iff it is an element of all the epistemologically most entrenched maximal subsets of **B**. (Gärdenfors 1988: 80)

And now the guts of the model's transition theory are easy to state. It says that shift between epistemic states should boil down to expansion by logic, contraction, and their iteration in reverse order. That is all there is to it.

## 5.6 Postulates

The Belief Model's transition theory is built from three basic ideas:

1. When shifting view, don't give up something unless forced to by logic;
2. When shifting view, don't take on something unless forced to by logic;

3. Where ever possible measure the 'size' of what is given up or taken on by inclusion relations between belief sets.

These ideas drive the construction of the model in two different ways. They motivate the Levi identity, as we'll see, and they motivate various *Postulates* for revision, expansion, and contraction. These Postulates are rules which specify how a rational shift in view should proceed. In his landmark book *Knowledge in Flux* Gärdenfors proves that the Postulates and the Levi identity 'hang together' in a mutually supporting way (which we'll explain in a moment).

In constructing his Postulates, however, it is important to emphasize that Gärdenfors appeals time and again to informational economy. In turn this leads him to a system of rules for expansion, revision, and contraction. Here is the system:

*Expansion Postulates*
(+1)  (B+P) is consistent and fully logical.
(+2)  P is in (B+P)
(+3)  Everything in B is also in (B+P)
(+4)  If P is in B, then (B+P) = B
(+5)  If everything in B is also in B*, then everything in (B+P) is also in (B*+P)
(+6)  (B+P) is the smallest set satisfying (+1)−(+5).

*Revision Postulates*
(*1)  (B*P) is consistent and fully logical
(*2)  P is in (B*P)
(*3)  Everything in (B*P) is also in (B+P)
(*4)  If ¬P is not in B, then everything in (B+P) is also in (B*P)
(*5)  (B*P) is logically inconsistent if but only if P is logically inconsistent
(*6)  If P and Q are logically equivalent, then (B*P) = (B*Q)
(*7)  Everything in [B*(P&Q)] is also in [(B*P)+Q]
(*8)  If ¬Q is not in (B*P), then everything in [(B*P)+Q] is also in [B*(P&Q)]

*Contraction Postulates*
(−1)  (B-P) is consistent and fully logical
(−2)  Everything in (B-P) is also in B
(−3)  If P isn't in B, then (B-P) = B
(−4)  If P is not a logical truth, then it is not in (B-P)
(−5)  If P is in B, then everything in B is also in [(B-P)+P]
(−6)  If P and Q are logically equivalent, then (B-P) = (B-Q)
(−7)  Everything in both (B-P) and (B-Q) is also in [B-(P&Q)]
(−8)  If P isn't in [B-(P&Q)], then everything in [B-(P&Q)] is also in (B-P)

These Postulates are justified by loose intuition and the principle of informational economy. The idea is put forward repeatedly that information is precious, that one should not lose information in changing one's mind unless forced to do so, and that logic is the source of such force. These thoughts are quickly used to codify the Postulates above and then Gärdenfors sets about proving various non-trivial technical things about the Postulates. Often those things are quite interesting. We shall focus on two results.

First: Expansion Postulates fit together with the idea, used in §1.4, that expansion works like set-theoretic union plus deduction:

*Expansion-as-Deduction Theorem*
A function '+' obeys (+1)–(+6) iff $(B + P) = \{\emptyset : \{B \cup \{P\}\} \Rightarrow \emptyset\}$.
Recall §1.4's rule for expansion

$$(+) \quad (B + P) = \{\emptyset : \{B \cup \{P\}\} \Rightarrow \emptyset\}.$$

This is the right-hand side of the Expansion-as-Deduction Theorem. Hence that Theorem shows that Expansion Postulates go hand in hand with (+), pinning down the fact that expansion works like set-theoretic union plus logic. Since the rule (+) is itself motivated by the principle of informational economy, it is nice to see likewise-motivated Postulates fit into place. That is what the Expansion-as-Deduction Theorem shows.

Second, Gärdenfors proves something interesting about revision:

*Revision Theorem*

If          (1) '–' obeys (–1)–(–4) and (–6)–(–8),
&            (2) '+' obeys (+1)–(+6),
&            (3) '*' obeys the Levi identity,
then     (4) '*' obeys (*1)–(*8).

This motivates the overall Belief Model construction in several directions at once. It makes the Levi identity look right, shows how Postulates fit together as a group, and demonstrates that the model is internally coherent. This is exactly what you would expect when technically astute philosophers such as Carlos Alchourrón, Peter Gärdenfors, and David Makinson bring similar intuitions to bear on a particular formalism.

## 5.7 Linking States and Transitions: Conditional Belief

All in all, then, we've seen the following:

- The Belief Model boils down its transition theory to three types of shift in view: Expansion, Revision, and Contraction.
- In each case, the model claims that shift in view should be minimal, that it should involve the smallest epistemic change brought on by the context to hand.
- Whenever possible, the model adopts a purely logical and/or set-theoretic take on 'smallest change', which leads to the Levi identity and Postulates for shift-in-view.
- Those Postulates together with that identity jointly imply:
    - Expansion works like set-theoretic union plus deduction,
  and so
    - Revision collapses to contraction plus expansion.
- The Belief Model says contracting **B** by P involves movement to the belief set which consists in what is common to the most entrenched maximal non-P belief subsets of **B**.

176  THE BELIEF MODEL (AGM)

On this sort of approach, intuitively, rational configurations of epistemic attitudes should be logically kosher; and rational shifts between such configurations of attitude should themselves be minimal.

Yet nothing has been said so far about whether these prescriptions are linked systematically. So we shall ask: does the Belief Model see any direct link from its theory of states to its transition theory or vice versa?

Yes, the model sees a direct link in both directions: from its theory of states to its transition theory, and from its transition theory to its theory of states. To see how this works, consider the frame

(B)  S believes that—.

Various sentences can be used to fill it. Each of the following sentences, for instance:

- You struck the match.
- You caused the fire.
- Oswald didn't kill Kennedy.
- Someone else killed Kennedy.

Plugging any of these sentences into frame (B) yields an ordinary belief attribution:

- S believes that you struck the match.
- S believes that you caused the fire.
- S believes that Oswald didn't kill Kennedy.
- S believes that someone else killed Kennedy.

The Belief Model sees no direct link between such beliefs and rational shift in view.

But it does see a direct link between certain extraordinary beliefs and its transition theory. And these extraordinary beliefs are described when certain *conditional sentences* are put into (B). For instance, when either of the following two sentences is put into (B)

- If you struck the match, you caused the fire.
- If Oswald didn't kill Kennedy, someone else killed Kennedy.

the result is conditional-belief attribution:

S believes that if you struck the match, you caused the fire.
S believes that if Oswald didn't kill Kennedy, someone else did.

The Belief Model sees a very deep link between such conditional beliefs and rational shift-in-view. It uses its take on such conditional beliefs to build a two-way bridge linking belief sets on the one hand and rational state transitions on the other.

In turn this is because the model is heavily influenced by the most influential remark ever made on conditional belief. Almost a century ago the great philosopher F. P. Ramsey wrote:

If two people are arguing 'If $p$ will $q$?' and are both in doubt as to $p$, they are adding $p$ hypothetically to their stock of knowledge and arguing on that basis about $q$...

Throughout formal epistemology this has become known as the 'Ramsey Test' for conditional belief. Gärdenfors describes it in the following way:

In order to find out whether a conditional sentence is acceptable in a given state of belief, one first adds the antecedent of the conditional hypothetically to the given stock of beliefs. Second, if the antecedent together with the formerly accepted sentences leads to a contradiction, then one makes some adjustments, which are as small as possible without modifying the hypothetical belief in the antecedent, such that consistency is maintained. Finally, one considers whether or not the consequent of the conditional is accepted in this adjusted state of belief. The Ramsey test can be summarized by the following rule: accept a sentence of the form 'If A, then C' in a state of belief **B** if and only if the minimal change of **B** needed to accept A also requires accepting C.     (Gärdenfors 1988: 147)

By the Belief Model's lights, of course, minimal change is partial-meet contraction as described by the model's transition theory, as characterized by its Postulates, and so forth.

Let **min-rev** be the process of minimal revision, whatever it turns out to be exactly. The Ramsey Test for conditional belief then becomes:

(RT)   (A→C) belongs to an agents set of beliefs **B** iff C belongs to **min-rev**(**B** by A).

This principle builds a bridge between epistemic states and their rational revision, with the bridge being conditional belief. The Ramsey Test ensures that a given epistemic state will mark its own rational revision by the conditional beliefs within it.

## 5.8 A Matching Psychology: Bella

In Chapter 1 we noted that any full-dress theory of rationality will have three major moving parts: a theory of states, a transition theory, and a story about how the two fit together. The theoretical template is this

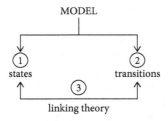

**Figure 5.2**

In this chapter we've seen how the Belief Model fills out the template

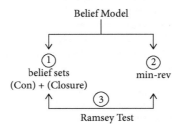

**Figure 5.3**

In Chapter 1 we also noted that it's best for three things to be true of a formal model of any target phenomena:

1. Basic facts in its target domain are explicitly marked by basic elements in the model;
2. Derivative facts in its target domain are explicitly marked by derivative elements in the model;
3. Derivative facts in the target domain are grounded in target basic facts so that grounding relations are mirrored by those between markers in the model.

When these things happen a model *metaphysically matches* its target domain; and when a model so matches its target domain one can read off from its surface how derivative and basic facts in that domain fit together. Question: what would it take for a target psychology to be metaphysically matched by the Belief Model?

Well, such a psychology would have to consist in basic states of mind marked explicitly by basic elements of the model; it would have to consist in derivative states of mind marked explicitly by derivative markers in the model; and these two aspects of the target domain would have to fit together grounding-wise as their markers do in the model. If we assume the model metaphysically matches a target psychology, therefore, we assume one can read off its surface what the basic facts are about rationality. So ask yourself this: what is the fundamental moving-part of the Belief Model?

Answer: the sentence.[5] The model groups collections of sentences together into belief sets. It then uses these sets to construe rational configurations of belief, and rational transitions between such configurations. The basic mental kind marked by the Belief Model is thus the propositional attitude of belief. Belief sets are the model's surface-level marker for collections of individual states of belief. And the model's revision function **min-rev** is its surface-level marker for rational shift in configurations of belief. The model's Ramsey Test is then its story about how its theory of states fits together with its transition theory. Conditional sentences in belief sets link input and output of **min-rev**. This is how the Belief Model fleshes out parts ❶-thru-❸ of the theoretical template with which we began this section.

For the model to metaphysically match a domain of fact, therefore, its target will need to consist in basic states of belief. Groups of those states will need to shift en masse, upon receipt of new input, as specified by **min-rev** function. And the **min-rev** function will need to work out in line with conditional belief. To see how this might be so, we shall augment an influential thought-experiment by Stephen Schiffer:

> Suppose we are faced with a rather unusual individual: Bella. She has beliefs in whatever sense we do, and those beliefs are psychologically basic to her mind. Bella thinks in a language-like internal system of representation—her language-of-thought—and she has a giant transparent head. Within her giant transparent head there is a transparent box marked 'B'. This is Bella's belief-box. She thinks in an internal language-of-thought; and

---

[5] Or better still: the sentence-letter, something which functions in in the model as a name for a normal sentence which might codify what one believed. We move back and forth without comment between talk of sentences like this and talk of letters which name them, since keeping track of the distinction between them is not necessary for our discussion.

she lends the attitude of belief to a claim C by placing a C-meaning sentence of that language in her belief-box. We stipulate that whenever a C-meaning sentence is in Bella's belief-box she manifests the signature function of belief in C. This is just a fancy way of saying that Bella's belief-box is functionally individuated so that its cash value is identical to that of our states of belief.[6]

Let us suppose that Bella's language-of-thought is similar to the language used by the Belief Model—in both cases, say, a sentential language of propositional logic. Let us also suppose that sentences in Bella's belief-box—including conditional sentences—shift as a group in one step, exactly in line with the **min-rev** function. Then the model will metaphysically match Bella's psychology. We have reverse engineered her to ensure that is so.

The fundamental marking element in the Belief Model's theory of states is sentence membership in a belief set. This corresponds to the fundamental mental kind in Bella's psychology: the individual state of belief. The fundamental marking element in the model's transition theory is the **min-rev** function. This corresponds to how content-bearing sentences in Bella's belief-box shift upon perturbation. And the details of Bella's belief-transitions are marked exactly by conditional sentences in her belief box. This corresponds to the Ramsey-style role conditional sentences play in the Belief Model.

Further still—we may stipulate—Bella's psychology involves a pair of derivative propositional attitudes which are subject to epistemic appraisal: disbelief and suspended judgement. But these states only occur in Bella because and in virtue of her belief-box working a certain way. We stipulate that the disbelief-as-belief hypothesis is true of Bella:

(D-as-B)   A subject S disbelieves $\Phi$ by believing $\neg\Phi$.

And we stipulate that the suspended-judgement-as-belief hypothesis is true of Bella:

(SJ-as-B)   A subject S suspends judgement in $\Phi$ by failing to believe or disbelieve $\Phi$.

This corresponds to the Belief Model's portrayal of disbelief and suspended judgement, since the model marks the former propositional attitude with a negated sentence in a belief set, and the latter propositional attitude with the absence of a sentence or its negation in a belief set.

By design, then, the Belief Model metaphysically matches Bella's psychology. It marks fundamental aspects of her mind with basic elements of its machinery, derivative aspects of her mind with derivative elements of its machinery, and ensures that fundamental and derivative facts in its target domain fit together exactly like their markers do in the model.

---

[6] (Schiffer, 1981, p. 212). The hero of Schiffer's thought-experiment is Hilarious Meadow rather than Bella. Schiffer notes—rather implausibly, in my view—that Meadow is no relative of Hilary Putnam or Hartry Field. See also (Fodor, 1975) for the language-of-thought hypothesis.

# 6
# Critical Discussion of the Belief Model

## 6.1 Preview

The Belief Model is the best-known model of rational coarse-grained attitudes. Its mathematical properties are elegant, extensively investigated, and of permanent use in many areas of theoretical concern (e.g. the theory of data-management). The model has proved to be of intrinsic interest and practical worth. It is not though—or at least not as it stands, anyway—a good formalism of our rational coarse-grained attitudes. This chapter canvasses some of the main reasons why that is so. We'll not look at every serious worry for the Belief Model, since later chapters make clear that some of them cover popular models of fine-grained attitudes too. But we'll focus on some worries intrinsic to the Belief Model itself. These have to do with both its theory of states and its transition theory.

Our discussion will function not only as a critique of the Belief Model but also as a warm-up for tackling general aspects of rationality. Those aspects are to be emphasized repeatedly in later chapters of the book, so it's good to be clear about them here. In the next two sections we focus on the Belief Model's theory of states, and then we turn to its transition theory.

## 6.2 States in the Belief Model: Only One Coarse-Grained Attitude?

There is a curious asymmetry in the epistemology of coarse- and fine-grained attitudes. This asymmetry holds as much in informal discussions of the phenomena as it does in formal ones. The running motif in the literature on coarse-grained attitudes is that there is deep down only one such attitude: belief. It is not that philosophers reject the very idea of disbelief or suspended judgement—that would fly in the face of common sense, after all—it is rather that philosophers simply assume a reduction of these attitudes to belief. This means they assume, as we put in in §2.8, both the disbelief-as-belief hypothesis and the suspended-judgement-as-belief hypothesis:

(D-as-B)  A subject S disbelieves Φ by believing ¬Φ.
(SJ-as-B) A subject S suspends judgement in Φ by failing to believe or disbelieve Φ.

Nothing like this happens in the epistemology of fine-grained attitudes. As we'll see in subsequent chapters, it is not generally assumed that one kind of fine-grained attitude, nor even a sub-collection of fine-grained attitudes, is explanatorily basic.

We may picture the relevant perspective on coarse-grained attitudes with a pair of grounding schemata:

*Grounding-of-suspended-judgement schema*

$$SJ(\Phi)$$

⇛

$$\{\neg B(\Phi) \ \& \ \neg DB(\Phi)\}$$

*Grounding-of-disbelief schema*

$$DB(\Phi)$$

⇛

$$B(\neg \Phi)$$

The idea behind the first schema is this: suspended judgement is nothing over and above the absence of belief and disbelief. This is the suspended-judgement-as-belief hypothesis. The idea behind the second schema is analogous: disbelief is nothing over and above belief in negation. This is the disbelief-as-belief hypothesis. If both of these schemata are valid, if all of their instances are true, there is only one basic kind of coarse-grained attitude: belief. The Belief Model proceeds as if that is so.

Consider the analogue view in the epistemology of fine-grained attitudes. Within a probabilistic setting—of the kind we explained from scratch in Chapter 2—this would amount to the idea that for any real-number $n$ (not less than 0 but less than .5):

*Grounding of low credence schema*

$$Cr(\Phi) = n$$

⇛

$$Cr(\neg \Phi) = (1-n).$$

The thought here would be that low credence is deep down nothing but high credence in negation. This is a credal analogue of the idea that disbelief is deep down nothing but belief in negation.

The analogue seems obviously wrong. Low credence doesn't look or feel like high credence in negation, and in the next section we'll see that low credence doesn't fully function like high credence in negation either. Instead low credence looks and feels (and functions) like a proprietary kind of attitudinal stance. Being one-quarter sure that it will snow, for instance, is not really the same thing as being three-quarters sure that it will not snow.[1] The latter take on the weather may itself be forced upon

---

[1] See Chapter 9 for a general argument that attitude and operator are not fully fungible.

one, rationally, when the former take on the weather is adopted, but the low-credence attitudinal stance seems to be something distinct from its high-credence analogue, psychologically speaking. And so it goes with other states of low credence. They seem to be metaphysically distinct from states of high credence, even states of high credence lent to the negation of their contents. The grounding of low credence schema is implausible on its face.

This fact casts doubt on the grounding of suspended judgement and the grounding of disbelief schemata. It is unsurprising, therefore, that neither of the latter schemata are plausible after reflection. To see this, recall the schema which grounds suspended judgement in belief:

*Grounding-of-suspended-judgement schema*

$$SJ(\Phi)$$
$$\Rightarrow$$
$$\{\neg B(\Phi) \,\&\, \neg DB(\Phi)\}.$$

The lower condition here is clearly *in*sufficient for its upper condition—or, put another way, the upper condition is clearly something over and above the lower one. When you fail to consider whether Caesar crossed the Rubicon carrying nuclear weapons, for instance—say because you lack the concept of a nuclear weapon—you fail to believe or disbelieve that Caesar crossed the Rubicon carrying nuclear weapons. This does not mean that you've suspended judgement in whether he did so. In these circumstances not only would it be the case that you have no view of the matter—belief, disbelief, or suspended judgement—it would also be the case that you lack the conceptual resources to have a view on the matter.

Suspended judgement is not the absence of belief and disbelief. It is the presence of a proprietary kind of neutral commitment, something more than a mere absence or lack. Suspended judgement is the propositional attitude of *committed neutrality*. It will be our job to flesh out what this comes to.[2]

Now recall the schema which grounds disbelief in belief in negation:

*Grounding-of-disbelief schema*

$$DB(\Phi)$$
$$\Rightarrow$$
$$B(\neg\Phi).$$

The idea here is that disbelief is nothing over and above belief in negation. But that too seems plainly false after reflection. The lower condition of the schema concerns the endorsement or acceptance of $\neg\Phi$. Disbelief in $\Phi$ does not intuitively concern the endorsement or acceptance of anything: it seems to involve the pushing-away of $\Phi$ in

---

[2] In the fall of 2002 I went through this material in a grad-seminar at Harvard. I confessed frustration at not having a good label for the conception of suspended judgment I was defending. After listening for a while Selim Berker offered the helpful phrase 'committed neutrality'. Thanks Selim!

thought. Disbelief seems to involve a proprietary type of attitudinal condemnation. This too will take some explaining.

But our initial impression in the area is clear enough: belief, disbelief, and suspended judgement are each their own kind of thing. None of them seems to reduce to the others. We need a philosophical conception of coarse-grained attitudes which underwrites this initial impression. Developing one is our next task.

## 6.3 Coarse-Grained Attitudes

Each of the three coarse-grained attitudes—belief, disbelief, and suspended judgement—seems to have a psychological life of its own. To unearth a conception of how this can be we shall first lay out a pair of thought experiments. Then we'll reflect on the conception of coarse-grained attitudes which falls out of them if one is a functionalist about the attitudes (in line with the Cash-Value Assumption of Chapter 1). The initial thought experiment is

### THREE DOORS

You are told to exit a room by one of three doors: the $\underline{L}$eft door, the $\underline{M}$iddle door, or the $\underline{R}$ight door. Hence there are four things that you might do: exit by the left door $\underline{L}$, exit by the middle door $\underline{M}$, exit by the right door $\underline{R}$, or fail to act. So we can define a condition C by appeal to a double failure:

$$C =_{df.} (\neg \underline{L} \& \neg \underline{R}).$$

C is the condition of failing to leave by the left and failing to leave by the right door. There are two ways to get into C: you can do so by exiting via the middle door $\underline{M}$, you can do so failing to exit at all.

Intuitively, a similar structure plays out with coarse-grained attitudes. Suppose you are given some data relevant to claim Φ. You are instructed to examine the data carefully and adopt the take on Φ which best reflects their relevance concerning whether or not Φ is true. In the event, there are three coarse-grained options before you: belief, disbelief and suspended judgement. Hence there are four psychological possibilities to hand. You might come to believe Φ after studying the data. You might come to disbelieve Φ after doing so. You might come to suspend judgement in Φ after studying the data. Or you might fail to adopt a view about Φ at all (say because you get distracted and start thinking about something else). There are two ways, therefore, to fail to believe Φ while failing to disbelieve Φ: this happens when you suspend judgement in Φ, and also when you have no Φ-commitment whatsoever. While going through the data and trying to decide how they relate to Φ's truth-value—as well as before the question of that truth-value has even occurred to you—you have no Φ-commitment at all. In neither case do you suspend judgement in Φ. In neither of them do you adopt the attitude of committed neutrality to whether Φ is true.

Our second thought experiment is

### THE JUDGE

You are a pre-trial judge meant to assess evidence gathered by police. You must decide if the evidence makes for an initial indication of guilt, innocence, or neither. And there are three verdicts available to you: evidence indicates guilt, evidence indicates innocence, evidence does neither of these things. Suppose Mr. Big has been charged with stealing the cookies and you have been contacted by one of his powerful allies. You are urged to reach a verdict immediately so as to dampen public discussion of the case. But you haven't received the evidential dossier from the police yet. In the event, there are four options to hand. You might commit to the view that the evidence makes for an initial indication of guilt. You might commit to the view that the evidence makes for an initial indication of innocence. You might commit to the view that the evidence does neither of these things. Or you might steadfastly refrain from any such commitment at all. In the envisaged circumstances it is clear that you should opt for the last of these choices, since you've not received the evidential dossier from the police and thus have no clue about the relevant evidence. But you have four options before you rather than three.

The same structure plays out in the epistemology of coarse-grained attitudes. There are four attitudinal stances available. Intuitively:

settled endorsement = belief
settled denial = disbelief
settled neutrality = suspended judgement
unsettled stance = no epistemic attitude.

There is a clear psychological difference between these four scenarios. The first one involves the settled intellectual embrace of a claim, the kind of endorsement-like state which is incompatible with a fleeting or unstable take on its truth-value. The second scenario involves a settled intellectual pushing-away of a claim, a kind of rejection-like state likewise incompatible with a fleeting or unstable take on its truth-value. The third scenario involves settled intellectual neutrality about a claim, a kind of stable reserve also incompatible with any fleeting take on its truth-value. And the fourth scenario involves no epistemic attitude at all, for it involves too much psychological instability.

None of these states seem to inter-reduce. For example, disbelief does not seem to be any combination of belief, suspended judgement, or lack of commitment. And nor do any of the other coarse-grained states look to boil down to a combination of their coarse-grained cousins. Moreover, a lack of stable attitudinal commitment obviously does not reduce to any combination of stable commitments. So none of the four possibilities above reduce to the others.

We can make ready sense of this from a functionalist perspective. The following is one way to do so (there are many others). First, we align belief lent to a particular content with the strong and stable disposition to rely on that content in various ways. For instance, we align belief in $\Phi$ with the strong and stable disposition to take bets on Φ, to say things like 'Yes, of course!' when asked whether Φ is true, to make use of Φ in our practical and theoretical reasoning, and so on.[3] This sort of functionalism about belief-in-Φ aligns that particular kind of belief with a constellation of 'signature functions'. In turn these functions are always indexed somehow to Φ being true. And each of these signature functions generates a particular disposition, namely, the one defined as a disposition to carry out the Φ-related signature function in question. These signature dispositions are constituent elements of belief-in-Φ. The state of believing Φ itself is identified as the manifestation of enough of these signature dispositions.[4]

Second, we align disbelief in a particular content with the strong and stable disposition to rule-out that content in various ways. For instance, we align disbelief in Φ with the strong and stable disposition to reject bets on Φ, to say things like 'No, don't be stupid!' when asked whether Φ is true, to rule out anything which clearly entails Φ in our practical and theoretical reasoning, and so on. This sort of functionalism about disbelief-in-Φ likewise aligns that particular kind of disbelief with a constellation of signature functions. In turn these functions are indexed to Φ being false; and once more each of them generates a particular signature disposition. These signature dispositions are thought of as constituent elements of disbelief-in-Φ. And the mental state in question is itself identified as the manifestation of enough of the Φ-relevant signature dispositions.[5]

Third, we align suspended judgement with the strong and stable disposition to *refrain* from activities the strong and stable presence of which make for belief or disbelief. This means we align suspended judgement in Φ with the strong and stable disposition to refrain from accepting or rejecting bets on Φ, the strong and stable disposition to say things like 'Oh, I haven't the slightest idea!' when queried about Φ's truth-value, the strong and stable disposition to refrain from using Φ or its negation in any sort of reasoning, and so on. The thought here is to align suspended judgement in Φ with a constellation of signature disposition. Possession of enough of them rules-out functioning as someone who believes or disbelieves in Φ.

And finally, we align attitudinal unsettledness with the absence of dispositions the strong or stable presence of which make for belief, disbelief or suspended judgement. In turn this means being unsettled about Φ is a kind of attitudinal lack about whether Φ is true. More specifically, it's the lack of dispositions the presence of which make for the endorsement of a content, the rejection of a content, or committed neutrality

---

[3] Chapter 13 sketches a view about how this works for humans despite two further things being true of us: states of believing are states of confidence deep down, and states of confidence do not figure in reasoning.

[4] We take no stand in this book on which pro-Φ functions, exactly, are constitutive of the attitudes? Some kind of functionalism about them will be assumed, but nothing need be specified about whether that functionalism is of the common-sense variety, the scientific variety, or something else yet again. For elegant discussions of functionalism see (Loar, 1981), (Lewis, 1966) and especially (Lewis, 1994), and (Schiffer, 1987).

[5] Something very like the take on disbelief found here often makes an appearance in philosophical logic. Those who make use of it normally do so to reduce or explicate negation. But nothing follows about the semantics of negation, or the nature of logic, from the view that disbelief has a psychological life of its own, that it is metaphysically distinct from belief in negation. For a useful guide to the relevant literature see (Ripley, 2011). See also (Rumfitt, 2000).

about a content. Attitudinal unsettledness involves functional instability. Such instability is the signature of an attitudinal lack, given functionalism about the attitudes.

These are the beginnings of a functional understanding of our coarse-grained attitudes. They underwrite the idea that such attitudes fail to inter-reduce, which in turn makes it reasonable to affirm our initial impression of the coarse-grained attitudes, namely, that belief is a proprietary kind of positive commitment, disbelief is a proprietary kind of negative commitment, and suspended judgement is a proprietary kind of committed neutrality. When it comes to the relation between belief, disbelief and suspended judgement, therefore, the most we can hope for is systematic alignment when the attitudes are fully rational.

For instance, it is plausible to suppose that the following schema is true of fully rational agents who consider whether or not $\Phi$:

(a) $SJ(\Phi)$ iff $\neg B(\Phi)$ & $\neg DB(\Phi)$.

It seems plausible to suppose, that is to say, that such agents will suspend judgement exactly when they fail to believe and fail to disbelieve. But this sort of normative alignment between suspended judgement and the absence of belief and disbelief is itself compatible with anti-reductionism about suspended judgement. Just because fully rational suspended judgement (on a question being considered) lines up with the absence of belief and disbelief, after all, it does not follow that suspended judgement itself reduces to the absence of belief and disbelief. And we have seen good reason to think that it does not so reduce. We thus duly conclude that only an (a)-style correlation exists between them.

Similarly, it seems plausible to suppose that the following schema is true of fully rational agents like us:

(b) $DB(\Phi)$ iff $B(\neg\Phi)$.

It seems plausible to suppose, that is to say, that such agents will disbelieve exactly when they believe a negation. But this sort of normative alignment between disbelief and belief in negation is compatible with anti-reductionism about disbelief. Just because fully rational disbelief in humans lines up with belief in negation, after all, it does not follow that disbelief itself is grounded by belief in negation. And we have seen good reason to think that it is not so grounded. We duly conclude that only an (b)-style correlation exists between them.

We are left, then, with a pair of interim conclusions: coarse-grained attitudes stand on their own with respect to one another, and they are subject to proprietary epistemic norms. In this sense there is symmetry between coarse- and fine-grained attitudes: when it comes to how elements within a given attitudinal space relate to one another—i.e. how course-grained attitudes relate to one another, and how fine-grained attitudes relate to one another—anti-grounding seems the best bet. Both coarse- and fine-grained attitudes look to be on an explanatory par with their level-mates, and, for this reason, attitudes within a given level look to be subject to proprietary epistemic norms.

If this is right—and from now on we'll assume that it is—the Belief Model's theory of states fails to match its target domain. After all, the theory's approach to mental states regards suspended judgement and disbelief as derivative phenomena, at best; but they are *bona fide* propositional attitudes which stand on all fours with belief. And they are subject to proprietary epistemic appraisal in light of the evidence. By marking them in a derivative way, the Belief Model's theory of states fails to match its target domain of fact.

To make it do so we'd need to add disbelief and suspended-judgement sets to the model's machinery; and we'd need to add rules for how the new sets should be structured. Then we could codify an agent's states with an ordered triple <B, D, SJ>. B would represent the agent's states of belief, D her states of disbelief, and SJ the contents about which the agent suspends judgement. And just as the consistency rule (Con) and the entailment rule (Entail) are general rules for the overall structure of a belief set, a metaphysically matching Belief-Model-style theory of states would need analogue rules to do with the structure of rational disbelief and suspended judgement.

Think of it this way. Disbelief and suspended judgement are propositional attitudes subject to epistemic appraisal. Belief-Model-style modelling of propositions takes place with sentences. Like their belief-theoretic counterparts, therefore, disbelief and suspended-judgement sets in a matching approach can be represented by sets of sentences. Just as a belief set B can be thought of as a set of sentences which express claims believed by a rational agent, disbelief set D can be thought of as a set of sentences which express claims disbelieved by a rational agent, and suspended-judgement set SJ can be thought of as sets of sentences which express claims in which an agent is neutrally committed. This much is easy when it comes to creating an AGM-style theory which matches our psychology. What is not so easy is specifying the norms which structure rational disbelief and suspended-judgement when we do so. What should they look like?

Well, recall the norms used in the Belief Model's theory of states:

(Con-for-belief)      Belief sets are logically consistent.
(Entail-for-belief)      For any belief set B and sentence S: if the members of B logically entail S, then S belongs to B.

The first rule ensures that as a matter of logic all the members of a belief set can be true together. The second rule ensures that belief sets are closed by logical implication: intuitively, this means that you cannot walk your way out of a belief set by chasing down its logical implications.[6] Each of these rules is meant to apply to a rational agent, and that is a plausible thought on its face. What is equally plausible, however, is that direct analogues of them should *not* apply to rational states of disbelief or suspended judgement.

To see why, consider the analogue rules for disbelief. Neither of them withstands a moment's reflection:

(Con-for-D)      Disbelief sets are logically consistent.
(Entail-for-D)      For any disbelief set D and sentence S: if the members of D logically entail S, then S belongs to D.

---

[6] See §5.2 for details.

Since disbelief is a kind of stable rejection of a claim, the attitude of disbelief can rationally occur when a claim turns out to be impossible. It might be explicitly inconsistent, for instance, or a truth-functional falsity, or a conceptually incoherent claim (e.g. the claim that a given shoe is red but uncoloured). In any of these cases a rational agent will disbelieve the claim to hand; but this means that the set which represents their states of disbelief will itself be inconsistent. Our approach should definitely permit rational agents to disbelieve such impossible claims. Any acceptable extension of the Belief Model to handle disbelief will thus allow disbelief sets to be inconsistent. The rule (Con-for-D) is a mistake.

Similarly, just because disbelieved contents logically imply a given claim, it does not follow that disbelievers should rule-out that claim. After all, a set of things rationally disbelieved will doubtless contain formal contradictions. Those contradictions will entail basically everything, including simple truth-functional tautologies. Disbelief sets are closed by implication, therefore, only if rational agents disbelieve simple truth-functional tautologies. But that does not look to be possible. We should thus reject the idea that disbelief sets are closed under implication.

What seems true is that rational disbelief is closed under some kind of negative reverse implication. Here is one way to spell out the idea:

(Rev-D-1)   For any disbelief set **D** and sentence S: if S entails something in **D**—or entails that something in **D** is true—then S is in **D**.

Here is a more general way to spell out the idea:

(Rev-D-2)   For any disbelief set **D** and sentences $S_1 \ldots S_n$: if $S_1 \ldots S_n$ jointly entail something in **D**—or jointly entail that something in **D** is true—then, $(S_1 \& \ldots \& S_n)$ is in **D**.

We do not need to explore how best to spell out the relevant idea; for it is clear enough that entailing something rejected is itself a way of meriting rejection. Any complete model of rational coarse-grained states should respect that insight.

It also seems clear that rational suspended judgement is not consistent. For instance the following rule seems plainly silly:

(Con-for-SJ)   Suspended-judgement sets are logically consistent.

After all, suspended judgement is stable neutrality about the truth-value of a content. It would be daft to maintain neutrality toward a content C without also doing so toward its negation. The moment you ruled in or out ¬C, after all, you'd be in position to rule out or in C. Suspended-judgement sets should be *in*consistent sets par excellence, as contradictory as you please.

This means that the following rule is dead on arrival:

(Entail-for-SJ)   For any suspended-judgement set **SJ** and sentence S: if members of **SJ** logically entail S, then S belongs to **SJ**.

Since suspended-judgement sets are logically inconsistent, they entail every claim: it is not logically possible for their members all to be true while a given claim is false, since it is not logically possible for their members all to be true. If suspended-judgement sets were closed by implication, therefore—in line with the rule (Entail-for-SJ)—it would follow that such sets contain every claim whatsoever. But that is absurd. Fully rational agents do not to suspend judgement in everything.

A theory of coarse-grained states metaphysically matches its target domain of fact only if the approach deals explicitly with belief, disbelief and suspended judgement. Fully rational states of belief look to be consistent and closed by logical implication. In this way logic itself plays a crucial role in how fully rational belief is shaped. It is also plausible that two further norms link fully rational belief, disbelief, and suspended judgement. The first links suspended judgement to belief and disbelief about contents being considered:

(a)   $SJ(\Phi)$ iff $\neg B(\Phi)$ & $\neg DB(\Phi)$.

And the second links disbelief to belief itself in beings like us:

(b)   $DB(\Phi)$ iff $B(\neg\Phi)$.

These are plausible norms linking fully rational belief, disbelief and suspended judgement. If a model is to metaphysically match the links they detail, it must have explicit analogues of them amongst its marking elements.

## 6.4 The Belief Model's Transition Theory

Recall that the Belief Model's transition theory is built atop three ideas:

1. When shifting view, don't give up something unless forced to by logic;
2. When shifting view, don't take on something unless forced to by logic;
3. Whenever possible, measure the size of what is given up or taken on by inclusion relations between belief sets.

We saw in the previous chapter that these ideas shape the Belief Model's transition theory in several ways. They motivate the Levi identity aligning revision with a two-step process (of contraction and then expansion). They loosely motivate Postulates for modelling revision, expansion and contraction. And their net effect is meant to ensure that the model's transition theory captures something like *purely logical constraints* on the ordinary shift in rational opinion.

As we'll now see, however, there are no such constraints on ordinary rational shift-in-view. One cannot use loose intuition about informational economy, spelled out via logical-cum-set-theoretic machinery, in an effort to track what happens in the ordinary shift of rational opinion. To see why, recall it is by appeal to such machinery that the Belief Model motivates expansion postulates:

(+1)   (**B**+P) is consistent and fully logical.
(+2)   P is in (**B**+P)
(+3)   Everything in **B** is also in (**B**+P)
(+4)   If P is in **B**, then (**B**+P) = **B**

190   CRITICAL DISCUSSION OF THE BELIEF MODEL

(+5)   If everything in **B** is also in **B***, then everything in (**B**+P) is also in (**B***+P)
(+6)   (**B**+P) is the smallest set satisfying (+1)–(+5).

But these Postulates do not accurately track rational expansion of opinion. They entail, for instance, that adding P to the intersection of two belief sets yields the same thing as taking the intersection of the states got by adding P to each of them. Or in other words: the Belief Model expansion postulates entail that the result of expanding what two belief sets have in common by P is itself identical to expanding each of the belief sets by P and then gathering up what they have in common. Or in still other words:

(⊗)   $[(\mathbf{B} \cap \mathbf{B}^*) + P] = [(\mathbf{B} + P) \cap (\mathbf{B}^* + P)]$.

This is a sad consequence of the Belief Model's transition theory. We may picture it this way

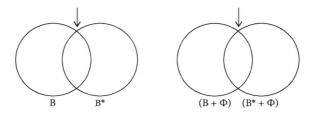

**Figure 6.1**

Adding Φ to here and then updating ≠ What you find here

It is easy to see that rational shift-in-view does not work this way. Just consider a case about Canada and its speakers.

*The Canada Case*

Let **B** equal the belief set got from the consequences of (i) and (ii):

(i)   99% of Canadians speak English and not French.
(ii)  Montreal is in Canada.

Let **B*** equal the belief set got from the consequences of (i), (ii), and (iii):

(iii)  50% of Montreal Canadians speak French and not English.

Now let P be the claim that Pierre is a Montreal Canadian. Obviously, the intersection of **B** and **B*** is **B** itself:

(a)   $(\mathbf{B} \cap \mathbf{B}^*) = \mathbf{B}$.

So the expansion of each by P must yield the same state:

(b)   $[(\mathbf{B} \cap \mathbf{B}^*) + P] = (\mathbf{B} + P)$.

But let E be the claim that Pierre speaks English and not French.

Intuitively, E belongs to (B+P). If one starts out rational, believes (i) and (ii) and their consequences, and nothing else relevant to the case, then, by coming to believe merely that Pierre is a Montreal Canadian (i.e. P), one should also come to believe that Pierre speaks English and not French. That is why E belongs to the expansion of **B** by P. In symbols, that is why

(c)  $E \in (\mathbf{B} + P)$.

But claim (c) and (b) together ensure

(d)  $E \in [(\mathbf{B} \cap \mathbf{B}^*) + P]$.

After all, claim (b) insists that the epistemic state got from expanding **B** by P is itself identical to the one got by expanding what's in common to **B** and **B*** by P. It follows from this thought and (c) that E belongs to the overall state got by expanding what's in common to **B** and **B*** by P, i.e. it follows that claim (d) is true.

On the other hand, it is obvious that E will *fail* to be in the expansion of **B*** by P. If one starts out with fully rational belief in (i), (ii) *and* (iii), plus their consequences, and nothing else relevant to the case, then, by coming to believe that Pierre is a Montreal Canadian—i.e. by coming to believe P—one should *not* end-up believing that Pierre speaks English and not French. That is why E will not belong to the expansion of **B*** by P, i.e. why the following claim is true

(e)  $E \notin (\mathbf{B}^* + P)$.

But this claim entails that E cannot be in the intersection of a set **X** and (**B***+P). After all, to be in the intersection of two sets **X** and **Y**, a claim must start out in both **X** and **Y**. Claim (e) insists that E is not in the expansion of **B*** by P; so it cannot be in the intersection of that expansion and something else. For any set at all **X**, therefore, we have the following:

$$E \notin [\mathbf{X} \cap (\mathbf{B}^* + P)],$$

which guarantees that this claim is true:

(f)  $E \notin [(\mathbf{B} + P) \cap (\mathbf{B}^* + P)]$.

Thus we find a counter-example to the Sad Consequence mentioned earlier:

(⊗)  $[(\mathbf{B} \cap \mathbf{B}^*) + P] = [(\mathbf{B} + P) \cap (\mathbf{B}^* + P)]$.

This consequence of the expansion postulates is not right. It does not mark an aspect of rational expansion of belief. We know by claim (d) that E belongs to the left side of (⊗), and by claim (f) that E does not belong to the right side of (⊗). It follows that the left- and right-sides of (⊗) are not the same: the former contains the belief that Pierre speaks English and not French, the latter does not. The Belief Model expansion postulates entail mistakenly that these epistemic states are identical. Hence the Canada Case shows that the model's expansion goes wrong, placing mistaken demands on rational expansion. Or in other words: the model's transition theory mischaracterizes rational shift-in-view from suspended judgement to belief.

Moreover, the Canada Case makes clear *where* Belief Model expansion postulates go wrong. The case points to a major flaw in those postulates. Consider the main moving parts in the case:

(i) 99% of Canadians speak English and not French.
(ii) Montreal is in Canada.
(iii) 50% of Montreal Canadians speak French and not English.
P = The proposition that Pierre is a Montreal Canadian.
E = The proposition that Pierre speaks English and not French.

A fully rational agent who accepts (i), (ii), and P—but nothing else relevant to the issues at hand—thereby has enough information rationally to accept E. A fully rational agent who believes (i), (ii), P and (iii), however—but nothing else relevant to the issues at hand—does *not* thereby have enough information rationally to accept E. Yet the second fully rational agent has all the information possessed by the first fully rational agent, plus further information relevant to the issue at hand. But the extra information had by the second fully rational agent itself undermines information used by the first agent to accept E. That is why the second agent should not join the first in accepting E.

Think of it this way. The following is a perfectly rational line of thought:

'99% of Canadians speak English and not French; Montreal is in Canada; Pierre comes from Montreal; no other information to hand seems relevant. Conclusion: Pierre speaks English and not French.'

But the following is *not* a rational line of thought:

'99% of Canadians speak English and not French; Montreal is in Canada; Pierre comes from Montreal; 50% of Montreal Canadians speak French and not English; nothing else to hand seems relevant. Conclusion: Pierre speaks English and not French.'

What the Canada Case shows is that good reckoning isn't like logical proof.

Here's why: good reckoning can be spoilt by the introduction of new information which is logically consistent with information to hand. Logical proof cannot be spoilt in that way. If a conclusion C is established logically by premises $P_1 \ldots P_n$, then, that conclusion is established logically from those premises together with any further information added to them. A fortiori C is established logically from the premises in question plus information which doesn't conflict with those premises.

This is very important. The key fact here can be unearthed by considering two arguments:

|     | (A) |     | (B) |
| --- | --- | --- | --- |
| 1a | *All* Texans have a Texas accent. | 1b | *Most* Texans have a Texas accent. |
| 2 | Guido's a Texan | 2 | Guido's a Texan |
| C | ∴ Guido has a Texas accent. | C | ∴ Guido has a Texas accent. |

THE BELIEF MODEL'S TRANSITION THEORY   193

The two arguments share a conclusion, of course, and each of them provides intuitive support for that shared conclusion. But the two arguments support their conclusion in strikingly different ways. The premises of argument (A) link to the conclusion C in what we might term 'an unbreakable way', while the premises of argument (B) do not do anything like that. It is possible to expand (B)-premises with new information—adding nothing which makes for logical conflict—yet break the overall argumentative support for conclusion C. That would happen were you to learn, for instance, that Guido was not raised in Texas but in some place with a differing kind of accent. Although (B)'s premises do support C, they allow for consistent expansion which wipes out that support. (A)'s premises do not allow for this sort of wipe-out. They logically support C no matter how they are expanded.

Think of it this way. Suppose you build a column of claims. First you list a set of claims S and then draw a line under those claims. Then under that line you list S's logical consequences L(S). Next you build a new column just to the right, only this time you start with the members of S plus a new claim N, drawing a line under the embellished collection of premises. Under that new line you then list the logical consequences of the expansion of S by N. Since that expansion contains everything in S, you are guaranteed that everything below your first line appears below your second, i.e. you are guaranteed that L(S+N) contains L(S)

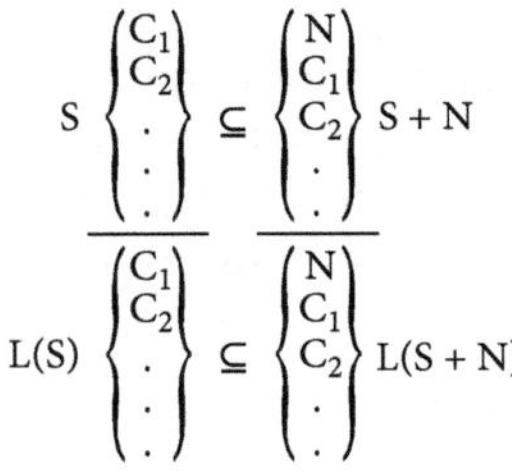

$$S \begin{Bmatrix} C_1 \\ C_2 \\ \vdots \end{Bmatrix} \subseteq \begin{Bmatrix} N \\ C_1 \\ C_2 \\ \vdots \end{Bmatrix} S+N$$

$$L(S) \begin{Bmatrix} C_1 \\ C_2 \\ \vdots \end{Bmatrix} \subseteq \begin{Bmatrix} N \\ C_1 \\ C_2 \\ \vdots \end{Bmatrix} L(S+N)$$

**Figure 6.2**

Rational expansion of opinion is not generally like that. Start a column with a set of premises S, draw a line and then list what is rationally supported by S (either logically or non-logically). Then start a new column with the members of (S+N). There will be no guarantee that what is below your first line appears below your second

$$S \begin{Bmatrix} \Phi_1 \\ \Phi_2 \\ \vdots \end{Bmatrix} \subseteq \begin{Bmatrix} N \\ \Phi_1 \\ \Phi_2 \\ \vdots \end{Bmatrix} I(S+N)$$

$$I(S) \begin{Bmatrix} I_1 \\ I_2 \\ \vdots \end{Bmatrix} \text{...?...} \begin{Bmatrix} \Delta_1 \\ \Delta_2 \\ \vdots \end{Bmatrix}$$

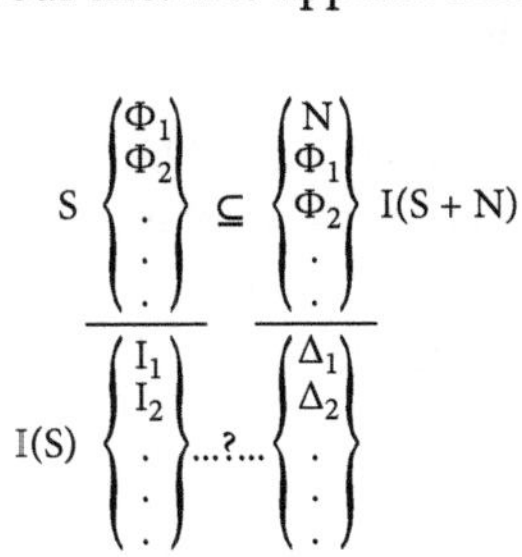

**Figure 6.3**

As one says in this area of inquiry, logical proof is *strictly increasing* (aka *monotonic*).[7] Intuitively this means that one never has to retract something logically proved simply because one has added information to one's premises. But we have seen that rational expansion of opinion is not strictly increasing: it is *non*-monotonic.

We can make this precise in the following way. Let us say that

a rule for shift-in-view **R** is *strictly increasing* (or *monotonic*) $=_{df.}$ when a belief set **B** is contained in another **B***, then, for any information I, the result of **R**-revising **B** by I is itself contained in the result of **R**-revising **B*** by I.

In other words, a rule for fully rational shift-in-view is strictly increasing when its picture appears this way

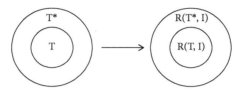

**Figure 6.4**

Belief Model expansion is strictly increasing. In this respect it works like logical proof. But rational expansion of opinion is not strictly increasing. As the Canada Case makes clear—and countless others like it—rational movement from suspended judgement to belief is a non-strictly-increasing process.

This is our first major lesson about the transition theory for coarse-grained attitudes:

*Lesson 1:*   Rational expansion is non-monotonic.

This conflicts with the fifth expansion postulate of the Belief Model's transition theory:

(+5)   If everything in **B** is also in **B***, then everything in (**B**+P) is also in (**B***+P)

But that doesn't seem right at all. Rational expansion does not intuitively work like logical proof. Sometimes when expanding rationally one has to *take things back*; and that is true even when new information is compatible with information already in one's possession.

For this reason, rational expansion is not like logical proof: it is non-monotonic rather than strictly increasing. Rationally accepting something about which you were previously neutral can oblige shrinkage as well as inflation of opinion. After all, new information can override old information. This is sometimes put by saying that

---

[7] The monotonicity of a function turns on whether it preserves the inclusion relation. An arithmetical function of natural numbers, for instance, is monotonic when the following is true: whenever a set of natural numbers S is a subset of another set of natural numbers S*, the set got by applying f to S's members is itself a subset of the set got by applying f to S*'s members.

new information can 'defeat' old information, and that's why fully rational expansion is sometimes called a 'defeasible' process. The Belief Model's transition theory mistakenly treats it as an indefeasible process.

How might a defender the model push back against this sort of criticism?

Well, he cannot disallow critique of the Belief Model's transition theory based on thought experiment or intuition. Discussion exactly like that surrounding our Canada Case was used by proponents of the Belief Model to motivate its postulates in the first place. Consider the follow proposal about rational expansion:

(*M)  If $B_1 \subseteq B_2$, then $(B_1 {}^*P) \subseteq (B_2 {}^*P)$.

This rule echoes the Belief Model's postulate (+5), a postulate heartily endorsed by Gärdenfors. But just as (+5) insists that fully rational shift-in-view—from suspended judgement to belief—is itself monotonic, (*M) insists that fully rational shift from rejection to belief, or vice versa, is likewise monotonic. Gärdenfors accepts the first of these ideas but rejects the second. Yet his reason for rejecting (*M) is like ours for rejecting (+5). He constructs thought-experiments to put pressure on the idea that revisions are monotonic.[8] Of course I agree that this can be done: strong intuition about particular cases indicates clearly that fully rational revision is not like logical proof. It is non-monotonic or defeasible. By similar reasoning, however, strong intuition about situations like the Canada Case shows clearly that fully rational expansion is likewise non-monotonic or defeasible. Postulate (+5) is plainly wrong.

Here is a final way to see the bother. Recall the third and fourth postulate for rational revision:

(*3)  Everything in (B*P) is also in (B+P)
(*4)  If ¬P is not in B, then everything in (B+P) is also in (B*P)

As Gärdenfors notes, Postulates for revision jointly entail

(g)  When   $\neg P \notin B$, (B*P) = (B+P).

By the time Gärdenfors gets around to proving this in his book, however, he's already proved that Belief Model expansion is monotonic! His overall position is thus committed to the view that all counter-examples to (*M) occur when the epistemic shift of opinion involves accepting something previously rejected. Why on Earth should *that* be? So far as I can see there is no rhyme nor reason to this constellation of commitments. We need a better theory of rational shift in coarse-grained attitudes.

Recall the guiding ideas behind the Belief Model transition theory:

- When shifting view, don't give up something unless forced to by logic;
- When shifting view, don't take on something unless forced to by logic;
- Whenever possible, measure the 'size' of what is given up or taken on by inclusion relations between belief sets.

---

[8] (Gärdenfors 1988: 59ff).

None of these ideas is correct. Often a fully rational agent should give up a belief consistent with all else she believes, often she should accept things not entailed by her new information, and minimal epistemic disturbance should definitely *not* be seen through the lens of logic and/or set theory.

At bottom the Belief Model transition theory is meant to capture something like 'purely logical' constraints on rational shift-in-view. But there is basically no reason to suppose that there *are* purely logical constraints on rational shift-in-view. The underlying assumptions of the theory seem deeply flawed.

# 7
# Conditional Commitment and the Ramsey Test

## 7.1 Linking Theory and Conditional Commitment

As we saw in Chapter 1, formal models of rationality tend to instantiate a single theoretical form

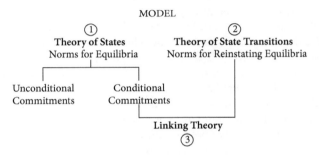

Figure 7.1

As this map makes clear there are three major moving parts to full-dress epistemic theory. One is a theory of states describing how rational commitments are to be configured in equilibrium. One is a transition theory describing how epistemic states are to change when equilibria are perturbed by input. And one is a linking theory which forges connections between the model's theory of states and its transition theory.

A running theme throughout formal epistemology is that conditional commitment is central to linking theory. This chapter discusses some well-known technical problems which arise when that theme is made precise in various ways. Specifically, we shall look at technical Bombshells deriving from the work of Peter Gärdenfors and the work of David Lewis. The former makes mischief for orthodox linking theory within the formal epistemology of belief. The latter makes mischief for such theory within the formal epistemology of credence. Eventually we'll question the main idea underneath the entire discussion, and we'll suggest that there is no deep tie between conditional commitment and rational shift-in-view.

*The Rational Mind.* Scott Sturgeon, Oxford University Press (2020). © Scott Sturgeon.
DOI: 10.1093/oso/9780198845799.001.0001

## 7.2 The Issue

Consider the following sentence frame:

Obama lends attitude A to the claim that —.

Now fill it with an indicative conditional, something like

If Putin eats an Apple, he'll drink a Coke.

The result is

Obama lends attitude A to the claim that if Putin eats an Apple, he'll drink a Coke.

What makes something like this true? What sort of facts are marked by instances of our initial sentence frame?

In one sense the answer is obvious: facts about attitudes are so marked. We have seen, though, that in formal epistemology there are competing schools of thought when it comes to epistemic attitudes; and this rides atop the fact that common sense thinks of such attitudes in two very different ways. On the one hand it sees them as a three-part affair: belief, disbelief, and suspended judgement. This way of thinking about epistemic attitudes is decidedly *coarse-grained*. On the other hand common-sense sees them as much more subtle: 'How strong is your faith?' can be apposite between believers, after all, something which signals that ordinary practice also treats epistemic attitudes as a fine-grained affair. This is what happens when we speak of confidence and make use of a fine-grained conception of the attitudes. There are two ways, then, that such attitudes are seen in everyday life: coarse-grained and fine-grained.

Both of these conceptions are used in formal treatments of rationality. When the attitudes are viewed in the coarse-grained way an agent's overall epistemic state is normally modelled by a *set of sentences* (as we saw with the Belief Model). Sets like this are said to codify what an agent believes; and rationality is then modelled by constraints on them as well as shifts between them. When the attitudes are viewed in a fine-grained way, however, an agent's overall epistemic state is normally modelled by a *probability function* (as we saw with the Bayesian model). Functions like this are said to measure how much one lends confidence; and rationality is then modelled by constraints on the functions as well as shifts between them. This Janus-faced approach spills over to work on the attitude-frame with which we began. We really face two questions about it not one: what are its truth-makers when the attitudes are viewed in a coarse-grained way? and what are its truth-makers when the attitudes are viewed in a fine-grained way?

The most influential remark on this comes in a footnote by F. P. Ramsey:

If two people are arguing 'If p will q?' and are both in doubt as to p, they are adding p hypothetically to their stock of knowledge and are arguing on that basis about q.

(1929: 143)

Both coarse- and fine-grained epistemology take inspiration from this passage. Both of them find in it a so-called 'Ramsey Test' for (indicative) conditionals. This Test is meant to say what it is (or at least when one should) believe a conditional or lend it a certain level of confidence.

In making theirs precise, however, both coarse- and fine-grained epistemology are hit with technical Bombshells. Peter Gärdenfors used one Ramsey Test to derive absurdity within coarse-grained epistemology; and David Lewis used another to do so within fine-grained epistemology.[1] This makes one wonder: why do such Tests lead to trouble? Why do they generate conflict within precision epistemology? What is the underlying assumption about conditional commitment, if any, which leads to Gärdenfors' result when Ramsey is read in the coarse-grained way and Lewis' result when he's read in the fine-grained way? That will be our question. Now for its background.

## 7.3 The Coarse-Grained Bombshell

Suppose we model epistemic attitudes with sentences, representing the overall epistemic state of an agent with a set of them. Then our model will be a *theory* in the old-fashioned sense of 'theory', and within this framework the Ramsey Test will become:

(A→C) belongs to an agent's theory T iff    C belongs to the minimal revision of
                                             T induced by the addition of A.

The basic idea here is that a rational agent believes a conditional (A→C) when its consequent, C, belongs to the minimal perturbation of her overall view brought on by the introduction of its antecedent: A. This is not only a coarse-grained take on Ramsey's idea it is a *belief-revision* take as well. The indented biconditional spells out the Ramsey Test by appeal to the idea of a 'minimal revision' of an agent's theory or worldview.

Let **min-rev** be a function which so revises belief sets. The coarse-grained Ramsey Test is then

(RT)    (A→C) belongs to an agent's theory T    iff    C belongs to **min-rev**(T by A).

Of course it is not yet clear what **min-rev** comes to, but it turns out that we need just two assumptions about it to set off Gärdenfors' Bombshell. One is a principle of Contradiction Avoidance;

(CA)    If an agent's theory T is self-consistent, and her input I is too, then **min-rev**(T by I) is likewise self-consistent.

The other is a principle of Epistemic Conservatism;

(EC)    If an agent's theory T contains Φ, and her input I doesn't conflict with Φ, then **min-rev**(T by I) contains Φ as well.

The first principle aims to capture the idea that rational agents do not endorse contradictions unless they are forced to do so. The second principle aims to capture the idea that rational agents do not throw out information unless prompted to do so.

---

[1] (Gärdenfors, 1986) and (Lewis, 1976). See also (Bennett, 2003), (Edgington, 1995), and (Edgington, 2014) for discussion.

200  CONDITIONAL COMMITMENT AND THE RAMSEY TEST

With these resources Gärdenfors dropped a Bombshell on the formal epistemology of coarse-grained attitudes. Through a complex derivation he showed that its Ramsey Test—together with Contradiction Avoidance and Epistemic Conservatism—leads to absurdity. In particular, he showed these elements generate contradictory predictions about belief revision. But he did not diagnose why. We'll do so in §7.5.

## 7.4 The Fine-Grained Bombshell

Suppose we model confidence with a probability function and see the overall epistemic state of a rational agent as measured by one. Within this framework the fine-grained Ramsey Test says that when **cr**(A) is nonzero:

$$(R_tT) \qquad \mathbf{cr}(A \rightarrow C) = \mathbf{cr}(C/A).$$

The basic idea is that a rational agent lends credence to (A→C) which matches in strength the conditional credence she has for C given A. In other words, for rational agents indicative credence is equal to conditional credence. This is a fine-grained take on what Ramsey had in mind; and in the Bayesian model it likewise yields an internal connection between conditional commitment and rational shift in view. But this takes some explaining.

The fine-grained epistemology used by Lewis says that one should update credence in C after learning A by the rule known as *Conditionalization* (C).[2] This rule runs the update process off the right-hand side of the fine-grained Ramsey Test ($R_tT$). The resulting picture agrees with the coarse-grained model in thinking that for rational agents, at least, commitment to the indicative conditional (A→C) aligns with the upshot of rational shift-in-view. Specifically, it aligns with how one should view C after learning A. But there is a difference in the coarse- and fine-grained approaches when it comes to their update rules. The former uses **min-rev** and the latter uses Conditionalization.

There's an easy way to picture the latter update rule, one which proves useful in diagnosing Lewis' Bombshell. To see it suppose you've got a marble for each 'percent of credence' you have to lend; and you distribute your marbles this way (so to say).

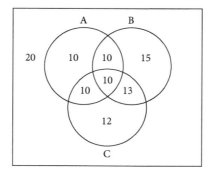

Figure 7.2

---

[2] See §4.6 for an explanation of how this rule relates to Jeffrey's.

Think of the box as logical space and its points as possible worlds. Then circles collect worlds at which propositions are true, and they partition logical space into mutually exclusive and jointly exhaustive cells (which correspond, of course, to lines in a three letter truth-table). Numerals within each cell show your spread of credence for the conjunctive proposition which corresponds to the cell. And they indicate, among other things, that you see four ways that A might be true: with B and C, with neither, and with just one of them. The numerals also show that within A-worlds you see only symmetry:

$$cr(A\&B\&C) = cr(A\&\neg B\&\neg C) = cr(A\&B\&\neg C) = cr(A\&\neg B\&C) = 10\%.$$

You're 40% sure A will happen, 60% sure it won't.

Suppose you rationally become certain that A is true, but nothing else changes in your epistemic commitments. Then you have gone from an equilibrium state to one of disequilibrium. Conditionalization says, in effect, that in these circumstances you should regain equilibrium by adopting the overall position most like the one you started with consistent with certainty for A. Intuitively, this means you should scoop-up credence lent to ¬A, distribute it within A-worlds, and preserve the credal symmetry with which you began. The easiest way to picture this is to lop off the non-A bit of Figure 7.2 and reinterpret the marbles. In other words: zoom in on the A-bit of Figure 7.2

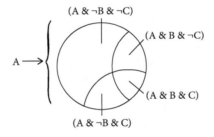

**Figure 7.3**

Now we have 40 marbles in our model rather than 100, so each marble now represents l/40th of the credence you can lend rather than 1/100th. Note also that your new credal distribution preserves symmetry within A: your old credence lent equal weight to four ways that A might be true, and your new credence distribution does too, for it says this about the credence you have upon learning A for sure:

$$cr_A(A\&B\&C) = cr_A(A\&\neg B\&\neg C) = cr_A(A\&B\&\neg C) = cr_A(A\&\neg B\&C) = 25\%.$$

Pictorially, then, Conditionalization is a 'zoom in' rule of credence revision. It takes a credence distribution as input and yields another as output, with the output focused on one of the original distribution's cells; and the new distribution is got by zooming in on the cell which corresponds in the old distribution to what is learned for sure. Conditionalizing on A is thus the minimal way to become certain that A without disrupting prior-to-learning credal structure within the A-zone of one's initial epistemic space.[3]

Thus it is that Bayesian fine-grained epistemology has a credal-revision take on Ramsey. It marks a rational agent's view of (A→C) by her view of C after doing no more nor less than zooming in on the A-portion of her initial epistemic space. With these resources, however, David Lewis dropped a Bombshell on the resulting epistemology of fine-grained epistemic commitment. Through a complex derivation he showed that the fine-grained Ramsey Test and Conditionalization lead to absurdity: in particular, they are consistent only if credence is utterly trivial (in a way we'll explain). But Lewis did not diagnose why he arrived at his Bombshell. We shall do so in §7.6. Before that we turn our diagnostic attention to the coarse-grained difficulty.

## 7.5 Diagnosing Gärdenfor's Bombshell

The key to this explosion is a technical property of belief revision emphasized in Chapter 5. We can unearth it by considering two arguments:

| (A) | (B) |
|---|---|
| 1a *All* Texans have a Texas accent. | 1b *Most* Texans have a Texas accent. |
| 2   Fred is a Texan. | 2   Fred is a Texan. |
| C   ∴ Fred has a Texas accent. | C   ∴ Fred has a Texas accent. |

The arguments share a conclusion which they both intuitively support. But the arguments support their shared conclusion in rather different ways. The premises of (A) link to C in an 'unbreakable' way. Those of (B) do not. You can supplement the latter with new information, add nothing which makes for conflict, yet break the (B)-style support for the shared conclusion C. That would happen were you to add to (B)'s premises that Fred was not raised in Texas (say). Although (B)'s premises do support C, they allow for consistent supplementation which wipes out that support. (A)'s premises do not permit this sort of supplementation. They support the shared conclusion C no matter how they're embellished.

Think of it this way. Suppose you build a column of claims. First you list a set of claims S, then you draw a line under which you list S's logical consequences L(S). Next you build a new column just to the right, but this time you start with S plus a new claim N. Then you draw a line under which you list the logical consequences of (S+N). Since (S+N) contains S, you're guaranteed that L(S+N) contains L(S). You're guaranteed everything below your first line appears below your second (Figure 7.4).

Induction isn't like that. To see why start a column of claims S, draw a line underneath it, then list whatever is inductively supported by the claims in S. Now start a new column with everything in S plus a new claim N: (S+N). There will be no guarantee that inductively supported claims I(S+N) contain in the inductively supported claims I(S). There will be no guarantee that what is below your first line will also appear below your second (Figure 7.5).

---

[3] §4.8. explains how Jeffrey Conditionalization is likewise motivated, and how to use that motivation to create an update rule for when conditional credence is the contact-point of rational shift-in-view.

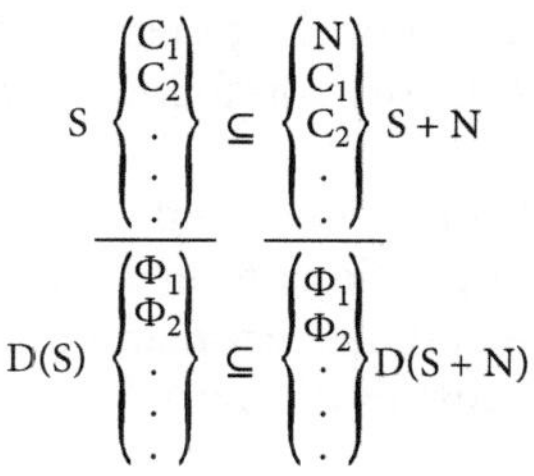

$$S \left\{\begin{matrix} C_1 \\ C_2 \\ . \\ . \\ . \end{matrix}\right\} \subseteq \left\{\begin{matrix} N \\ C_1 \\ C_2 \\ . \\ . \end{matrix}\right\} S+N$$

$$D(S) \left\{\begin{matrix} \Phi_1 \\ \Phi_2 \\ . \\ . \\ . \end{matrix}\right\} \subseteq \left\{\begin{matrix} \Phi_1 \\ \Phi_2 \\ . \\ . \\ . \end{matrix}\right\} D(S+N)$$

**Figure 7.4**

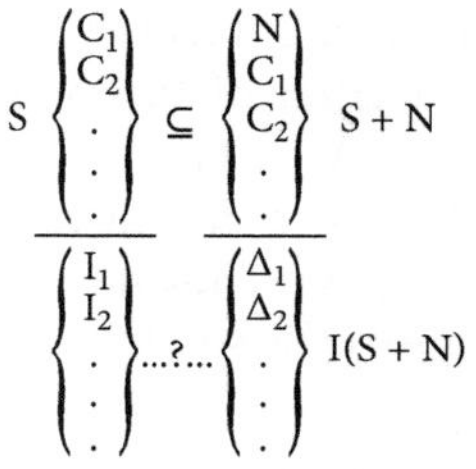

$$S \left\{\begin{matrix} C_1 \\ C_2 \\ . \\ . \\ . \end{matrix}\right\} \subseteq \left\{\begin{matrix} N \\ C_1 \\ C_2 \\ . \\ . \end{matrix}\right\} S+N$$

$$\left\{\begin{matrix} I_1 \\ I_2 \\ . \\ . \\ . \end{matrix}\right\} ...?... \left\{\begin{matrix} \Delta_1 \\ \Delta_2 \\ . \\ . \\ . \end{matrix}\right\} I(S+N)$$

**Figure 7.5**

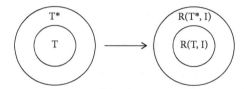

**Figure 7.6**

This is a basic difference between induction and deduction. It proves the key to Gärdenfors' Bombshell. Let's say

A revision rule **R** is *strictly increasing* $=_{df.}$ when theory T is contained in theory T*, R(T by I) is contained in R(T* by I).

In other words, update rule **R** is strictly increasing when its picture appears as in Figure 7.6. Deduction is strictly increasing, induction is not.

Now recall the coarse-grained Ramsey Test:

(RT)   (A→C) belongs to an agent's theory T iff   C belongs to **min-rev**(T by A).

It says, in effect, that a rational agent is disposed to infer C upon learning A exactly when her theory *marks* the inferential disposition. More specifically, the coarse-grained Ramsey Test says that a rational agent is so disposed when her theory marks the disposition with the indicative conditional (A→C). That is tantamount to the idea that update dispositions are *part* of her overall epistemic state. And it turns out that *that*, somewhat surprisingly, guarantees that belief revision is strictly increasing.

If inferential dispositions are part of one's epistemic state—if they are even so much as marked somehow in one's theory—it follows that belief revision works like deduction rather than induction.

To see this, suppose theory T is contained within theory T*. (RT) then ensures that T uses conditionals to mark dispositions to endorse claims on the basis of input. Since T* contains T, it follows that those very marks are in T* too. Hence a claim is in **min-rev**(T by I) only if it's in **min-rev**(T* by I). We have

Fact 1: The coarse-grained Ramsey Test (**RT**) implies that the minimal-revision function **min-rev** is strictly increasing, i.e. that it works like deduction rather than induction.

*Proof.* Suppose theory T is included in theory T* and claim C is in **min-rev**(T by A). The right-to-left direction of the coarse-grained Ramsey Test (**RT**) ensures that the indicative (A→C) is in T. Since T is included in T*, though, (A→C) is in T* as well. Hence the left-to-right direction of (**RT**) ensures that C is in **min-rev**(T* by A). Thus **min-rev**(T by A) is included in **min-rev**(T* by A). Hence **min-rev** is strictly increasing. ∎

*Comment.* The proof relies on nothing more than the idea that one's epistemic state includes two-place updating dispositions. It does not rely on the idea those dispositions are part of one's *theory*, that something one accepts marks them. It just needs the thought that one's epistemic state *includes* two-place updating dispositions (however managed).

To see this, suppose we model epistemic states with sentences. This time, though, we embellish our sets of sentences with two-place updating dispositions. We say that an epistemic state E is a combination of sentences and such dispositions. The former codify what one believes, and the latter mark tendencies to endorse specific claims on the basis of specific input. E will then look this way:

$$E = \{T + D\}.$$

T will be the worldview of those in epistemic state E, and D will be the two-place updating dispositions of those in that epistemic state. Moreover, we now can say that epistemic state E is included in epistemic state E* exactly when two things happen: T is included in E*'s worldview T*, and D is included in E*'s disposition set D*. Now, suppose we endorse the Ramsey-like view

(**RT**)* Inferential disposition D(A,C) belongs to an agent's epistemic state E iff C belongs to **rev**(the T in E by A).

Then we can show that the revision rule **rev** is strictly increasing; and the proof goes just as before:

*Proof:* Suppose E is included in E* and C is in **rev**(the T in E by A). The right-to-left direction of (**RT**)* ensures that D(A,C) is part of E. Since E is included in E*, it follows that D(A,C) is in E* too. Hence the left-to-right direction of (**RT**)* ensures that C is in **rev**(the T* in E* by A). Thus **rev**(the T in E by A) is included in **rev**(the T* in E* by A), **rev** is strictly increasing. ∎

In a nutshell: (**RT**)* entails that the revision rule **rev** works like deduction. So the take-home lesson is stark: rational inductive update requires that updating dispositions be *ternary*. It obliges them in essence to be relativized to one's background theory. It turns out that this lesson can be used to block Gärdenfors' Bombshell, so let's get that Bombshell on the table and then see how it can be blocked.

Recall the other two constraints placed on the minimal-revision function **min-rev** by Gärdenfors. We had the contradiction avoidance principle

(CA) If an agent's theory T is self-consistent, and her input I is too, then **min-rev**(T by I) is likewise self-consistent.

And we had the epistemic conservatism principle

(EC) If an agent's theory T contains Φ, and her input I doesn't conflict with Φ, then **min-rev**(T by I) contains Φ as well.

These principles jointly imply that **min-rev** is *not* strictly increasing, that minimal revision works like induction. That is why putting the two principles with the coarse-grained Ramsey Test sets off a technical explosion.

To see how this works, suppose three guys are walking down a road. They come to a three-way fork

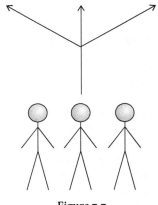

**Figure 7.7**

Leftie then thinks: 'Either we're going left or down the middle.' Rightie then thinks: 'Either we're going right or down the middle.' And Middleman thinks: 'We're going down the middle.' These are super-boring guys, but they are also super-logical: they think only these thoughts and whatever follows from them. Note each fellow ends up with a consistent view, and that Middleman's view *contains* both Leftie's and Rightie's. After all, Middleman's view logically implies Leftie's view—since going down the middle entails either going left or down the middle—and it logically implies Rightie's view as well—since going down the middle entails going right or down the middle. But consider what happens when an Oracle they all trust says that Middleman is wrong, i.e. that they are not going down the middle path. How should our heroes update on the news?

Well, the new information is internally consistent; and all three of our heroes began with a self-consistent view. Contradiction Avoidance thus insists that their views should remain self-consistent after taking on board that Middleman is wrong in initially thinking that they will go down the middle. Yet the Oracle's new information is compatible with both Leftie's and Rightie's initial take on things. Epistemic Conservatism thus insists that they *add* what the Oracle's says to their extant stock of beliefs. Logic then leads them in opposite directions (as it were). Leftie thinks: 'We're going left'; and Rightie thinks: 'We're not going left.' Since Middleman's view must remain consistent after revision, his revised view *cannot* contain both Leftie's and Rightie's, since theirs now conflict with one another. Although Middleman began with a view which contained that of his cohorts, after revision Middleman can no longer hold a consistent view which does so. Thus we have

**Fact 2:** (CA) & (EC) imply **min-rev** is *not* strictly increasing.[4]

It turns out, then, that Gärdenfors' Bombshell has a simple source: Contradiction Avoidance, Epistemic Conservatism and the coarse-grained Ramsey Test place inconsistent demands on minimal belief revision. The first two jointly force it to deflate as well as expand, like good induction. The last principle forbids deflation, like good deduction.

## 7.6 Diagnosing Lewis' Bombshell

The key to this explosion is the Bayesian update rule of Conditionalization. Recall that it's a zoom-in rule of revision. Suppose you start with a distribution of credence as in Figure 7.8. Conditioning on A amounts to zooming in on the A-portion of epistemic space without disrupting its internal structure. Conditioning on B amounts to zooming in on the B-portion of epistemic space without disrupting its internal structure. And so forth. Hence conditioning on A *and then* conditioning on B yields the same thing as conditioning *once* on (A & B). After all: zooming in on the A-portion of epistemic space—without disrupting anything internal to it—and then zooming in on the B-portion of epistemic space—without disrupting anything internal to it—should yield the same thing as zooming in once on the (A & B)-portion of epistemic space—again without disrupting anything internal to that portion of space. Pictorially put: lopping

---

[4] A bit more formally: Let A be a contingent proposition. Consider three theories: T1 = {the consequences of A}, T2 = {the consequences of (A v C)}, and T3 = {the consequences of (A v ¬C). T2 and T3 are included in T1. Consider the minimal revision of each by ¬A. Since ¬A is consistent with (A v C), Epistemic Conservatism ensures that both claims are in **min-rev**(T2 by ¬A). So C is in **min-rev**(T2 by ¬A) too. Similarly: ¬A is consistent with (Av¬C). So Epistemic Conservatism ensures that both claims are in **min-rev**(T3 by ¬A). Hence ¬C is in **min-rev**(T3 by ¬A). Yet Contradiction Avoidance implies the minimal revision of T1, T2 and T3 by ¬A are each consistent. So it *can't* be that **min-rev**(T2 by ¬A) and **min-rev**(T3 by ¬A) are each included in **min-rev**(T1 by ¬A). That would mean C and ¬C are both in **min-rev**(T1 by ¬A), in conflict with Contradiction Avoidance, so **min-rev** is *not* strictly increasing.

off the non-A bit of Figure 7.8 and then lopping off the non-B bit of the result should yield the same thing as lopping of the non-(A & B) bit of the original figure. Either way the result is as shown in Figure 7.9.

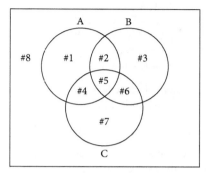

Figure 7.8

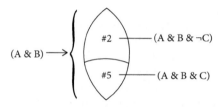

Figure 7.9

This is a key fact about Conditionalization. Running the process twice over lands you in the same place as running it once on a related conjunction.

Now recall the fine-grained Ramsey Test.

$R_f T$  $\qquad$ $\mathbf{cr}(A \rightarrow C) = \mathbf{cr}(C/A)$.

This view and Conditionalization jointly entail, in effect, that the conditional (A→C) *marks within* cr(-) the view of C taken in the new credence distribution which should be adopted after learning A for certain. In other words, the fine-grained Ramsey Test plus Conditionalization jointly entail that indicatives mark within a rational agent's credence distribution the attitude taken to its consequent once equilibrium has been regained after the agent has become certain of its antecedent. Of course this is because ($R_f T$)'s right-hand side is the item used by Conditionalization to pin down one's take on C after learning A for certain.

We've just seen, though, that two applications of Conditionalization end up equal to one application on a related conjunction. The fine-grained Ramsey Test and Conditionalization thus jointly imply that when cr(A & B) is non-zero:

**Fact 3:** $cr[A \rightarrow (B \rightarrow C)] = cr[(A \& B) \rightarrow C]$.

*Proof:* Suppose $(R_*T)$, (C) and $cr(A \& B)$ is non-zero. Then

$$\begin{aligned}
cr[A \rightarrow (B \rightarrow C)] &= cr[(B \rightarrow C)/A] & \text{by } (R_*T) \\
&= cr_A(B \rightarrow C) & \text{by (C)} \\
&= cr_A(C/B) & \text{by } (R_*T) \\
&= cr[(C \& B)/A] \div cr(B/A) & \text{by (C)} \\
&= cr[C \& B \& A] \div cr(B \& A) & \text{by algebra} \\
&= cr[C/(A \& B)] \\
&= cr[(A \& B) \rightarrow C] & \text{by } (R_*T). \blacksquare
\end{aligned}$$

As we saw in Chapter 4, though, Fact 3 is a probabilistic analogue of the so-called Import-Export law for indicative conditionals:

$$[A \rightarrow (B \rightarrow C)] \Leftrightarrow [(A \& B) \rightarrow C].$$

Allan Gibbard has shown how this latter rule entails that indicative conditionals have material truth-conditions, if they have truth-conditions at all.[5] His argument can be aped to show that the credal analogue of Import/Export—i.e. Fact 3—entails a credal analogue of Gibbard's result:

**Fact 4:** $cr(A \rightarrow C) = cr(A \supset C)$.

*Proof:* Assume $cr(A \& C)$ is non-zero. Since $(A \& C)$ is truth-functionally equivalent to $[(A \supset C) \& A]$, it follows that $cr[(A \supset C) \& A]$ is nonzero. An instance of Fact 3 is thus

$$cr[(A \supset C) \rightarrow (A \rightarrow C)] = cr\{[(A \supset C) \& A] \rightarrow C\}$$

Now apply $(R_*T)$ to both sides:

$$cr[(A \rightarrow C)/(A \supset C)] = cr\{C/[(A \supset C) \& A]\}.$$

The right-hand side of this equation is unity. Hence

$$cr[(A \rightarrow C) \& (A \supset C)] = cr(A \supset C).$$

This entails

$$cr(A \supset C) \leq cr(A \rightarrow C).$$

By $(R_*T)$, then,

$$cr(A \supset C) \leq cr(C/A).$$

Yet $cr(C/A)$ cannot exceed $cr(A \supset C)$. Hence

$$cr(A \rightarrow C) = cr(A \supset C). \blacksquare$$

In light of the fine-grained Ramsey Test, however, Fact 4 means

$$cr(C/A) = cr(A \supset C).$$

But recall that the Bayesian model insists that rational credence distributes like a probability function. It is simple fact about probability functions that whenever

$$cr(C/A) = cr(A \supset C),$$

one of two things happens. Either

(i) $cr(A) = 1$

---

[5] (Gibbard, 1981).

or

(ii) $cr(A\&\neg C) = 0$.

But that means that the function we are dealing with fails to spread across cells in a space like this

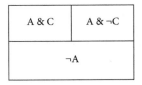

Figure 7.10

After all, if a probability-like credence function did spread across such cells, neither (i) nor (ii) would hold. Lending credence to ¬A would violate (i), lending credence to (A & ¬C) would violate (ii). In a nutshell, then, cr(-) must fail to spread across more than two disjoint cells built from A and C. Yet A and C were chosen at random. Hence we've shown

**Fact 5:** ($R_cT$) and (C) jointly imply that cr(-) carves epistemic space into less than three disjoint cells.

We can now explain Lewis' initial 'triviality' results. The fine-grained Ramsey Test plus Conditionalization together entail the credal analogue of Import/Export. This is what Fact 3 is all about. Yet Fact 3 ensures that conditional credence aligns with credence lent to material truth-conditions. The only way *that* can happen, however, is if credence spreads across less than three disjoint cells in epistemic space. That is why the fine-grained Ramsey Test and Conditionalization jointly lead to the absurd thought that epistemic space is trivial.

## 7.7 The Rumpus

Drawing all this together, we've seen that two precision epistemologies latch onto Ramsey's footnote, use it to forge a link between conditional commitment and shift-in-view, and run smack into trouble in the process. This suggests that there is no internal link from conditional commitment to shift-in-view—or vice versa—that the two phenomena are independent of one another. The technical difficulties we've rehearsed do not *prove* that this is so, of course; but they burden those who think otherwise by obliging an explanation which roots the source of the Bombshells without fingering a link between conditional commitment and shift-in-view. This holds for Ramsey Test loyalists in both the coarse- and fine-grained traditions.

But that is where the symmetry between them ends. To see why, recall the two Ramsey Tests before us:

(**RT**)  (A→C) belongs to an agent's theory T iff C belongs to **min-rev**(T by A).
($R_cT$)  $cr(A \to C) = cr(C/A)$.

The left-hand side of the coarse-grained Ramsey Test concerns belief in a conditional and its right-hand side concerns belief revision. The Test thus forges a direct link between indicative belief and shift-in-view. Nothing like that happens with the fine-grained Ramsey Test. Its left-hand side concerns credence lent to a conditional—called 'indicative credence' in the previous two chapters—but its right-hand side does not concern shift-in-view. Instead it concerns conditional credence. The link from such credence to shift-in-view—and thus from indicative credence to shift-in-view—is forged by something off-stage so far as the fine-grained Ramsey Test is concerned, namely, the update rule Conditionalization. For this reason, the fine-grained Ramsey Test sees no direct link from indicative credence to shift-in-view.

When hit with technical Bombshells, therefore, Ramsey Test loyalists enjoy differing lines of defence. Coarse-grained loyalists must drop the heart and soul of their view, since they see an explicit tie between indicative belief and shift-in-view. Defenders of the fine-grained Ramsey Test are in no such position, for they do not accept such a link in their Ramsey Test. On their view, there is at most an indirect link from indicative credence to shift-in-view, and, for this reason, technical Bombshells do not force them to drop the heart and soul of their Ramsey Test. They can simply reject presuppositions found in the reasoning which lead to the bother. In the next section we sketch how this might be done.

## 7.8 Conditionals and Lewis' Bombshell

A huge range of human practice can be usefully approached with two broad theoretical resources. The resources can be brought into focus by appeal to our capacity to think and speak of the world (and much else besides). In understanding this capacity, it is natural to make appeal to a certain kind of theoretical resource—a range of bespoke objects, say, or bespoke properties—the essence of which is to be or to determine or to code for *what* we can think and speak of. Theoretical resources in this neighbourhood go under many names in the literature: propositions, contents, senses, guises, modes of presentation. All of these theoretical gizmos are meant to help clarify *what*, exactly, we can think about, and *what*, exactly, we can talk about.[6]

A full understanding of our capacity to think and speak, however, requires more than a theoretical grip on what we can think and speak of. It also requires a view about how we engage with topics we can think and speak of. Minimally there is also a need to understand how we make use of the theoretical gizmos which help us make sense of what we can think and speak of. If we use a particular type of entity when dealing with the first issue—sets of possible worlds, for example—we'll also need to say something about what agents do with entities of that type (or at least what they are doing when they are usefully modelled with them). This is what the attitude-focused part of the theory of propositional attitudes is all about, for instance, and what the act-part of speech-act theory is too. In both cases the bit of theory before us specifies which states or acts of an agent are to be individuated by the gizmos which help us understand what we can think and speak of. It specifies the *arena* in which claims or contents or propositions do their work.

---

[6] For useful discussion of this see (Crane, 2001), (Schiffer, 1987) and (Schiffer, 2003), (Yablo, 2014).

In a nutshell, then, when theorizing about our capacity to think and speak of the world (and much else besides), part of our approach will answer a *what*-question—what can we think and/or speak of?—and part of our approach will answer a *where*-question—where in practice do we engage with whatever answers the what-question? When it comes to the theory of conditionals, moreover, the two main approaches to them disagree precisely in where they locate their proprietary treatment of conditionality. One approach puts forward a view on which the home of conditionality is in the theory needed to answer the what-question. The other put forward a view on which the home of conditionality is in the theory needed to answer the where-question. The first sort of approach is more traditional than the second, but it is the second which works best in epistemology.

Philosophers who spell out the distinctive nature of conditionals while answering (at least part of) the what-question put forward a version of what I call *Aletheism* about conditionals. This is the view that conditionals are in the business of being true or false—that they are alethic items, so to say—and thus that conditionals stand for claims (or propositions or contents or whatever) which chop logical space into zones. One of the zones will be filled with possible worlds at which a conditional is true, the other will be filled with worlds at which the conditional is false. The meat and potatoes of any particular version of Aletheism have to do with the specific truth-conditions that version proposes for conditionals. On all versions, though, when a person lends credence or belief to a conditional, the point of their practice is to use an item which chops logical space into cells corresponding to truth and falsity.

Moreover, defenders of Aletheism maintain that conditionals stand for truth-evaluable contents which are *built* from truth-evaluable contents. Hence the approach sees conditionals as complex claim-forming devices. To see how this works, let

L = the claim that Lewis didn't kill Leibniz,
S = the claim that someone else did.

Note that L and S are typical alethic items: by stipulation they are in the business of being true or false. Aletheism associates L and S with the antecedent and consequent of

(\*)   If Lewis didn't kill Leibniz, someone else did.

Then it sees (\*) as standing for a proposition of the form COND<L,S>. This proposition is meant to be a logical-space divider built from other such dividers. Versions of Aletheism differ from one another in how they spell out COND<L,S>.

For these reasons, Aletheism sees everyday production and consumption of conditionals as very like quotidian production and consumption of other truth-evaluable sentences. The position entails that the major point of practice with alethic items is to traffic in accurate contents; and it points out that sometimes such practice is well served with a conditional, while other times it is not. The distinctive nature of conditionality as such has only to do with the kind of truth-conditions in use.

The alternative approach goes in precisely the other direction, insisting that what is distinctive about conditionals is the context they set for the use of alethic items. The approach insists that this is a proprietary kind of conditional context. The distinctive nature of conditionality is said to turn on resources which answer the where-question rather than the what-question. For obvious reasons, I call this approach *Contextism* about conditionals, since it's the view that their distinctive function is to create a proprietary kind of context—an essentially conditional context—in which alethic items go to work. According to contextism: when a person lends credence or belief to a conditional, the point of doing so is to create a conditional setting in which alethic items associated with a conditional's antecedent and consequent function in various ways.

The key difference, then, between the two major approaches to conditionals has to do with where they locate conditionality. Aletheism finds it in resources which help to answer the what-question. Contextism finds it in resources which help to answer the where-question. Let

A = the claim that you will eat an Apple,
C = the claim that you will drink a Coke.

Then we can spell out each of these approaches for belief and assertion in the following way.

- Aletheists say that belief in (A→C) is the ordinary binary relation of belief holding between a subject and a conditional alethic item: the truth-evaluable claim that if you eat an Apple, you'll drink a Coke. And like other alethic items, the view has it that this one is a logical-space-divider, chopping epistemic possibilities into those at which (A→C) is true and those at which (A→C) is false. In this way Aletheism construes belief in (A→C) as a regular state of belief, just like belief in A or belief in C. But proponents of Contextism take the opposite view, saying that belief in (A→C) is the extraordinary relation of conditional belief holding between a subject, A, and C. The latter two things are said to be logical-space-dividers, of course, in the usual way; but the ternary relation is said to be where conditionality is truly located. Contextism construes belief in (A→C) as unlike belief in A or belief in C. The latter involve the ordinary binary relation of belief holding between a subject and a logic-chopping content. The former involves the ternary relation of conditional belief holding between a subject and two such contents. Aletheists understand talk of belief in general by appeal to one propositional attitude and two types of logical-space-divider (conditional and unconditional). Context-theorists understand such talk by appeal to two propositional attitudes—the binary and ternary relations of belief—and one type of logical-space-divider.
- Aletheists say that assertion of (A→C) is the ordinary binary relation of assertion holding between a subject and a conditional alethic item: the truth-evaluable claim that if you eat an Apple, you'll drink a Coke. Like other alethic items the view has it that this conditional one is a logical-space-divider, chopping epistemic possibilities into those at which (A→C) is true and those at which (A→C) is false. Aletheism construes assertion of (A→C) as an unconditional speech-act, just like assertion of A or assertion of C. Proponents of Contextism take the opposite view, claiming that assertion of (A→C) is the relation of conditional assertion holding between a subject, A, and C. The latter two things are said to be logical-space-dividers, but the ternary relation is said to be where conditionality itself is located. Contextism construes assertion of (A→C) as unlike assertion of A or assertion of

C. The latter involve the ordinary binary relation of assertion holding between a subject and a content. The former involves the ternary relation of conditional assertion holding between a subject and two contents. Aletheists understand talk of assertion in general by appeal to one type of speech-act and two types of logical-space-divider (conditional and unconditional). Context-theorists understand such talk by appeal to two types of speech-act—unconditional and conditional assertion—and one type of logical-space-divider.[7]

There is no space to adjudicate the debate between Aletheism and Contextism here, since that's a job which stretches well beyond the scope of this chapter.[8] We can, though, usefully connect the debate between these two views with topics seen in the last chapter.

Recall how we laid out the logical geography of issues to do with the fine-grained Ramsey Test

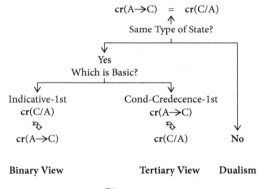

Figure 7.11

We noted in §4.8 that it is highly unlikely that indicative and conditional credence are two kinds of thing: dualism about conditionality—within a confidence-theoretic setting, at least—is almost certainly wrong. Once it is granted that monism about confidence-theoretic conditionality is correct, however, and hence that indicative and conditional credence are the same kind of thing, it is unclear which of them is explanatorily basic.

Having said that, we also saw that if the binary view of conditionality is true, and indicative credence is both binary in nature and the fundamental moving part in the

---

[7] In addition to conditional sentences which are put forward in the 'indicative mood', there are conditional sentences which are put forward in the 'interrogative' and 'imperative' moods too. These are conditional questions and commands respectively. By my lights one of the strongest reasons to adopt a ternary approach to conditionals is what I call the mood constraint: our treatment of conditionals in the indicative mood should dovetail gracefully with our treatment of conditional questions and conditional commands. To my knowledge only the ternary approach satisfies this constraint. See (Bennett, 2003), (Edgington, 1997) in (Woods, 1997), Woods himself in that book, and my review article on it (Sturgeon, 2000).

[8] It's a book-length task, in fact, and the best book on the topic is Bennett's op cit.

area, it should be relatively easy to concoct a case showing that *Modus Ponens* functions like other two-part rules of entailment, namely, in being merely a rule of entail rather than an obligatory path forward in rational shift-in-view. But it turns out that it is not at all easy to concoct a case showing that, as we saw in the last chapter—in fact we were unable to do so after repeated efforts. This suggests that conditional credence is the basic moving part in the area and that indicative credence reduces to conditional credence.

If that is right, however, the ternary view of confidence-theoretic conditionality is correct, in which case the right-hand side of the fine-grained Ramsey Test is to be thought of as reducing to its left-hand side. In other words, facts of this form

$$cr(A \to C)$$

are to be thought of as reducing to facts of this form

$$cr(C/A),$$

and the latter are to be understood as fine-grained ternary facts which hold between a thinker, C, and A.

This puts us squarely in line with Contextism about conditionals. It also means we should hear *other* claims about credence in a reductive spirit (once the Ramsey norm is in place). For instance each of these provable equivalences should be heard so that their left-hand sides reduce to their right-hand sides:

$$(\neg) \quad cr[\neg(A \to C)] = cr(A \to \neg C)$$
$$(cr\text{-}I/E) \quad cr[A \to (B \to C)] = cr[(A\&B) \to C].$$

And this is important. Since the conditional sign '$\to$' is the main connective on the right-hand side of both these schemata, and since that sign is thought to be nothing but a marker of conditional credence, ternary theorists of conditionality see the left-hand sides above as decidedly *misleading*. For they see them as having to do, at bottom, only with the state of conditional credence, a fundamental kind of state in the present discussion.

The ternary approach to conditionality does not see the conditional as a logical-space-divider. It sees it instead as notation for conditional states of mind. If that is right, though, certain steps in the reasoning which led to Lewis' Bombshell should be rejected, for they illicitly treat the conditional as if it is an alethic item, as if it is a logic chopper (so to say). For instance, recall the reasoning behind **Fact 3**:

*Proof:* Suppose $(R_cT)$, (C) and $cr(A\&B)$ is non-zero. Then

$$
\begin{aligned}
cr[A \to (B \to C)] &= cr[(B \to C)/A] && \text{by } (R_cT) \\
&= cr_A(B \to C) && \text{by (C)} \\
&= cr_A(C/B) && \text{by } (R_cT) \\
&= cr[(C\&B)/A] \div cr(B/A) && \text{by (C)} \\
&= cr[C\&B\&A] \div cr(B\&A) && \text{by algebra} \\
&= cr[C/(A\&B)] \\
&= cr[(A\&B) \to C] && \text{by } (R_cT). \blacksquare
\end{aligned}
$$

The initial step in this line presupposes that the conditional is an alethic item. That presupposition is mandatory if the move from

$$cr[(B \to C)/A]$$

to

$$cr_A(B \to C)$$

by Conditionalization is to be kosher. After all, Conditionalization is defined only for alethic items (claims, propositions, etc.). When the rule says in a given case that your new view of X should equal your old view of X conditional on Y, both X and Y must be a claim, or a proposition, or something like that. Both X and Y must be in the truth-value business. Proponents of the ternary view deny that conditionals are such items, hence they reject the first step in the reasoning above, seeing it as based on a false presupposition.

This does not mean that defenders of the ternary approach must reject **Fact 3**, of course. Just because a line of thought for a view is thought to be bogus it does not follow that the view itself is bogus. And in this case there is good reason to think that defenders of the ternary view will be happy with the credal Import-Export Law. For anyone who thinks that psychological situations canonically described as

$$cr(A \to C)$$

are really just psychological situations better described as

$$cr(C/A),$$

and also thinks that the latter situations are ternary in nature, will likely endorse the idea that *iterated* conditionals are notation for conditional credence involving conjunctions. Their commitment to the ternary approach to conditionality will likely lead them to the view that psychological situations of the form

$$cr[A \to (B \to C)]$$

are really just situations of this form

$$cr[(A\&B) \to C]$$

deep down, which are in turn really just situations of the form

$$cr[C/(A\&B)],$$

where the latter are expressly thought of as ternary facts to do with a thinker, C, and (A & B). Hence defenders of the ternary view will likely endorse the credal Import/Export Law on their own. But they will not do so on the basis of reasoning that treats the conditional as an alethic item. They will view that reasoning as spurious.

Or again: consider the reasoning used earlier for the view that conditionals have material truth-conditions (what we called **Fact 4** before):

*Proof:* Assume $cr(A \& C)$ is non-zero. Since $(A \& C)$ is truth-functionally equivalent to $[(A \supset C) \& A]$, it follows that $cr[(A \supset C) \& A]$ is nonzero. An instance of Fact 3 is thus

$$cr[(A \supset C) \rightarrow (A \rightarrow C)] = cr\{[(A \supset C)\&A] \rightarrow C\}$$
Now apply (RT) to both sides:
$$cr[(A \rightarrow C)/(A \supset C)] = cr\{C/[(A \supset C)\&A]\}.$$
The right-hand side of this equation is unity. Hence
$$cr[(A \rightarrow C)\&(A \supset C)] = cr(A \supset C).$$
This entails
$$cr(A \supset C) \leq cr(A \rightarrow C).$$
By (RT), then,
$$cr(A \supset C) \leq cr(C/A).$$
Yet $cr(C/A)$ cannot exceed $cr(A \supset C)$. Hence
$$cr(A \rightarrow C) = cr(A \supset C). \blacksquare$$

When the fine-grained Ramsey Test is applied to the reasoning's first equation, $(A \rightarrow C)$ is treated as an alethic item; for the move presupposes that the conditional is something which can hold on condition that material truth-conditions obtain. Hence the step in the reasoning presupposes that $(A \rightarrow C)$ is a logical-space divider. But the very idea of $(A \rightarrow C)$ holding on condition that $(A \supset C)$ *makes no sense* if '→' is but a marker for conditional context. If that is its job all one can get out of psychological situations of the form

$$cr[(A \supset C) \rightarrow (A \rightarrow C)]$$

are situations of the form:

$$cr\{C/[(A \supset C)\&A]\}.$$

Hence the reasoning above breaks down at its first major step.[9]

The ternary approach to conditionality entails that conditionals do not have truth-conditions. This means conditionals should not be allowed to function in thought as if they have truth-conditions. At several places the reasoning which leads to Lewis' Bombshell presupposes that conditionals have truth-conditions. For this reason, defenders of the ternary approach to conditionality reject the reasoning. They do not take it to show that there is anything wrong with the fine-grained Ramsey Test. Rather, they jettison the view that conditionals chop logical space into worlds at which conditionals are true and those at which conditionals are false. Defenders of the ternary approach replace this view with the idea that conditionals set up an irreducibly conditional context in which logic choppers can function.

Suppose this is so. Then it makes perfect sense of the idea that conditionals are central to linking theory. After all, linking theory must specify how states and state-

---

[9] Further still: when $(A \rightarrow C)$ appears as a conjunct in a conjunction—as it does in the reasoning which led to **Fact 4**—we also find the conditional acting as if it were an alethic item. The context of conjunction, after all, only makes literal sense when logical-space dividers are put into it. If '→' does nothing but mark conditional context, however, it does not divide logical space, and, for this reason, it should not appear as a conjunct in a conjunction. The result is no good even if harder to see because the relevant formulae look syntactically ok, and they look like analogues to do with truth-functional conditionals (which of course are logical-space dividers). As with left-nested conditionals, conjunctions with conditional conjuncts look OK but deep down they are not. See §6.4 for discussion of left-nested conditionals as well as (Bennett, 2003) and (Edgington, 1995) for the larger context.

transitions are meant to relate to one another. If lending an attitude to a conditional is in fact entering into a ternary relation between the agent and two contents, then, lending an attitude to a conditional can well function as a state marking how update is to proceed. This would make sense of why we found it so hard (in §4.7) to treat *Modus Ponens* like other two-premise rules of entailment; and it would fit nicely with the story to be told later (in Chapter 12) about why kinematics is a forward-looking affair.

# PART II
# Coarse- and Fine-Grained Attitudes

# 8
# Puzzling about Epistemic Attitudes

## 8.1 Two Questions about Epistemic Attitudes

Certain propositional attitudes are capable of being well taken or rational in light of the evidence. These are the epistemic attitudes. It is not a trivial hypothesis that we manifest any of them in everyday life. It is a trivial hypothesis that by doing so we open aspects of that life to epistemic evaluation. Common sense insists that we do manifest epistemic attitudes with great frequency, of course, but it conceptualizes them in at least two different ways.

On the one hand, common sense recognizes a coarse-grained space of epistemic attitudes consisting in belief, disbelief, and suspended judgement. This is the attitudinal space we tap into when we wonder if someone is a theist, atheist, or agnostic. On the other hand, common sense recognizes a fine-grained space of epistemic attitudes consisting in countless levels of confidence. This is the attitudinal space we use when we wonder how confident someone is that it will rain (say).

The fact that common sense uses these two attitudinal spaces itself raises a number of interesting questions. Two of them jump out right away:

(A) How do elements within one of these attitudinal spaces relate to one another?
(B) How do elements across such spaces do so?

Question (A) concerns how the metaphysics of belief, disbelief and suspended judgement relate to one another, and how the metaphysics of levels of confidence do too. These intra-level topics apply within a given space of epistemic attitudes. Question (B) concerns how the metaphysics of coarse- and fine-grained epistemic attitudes relate to one another. This inter-level topic applies across attitudinal spaces. Naturally there are reductionists and anti-reductionists about each of these issues.

Intra-level reductionists about coarse-grained attitudes say that one of belief, disbelief, or suspended judgement is more basic than its coarse-grained cousins. They use their take on the putatively more basic attitude to build an approach to the nature and norms of coarse-grained attitudes said to be less basic. Similarly, intra-level reductionists about fine-grained attitudes say that high or low levels of confidence are more basic than their opposite number. And they use their take on the putatively more basic attitudes to build an approach to the nature and norms of fine-grained attitudes said to be less basic.

Intra-level anti-reductionists reject this picture. They maintain that coarse- and fine-grained attitudes are on an explanatory par with their level-mates, and, for this reason, that attitudes within each level are subject to proprietary epistemic norms. A familiar dialectic then plays out. Reductionists plump for a line blessed with ontic

*The Rational Mind.* Scott Sturgeon, Oxford University Press (2020). © Scott Sturgeon.
DOI: 10.1093/oso/9780198845799.001.0001

and explanatory unity; but they pay for these signature theoretical virtues with substantive hostages to fortune. Anti-reductionists avoid the hostages to fortune by admitting a wider expanse of self-standing mental and evaluative fact.

The dialectic carries over, *mutatis mutandis*, to the inter-level issue. Some maintain that coarse-grained attitudes reduce to their fine-grained cousins, while others maintain that fine-grained attitudes reduce to their coarse-grained cousins. These are inter-level reductionists about epistemic attitudes. A given level of attitude is said to be more basic than its counterparts, with the more basic level of fact being used to build an approach to the nature and norms for attitudes said to be less basic.

Once again anti-reductionists reject the picture. They maintain that coarse- and fine-grained attitudes are on an explanatory par with one another, and, for this reason, that attitudes at each level are subject to proprietary epistemic norms. On their view: belief, disbelief and suspended judgement do not reduce to levels of confidence, and levels of confidence do not reduce to belief, disbelief or suspended judgement. Once again reductionists put forward a picture blessed with ontic and explanatory unitypaid for with non-trivial hostages to fortune. Once again anti-reductionists avoid the hostages to fortune by admitting a wider expanse of self-standing mental and evaluative fact.

Part I of the book put forward a case for the anti-reductive position on the intra-level issue. Chapters 2 and 3 presupposed such a view for fine-grained epistemic attitudes, with the presupposition playing out well; and Chapter 6 argued explicitly for anti-reductionism about coarse-grained epistemic attitudes (see §§6.2–3). Thus we have our answer to question (A) already: elements of a given attitudinal space do not inter-reduce. They are self-standing members of proprietary epistemic domains.

Part II of the book argues for a reductive position on the inter-level issue. Specifically it argues that coarse-grained attitudes reduce to their fine-grained cousins; but the reductive position defended itself manifests virtues had by *each* type of inter-level reductionism: those which ground coarse-grained attitudes in their fine-grained cousins, and those which do the reverse. Attractive aspects of each strategy are slotted into a unified whole for the first time, and this is done by locating explanatory resources even more basic than epistemic attitudes. Chapters 11 and 12 use those resources to build a fully reductive approach to the epistemic attitudes.

## 8.2 A Puzzle in Three Easy Pieces: the Lottery and the Preface

We begin with a familiar Puzzle about coarse- and fine-grained epistemic attitudes. At bottom it is a Puzzle about the relation between their metaphysics and their epistemology. As we'll see it is easy to generate conflict when the most plausible position about that metaphysics is put together with obvious-looking norms in the epistemology. The Puzzle is to sort out the least painful way to remove conflict from our overall picture.

Now, a plausible answer to question (B)—very often taken for granted in common sense and the philosophy of mind—spells out the idea that coarse-grained attitudes *grow metaphysically* from their fine-grained cousins. In particular it plumps for the following two thoughts:

(a) whether or not one believes, disbelieves, or suspends judgement is fixed entirely by how one lends credence,

and

(b) whether one's coarse-grained attitudes are rational is fixed entirely by the rationality of one's credence.[1]

On the approach I have in mind, one manages to have coarse belief by investing credence, and one manages to have rational coarse belief by investing rational credence.

Just as thermal phenomena can be represented by pictures of a thermometer, so the position I have in mind can represent confidence-theoretic phenomena with pictures of a 'credometer'. This is a machine which has liquid inside which goes up and down as a function of something else—just as a thermometer does—but unlike a thermometer the waxing and waning on the inside of a credometer is not a function of temperature but rather of credal strength. As an agent's credence goes up and down for a claim Φ, the liquid inside her credometer for Φ goes up and down systematically.

With that idea in mind we may picture an initially plausible answer to question (B) with a credometer

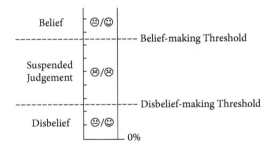

Figure 8.1

The position we'll call the *Threshold View* accepts this picture of the relation between coarse- and fine-grained attitudes. It is a picture on which the latter are grounded in the former. But there is one misleading aspect of the picture that we should flag straightaway, just to keep things clear.

On any plausible version of the Threshold View, the belief-making threshold is both vague and contextually variable. The view sees our chunking of confidence into a three-fold scheme—belief, disbelief, suspended judgement—on a par with our chunking of fine-grained heights into a three-fold scheme—tall, short, middling in height. And the position runs full-steam-ahead with the analogy: just as there is

---

[1] We'll run the position here in terms of credence, and generalize it later to include thick confidence.

nothing more to being tall, metaphysically, than having a sufficiently large specific height, for instance, the Threshold View insists that there is nothing more to believing, metaphysically, than lending sufficiently strong confidence. And just as what counts as sufficient height to make one tall can vary from context to context—someone might count as tall at an APA conference, for instance, without doing so at an NBA conference[2]—so it's the case that what counts as strong enough credence to make for belief can vary from context to context—you might count as believing that your car keys are on the mantel when it is contextually-salient that nothing turns on it, say, even though you would not so count if it is so salient that your life is at stake. Any plausible version of the Threshold View must take this as read, so we'll do that in what follows. Understood in this way the Threshold View is the first piece of our Puzzle.

The second turns on the quotidian fact that belief can be more or less reasonable, depending upon the evidence to hand. There seem to be rules or norms for how belief should be doled out as a function of the evidence. And while there is debate about what those rules say, exactly, two thoughts look hard to deny. The first is

*The Conjunction Rule*
For any claims P and Q: if one rationally believes P, and rationally believes Q, and considers the matter, one should also believe their conjunction: (P&Q).

This rule says there is something wrong in rationally believing each in a pair of claims, wondering about their conjunction, yet withholding belief in that conjunction. The rule is both plausible and widely held as a correct idealization in the epistemology of belief. And so is the following rule:

*The Entailment Rule*
For any claims P and Q: if one rationally believes P, and P logically entails Q, one should also believe Q.

This principle says there is something wrong with failing to believe the consequences of one's rational beliefs. It too is plausible and widely held as a correct idealization in the epistemology of belief. According to these two principles, then, rational belief is preserved by conjunction and by entailment. The position we'll call the *Coarse View* accepts that by definition. So understood it is the second piece of our Puzzle.[3]

The third turns on a well-known thought about rational credence

*The Partition Rule*
For any claims $P_1$-$P_n$: if $P_1$-$P_n$ are a logical partition—i.e. they break down possible worlds into exclusive and exhaustive cells, worlds at which $P_1$ is true, worlds at which $P_2$ is true, and so on—then, an agent's credence for the $P_i$ should add-up to 100%.

This rule says there is something wrong with investing credence in a way which does not 'sum to unity' across cells of a logical partition. If you are 20% sure that A is true, for instance, you should be 80% sure that ¬A is true, for the two claims are jointly a

---

[2] The APA is the American Philosophical Association and the NBA is the National Basketball Association. On average basketball players are far taller than philosophers (sadly).

[3] See Chapters 2 and 3 for further discussion of closure principles for belief.

logical partition. Or again; if you are 20% sure that A is true together with B, and 30% sure that A is true without B, then you should be 50% sure that A is not true, for (A&B), (A&¬B), and ¬A are jointly a logical partition. And so on. The Partition Rule generalizes this simple idea to finite logical partitions. The position we'll call the *Fine View* accepts this by definition. So understood it is the final piece of our Puzzle.[4]

So our Puzzle takes off from three easy pieces:

- The Coarse View
- The Fine View
- The Threshold View.

It is well known that they lead to trouble. Long ago Henry Kyburg kicked off the bother by focusing on situations in which one can be rationally sure that something improbable will happen. Shortly after that David Makinson turned up the heat by focusing on human fallibility and its relation to rationality. The first issue has come to be known as the Lottery Paradox. The second has come to be known as the Preface Paradox. Consider versions of them in turn.

Suppose you know a given lottery will be fair, have one hundred tickets, and exactly one winner. Let $L_1$ be the claim that ticket-1 loses, $L_2$ be the claim that ticket-2 loses, and so forth. Let W be the claim that one of the tickets wins. Suppose you are rationally all but certain that the lottery will take place as described. Then your rational credence in each L-claim will be 99%, since you know the lottery is fair that and each ticket has a 99% objective chance of losing. And your rational credence in W will be thereabouts too, since you are rationally all but certain that the lottery will take place, etc. Hence the Threshold View looks to entail that you have rational belief in each of these claims. After all, you are rationally all but certain of each of them—and the example could be changed, of course, to make you ever more close to certain of each of them. But consider the conjunction

$$\&_L = (L_1 \& L_2 \& \ldots \& L_{100}).$$

You rationally believe each conjunct. By repeated application of the conjunction rule you should also believe the conjunction. Yet think of the disjunction

$$V_{\neg L} = (\neg L_1 \vee \neg L_2 \vee \ldots \vee \neg L_{100}).$$

You rationally believe *one* of the tickets will win. That entails the disjunction $V_{\neg L}$, so by the entailment rule you should believe the disjunction too. Yet the conjunction $\&_L$ entails the disjunction $V_{\neg L}$ is false, so you should believe the disjunction's negation: $\neg V_{\neg L}$. Hence the conjunction rule ensures that you should believe an explicit contradiction: $(V_{\neg L} \& \neg V_{\neg L})$.

That looks obviously wrong, but things go from bad to worse at this point. After all, the negation of $(V_{\neg L} \& \neg V_{\neg L})$ is a truth-functional tautology. So it by itself is a logical partition, since logic alone guarantees that $\neg(V_{\neg L} \& \neg V_{\neg L})$ is true. Hence the Partition Rule ensures you should lend full credence to $\neg(V_{\neg L} \& \neg V_{\neg L})$. Yet that negation and the contradiction itself are a partition—logic guarantees that exactly

---

[4] Chapter 2 explains and motivates the Partition Principle from scratch.

one of them is correct as well, of course—so the partition rule also ensures you should lend the contradiction *no* credence. The Threshold View then precludes rational coarse belief, since it precludes belief of any sort when no credence is lent! In this way our three easy pieces have led to disaster. They entail that you should believe a certain claim, and they also entail that it is not the case that you should believe that claim. For our purposes this contradiction is the Lottery Paradox.

Or suppose you have written an unusual history book. Years of study have led you to various non-trivial claims about the past. Your book lists them in bullet-point style: *One Hundred Historical Facts*, it is called. You are aware of human fallibility, of course, and hence you are sure that you have made a mistake in the book somewhere, since any book of equal ambition will have doubtless gone wrong somewhere. So you add a preface saying exactly one thing: 'At least one of the following 100 claims is false.' This makes for trouble.

To see why, let the one hundred historical claims of the book be $H_1$–$H_{100}$. You spent years on each of them and have rational credence in each of them. You have so much rational credence in each of the historical claims, in fact, that we may suppose it makes the threshold for rational belief. So you rationally believing each H-claim as well as the claim in your preface. But consider the conjunction of historical claims:

$$\&_H = (H_1 \& H_2 \& ... \& H_{100});$$

and think of your preface claim P.

Things go just as before: the conjunction rule ensures you should believe $\&_H$. That claim entails ¬P, so the entailment rule ensures you should believe ¬P. The conjunction rule then foists the contradiction (P&¬P) on you, which is bad enough. But the negation of this contradiction is a truth-functional tautology, so by itself it is a logical partition. Hence the partition rule entails that you are rationally certain of ¬(P&¬P). Yet this tautology with the contradiction is a partition too, so the partition rule entails (in light of your full credence for the tautology), that you lend no credence to (P&¬P). The threshold rule then ensures that you do not believe (P&¬P). And once again we are led to disaster: our three easy pieces entail that you should believe a certain claim and that it is not the case that you should do that. For our purposes this contradiction is the Preface Paradox.

## 8.3 A Troika of Extreme Reactions

Something must be wrong with our three easy pieces. Lottery and preface situations refute the conjunction of Coarse, Fine, and Threshold Views. They lead to explicit contradiction in those situations. Since each of the Views looks correct on its own, the Puzzle is to reckon which isn't right as it stands. This is basically the task of locating the least painful way out of conflict.

There are three extreme reactions to our puzzle.

Some epistemologists take it to show that the very idea of rational belief is somehow specious, because they take it to show that the very idea of belief is specious. Others take the puzzle to show that the very idea of rational credence is specious, since the very idea of credence is specious. And still other epistemologists react to our puzzle by endorsing the view that belief and credence are metaphysically disconnected, that neither grows from the other, and, as a result, that each have disconnected epistemologies. For obvious reasons I call these the credence-only, belief-only, and divide-&-conquer reactions to our puzzle. Consider them in turn:

1. The credence-only reaction accepts the Fine View but denies that belief grows from credence. In turn that denial is itself sourced in a full-on rejection of belief as a psychological kind. The credence-only reaction to our puzzle throws out coarse-grained epistemology, rejecting any need for a link from it to its bona fide fine-grained cousin; for the credence-only reaction to our puzzle rejects the very idea of belief itself. The only psychological phenomenon in the ballpark it recognizes is credence.

How might such a view be defended? Richard Jeffrey puts it this way:

By 'belief' I mean the thing that goes along with valuation in decision-making: degree-of-belief, or subjective probability, or personal probability, or grade of credence. I do not care what you call it because I can tell you what it is, and how to measure it, within limits... Nor am I disturbed by the fact that our ordinary notion of belief is only vestigially present in the notion of degree of belief. I am inclined to think Ramsey sucked the marrow out of the ordinary notion, and used it to nourish a more adequate view.[5]

The line here rejects the epistemology of coarse-grained belief and replaces it with the epistemology of credence. In turn this is done because the very idea of belief is replaced with that of credence. The resulting position has no room for either the Coarse or Threshold Views. It runs everything of interest off the back of credence.[6]

2. The belief-only reaction accepts the Coarse View but denies that belief grows from credence. In turn that denial is itself sourced in a full-on rejection of credence as a psychological kind. The belief-only reaction to our puzzle throws out fine-grained epistemology, for reaction rejects the very idea of credence. The only psychological phenomenon it recognizes in the ballpark is belief.

How might such a view be defended? Richard Holton puts it this way::

My contention [is that] we cannot form credences at all. The Bayesian [model] is not an idealization of something we do. Instead, it is quite foreign to us. Just as our core native deliberative state is that of the simple intention, so our core native epistemic state is that of simple, all-out belief. This is what makes it possible for creatures with the limited cognitive powers that we have to deliberate and act as effectively as we do.[7]

The line here simply rejects credence and its epistemology, replacing them both with a coarse-grained approach. The resulting position sees it as a serious mistake to think

---

[5] See his (Jeffrey, 1970).
[6] See also (Urbach & Howson, 1993). After saying to a well-known Bayesian once that I was working on the puzzle of this section, he remarked: 'but the epistemology of belief is pre-scientific *Cartesian* epistemology. Why would anyone still be thinking about that?' This remark captures a good deal of the spirit of many Bayesians. And their belief-only colleagues are in the same spirit, of course, only endorsing the mirror-image psychology.
[7] (Holton 2014: 27).

that sensible credence makes for rational belief, since the resulting position rejects the very idea of credence as such.

3.The divide-and-conquer reaction to our puzzle accepts both the Coarse and the Fine Views but it rejects the Threshold View. The reaction has no difficulty with the bona fides of belief, of credence, or of their respective epistemologies. It just sees the metaphysics of belief and of credence as disconnected.

How might this last claim be defended? Patrick Maher puts it this way:

> What is the relation between belief and credence?... [I have shown that] no credence short of 100% is sufficient for belief, while credence of 100% is not necessary for belief. Together, these results show that belief cannot be identified with any level of credence.[8]

The divide-and-conquer reaction to our puzzle holds onto both the Coarse and the Fine Views. It drops the idea that there is an internal link between belief and credence, that the metaphysics of each is intertwined with the other.

In a nutshell, then, the credence-only reaction to our puzzle says that Threshold and Coarse Views are hopelessly wrong, locating their putative major mistake in reliance on the bogus notion of belief. The belief-only reaction to our puzzle says that Threshold and Fine Views are hopelessly wrong, locating their putative major mistake in reliance on the bogus notion of credence. The divide-and-conquer reaction to our puzzle takes a slightly-less-radical stance ontologically: it accepts the psychological bona fides of belief and credence, but rejects that their metaphysics are tethered together.

## 8.4 Critical Discussion

Unfortunately neither eliminativist position is at all plausible. Our everyday notions of belief and confidence simply work too well to take seriously the idea that they are unreal. Indeed only a bit of reflection makes it clear that we enjoy rather stunning success at predicting and explaining one another by appeal to beliefs, that we enjoy similar success at predicting and explaining one another by appeal to states of confidence, and—perhaps most importantly for our purposes—that these highly-successful explanatory schemes are tightly interwoven when at work. Further still, it is not as if the causal/explanatory work done by appeal to our coarse- and fine-grained attitudes is not worth doing or unimportant. On the contrary: the social world is what we care about most in life, and it is built primarily from individuals acting and reacting to one another. Without a causal/explanatory story about that we'd be literally lost in the layer of reality of fundamental significance to us. Yet the only story we have about this is entirely infused with coarse- and fine-grained attitudes. There is simply no way to navigate the social world successfully without making heavy use of belief, for instance, or heavy use of one agent being more confident of something than something else. It makes little-to-no methodological sense, therefore, to adopt a view on which there are no states of belief, or a view on

---

[8] (Maher 2008: 88).

which there are no states of confidence. Any such eliminativist position is quite obviously false.

The relevant point here is well known in the philosophy of mind, but it does not seem to be properly absorbed in epistemology. Abstractly put the point is this: *if* we use a given type of state in a seemingly successful causal-explanatory practice, and we have no means of getting that causal-explanatory work done save by appeal to instances of that type of state, then, it is simply unacceptable to deny there are instances of the type in question (the type we use in our successful practice). The only sensible position is one on which (a) the world contains instances of the type found in our seemingly successful causal-explanatory practice, and (b) those instances do basically whatever it is that they seem to do in our causal-explanatory practice.[9]

This methodological point applies directly to our practice involving coarse- and fine-grained attitudes, i.e. states of belief, suspended judgement, confidence and so on. The thing we care most to understand in the world, if we're honest—both causally and otherwise—is social reality. We want to understand people as such, action as such, when and why social things happen, the significance of it all, and more. And we can understand all of this rather well by appeal to coarse- and fine-grained attitudes. We can understand none of it well without making such an appeal. For this reason, eliminativism about the attitudes is unacceptable. This is true for coarse-grained states of belief, disbelief, and suspended judgement. It is true for their fine-grained cousins as well.

Here is an example (like one) given by Jerry Fodor long ago:

(*)We are both in a room when an object on the floor begins to vibrate. Your body moves in complex ways in reaction to the vibration. Those movements cause various things to happen which bring it about that (a) the vibrating object stops vibrating, and (b) it rests next to your ear. Sounds then come out of your mouth followed by further complex bodily movements. Those movements cause various things to happen which bring it about that (c) the initially-vibrating object ends-up back where it began, and (d) your mouth changes shape a certain way.

What does it all mean?

Well, if I deploy a loose collection of common-sense thoughts about how people and the social world work—sometimes known as 'folk psychology'—I will have no difficulty understanding the situation. I'll see the vibrating object as a phone and its vibration as a phone signal. I'll see your bodily movements as action aimed at answering the phone. I'll causally explain this action by appeal to a belief on your part that someone is trying to reach you by phone. I'll see you as chatting with someone about picking them up at the airport in one hundred days' time, as promising to do so out of a desire on your part to be helpful, together with high confidence that your interlocutor wishes you to pick them up, etc. And on the basis of

---

[9] The caveat is needed for a simple reason: although realism about Xs is entirely warranted in the situation envisioned—i.e. the view that there really are Xs in the world—it may turn out that Xs are different than we conceived them in our X-based explanatory practice. How different can they turn out to be, consistent with realism about Xs being warranted by practice? Good question. The answer is not too different, of course; but the devil is in the details. See chapter 1 of (Stich, 1996) for a good discussion of this.

all this I'll be able to predict—after watching for only a moment—that you'll be at a certain place at a certain time in one hundred days.

In the event, we have before us a good example of the causal-explanatory power of folk psychology. There does not seem to be a way to equal it save by appeal to folk-psychological notions, not even remotely. When it comes to the prediction and explanation in the social world, folk-psychological efforts are the only game in town. They are the only real means of dealing with target *explananda*. Yet folk psychological practice is knee-deep in epistemic attitudes. It predicts what people will do by appeal to doctrines they reject, makes sense of the past by appeal to confidence and evidence; and so on. If we take all this seriously—as we really should, given our interests and the lack of any serious alternative—we must admit the reality of coarse- and fine-grained epistemic attitudes. This is why it seems dead obvious that people believe, disbelieve, and suspend judgement, and equally obvious that our confidence waxes and wanes as we go through life.

Take another example. I venture that everyone reading this page is doing so inside a hollow material object. What *is* that object? Why is it there? How does it work? Why does it work *that* way? And so on. If I deploy folk psychological notions, there is no difficulty in answering these questions. The hollow object is an artefact—a university building, a coffee shop, a private home. It was built by architects, engineers, and builders precisely so that folks like you can do things like read this book inside it. The large artefact was put together in various ways because architects, engineers, and builders believed that it would serve its function well if it were built in that way. And various aspects of the artefact are back-up systems—say to do with electrical grounding in the building—because architects, engineers, and builders were not super-confident that the front-line mechanisms for these jobs would work. This overall story about the hollow object in which you are reading this book is knee-deep in epistemic attitudes. It retrodicts what people have done by appeal to what they believed, by appeal to their states of confidence, and so on. If we take the story seriously—as we really must, given the lack of alternatives—we should admit not only that there are buildings but that they were caused to exist by people with coarse- and fine-grained attitudes.

In a nutshell: we often use the full range of epistemic attitudes to predict and explain the social world; and we have no real idea how to get that job done save by appeal to the attitudes. For this reason it is unacceptable to endorse eliminativism about coarse- or fine-grained attitudes. The only sensible move is to embrace the existence of belief, disbelief, and suspended judgement—as well as their confidence-theoretic cousins—and to endorse the idea that such attitudes do basically what common sense sees them as doing.

It is likely true, of course, that our common-sense practice of predicting and explaining one another by appeal to coarse- and fine-grained attitudes goes wrong from time to time. But it is unacceptable to say—in light of the success of that practice and the palpable lack of alternatives—that the practice is based on mistaken vacuous psychological presuppositions. If the Coarse View is so based, after all, no one acts as they do because they believe it will get them what they want, or because they disbelieve something that someone has told them, or because they suspend judgement in the veracity of testimony. If the Coarse View is based on mistaken psychological presuppositions, in other words, our practice of predicting and explaining one another by appeal to belief, disbelief, and suspended judgement is hopelessly flawed, for there are no such psychological states. Similarly: if the Fine View is based on vacuous psychological presuppositions, no one ever acts as they do because they are unsure what the relevant truth is in a given area, or because they are certain of what they are doing. Hence our practice of predicting and explaining one another by appeal to such confidence-theoretic facts is likewise hopelessly flawed, for there are no such facts in the first place.

Each of these positions leads to eliminativism about a certain range of attitudes. One throws out coarse-grained attitudes in favour of their fine-grained cousins. The other does just the reverse. As Fodor remarked long ago, however, if eliminativism about the attitudes is true, then, 'practically everything [we] believe about anything is false and it's the end of the world'.[10] This is hyperbolic to be sure; but it marks the fact that our coarse- and fine-grained folk psychological practices are extremely effective. We would be entirely lost without them. No sensible methodology can underwrite eliminativism about their presuppositions.

The Coarse and Fine Views may well go wrong in their details—in which case they go wrong in their *norms*—but the success of everyday practice with the attitudes makes it all but impossible to accept that the practice is so hopelessly mistaken that it goes wrong in its ontology. Any epistemic perspectives which throw out all but fine-grained attitudes, or which throws out all but coarse-grained attitudes, is refuted by practice.

This means both the credence-only and the belief-only reactions to our puzzle should be rejected. The former entails that no one believes, disbelieves, or suspends judgement. The latter entails that no one invests confidence. Both stories are quite literally incredible. If there is a sensible reaction to our puzzle, therefore, it will either be the divide-and-conquer strategy mentioned earlier, or something yet to be discussed. Let us turn, then, to the divide-and-conquer strategy and see how it fares.

Although the divide-and-conquer approach finds more right in practice than its eliminativist cousins—and that is definitely a good thing—it is still hard to accept in light of everyday practice. For not only do coarse- and fine-grained attitudes do a huge amount of explanatory work in everyday life, they also *march in step* when they do that work. This is hard to understand if their metaphysics are as disconnected as the divide-and-conquer strategy would have us believe.

To see this, note that whenever someone goes to the fridge because they believe that it contains some beer, there is a clear and everyday sense in which they go to the fridge because they are confident that it contains some beer too. And whenever someone goes to the window because they are confident that someone has called out, there is a clear and everyday sense in which they go to the window because they believe that someone has done so. In general: whenever there is a coarse-grained spring of action recognized by common sense, there is a clear and everyday sense in which there is a fine-grained spring of that very action too; and vice versa. In this way coarse- and fine-grained attitudes give rise to action in harmony. They march in step

[10] (Fodor 1990: 156).

when at work in everyday practice. Common sense sees them as causally responsible for much the same things.

This cries out for explanation. Why should being confident that it will rain, for instance, cause you to take an umbrella pretty much exactly when belief in rain does the same thing? Or why should belief that there is beer in the fridge cause you to walk to the kitchen pretty much exactly when high confidence in beer causes you to do the same thing? When it comes to umbrella-taking or beer-fetching behaviour, after all, that is precisely what common sense says. The general datum here is simple: there is a coarse-grained spring of action pretty much exactly when there is a fine-grained analogue; and *vice versa*. Coarse- and fine-grained attitudes march in step as the causal springs of action.

If such attitudes are metaphysically disconnected, however—as the divide-and-conquer strategy insists—it is a mystery why coarse- and fine-grained attitudes march in step when at work. It is not logically impossible, of course, that there is no explanation of the marching-in-step phenomenon. Perhaps the world is just set up in this way and there is nothing more to be said about it. But this is a believe-it-if-you-can theory. If at all possible we should insist on an explanation of the fact that coarse- and fine-grained attitudes march in step when at work.

Chasing one down will take up the lion's share of the remainder of this book. In the next chapter we'll look at and reject the strategy which attempts to build levels of confidence out of states of belief. Chapters after that work up the best view which does the reverse. In the end we'll need such a view to do three things: find sufficient truth in the Coarse, Fine, and Threshold Views, dissolve the Lottery and Preface Paradoxes, and explain why coarse- and fine-grained attitudes march in step when at work.

# 9
# Belief-First Epistemology

## 9.1 Two Strategies

How do states of confidence relate to their coarse-grained cousins? Can the former be reduced to the latter? The approach which says that they can is an approach I call 'belief-first epistemology'. This is an approach which does not reject the very idea (or bona fides) of fine-grained attitudes, but rather attempts to explain them by appeal to their coarse-grained cousins. In this chapter we assess the prospects for the approach by looking at views which attempt to reduce credence to belief. Most everything we say generalizes to the broader project of reducing thick confidence to belief too. We'll stick with the more narrow discussion, since it is fraught with difficulties enough by itself.

Every attempt to reduce credence to belief takes the following form:

$$Cr(\Phi) = n$$
$$\leftrightarrows$$
$$\ldots B \ldots \Phi \ldots n \ldots$$

For each $n$ in the unit interval, the root idea is that $n$-level credence in $\Phi$ is nothing over and above some kind of belief-theoretic situation involving $\Phi$ and $n$. A key move in the reductive project involves locating something to plausibly ground the strength of $n$-level credence in $\Phi$. It is plain that such credence should be individuated by reference to the content $\Phi$, but that doesn't distinguish $n$-level credence in $\Phi$ from other attitudes lent to $\Phi$. What's distinctive about $n$-level credence in $\Phi$ vis-à-vis those other attitudes is its strength—the $n$-bit, so to say—the fact that the attitude in question is $n$% of certainty strength-wise. This aspect of the attitude must shine through any $\Phi$-indexed belief-theoretic situation if it's credibly to ground $n$-level credence in $\Phi$.

There are two natural strategies for locating such a grounder of credal strength. One involves locating some aspect of the *role* of belief to match credal strength. The other involves locating some aspect of the *content* of belief to do so. It turns out that neither strategy works very well, as we'll see. In the next section we spell out some problems with the first strategy, and in the following section we spell out some problems with the second. Eventually we reject the very idea that credence is grounded in belief—which means, of course, that there is no hope of explaining why credence and belief march in step by appeal to such a reduction. Since we've ruled out a dualistic approach credence and belief—on which neither is spelled out by appeal to the other—and since we've insisted that one must be spelled out by appeal

*The Rational Mind.* Scott Sturgeon, Oxford University Press (2020). © Scott Sturgeon.
DOI: 10.1093/oso/9780198845799.001.0001

## 9.2 Credence as Update-Disposition

The first strategy we'll consider here attempts to ground credence by fleshing out the following schematic idea:

$$Cr(\Phi) = n$$
$$\leftrightarrows$$
$$\text{Update-disposition}[Att(\Phi)]\ldots n \ldots$$

For each $n$ in the unit interval, the root idea is that $n$-level credence in $\Phi$ is nothing over and above some kind of $n$-strength disposition to update after receipt of input. When $n$ is high, of course, it's fairly clear how the line is most naturally spelled out. The thought is that high credence in a content is nothing over and above some kind of strong disposition to retain belief in that content upon update after receipt of new input. When $n$ is not high, though, it's unclear what the relevant reductive thought in the neighbourhood is. Suppose $n$ is low. We should not then plump for the cleanest of analogies, for that would mean going in for the view that low credence in $\Phi$ is nothing over and above weak disposition to retain belief in $\Phi$ upon update after receipt of new input. But then the view before us entails that low credence in $\Phi$ requires belief in $\Phi$, which it clearly does not. Presumably, when $n$ is low the relevant thought should be something like this: low credence in $\Phi$ is nothing over and above low-strength disposition to acquire belief in $\Phi$ upon update after receipt of new input. And similarly when $n$ is middling in strength the relevant thought should be that $n$-level credence in $\Phi$ is nothing over and above middling-strength disposition to acquire belief in $\Phi$ upon update after receipt of new input.[1]

We needn't settle on how to spell this out exactly, for any approach like this will fail, no matter how it is spelled out. After all, there is an important and obvious difference between attitude-taken-to-content and disposition-to-update-with-that-content. The present attempt to ground credence in belief elides that important and obvious distinction. For that reason it is doomed to failure.

To see this, recall an old exchange between Popper and Jeffrey.[2] The former claimed that an agent's epistemic state could not be well modelled with a single probability function. He noted that an agent might lend 50% credence by way of reaction to an utter lack of data, and contrasted that kind of case with one in which someone lent 50% credence by way of reaction to copious amounts of data. Popper

---

[1] See (Harman, 1986) for an endorsement of the high-credence part of this view. He remains silent on anything but high credence.

[2] (Popper 1959: 414–15), and (Jeffrey 1965: 195).

thought a single probability function was not capable of marking the obvious psychological differences between such agents; and this led him to conclude that more than one probability function was needed when attempting to model the agent's rationality.

Jeffrey responded by appeal to conditional credence. He noted that in Popper's scenario one agent's credence for the claim in question conditional on various bits of information look very different than the other agent's credence for that claim conditional on those bits of information. Jeffrey used this divergence in conditional credence to mark intuitive differences manifested by Popper's agents. And then Jeffrey endorsed the further idea that updating dispositions are themselves marked by conditional credence. So his response to Popper rested ultimately on the idea that two agents could invest the same credence in a claim yet manifest divergent credal-updating dispositions with respect to it.

Jeffrey is right to think that agents can invest equal credence in a claim yet diverge in their dispositions to update. There is an important and obvious difference between lending credence to a claim and any disposition one might enjoy to shift one's take on that claim upon receipt of new input. This is precisely the sort of difference needed to distinguish Popper's two agents (as Jeffrey saw clearly).

A similar point cuts against any attempt to reduce credence to the (rational) flux of coarse-grained states. For instance, two agents can adopt the same credence in $\Phi$ yet diverge in their disposition to update belief in $\Phi$, disbelief in $\Phi$, or an attitude of suspended judgement in $\Phi$. Perhaps they cannot do so without *also* differing in their conditional beliefs: that is not presently relevant. What matters here is that adopting credence is one thing and being disposed to update is another. This is true when the disposition in play is indexed to a shift in fine-grained states such as credence. It is also true when the disposition in play is indexed to a shift in coarse-grained states such as belief.

There is no way to ground credence in dispositions to update belief. Any such effort elides the important difference between attitude and disposition to change attitude. Since that difference is conceptually fundamental, there looks to be no way to spell out the nature of fine-grained attitudes by appeal to dispositions to change coarse-grained attitudes. It also suggests that if coarse-grained attitudes are to be used as credence makers, they should be used more directly. That is the strategy we now consider.

## 9.3 Credence-as-Belief

The second strategy for grounding credence in belief involves the following schematic idea:

$$\text{Cr}(\Phi) = n$$
$$\Downarrow$$
$$\text{belief in } [\text{prob}(\Phi) = n]$$

For each $n$ in the unit interval, the root idea is that $n$-level credence in $\Phi$ is nothing over and above belief in the view that the probability of $\Phi$ equals $n$. I call this sort of reductive position 'credence-as-belief'.[3] Before laying out the deepest problem with the view, three initial worries for it should be discussed, and one of its major advantages should be emphasized. As we'll see, two of the worries are fairly easy to handle, the third is quite interesting but ultimately not threatening to the credence-as-belief hypothesis, and the major advantage of the view is highly non-trivial. This all takes some explaining, of course, so consider the issues in turn.

*Worry 1: What Kind of Probability?*

When confronted with this position Bayesians usually insist that its proponents specify the *kind* of probability at work in their view; and by 'specify' they normally have a particular thing in mind. Bayesians usually demand that proponents of credence-as-belief give reductive truth-conditions for the probability claims at work in their view. They insist that proponents of credence-as-belief tell us if their notion of probability is to be spelled out in objective or subjective terms, by appeal to ideal or real frequencies, or some other reductive resource like that. The basic idea behind their demand is that the credentials of credence-as-belief turn on the plausibility of credence reducing to belief in some independently-articulated kind of probability: nomic, metaphysical, evidential, or whatnot.

But this is a mistake. After all, proponents of credence-as-belief can say that credence is nothing but belief in an everyday notion of probability, a notion which is no more detailed or theoretically articulated than any other ordinary notion. And it is certainly not true that ordinary notions are readily—or, arguably even ever—subject to reductive truth-conditions! Yet that does not make those notions illegitimate or unreal. It just means that they gain their cognitive significance without underpinning by an articulated set of reductive truth-conditions. Proponents of credence-as-belief can say that their notion of probability is no different than any other ordinary notion—such as a table, or a chair, or a nation, or a person. It is pinned down by its conceptual and/or functional role in life. Such theorists need only insist that belief in claims built from an ordinary notion of probability register functionally as states of credence do. That is the meat-and-potatoes of their view. It does not require reductive truth-conditions for the claims about probability it involves. To think otherwise is to be overly reductive in philosophy.[4]

*Worry 2: Not Enough Beliefs to Go Around*

The doctrine of credence-as-belief faces an obvious worry straightaway: we do not have enough explicit beliefs about probability to ground all our states of credence. Just consider the dead-obvious claim vocalized by this sentence: 'Either snow is white, it is not the case that snow is white, or I'm very confused.' As it happens I invest maximal credence in the claim which I make with the sentence. But I do not have an explicit belief about the probability of that claim. This is an instance of something much more general:there are not enough explicit beliefs about probability

---

[3] See (Holton, 2014), (Lance, 1995), and (Pollock, 1995) for sympathetic discussion of credence-as-belief.

[4] This sort of misplaced emphasis on reduction is rampant in areas of philosophy which make heavy use of modal notions (such as probability). See various entries under 'modality' in the *Stanford Encyclopedia of Philosophy*.

to cover our states of credence. This seems to show that credence cannot be reduced to explicit belief in probability.

In light of this worry defenders of credence-as-belief should maintain that credence reduces to belief in probability which is normally tacit (and maybe even always tacit). They should construe credal-making belief as routinely (and maybe even always) below the surface of our mental life, appearing on that surface, if at all, only in special settings, perhaps only when other probabilistic considerations are explicit, or whatever. Their view should be taken as a substantive hypothesis about how our cognitive life works, as the claim that below the surface there are a number of tacit coarse-grained attitudes. The content of those attitudes has to do with the probability of various claims. The view is then that credence lent to a claim is itself grounded in tacit belief about its probability. This is not obviously the case, of course, but nor should a defender of credence-as-belief take it to be. Such a theorist should put forward their view as a substantive working hypothesis about how our mind works.

*Worry 3: Functional Equivalence*
Recall the Cash-Value assumption discussed in the Chapter 1. This is the view that attitude-types are basically identical to signature functions. Those functions provide the 'cash value' of the types in question. Hence we begin with the view that notionally distinct attitude-types are genuinely distinct only if manifesting them essentially involves a functional difference of some kind; and we begin with the view that the functional identity of notionally distinct attitude-types is sufficient for their genuine identity deep down.

This sort of functionalism leads to a worry. After all, the doctrine of credence-as-belief is basically the mirror image of the credence-based view discussed in the last chapter. On the former position credence is lent to a content—metaphysically speaking—by believing a related content. On the latter position belief is lent to a content by investing credence in that content. Each view says that one kind of attitude is manifested solely in virtue of the other being lent; and each agrees that the two kinds of attitude are credence and belief. The views differ solely on which of these phenomena are explanatorily more basic. Credence-as-belief takes the coarse-grained attitude as more fundamental than its fine-grained cousin, and 'belief-as-credence' does the reverse: taking credence to be more basic. The *worry* about this—most definitely pressing in light of our functionalism about the attitudes—is that the two views are really just notational variants of one another, that there is no real psychological difference between belief-first and credence-first creatures.

Fortunately, this worry can be set aside. To see how let us stipulate that Bella is a belief-first creature for whom credence-as-belief is true, and that Creda is a credence-first creature for whom belief-as-credence is true. At the base of their respective psychologies, then, Bella lends credence by believing and Creda believes by lending credence. Moreover—and purely for illustrative purposes—we stipulate that Bella and Creda each thinks in a language-of-thought, and that at the base of their respective psychologies each of them lends attitude A to content C by placing a C-meaning sentence of their language-of-thought in a functionally-individuated 'attitude box': the **A**-box.[5] This box is defined so that whenever a C-meaning sentence is placed within it the agent functions in whatever ways happen to be signature functions for lending attitude **A** to claim C.

Bella has a single attitude box of relevance: the belief box. She adopts a psychologically basic belief in a claim C by placing a C-meaning sentence of her *lingua mentis* in the belief box. Credence-as-belief is also true of Bella, by hypothesis, so her psychological make-up involves lending credence as well as belief. Yet Bella lends credence in the first instance by having a sentence of her language-of-thought in the belief box, a sentence which speaks to the probability of the claim to which credence is thereby lent.

Likewise, Creda has many attitude boxes at the base of her psychology: one for each level of credence she can lend. Creda lends psychologically basic $\ell$-level credence to C by placing a C-meaning sentence of her *lingua mentis* in the $\ell$-box—the box individuated to ensure that whenever a sentence is placed within it, Creda functions in the signature ways associated with those who lend $\ell$-level credence to the meaning of that sentence. Belief-as-credence is also true of Creda, by stipulation, so her psychological make-up involves lending belief as well as credence. Yet Creda believes (in the first instance) by having a meaningful sentence of her language-of-thought placed in an aptly-strong credal box, a sentence which expresses the claim thereby believed.

Once it is assumed that belief-first creatures like Bella are possible, however, and also assumed that credence-first creatures like Creda are possible, it is natural to wonder if the two types of creature are notational variants of one another. After all, everyone agrees—who accepts that each type of creature is possible, anyway—that agents of both types end-up with belief and credence; and every theorist of this sort agrees that agents like Bella and Creda differ solely in how their psychologies get the job done: one ends up believing by lending credence, the other ends up lending credence by believing. For epistemic or moral or decision-theoretic purposes, then, the symmetry makes it seem as if salient differences between Bella and Creda show up, if at all, only at the base level of their respective psychologies. In turn this prompts the thought that differences between them make no real philosophical difference, that epistemology, ethics, etc. should see Bella and Creda as notational variants of one another. Their symmetry prompts the idea that it does not *matter*, when theorizing philosophically, whether we are creatures like Bella, creatures like Creda, or creatures like something else yet again.

The worry is pressing, of course, in light of our Cash-Value assumption. Recall that the language-of-thought and the attitude-boxes are meant to be functionally individuated. This makes it an open theoretical possibility—to put it mildly—that credence boxes in one creature are realized by complex mental sentences being placed in the belief box in that creature, while at the same time, in another creature, the belief box is itself realized by less complex mental sentences being placed within a complex array of credal boxes. The trade-off looks to be one between a relatively

---

[5] See the last section of Chapter 2 for a fuller explanation of Creda, and the last section of Chapter 5 for a fuller explanation of Bella. This sort of thought experiment was originally cooked-up by Stephen Schiffer, in his 'Truth and the Theory of Content' (1981).

complex array of mental sentences interacting with a single attitude box, on the one hand, and a potentially simpler array of mental sentences interacting with a relatively complex array of attitude boxes, on the other. But that looks to be *just* the sort of difference-in-implementation from which functionalism abstracts. Hence those making the Cash-Value assumption, like us, are prima facie motivated to view Bella and Creda as notational variants of one another. From our point of view differences between them look to turn on how functional states are realized in an agent's psychology, which in turn prompts the idea that nothing of philosophical substance depends on whether we are creatures like Bella, creatures like Creda, or something else yet again.

But this cannot be right.

Bella and Creda are *not* notational variants of one another. The demonstration of this fact is most easily given with a bit of terminology, so let us say that two agents are *like-minded* exactly when for any content C and level of credence $\ell$, either both believe C or fail to do so, and either both lend $\ell$–level credence to C or fail to do so. Intuitively put, like-minded agents manifest precisely the same beliefs and precisely the same states of credence. By supposing that Bella and Creda are like-minded it is easy to show that each of them manifests a configuration of epistemic states unlike any we could enjoy.

To see this suppose Bella and Creda are like-minded and that Bella believes C. Then Creda must also believe C by like-mindedness. Yet belief-as-credence is true of Creda, so her belief in C must itself be got by investing a level of credence in C. Suppose that level of credence is $\ell$. Since Bella and Creda are like-minded, it follows that Bella also invests $\ell$-credence in C. Yet credence-as-belief is true of Bella, so Bella manages to invest $\ell$-credence in C by believing a claim like **prob**(C)= $\ell$. Since Bella and Creda are like-minded, though, it follows that Creda also believes that claim. Since belief-as-credence is true of Creda, it follows that she ends-up believing the claim that **prob**(C)= $\ell$ by lending credence to that very claim. Suppose her credence in that very claim be $\ell^*$-level credence. Like-mindedness then ensures that Bella also lends $\ell^*$-credence to the claim that **prob**(C)= $\ell$. Since credence-as-belief is true of Bella, though, she ends-up lending $\ell^*$-credence to the claim that **prob**(C)= $\ell$ by believing the more complicated claim that **prob**[**prob**(C)= $\ell$]= $\ell^*$. And so on.

The bottom line is this: when like-minded belief- and credence-first agents believe an arbitrary claim C, and when the belief-first agent lends credence via belief in claims formed with something like a probability operator **prob**(-), then, for *every* natural number $n$, the two agents also believe a claim of the form

$$\mathbf{prob}_n\{\mathbf{prob}_{n-1}(\ldots\ldots[\mathbf{prob}_1(C) = \text{value}_1] = \text{value}_2\}\ldots\ldots\} = \text{value}_n.$$

Likewise, suppose Bella and Creda are like-minded and that Creda invests $\ell$-credence in C. Then Bella must also lend $\ell$-credence to C by like-mindedness. Since credence-as-belief is true of Bella, however, she will lend $\ell$-credence to C by believing a claim like **prob**(C)= $\ell$. Like-mindedness will then ensure that Creda also believes the claim that **prob**(C)= $\ell$. Yet belief-as-credence is true of Creda; so her belief in the claim that **prob**(C)= $\ell$ is got by lending credence to that very claim. Suppose her credence in that very claim is $\ell^*$-level credence. Like-mindedness then ensures that Bella also lends $\ell^*$-credence to the claim that **prob**(C)= $\ell$. Since credence-as-belief is true of

Bella, however, she lends $\ell^*$-credence to the claim that $\mathbf{prob}(C)= \ell$ by believing the more complicated claim that $\mathbf{prob}[\mathbf{prob}(C)= \ell]= \ell^*$. Like-mindedness then ensures that Creda also believes that more complicated claim. And since belief-as-credence is true of Creda, her belief in the more complicated claim is itself got by lending credence to that very claim: i.e., by lending credence to the claim that $\mathbf{prob}[\mathbf{prob}(C)= \ell]= \ell^*$. And so on.

The bottom line is this: when like-minded belief- and credence-first agents lend credence to an arbitrary claim C, and when the belief-first agent lends credence via belief in claims formed with something like a probability operator $\mathbf{prob}(\text{-})$, then, for *every* natural number $n$, the two agents also lend credence to a claim of the form

$$\mathbf{prob}_n\{\mathbf{prob}_{n-1}(\ldots\ldots[\mathbf{prob}_1(C) = \text{value}_1] = \text{value}_2\}\ldots\ldots\} = \text{value}_n.$$

Putting all this together, then, we have the following: for any claim C, and any natural number $n$, belief- and credence-first agents are like-minded only if

(a) whenever they believe C, they also believe the result of embedding C into an $n$-length iteration of the operator used by the belief-first agent to lend credence.

and

(b) whenever they lend credence to C, they lend credence to the $n^{\text{th}}$-length embedding mentioned in (a).[6]

Like-minded belief- and credence-first creatures manifest an *in*human configuration of attitudes. There is no finite upper bound on the number of attitudinal states they enjoy. There is no such bound on the surface complexity of contents to which they lend belief and/or credence.

Whenever a belief-first agent fails to manifest such a configuration of attitudes—say by having a human-like set of epistemic states—that agent cannot be replicated by a credence-first cousin. No such cousin can possess exactly the attitudes manifested by the human-like belief-first agent. Similarly, whenever a credence-first agent manifests a normal set of epistemic states, that agent cannot be replicated by a belief-first cousin. No such cousin can possess exactly the attitudes manifested by the human-like credence-first agent. Functionalism about the attitudes does not render differences between Bella and Creda benign. At most, one of them can model our epistemic states.

---

[6] It is easy to turn these intuitive lines of argument into proofs by induction on $n$. Back-and-forth arguments like this apply only to positions on which belief and credence fold into one another in an elegant one-by-one fashion. They do not apply—so far as I can see—to belief- or credence-first views which are shaped, for instance, like non-reductive materialism: i.e., views which claim that credence is belief deep down, or the reverse, but also claim only that something like global supervenience holds between them. Rather different views of this sort have recently been defended: see (Frankish, 2009) and (Leitgeb, 2014). See also (Baker, 2009) for a discussion of that position, and (McLaughlin, 1995) for a discussion of global supervenience.

It is clear why there is a doxastic explosion between like-minded belief- and credence-first creatures. The following form will be will true of any credence-first believer like Creda:

$$(\text{C-1}^{st}) \quad b(\Phi) \supset cr^+(\Phi).$$

Since belief-as-credence holds of any such agent, they manage belief in $\Phi$ by lending high credence to $\Phi$. Yet the following form will be true of any belief-first credal agent like Bella:

$$(\text{B-1}^{st}) \quad cr(\Phi) \supset b[\text{operator}(\Phi)].$$

Since credence-as-belief is true of any such agent, they lend credence to $\Phi$ by believing a content got by embedding $\Phi$ in a content-forming operator of some kind (such as a probability operator). Whenever two agents are like-minded, though, they share exactly the same beliefs and states of credence. If one of them is a credence-first creature, while the other is a belief-first creature, principles like (C-1$^{st}$) and (B-1$^{st}$) will each be true of a *single* set of attitudes. Jointly, they make for explosive schemata: one for belief, another for credence.

After all, (C-1$^{st}$) ensures that there is high credence lent to $\Phi$ whenever $\Phi$ is believed; and (B-1$^{st}$) ensures that there is belief in a content of the form [operator($\Phi$)] whenever credence is lent to $\Phi$. For any content $\Phi$ whatsoever, then, and any set of attitudes for which both principles hold, the following will also hold of belief:

$$(\text{B}) \quad b(\Phi) \supset b[\text{operator}(\Phi)].$$

That is why there is an explosion of things believed by like-minded belief-and credence-first agents. Schema (B) guarantees the explosion: any content found on the right-hand side of one of its instances is also found on the left-hand side of another of those instances.

Similarly, (B-1$^{st}$) ensures that there is belief in a claim of the form [operator($\Phi$)] whenever credence is lent to $\Phi$; and (C-1$^{st}$) ensures that high credence is lent to a content when that content is believed. For any content $\Phi$ whatsoever, then, and any set of attitudes for which both principles hold, the following will also hold of credence:

$$(\text{C}) \quad cr(\Phi) \supset cr^+[\text{operator}(\Phi)].^7$$

That is why there is an explosion of things to which credence is lent by like-minded belief- and credence-first agents. Schema (C) guarantees the explosion: any content found on the right-hand side of one of its instances is also found on the left-hand side of another of those instances.

---

[7] Here one should ask: what sort of high credence makes for belief? We obviously believe things of which we're not absolutely certain. Fully maximal credence should not be required for belief. Once that is granted, though, (C) will involve some sort of sub-optimality; for (C) will have instances with $cr(\Phi)$ unequal to $cr[\text{operator}(\Phi)]$. Yet the content-forming operator will be something like a probability operator, or a likelihood-of-truth operator, or some such. So with **cr** non-degenerate the relevant instances of (C) will be situations like being exactly 95% certain of $\Phi$ while being less than certain that the probability of $\Phi$ is 95%, or less than certain that the likelihood of $\Phi$'s truth is 95%, or whatever.

Normal belief-first creatures—i.e., those with human-like configurations of attitude—cannot be replicated in a credence-first way; and normal credence-first creatures— i.e., those with human-like configurations of attitude—cannot be replicated in a belief-first way. Every human-like configuration of attitudes is such that either it is impossible for a credence-first creature like Creda to manifest exactly those attitudes or it is impossible for a belief-first creature like Bella to do so. If both kinds of creature could manage the task, after all, like-minded creatures of each kind could manifest a human-like configuration of attitudes. But that is not possible.[8]

A natural response to the explosion arguments is this:

> OK, belief- and credence-first creatures cannot be like-minded if either exhibits a human-like configuration of attitude. It is still an *empirical* issue, though, whether our psychological architecture is like Bella, like Creda, or like neither of them. After all, belief- and credence-first creatures are obviously possible. Given well-known differences between cow-poke Texans and city-slicker Californians, for instance, science may well discover that Texans are Bellas and Californians are Credas (so to say). We'll just have to investigate.

But it turns out that part of this response is wrong; for it turns out that it is *not* true that belief- and credence-first creatures are each possible. Reflection on their metaphysics reveals that at most one type of creature is possible.

To see this the key place to start is with the following thought: both doctrines in play here—belief-as-credence and credence-as-belief—entail that facts about one kind of attitude come for free once facts about another kind of attitude are settled. This is true because both doctrines maintain that instances of one type of attitude are elegantly grounded, one-by-one, in instances of another type of attitude. The two doctrines diverge in which types of attitude they see as grounded, and they diverge in which they see as doing the grounding work, but belief-as-credence and credence-as-belief agree with one another that some attitudinal facts metaphysically derive, in an elegant way, from other attitudinal facts. It turns out that this symmetry itself precludes it being the case that each doctrine is possible.

To see why, recall that belief-as-credence ensures that belief in Φ comes for free once high credence in Φ is in place, and credence-as-belief ensures that high credence in Φ comes for free once belief in (something like) the high probability of Φ is in place. The doctrines are each possible only if each side of this picture is too:

---

[8] Suppose that for some number n it turns out that everyday purposes only concern the functioning of our attitudes taken to contents involving no more than n nested probability operators. Then the explosion argument does not rule out that like-minded belief- and credence-first creatures model attitudes up to but not exceeding n nested probability operators. In the event such creatures might model us for all practical purposes.

But the argument concerns more than practical interest. It covers all functionally-relevant aspects of our mental life. Those aspects might be difficult to discern—perhaps only a serious science could discern them. But functionalism about the attitudes, plus the paper's explosion argument, guarantee that like-minded belief- and credence-first creatures could not be like us in all functionally discernible respects.

$$b(\Phi) \qquad cr^+(\Phi)$$
$$\downarrow \qquad \downarrow$$
$$cr^+(\Phi) \qquad b[prob^+(\Phi)].$$

**Figure 9.1**

Downward arrows in Figure 9.1 continue to mean that once a lower attitudinal condition is in place, a higher attitudinal condition is nothing over and above the lower one. The higher one comes for free, being grounded in the lower attitudinal condition.

The key point is then drawn from the metaphysics of grounding, namely, that coming-for-free is a *modally invariant relation*. If, at any world, one condition comes for free once another is in place, then, at every world, that condition comes for free once the other is in place.[9] If it is so much as possible that belief in $\Phi$ comes for free once high credence in $\Phi$ is in place, therefore, it is necessarily the case that belief in $\Phi$ comes for free once high credence in $\Phi$ is in place. And if it is so much as possible that high credence in $\Phi$ comes for free once belief in the high probability of $\Phi$ is in place, therefore, it is necessarily the case that high credence in $\Phi$ comes for free once belief in the high probability of $\Phi$ is in place.

This means that if belief-as-credence and credence-as-belief are each possible, two further claims about grounding are the case. One is that belief in $\Phi$ comes for free once belief in $\Phi$'s high probability is in place. The other is that high credence in $\Phi$ comes for free once high credence in $\Phi$'s high probability is in place. Belief-as-credence and credence-as-belief are each possible, in other words, only if each side of this picture is too:

$$b(\Phi) \qquad cr^+(\Phi)$$
$$\downarrow \qquad \downarrow$$
$$B[prob^+(\Phi)] \qquad cr^+[prob^+(\Phi)],$$

**Figure 9.2**

where downward arrows continue to depict that a higher condition is grounded in a lower one. Figure 9.2's left-hand dependence is got by taking the right-hand and then the left-hand dependence of Figure 9.1, in that order. And Figure 9.2's right-hand dependence is got by taking the left-hand and then right-hand dependence of Figure 9.1, in that order, with the relevant content being $[prob^+(\Phi)]$.

These last depictions of grounding are obviously wrong. They are each of the form

$$@(\Phi)$$
$$\downarrow$$
$$@[prob^+(\Phi)].$$

---

[9] This is a modalized version of a popular principle in the grounding literature. That principle is often called 'Necessitation'. Rosen (2009) proposes it under the label 'Entailment'. See also relevant papers in (Schnieder, Hoeltje, & Steinberg, 2013).

The idea is that lending a given attitude to a content is itself grounded in that very attitude being lent to a second content—a second content which makes likely, but does not entail, the first content involved in the case. But that cannot be. Since a single attitude is meant to be involved in the putatively grounding and grounded fact, and since the content of the former does not entail that of the latter, the putative grounded condition—i.e. the one that is meant to come for free—should itself have *stronger* functional constituents than the putative grounding condition—i.e., the one meant to make for what is meant to be grounded. Yet a single attitude lent to a claim cannot be grounded in that very attitude being lent to a second claim which fails to entail the first.

For example, despite a good deal of disagreement about which functions are essential to belief in $\Phi$, most everyone agrees that such belief essentially involves a strong and immediate disposition to do at least one of the following:

(a) use $\Phi$ in practical deliberation,
(b) use $\Phi$ in theoretical deliberation,
(c) say 'yes' when asked whether $\Phi$ is true.

Belief in the high probability of $\Phi$ essentially involves none of these things. When you have such belief you may well be disposed to use $\Phi$ in (a)- or (b)-style deliberation, and you may well be disposed to say 'yes' when asked if $\Phi$ is true; but these dispositions will be recognizably weaker than the counterpart dispositions flowing directly from belief in $\Phi$. After all, the claim that $\Phi$'s probability is high makes it likely that $\Phi$ is true, but it does not ensure that $\Phi$ is true; so dispositions which flow directly from belief in the probabilistic content will be milder variants of those which flow directly from belief in $\Phi$. Hence the left-hand dependency of Figure 9.2 fails. We have seen, though, that that very dependency is entailed by the possibility of belief-as-credence together with that of credence-as-belief. One or both of those doctrines is not possible. Either Creda or Bella is an impossible agent.

Similarly, high credence in the claim that $\Phi$ is very probable is itself a weaker state than is equally high credence in $\Phi$. If you are 95% sure that the probability of $\Phi$ is 95%, for instance, then, typically, you will be less than 95% sure of $\Phi$. And while it is possible to be 95% sure of $\Phi$ while also being 95% sure that the probability of $\Phi$ is 95%, being in the latter condition is no guarantee of being in the former. Hence the right-hand dependency of Figure 9.2 also fails. Yet that dependency is itself entailed by the possibility of belief-as-credence together with that of credence-as-belief. One or both of those doctrines is not possible. Far from being notational variants of one another, either Bella or Creda is actually an impossible agent.

*Major Advantage: Reasoning with Credence*

Chapter 6 made it clear that there is a mismatch between rules like Jeffrey Conditionalization and standard cases of inference. In that discussion we made use of the Core Inference Principle:

(CIP) A mental-state transition is a bog-standard inference if

1. Its input is a small number of instances of an attitude taken to contents.
2. Its output is an instance of that attitude taken to a new content.

3. The output is formed on the basis of the input.
4. The shift from input to output reflects sensitivity to the fact that input-contents evidentially support output-content.

Each clause of this principle captures an essential element of certain kinds of ordinary inference, but not one of them is essential to transitions described by rules like Jeffrey's.[10]

The latter transitions concern total configurations of credence rather than small numbers of attitudes, contra clause 1 of the Core Inference Principle. They also routinely concern differing attitudes in the output-state than are found in the input-state, contra clause 2 of the Core Inference Principle. Moreover, nothing in Jeffrey's rule turns on the basing of one mental state on another, something essential to clause 3 of the Core Inference Principle. And Jeffrey-like transitions turn on how pre- and post-transitional *attitudes* hang together—not how their contents do—contra clause 4 of the Core Inference Principle.

Jeffrey Conditionalization and the like have to do with structural properties of overall epistemic positions. Those properties are meant to constitute epistemic equilibria when configured properly. Jeffrey Conditionalization and the like have to do with the recovery of equilibrium after it's been lost via the absorption of input. By contrast, rules of inference have to do with local properties of a small clutch of attitudes, properties meant to explain why local bits of cognition push forward in an evidentially well-done way. This is very different than anything found in the Bayesian Transition Theory. As we put the point in previous chapters: one kind of rule belongs to a theory's kinematics, the other belongs to its dynamics.

This makes it hard to see how there could be such a thing as reasoning with credal states. After all, epistemic rules for the update of credence do not look like rules in the literature on bog-standard inference.[11] To put the worry bluntly, there is no theory of credal inference in the literature, we're basically lost when it comes to genuinely inferential transitions between states of credence. This calls into question the bona fides of confidence-first epistemology.[12]

This difficulty vanishes, though, if we accept the doctrine of credence-as-belief. To see this consider an example: in its first stage a rational agent's states of credence are described by three in-between real numbers $x$, $y$ and $z$:

$$\begin{aligned} cr_1(\Phi) &= x \\ cr_1(\Psi/\Phi) &= y \\ cr_1(\Psi) &= z. \quad \smiley \end{aligned}$$

The smiley face indicates that the agent in Stage-1 has coherent credence. In Stage-2 we suppose that she gets new input to the effect that $\Phi$ is now true, and that she registers the news with certainty. Before anything else changes, then, we have:

---

[10] See Chapter 13 for a much fuller discussion of inference.
[11] See (Horty, 2014), or (Pollock, 1987).
[12] Chapter 13 puts forward a solution to this problem for confidence-first epistemology.

$$\begin{aligned} cr_2(\Phi) &= 1 \\ cr_2(\Psi/\Phi) &= y \\ cr_2(\Psi) &= z. \end{aligned} \quad \text{☹}$$

The frown indicates that our agent at this Stage has incoherent credence (since $z$ does not equal $y$).

There is only one way to recover coherence while preserving full credence in $\Phi$ as well as initial credence in $\Psi$ given $\Phi$. The result is a happy shift-of-view into Stage-3 credence:

$$\begin{aligned} cr_3(\Phi) &= 1 \\ cr_3(\Psi/\Phi) &= y \\ cr_3(\Psi) &= y. \end{aligned} \quad \text{☺}$$

The transition from Stage-1 to Stage-3 is in line with the update rule of Conditionalization.[13] Is the transition genuinely inferential?

Well, suppose Stage-3 credence in $\Psi$ is formed on the basis of new credence in $\Phi$—i.e. credence induced by worldly stimulation—together with extant credence in $\Psi$ given $\Phi$. The shift from State-1 to Stage-3 credence is then much like an inference. But there are still two reasons to worry:

- the transitioning states do not involve a single propositional attitude (as always happens in bog-standard cases of inference).
- it is very unclear how transition between them reflects contents supporting one another evidentially (as also happens in such inference).[14]

These things are central to the Core Inference Principle, since they look to be central to bog-standard inference. Without them it is unclear that a given mental-state transition is genuinely inferential. With them in place it is much clearer that it might be.

We can ensure both features are present in our example by endorsing credence-as-belief. Recall the view says that for any claim C and unit real $r$ an agent invests $r$-level credence in C by believing (something like) the claim that the probability of C equals $r$. If this is right then an agent invests credence by lending belief, what it is for an agent to invest credence is for them to believe things about probability. Suppose that is so. Then our example can be recast in the following way:

---

[13] Nothing in the argument here turns on it being Conditionalization that characterizes the transition. Jeffrey's rule would have worked just as well.

[14] In a Bayesian framework the most natural way to spell out evidential relations is with conditional probability. The strategy will be a success, though, only if a number of difficult issues can be resolved. For example, since conditional probability is a continent matter—varying from probability distribution to probability distribution—it is unclear such probability can ground non-contingent evidential relations between contents (of a sort which drive inference in everyday life). Since conditional probability is derivative in the Bayesian model–reducing to ratios of unconditional probability—and since unconditional probability is a global feature of a probability distribution—being fixed by everywhere within it, so to say—it is unclear conditional probability can ground local evidential relations between contents (of a sort which drive inference). And so on.

| Stage 1 | → | Stage 2 | → | Stage 3 |
|---|---|---|---|---|
| $\text{bel}_1[\text{prob}(\Phi) = x]$ | | $\text{bel}_2[\text{prob}(\Phi) = 1]$ | | $\text{bel}_3[\text{prob}(\Phi) = 1]$ |
| $\text{bel}_1[\text{prob}(\Psi/\Phi) = y]$ | | $\text{bel}_2[\text{prob}(\Psi/\Phi) = y]$ | | $\text{bel}_3[\text{prob}(\Psi/\Phi) = y]$ |
| $\text{bel}_1[\text{prob}(\Psi) = z]$ | | $\text{bel}_2[\text{prob}(\Psi) = z]$ | | $\text{bel}_3[\text{prob}(\Psi) = y]$. |
| ☺ | | ☹ | | ☺ |

Note that Stage-2 belief is conceptually inconsistent: if the probability of R is 1, after all, and the conditional probability of W given R is $y$, it follows (by the probability calculus) that the probability of W is $y$ too (and not $z$, since we're stipulating that $y \neq z$). The doctrine of credence-as-belief allows us to construe the shift from Stage-2 to Stage-3 credence as genuinely inferential, since it allows us to see that shift as the adjustment of belief due to conceptual entailment.

Put another way: credence-as-belief allows us to view shift from Stage-2 to Stage-3 credence as a local step-wise approximation of Bayesian updating. We can thus see localized shifts in credence as both Bayesian in spirit and inferential in nature. They are Bayesian in spirit because they are approximations of Conditionalization. They are inferential in nature because they satisfy each aspect of the Core Inference Principle. If our aim is to locate genuinely inferential phenomena within a credence-theoretic setting, therefore—and to do so in a way that respects (something like) the Core Inference Principle—we can do no better than to endorse credence-as-belief. The doctrine entails that reasoning with credence is no more puzzling than reasoning with belief.

This is a major advance.

It is something of a scandal that the epistemology of confidence has no real grip on the notion of inference involving states of confidence. The moment we fix on that topic directly, though, it looks tricky indeed, for there look to be serious differences between our conception of inference in bog-standard cases and our conception of shift in credence. This calls into question the very idea of reasoning with credence. The bona fides of that idea can be secured with the doctrine of credence-as-belief.[15]

Drawing everything together, then, here's where we are. There are two main strategies for reducing credence to belief. One involves locating an aspect of the cognitive role of belief to match credal strength. The other involves locating an item in the content of belief to do so. The former strategy elides an obvious and needed distinction between the nature of a standing state and that of a disposition to change standing states. The latter turns out to be more robust than one might initially expect. In particular:

- Credence-as-belief does not fall prey to outdated worries about truth-conditions for its brand of probability.
- The doctrine is consistent with the fact that agents have too few explicit beliefs about probability to ground states of credence.

---

[15] The approach to reasoning within a confidence-based setting discussed in Chapter 13 does not really solve this problem, for it does not detail how steps in reasoning lead rationally to shift of credence. That is further work to be done left on the table by this book.

- It does not trivialize debate between its proponents and their opposite order—i.e. those who aim to ground coarse-grained attitudes in their fine-grained cousins—for it can be shown that only one of the approaches can be true of us, indeed, that only approach can be true at all.
- Credence-as-belief does an excellent job of underwriting the idea that we reason with credal states.

This is a promising start. In light of the difficulties with the alternatives, then, the best strategy for grounding fine-grained attitudes in their coarse-grained cousins involves the idea that credence is really belief about probability deep down.

## 9.4 A Dilemma

Unfortunately, this promising strategy faces a dilemma connected with what I see as its most basic challenge. First we lay out the dilemma in detail and then we move to the major difficulty for credence-as-belief.

To see everything clearly it helps to work with an example. So consider an agent who is 70% sure that it will rain—**cr**(R) = 70%—and suppose that the signature function of that state of credence is the property of being 70% disposed to say that it will rain. These suppositions make vivid the functional signature targeted for reduction by defenders of credence-as-belief. They are made solely for illustrative purposes. Nothing in the example turns on them.

The doctrine of credence-as-belief then entails a picture like this in the case:

$$\mathbf{cr}(R) = 70\%$$
$$\Downarrow$$
$$\mathbf{bel}[\text{prob}(R) = 70\%]$$

Or in other words

(i) 70% credence in R is nothing but belief in [prob(R) = 70%].

Defender of credence-as-belief cannot rest with this claim. *If* they are to place a serious proposal before us, they must tell us more about the putatively credal-making belief toward the end of (i). Only after they have done so—and in no small detail, I'd say—will we understand what 70% credence in R is being said to be. So how would a defender of credence-as-belief make sense of the putatively credal-making belief in her view?

Well, let us spell out the example by continuing to draw on the computational theory of mind and the language-of-thought hypothesis. For illustrative purposes suppose that belief in the claim that it will rain is itself a computational state involving a mental sentence which means that it will rain, and, similarly, that belief in the claim that the probability of rain is 70% is itself a computational state involving a mental sentence which means that the probability of rain is 70%. More generally suppose that our defender of credence-as-belief says—again, purely for illustrative purposes—that for any claim Φ, belief in Φ is a computational state involving a mental sentence which means Φ.

Let the computational relation in play be **B** and let σ be a sentence in the language of thought. The picture is then one on which

$$\textbf{bel}[\text{prob}(R) = 70\%]$$
⇨
$$\textbf{B}(\sigma) \text{ when } \sigma \text{ means } [\text{prob}(R) = 70\%]$$

Or in other words,

(ii) belief in [prob(R) = 70%] is nothing but **B**(σ) when σ means [prob(R) = 70%].

This illustrative hypothesis joins with (i) to entail a picture on which

$$\textbf{cr}(R) = 70\%$$
⇨
$$\textbf{B}(\sigma) \text{ when } \sigma \text{ means } [\text{prob}(R) = 70\%]$$

Or in other words,

(iii) 70% credence in R is nothing but **B**(σ) when σ means [prob(R) = 70%].

Any proponent of a view like this will face a nasty dilemma.

After all, they must tell us *something* about its explanatory resources. Failure to do so will leave us ill-equipped to understand what it is they think reduces 70% credence in rain. In spelling out the explanatory resources in (iii), however, the proponent of credence-as-belief will either make appeal to the signature function of being 70% sure that it will rain or they fail to do so. But there are problems for them no matter which it is. In the first case, their story will vitiate the reductive ambitions of credence-as-belief; and in the second case, there will be little-to-no reason to suppose that standing in **B** to a mental sentence which means that the probability of R is 70% guarantees that one functions as those who are 70% sure that it will rain thereby function—in other words, in the second case there will be little-to-no reason to think that the signature function of 70% credence in rain will be entailed by belief in the claim that the probability of rain is 70%. Consider each horn of this dilemma.

## Horn 1

Suppose our defender of credence-as-belief spells out the explanatory resources in (iii) by appeal to the signature function of 70% credence that it will rain. The simplest way for her to do so would be to identify the relevant explanatory resources with that signature function. The picture would then be

$$\textbf{B}(\sigma) \text{ when } \sigma \text{ means } [\text{prob}(R) = 70\%]$$
⇨
70% disposition to say that it will rain.

Or in other words,

(iv) **B**(σ) when σ means [prob(R) = 70%] is nothing but a 70% disposition to say that it will rain.

There are a number of problems for any view like this.

For one thing (and most obviously), (iv)'s explanatory resources—i.e. the items after 'nothing but'—do not specify a computational relation of any kind, much less one taken to a mental sentence, very much less one taken to a mental sentence which means that the probability of rain is 70%. Hence (iv) looks straightforwardly false from the beginning. More importantly for our purposes, however, (iv) is incompatible with the reductive ambitions of credence-as-belief; for it joins with (iii) to entail the relevant theorist's take on 70% credence in rain:

$$cr(R) = 70\%$$
$$\Rightarrow$$
$$70\% \text{ disposition to say that it will rain}$$

Or in other words,

(v) 70% credence in R is nothing but a 70% disposition to say that it will rain.

Relative to the illustrative assumptions we are making, of course, (v) is perfectly true. But that's only because (v) states what any functionalist must say relative to those assumptions, namely, that 70% credence in rain is individuated by its signature function, which we have stipulated is a 70% disposition to say that it will rain. Once the explanatory resources in (iv) are equated with the signature function of 70% credence in rain, the resulting view is not one on which credence reduces to belief in probability, it is one on which belief in probability reduces to credence! The result badly conflicts with the reductive ambitions of credence-as-belief, for those ambitions aim to take belief as explanatorily prior to credence.

Suppose, then, that our defender of credence-as-belief forges a more subtle connection between the explanatory resources in (iv) and the signature function of 70% credence in rain. Suppose she does not crudely equate the former with the latter but instead uses the signature function of 70% credence in rain to explain, say, how a mental sentence gets its meaning, how it comes to mean that there is a 70% probability of rain. Her line would then something like this:

Lending 70% credence to rain is nothing but believing that the probability of rain is 70%. Believing that the probability of rain is 70% is nothing but bearing computational relation **B** to a mental sentence σ which means that the probability of rain is 70%. σ's meaning that the probability of rain is 70% is itself nothing but it's owner being 70% disposed to say that it will rain when she stands in **B** to σ.[16]

This story does not equate the explanatory resources of (iv) with the signature function of 70% credence in rain. It makes a more subtle move, deploying the signature function of 70% credence in rain in a story about the meaning-investing use of σ. Put another way: the story uses the signature function of 70% credence in rain to reveal what makes it the case that a mental sentence like σ comes to mean that the probability of rain is 70%.

---

[16] Cian Dorr suggested that the defender of credence-as-belief might take this line.

This too vitiates the reductive ambitions of credence-as-belief. After all, the very credence targeted for reduction by the defender of credence-as-belief is itself an explanatory primitive—an unexplained explainer—in her approach to a key resource meant to effect the reduction. This is no good. The picture put forward maintains that manifesting the very function targeted for reduction is part of what it is for a mental sentence to mean what it does; but the picture continues that standing in **B** to a mental sentence with that meaning is what reduces the credence associated with the signature function. The result is manifestly at odds with the reductive ambitions of credence-as-belief.[17]

Similar ways to spell out credence-as-belief suffer similar difficulties, for they all make appeal—either explicitly or more subtly—to the functional property which is 70% credence in R. No story like that successfully reduces credence to non-credal fact. It may look as if it does, initially, because the signature functions of credence are specified in functional rather than credal terms; but once the Cash-Value assumption is in place it's clear that views of this sort fail in their reductive ambitions.

## Horn 2

To avoid these problems a defender of credence-as-belief must do three things:

1. Specify the signature function of credal-making belief in a way which makes sense of that belief in its own terms;
2. Fail to make direct or indirect use of the signature function of targeted credence;
3. Show how manifestation of the signature function of credal-making belief brings with it the manifestation of the signature function of credence.

Only then will the view on offer be plausible. Yet doing the first two of these things makes doing the third one much harder.

To see this, suppose that for any claim $\Phi$ the signature function of belief in $\Phi$ is the disposition to say that $\Phi$ is true. Then a defender of credence-as-belief can make sense of the signature function of putative credal-making belief independently of the signature functions of credence. She can note that 70% credence in rain, for instance, is nothing but belief that the probability of rain is 70%; and she can use the supposition at the start of this paragraph to make non-circular sense of the signature function of this credal-making belief. But the resulting position entails that the signature function of the putative credal-making belief is

(SFB) = the disposition to say that the probability of rain is 70%,

whereas the (illustrative) signature function of 70% credence in rain is

(SFC) = the 70% disposition to say that it will rain.

One can easily makes sense of the first signature function without appeal to the second, so one can easily make sense of the putative credal-making belief without appeal to the

---

[17] Further: contrary to common sense, the picture before us strongly suggests that credence is not subject to epistemic evaluation at all; for it locates credence as an explanatory primitive in psychosemantics, not as an attitudinal component of a psychology involving states subject to such evaluation.

signature function of its reductive target. This means the first two tasks mentioned in the previous paragraph are done without difficulty. But the third task is now out of reach.

After all, possession of (SFB) does not guarantee possession of (SFC): being disposed to say that the probability of rain is 70% does not ensure a 70% disposition to say that it will rain. Relative to our illustrative suppositions, then, manifestation of the signature function of the putative credal-making belief does not guarantee manifestation of the signature function of its reductive target. That means the putative credal-making belief is no such thing: it does not make for credence. We have before us another failed defence of credence-as-belief.

I have no proof that every such defence will fail, much less proof that they will do so in a fashion like the failures we've seen. I do think, though, that working through the detailed failures before us generates rational scepticism that credence-as-belief can be made to work. And I think that a diagnosis of why this is so is to hand.

Here it is.

There are three things that any full-dress defender of credence-as-belief must do:

(A) She must specify the signature function of putative credal-making belief.
(B) She must show that this function is neither identical to nor built from the signature function of its reductive target; and
(C) She must show that possession of this function entails possession of the signature function of that target.

Doing (A) ensures that credence-as-belief is more than just talk. Any defender who fails to do (A) will not have been clear about what credence is meant to be. Doing (B) ensures that a defender of credence-as-belief avoids using credence in her understanding of credal-making belief. Failure to do so—either by equating the signature function of credal-making belief with the signature function of its reductive target, or by building the signature function of credal-making belief from the signature function of that target—vitiates the reductive ambitions of credence-as-belief. Either move undermines the point of credence-as-belief. Yet a defender of the view must also do (C) to ensure that credence-as-belief is a genuinely reductive position, to ensure that it succeeds in making clear that credence is not only real but really something else.

The challenge is to do (A), (B), and (C) together. Our discussion shows that meeting it is no easy thing. It is not obvious how to understand belief-in-probability so that our take on it is independent of the signature function of credence, yet our take on belief-in-probability underwrites the idea that so believing ensures that we function as a credence-lender functions, i.e. ensures that we manifest those functional properties constitutively possessed by those who lend credence.[18]

## 9.5 The Marching-in-Step Problem

It is a datum of everyday life that we act from our epistemic commitments. A moment ago I got up and flipped on the expresso machine in my kitchen. This

---

[18] Conditions very like (A) thru (C) must be satisfied, *mutatis mutandis*, by any view which aims to reduce coarse-grained attitudes to fine-grained ones. Chapter 11 will detail one way to do so.

I did because I believed that doing so would help me to make a coffee. That belief is quite obviously part of what *caused* me to get up and flip on the machine. It's not as if *other* factors yield a full story about why I behaved as I did. If common sense about this kind of situation is to be respected, we must say that my getting up and flipping on the machine was itself caused, at least in part, by my belief that doing so would help me to make a coffee.

But notice: an entirely similar story is available by appeal to confidence rather than belief. We can also say with common sense that I got up and flipped on the expresso machine because I was confident that doing so would help me to make a coffee; and this story is likewise obviously causal. If common sense is to be respected about this too, we must say that my getting up and flipping on of the machine was itself caused, at least in part, by my confidence that doing so would help me to make a coffee.

Common sense recognizes notionally distinct springs of action: one belief-theoretic, the other confidence-theoretic. It seems that whenever someone acts a certain way because they believe a certain thing is the case, there is an obvious and everyday sense in which they act that way because they're confident that that thing is the case. And whenever someone acts a certain way because they're confident that a certain thing is true, there is an obvious and everyday sense in which they act that way because they believe that thing is true. For this reason it's a datum of everyday life that belief and confidence march in step when causally explaining our actions.[19]

Given the Cash-Value assumption of Chapter 1, however, it follows that the nature of belief and high confidence are causally congruent—that they gracefully fit together—at least in so far as belief and confidence are the springs of action. A story about the relation between their metaphysics will be plausible, therefore, only if it squares with the fact that belief and confidence march in step in this way. Any story about the relation between them which does not fit with their causal congruence—say by conflicting with it or requiring ad hoc extra resources to dovetail with it—will thereby be difficult to believe. The causal congruence of belief and confidence is precisely the sort of thing that should fall out of the relation between their metaphysics.

This is bad news for credence-as-belief, for their marching-in-step comes basically to this:

(M-in-S)   For any claim $\Phi$ and action $\alpha$: belief in $\Phi$ causes $\alpha$ exactly when high confidence in $\Phi$ causes $\alpha$.

Our Cash-Value assumption ensures that this principle holds of necessity, that it's not merely true in the actual world but in every possible world. After all, causal marching-in step has to do with functional congruence. The Cash-Value assumption ensures that the nature of belief and confidence is pinned down by their function. So their functional congruence, if any, is not a contingent matter.

---

[19] There is an analogous sense in which disbelief and low confidence march in step; but, it is not the case that suspended judgement and middling-strength confidence march in step. This is a major puzzle for Lockeans about coarse-grained attitudes to solve. See Chapters 10 and 11 for its presentation and solution respectively.

This leads to a stronger marching-in-step principle:

(□M-in-S)   Necessarily, for any claim $\Phi$ and action $\alpha$: belief in $\Phi$ causes $\alpha$ exactly when high confidence in $\Phi$ causes $\alpha$.

And this principle, together with credence-as-belief, entails something that looks wrong from the latter's point of view:

(☹)   Necessarily, for any claim $\Phi$ and action $\alpha$: belief in $\Phi$ causes $\alpha$ exactly when belief in $\Phi$'s high probability causes of $\alpha$.

This principle looks wrong from the perspective of credence-as-belief. It requires that causally efficacious belief in $\Phi$ necessarily goes with causally efficacious high confidence in $\Phi$, which in turn requires that belief in $\Phi$ necessarily goes with high confidence in $\Phi$. But credence-as-belief looks to entail the possibility of high credence in $\Phi$ without belief in $\Phi$, and vice versa.

This is easy to see by appeal to the language-of-though hypothesis and the belief-box metaphor (again purely for illustrative purposes). Just because an agent has a mental sentence in her belief-box which means that the probability of $\Phi$ is high it does not follow that she has a mental sentence in her belief-box which means $\Phi$. And just because an agent has a mental sentence in her belief-box which means $\Phi$ it does not follow that she has a mental sentence in her belief-box which means that the probability of $\Phi$ is high. Credence-as-belief entails that belief in $\Phi$ and high credence in $\Phi$ are *doubly dissociable*. The doctrine entails that you can manifest either type of state without manifesting the other.

This is reason to reject the doctrine of credence-as-belief. The doctrine conflicts with functionalism about the attitudes in light of obvious facts about how the attitudes function. Since we're assuming functionalism about the attitudes here, the conflict is really between credence-as-belief and common-sense facts about how coarse- and fine-grained attitudes function. When there is competition between a doctrine like credence-as-belief and everyday facts about the function of credence and belief, it is the philosophical doctrine which should give way. After all, no doctrine like credence-as-belief is nearly so obvious as the fact that belief and confidence causally march in step with one another.

# 10
# Credence-First Epistemology
Strengths and Challenges

## 10.1 The Basic Picture

Suppose you listen to a conversation between two prosecuting attorneys: Cave and Incerta. They're discussing whether to ask for the death penalty in a case:

CERTA: We should definitely ask for the death penalty.
INCERTA: Really? I don't know...
CERTA: Don't you think Mr. Bad is guilty?
INCERTA: Of course I do! I wouldn't have prosecuted otherwise.
CERTA: Don't you think his dirty deed merits the death penalty?
INCERTA: Yes, of course, I think that as well.
CERTA: So why the hesitation? Why are you unsure about the death penalty?
INCERTA: Well, even though I believe Mr. Bad is guilty—I've seen the evidence, after all—I don't really believe as *strongly* as you do. I'm basically not sure he's guilty, and I only feel comfortable seeking the death penalty when I'm certain.
CAVE: Well I'm sure he's guilty, so I have no trouble asking for the death penalty.

Even though this dialogue concerns a quasi-technical bit of professional practice—attorneys discussing a case and the verdict they'll seek—it is not hugely off the way we speak of coarse- and fine-grained attitudes in everyday life. Our talk often slips from belief to credence and back again, without any whiff of ambiguity, sleight-of-hand, or other sort of defect. I believe I'll finish this book before the year is out, for instance, and my wife believes that too; but she believes it more strongly than I do, thank goodness, for her confidence helps to create ballast in dry writing periods. This sort of quotidian fact is a sign that common sense locates a very intimate link between coarse- and fine-grained attitudes.

Credence-first epistemology makes good on that link in a particular way. The approach offers a metaphysical integration of coarse- and fine-grained attitudes by grounding the former in credence. Since the idea was put forward by John Locke, evidently, we call it *credal-based Lockeanism* ('CBL' for short). The picture behind the view is shown in Figure 10.1.

On this picture coarse-grained states are just credence in the rough.[1] Belief is nothing more than sufficiently strong credence, disbelief is nothing more than

---
[1] Credal-based Lockeanism is endorsed by (Field, 2003), (Foley, 1992), (Schiffer, 2003), and many others. Something like the view is very often taken as read in the philosophy of mind.

*The Rational Mind.* Scott Sturgeon, Oxford University Press (2020). © Scott Sturgeon.
DOI: 10.1093/oso/9780198845799.001.0001

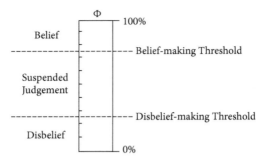

Figure 10.1

sufficiently weak credence, and suspended judgement is nothing more than middling-strength credence.

As we saw in Chapter 8, any plausible version of the view will have to admit that credal thresholds are vague and contextually-variable. The position will see our chunking of credence into a three-fold scheme—belief, disbelief, and suspended judgement—on a par with our chunking of heights into a three-fold scheme—tall, short, and middling in height. Just as there is nothing more to being tall, short, or middling in height—metaphysically speaking—than having a large, small, or middling specific height, respectively, plausible versions of credal-based Lockeanism will say that there is nothing more to believing, disbelieving, or suspending judgement than having a high-, low-, or middling-strength credence, respectively. And just as it is vague and contextually-variable what specific heights make for being tall, short, or middling in height, it is likewise vague and contextually-variable which credal strengths make for belief, disbelief, or suspended judgement.

## 10.2 The Strengths of Credal-Based Lockeanism

There are a number of reasons to think that credal-based Lockeanism is on the right track. Many but not all of them we've seen before; so the familiar ones will be sketched by reference to our earlier more detailed discussion, and the less familiar ones will be laid out in more detail here.

### Realism About the Attitudes

As we saw in Chapters 1, 8, and 9, folk psychology is shot through with both coarse- and fine-grained attitudes. Those attitudes are routinely used in a highly successful predictive and explanatory practice. The scope and power of that practice is great—so much so, in fact, that it is normally taken for granted. But our use of the attitudes in negotiating social reality is in fact a significant cognitive achievement. It's a very good thing, then, that credal-based Lockeanism takes realism about the attitudes to heart. Anything less would render the success of our practice a mystery, and, for that reason, would render the view implausible. Since it underwrites a healthy realism about coarse- and fine-grained attitudes, though, credal-based Lockeanism fits well with common sense.

## Underwrites Our Talk of the Attitudes

We say things like: 'Sascha and Fritz each believe that the trip will be fun, but Sascha believes it more firmly than Fritz does' or 'Maja disbelieves the witness is truthful, but she does not fully disbelieve her.' In these and other ways everyday description of coarse-grained attitudes prompts the idea that belief and disbelief are *graded states* that come in strengths. Ordinary talk of belief allows that you and I might each believe the same thing yet insist that this commonality between us somehow comes off more strongly in your hands than it does in mine; and the same point holds, *mutatis mutandis*, for disbelief. Given that the belief-making threshold is less than certainty, this is exactly what credal-based Lockeanism entails. So the view squares perfectly with this aspect of our everyday talk of the attitudes.[2]

## Intra-level Irreducibility

Formal approaches to coarse- and fine-grained attitudes are curiously asymmetric. Those centring on coarse-grained states routinely take one psychological kind in their domain—typically belief—to be explanatorily basic and then try to reduce other such kinds to the putatively basic attitude. Nothing like that occurs in formal approaches to fine-grained attitudes. None of them singles out a kind of state—or even a range of such kinds—as explanatorily basic and then tries to reduce other psychological kinds to the putatively basic attitudes. Intra-level irreducibility is assumed in fine-grained epistemology even though exactly the opposite is true in coarse-grained epistemology.

§6.2 argued by appeal to common sense, however, that intra-level reductionism about coarse-grained attitudes is wrong-headed, that all three coarse-grained attitudes have psychological bona fides of their own. If we take this aspect of common-sense at face value, then—as we should, *ceteris paribus*—belief is no more explanatorily basic than disbelief or suspended judgement; and vice versa. Coarse-grained attitudes stand to one another as their fine-grained cousins stand to one another: as independent siblings in an explanatorily useful psychological scheme. It's a very good thing, then, that credal-based Lockeanism squares with this aspect of common sense. Since the view entails that coarse-grained attitudes are grounded in their fine-grained cousins—in a simple, elegant, threshold-based way—the intra-level irreducibility of coarse-grained attitudes follows from the intra-level irreducibility of fine-grained attitudes. Or put differently: since credal-based Lockeanism maintains that belief, disbelief, and suspended judgement are grounded respectively in high, low, and middling-strength credence, and since no credence is taken to be more fundamental than any other, it follows that no coarse-grained attitude is more fundamental than any other. This is exactly in line with common sense. Credal-based Lockeanism does better at respecting our ordinary conception of coarse-grained attitudes—with respect to their internal relations, anyway—than do standard formal approaches to belief, disbelief, and suspended judgement.

---

[2] See (Stanley, 2005) for further discussion of this sort of linguistic practice.

## *Underwrites the Marching-in-Step Phenomenon*

Perhaps most importantly the view also yields an obvious and pleasing story about the causal harmony between coarse- and fine-grained attitudes. Since the position has it that coarse- and fine-grained attitudes are conceptually proximal determinables and determinates, respectively, we have an immediate story about why such harmony exists between them. After all, that is precisely how conceptually proximal determinables and determinates often relate to one another causally.[3]

To see the point clearly, compare the causal profile of being red with that of being crimson. These are conceptually proximal determinable and determinate conditions. For our purposes that just means it's dead obvious that satisfying the determinate condition (being crimson) is a particular way of satisfying the determinable condition (being red), and it is dead obvious that satisfying the determinable condition is not a way of satisfying the determinate condition. It is clear from common sense that both conditions are causal-explanatory—or at least it is clear that they both are *because-al*-explanatory, so to say: things routinely happen because objects are red, things routinely happen because objects are crimson.

How do these because-facts fit together?

Well, they overlap in obvious ways. It might be true, for instance, that a driver stops because she sees a light to be crimson even though it is also true that she would have stopped had she seen the light to be any shade of red whatsoever. On the other hand a man may well opt for a particular tie when dressing precisely because it is crimson, even when he would definitely pass on the tie were it to be any other shade of red. Intuitively, red-based explanations like this form into a relatively coarse-grained explanatory scheme, one which is partially underwritten by finer-grained crimson-based explanations. There is causal (or at least because-al) harmony between conceptually-proximal determinable and determinate here. Things happen because objects are red; and sometimes but not always this is so because the red objects are crimson. Things happen because certain objects are crimson; and sometimes but not always this is so because only crimson is relevant to what happens.

Similarly: it may well be true that a rambler takes her brolly because she believes with 95% certainty that it will rain, even though it is also true that she would have taken her brolly had she believed in rain with less or more credence. On the other hand, a man may opt to let his child take a trip because he believes with 99% certainty that the trip is safe, even though he would not give permission were he even slightly less confident in safety. Intuitively, belief-based explanations like this form into a relatively coarse explanatory scheme, one which is partially underwritten by finer-grained credence-based explanations. There is likewise causal (or at least because-al) harmony between conceptually proximal determinable and determinate. Things happen because certain people believe; and sometimes but not always this is so because believers lend 95% credence. Things happen because people lend 95% credence; and sometimes but not always this is so only because they lend exactly that credence.

---

[3] See (Wilson, 2017).

Credal-based Lockeanism sees coarse- and fine-grained attitudes as relating to one another as conceptually proximal determinates and determinables. For this reason, the view has no difficulty making sense of the common-sense fact that two attitudinal schemes march-in-step when explaining what happens. That is often how conceptually proximal determinables and determinates work. They explain things in an overlapping and mutually supportive way. When it comes to explaining our actions, this is exactly how common sense sees belief and high credence. This is strong evidence that something is right about credal-based Lockeanism.

## Underwrites the Rationalizing-in-Step Phenomenon

Further, the view yields an obvious and pleasing story about the rational harmony that exists between coarse- and fine-grained attitudes; for it prompts the natural thought that coarse- and fine-grained attitudes rationalize in parallel precisely because they are conceptually proximal determinable and determinate. This makes for harmony in their rationalizing powers as well as their causal powers.

To see why, suppose I have reason to raise my hand—perhaps I want to get the waiter's attention. Wanting to get the waiter's attention happens to be one way of being psychologically. Any way of being psychologically is also a way of being as such, a way of existing full stop. Wanting to get the waiter's attention is thus a way of existing full stop. But that doesn't mean that I have a reason to raise my hand simply because I exist as such, even though one of my reasons for raising my hand—namely, my desire to get the waiter's attention—metaphysically grounds my existence as such.

The explanation for this is simple: existence as such is too far removed, conceptually speaking, from wanting to get the waiter's attention for the former to rationalize action when the latter does so. On the credal-based Lockean story, however, coarse- and fine-grained attitudes are not conceptually distal in this way. They are conceptually proximal determinable and determinate states: they are basically the same kind of thing differing only at the level of grain. This is why the position underwrites the fact that coarse- and fine-grained attitudes rationalize-in-step; for that is how conceptually proximal determinable and determinate reasons relate to one another. This too strongly suggests that credal-based Lockeanism is on the right track.[4]

So we have a non-trivial amount of good news. With common sense credal-based Lockeanism underwrites realism about the attitudes and how we speak of them. It also underwrites the intra-level irreducibility of both coarse- and fine-grained attitudes, again in line with common sense. And most importantly of all, the view clarifies how causal and rational profiles of coarse- and fine-grained attitudes fit together. These good-making features jointly do more than make credal-based Lockeanism an attractive position. Together they make it hard to believe that the view is barking up the wrong tree. The sum total of good news before us is strong enough to suggest that there is something deeply right in the threshold approach to coarse-grained attitudes.

---

[4] For classic discussion of causal and rational harmony between determinable and determinate, see (Yablo, 1992) or his (Yablo, 1992). For similar thoughts in embryonic form, developed independently, see (Sturgeon, 1994).

## 10.3 Answerable Challenges for Credal-Based Lockeanism

Having said that, credal-based Lockeanism faces a number of challenges. In this section we lay out two which can answered directly. In the next section we sketch two further challenges which cannot be easily answered. Then in the next chapter we construct a version of threshold-based epistemology which does better with those challenges while preserving what's good in credal-based Lockeanism.

*The Conjunction Worry*

Suppose you rationally believe two things: it will rain tomorrow, and Obama was an effective president. Then you ask yourself if the two things are both true: is it the case that it will rain tomorrow *and* Obama was an effective president? It seems plausible—to put it mildly!—that that you should believe the conjunction as well as each of the conjuncts; and the obviousness of this makes it look as if rational belief is closed by conjunction. As we put the point in Chapter 8: for any rational agent and any claims P and Q, if the agent rationally believes P, and rationally believes Q, and considers whether (P&Q), the agent should also believe (P&Q).

This is a plausible principle. Indeed it is so plausible that many feel we should reject any view of rational belief which is inconsistent with it. Since credal-based Lockeanism is inconsistent with the closure principle—as we'll see in a moment—this leads them to reject the position. But I think that rejection is an over-reaction, for we can find a good deal of truth in the closure principle without rejecting credal-based Lockeanism. Indeed we can see the principle as approximately right—or at least as right enough *in situ* to generate the strong impression of truth—even while accepting credal-based Lockeanism.[5]

Assume that the belief-making threshold is less than certainty. Then credal-based Lockeanism entails that rational belief is not closed under conjunction. Consider a lottery for which the following is true:

- a single letter 'P' is printed on five tickets
- a single letter 'Q' is printed on five tickets
- the formula 'P&Q' is printed on eighty-five tickets
- the remaining five tickets are blank.

Now think of the winning ticket: what is the chance 'P' will be on it either alone or in the formula? and what is the chance 'Q' will be on it either alone or in the formula? For short: what are the chances of P and Q?

The chances look this way.

---

[5] And as Ralph Wedgwood reminded me, contextualism about the threshold might also help explain why the closure principle looks true despite being not true. The idea is that when we consider a normal instance of conjunction introduction, doing so moves the salient threshold so that it's not the case that credence for conjuncts is above it while credence for conjunction is not.

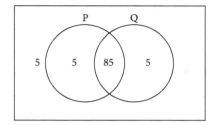

**Figure 10.2**

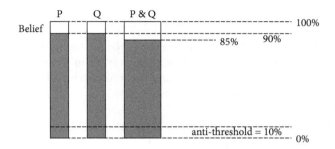

**Figure 10.3**

In these circumstances you should be 90% sure of P, 90% sure of Q, but only 85% sure of their conjunction.[6] Suppose for illustrative purposes that the belief-making threshold is 90%. Then you should have belief-level credence in both P and in Q but not in their conjunction (P&Q). Your rational credence will flout the conjunction rule as in Figure 10.3

Since rational credence is not preserved by conjunction, credal-based Lockeanism entails that rational belief isn't either. On plausible assumptions the view is flatly incompatible with the conjunction rule.

Yet credal-based Lockeanism entails something very like the conjunction rule for rational belief—or at least it does if we make standard assumptions about rational credence. To see this, let the risk of a proposition be the probability that it is false, and recall that the probability of falsity equals one minus the probability of truth. Then it is easy to prove a lower bound on the risk of a conjunction:

$$r(P\&Q) \leq [r(P) + r(Q)].^{7}$$

---

[6] This is because you are rationally certain about the chances just mentioned and you have no other relevant data about P or about Q. So you should set your credences in them equal to their respective chances of being true. See (Lewis, 1980) for classic discussion.

[7] Proof: As a matter of logic P is either true with Q, without Q, or it's not true at all. So P is logically equivalent to [(P&Q) ∨ (P&¬Q)]. Probability theory thus ensures that cr(P) equals cr[(P&Q) ∨ (P&¬Q)]. Since the disjuncts are logically exclusive, probability theory ensures that cr(P) equals [cr(P&Q) + cr(P&¬Q)]. Since (P&¬Q) entails ¬Q, probability theory ensures cr(P&¬Q) ≤ cr(¬Q). But probability theory also ensures that cr (¬Q) equals [1-cr(Q)]. Algebra then yields a lower bound for rational credence in (P&Q): [cr(P) + cr(Q) − 1] ≤ cr(P&Q). And this plus algebra and the definition of risk jointly yield the lower bound in the text. Then one can generalize the result by induction on the number of conjuncts.

The risk of a conjunction cannot exceed the cumulative risk of its conjuncts. Put another way: the chance of going wrong with a conjunction cannot exceed the cumulative chance of doing so with the conjuncts.

Suppose, then, that the threshold for coarse belief is τ. Let Δτ be the difference between τ and certainty. Suppose the risk of P plus that of Q does not exceed Δτ. Then the risk of (P&Q) cannot be greater than Δτ; so the probability of (P&Q) must reach the belief-making threshold. When credence starts out this way, credal-based Lockeanism entails that belief in P together with belief in Q bring with them belief in (P&Q). If one begins with rational credence, then, instances of the conjunction rule hold. The approximation requires just this:

$$[\mathbf{r}(P) + \mathbf{r}(Q)] \leq \Delta\tau.^8$$

In these circumstances credal-based Lockeanism entails instances of the conjunction rule. That is why proponents of the view can see truth in the rule. They can say instances hold when conjuncts are sufficiently closer to certainty than is the threshold for belief. Instances hold when things look like this.

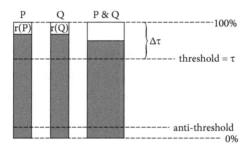

Figure 10.4

In a standard setting, therefore, credal-based Lockeanism explains not only why the conjunction rule is close to right, why it is not hopelessly false, but also why the rule looks generally true. When we consider an arbitrary case like the one with which we began this sub-section, after all, we don't think of beliefs which are weak or tenuous or borderline in the character. We think of solid or firmly-established beliefs, which normally have nothing to do with one another. In those circumstances the conjunction rule applies, and this generates the general impression that the rule always applies, no matter what the epistemic setting. Credal-based Lockeanism is inconsistent with that general impression, though it can explain how it gets off the ground.[9]

*The Conflict Worry*
A closely related worry for credal-based Lockeanism springs from a consequence of the view, namely, that it permits rational belief to conflict with itself. Just think back

---

[8] Ernest Adams has done more than any other to explain why rules such as the conjunction rule strike us as intuitively correct despite foundering within a probabilistic setting. For a good introduction to that work see (Adams, 1998), and for his classic treatment of conditional logic see (Adams, 1996).

[9] And as we'll see in Chapter 12, there are further ways a Lockean can find truth in the conjunction principle.

to the lottery from before. You believe of each ticket that it will lose—we suppose for illustrative purposes—because you set credence in line with objective chance. You also believe that a ticket will win, since you're basically certain of the set-up. You know how many tickets there are in the lottery. From these things it follows that your beliefs are in conflict with one another.

Without the conjunction rule that conflict stays implicit, of course—you cannot be drawn into believing an explicit contradiction by conjoining things you believe together—but the conflict in your overall state of belief is there all the same. Nothing in credal-based Lockeanism obliges a shift-in-view to correct for it. In fact, the view (together with standard assumptions) entails that your epistemic states are exactly as they should be, that they are in equilibrium.

Many find this unacceptable, and they point to our use of *reductio* in defence of their view. This style of argument—*reductio ad absurdum*—is used to damn another's opinion by exposing conflict within it. The practice is thought by some to indicate that even tacit conflict is ruled out by our epistemic norms. Here is Mark Kaplan with characteristic brio:

> In putting forth a *reductio* argument, a critic derives a contradiction from the conjunction of a set of hypothesis which an investigator purports to believe. The idea is supposed to be that the critic thereby demonstrates a defect in the investigator's set of beliefs—a defect so serious that it cannot be repaired except by the investigator's abandonment of at least one of the beliefs on which the *reductio* relies... But [without something like the conjunction rule] it is hard to see how *reductios* can possibly swing this sort of weight. [For then] the mere fact that the investigator's set of beliefs has been shown to be inconsistent would seem to provide no reason for her to experience the least discomfort. 'The fact that I believe each of the hypotheses in this set,' she should respond to her critic, 'does not commit me to believing their consequences. So your having shown that a contradiction lurks among those consequences casts no aspersion on my believing the hypotheses in the set.'[10]

But we can make good sense of *reductio* without anything like the conjunction rule. In fact we can make better sense of our *reductio*-based practice within a Lockean-setting than we can otherwise, in my view. The *reductio*-based worry has things exactly back-to-front.

The key point is simple: some *reductios* are much more potent than others. When it comes to dialectically-driven belief revision, in fact, the potency of a *reductio* argument hangs on its size. The most glaring thing about *reductio* is that its punch is inversely proportional to the number of claims in use. When a *reductio* is drawn from a small number of beliefs—two or three, say—it automatically obliges a shift-in-view on the part of its victim, irrespective of subject matter, irrespective of epistemic history, irrespective of anything else. Put another way: when a *reductio* is drawn from a small number of beliefs, it is sufficient on its own to oblige epistemic movement on the part of its victim, sufficient to mandate a shift-in-view on their part. When a *reductio* is drawn from a large number of beliefs—two hundred, say, or a million—none of this is true. Large *reductios* do not oblige a shift-in-view irrespective of subject matter or epistemic history. They do not mandate epistemic movement on

---

[10] (Kaplan, Decision Theory as Philosophy, 1983: 96–7), see also chapter 6 of (Maher, 2008).

their own. We rightly feel compelled to change our opinion when faced with a *reductio* drawn solely from a pair of our beliefs, for instance, but we do not feel that way when faced with a *reductio* drawn from a million of our Lottery beliefs. And nor do feel that way after being told that the apology in the preface of our book (for its mistakes) renders the book as a whole inconsistent.

This dialectical difference is central to our *reductio*-based practice. Credal-based Lockeanism explains it well.[11] To see this, suppose **B** is a *reductio* set of beliefs $\{B_1, \ldots, B_n\}$ As such **B** is inconsistent, which means in turn that certain *arguments* drawn from it will be valid. For instance, the negation of $B_n$ will follow from the rest of **B**:

$$B_1$$
$$\cdot$$
$$\cdot$$
$$\cdot$$
$$B_{(n-1)}$$
$$\overline{\quad\quad\quad}$$
$$\therefore \neg B_n$$

The negation of $B_1$ will follow from the rest of **B**:

$$B_2$$
$$\cdot$$
$$\cdot$$
$$\cdot$$
$$B_n$$
$$\overline{\quad\quad\quad}$$
$$\therefore \neg B_1$$

And so on. In general **B** is a *reductio* set only if the negation of each member is entailed by the others.

There is an easy-to-prove link, though, between validity and risk inheritance. Specifically: the risk of a conclusion cannot exceed the cumulative risk of premises from which it follows.[12] That means **B** is a *reductio* set only if the risk of a member's negation cannot exceed the cumulative risk of other members. Yet risk of negation is probability of truth. We thus reach the key technical fact behind the dialectical phenomenology of our *reductio*-based practice:

---

[11] As Kaplan points out in 'Decision Theory and Epistemology' (2005), we do sometimes feel obliged to shift our opinion when hit with fairly large *reductios*. But as lottery and preface cases make clear, we do not always feel obliged to shift our view when hit with really large ones. We do, though, always feel obliged to shift our view when hit with small *reductios*. Factors determining which way it will go are the subject matter involved, the epistemic history involved, and so on.

[12] Suppose a conclusion C is entail by premises $P_1, \ldots, P_n$. Then $(P_1 \& \ldots \& P_n)$ entails C. So $cr(P_1 \& \ldots \& P_n) \leq cr(C)$. So $r(C) \leq r(P_1 \& \ldots \& P_n)$. We've already proved, though, that the risk of a conjunction cannot exceed the cumulative risk of its conjuncts. So $r(C) \leq r(P_1) + \ldots + r(P_n)$.

(↪) B is a *reductio* set only if the probability of a B-member cannot exceed the cumulative risk of other B-members.

Assuming that rational credence works like probability, this principle constrains how credence can distribute across *reductio* sets. Credal-based Lockeanism then explains the phenomenology of *reductio*. Consider (↪)'s thrust in pictures (Figure 10.5).

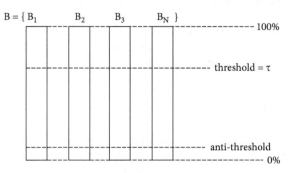

**Figure 10.5**

Suppose a *reductio* can be drawn from **B** while credence in each B-member meets the threshold for belief. In the event, credence in each B-member cannot exceed the cumulative risk of the others. Yet the belief-making threshold is fairly high, so there must a great many beliefs for (↪) to be true. Put back-to-front: the smaller **B** turns out to be, the less capable credence will be of satisfying (↪) while reaching the threshold for each B-member.

To see how this works in more detail simply idealize a bit. Assume each B-member gets equal credence (as would roughly hold, for instance, were the threshold for belief to be very high). Then (↪) places an upper bound on each member's credence that is a simple function of the number of beliefs in play:

| #(B) | Maximal equi-credal B-members | |
|---|---|---|
| 1 | 0 | 0% |
| 2 | $1/2$ | 50.0% |
| 3 | $2/3$ | 66.6% |
| 4 | $3/4$ | 75.0% |
| 5 | $4/5$ | 80.0% |
| 6 | $5/6$ | 83.3% |
| 7 | $6/7$ | 85.7% |
| 8 | $7/8$ | 87.5% |
| 9 | $8/9$ | 88.8% |
| 10 | $9/10$ | 90% |
| n | $n-1/n$ | |

This shows how *reductios* work under standard Bayesian assumptions. When

- the threshold for belief is high, say 90%, and
- one lends equal credence to things believed, then,
- a *reductio* cannot be drawn from less than 10 rational beliefs.

If a critic succeeds in producing one from nine or fewer beliefs, therefore, credence is thereby shown to be incoherent. Since we are assuming that rational credence is coherent, it follows that the *reductio* demonstrates credal irrationality. Credal-based Lockeanism then implies that the relevant beliefs are also irrational. And the fewer of them the critic uses in her *reductio* the more potent is her point.

This is why we feel compelled to change our view when faced with a *reductio* drawn from one or two beliefs, say, but we do not automatically feel that way when faced with a *reductio* drawn from many beliefs (as in the Lottery and the Preface). Since the threshold for belief is relatively high, a *reductio* drawn from a small number of beliefs shows credal incoherence, which in turn shows credal irrationality and thereby the irrationality of credal-based belief. Large *reductios* are not guaranteed to do this. Small *reductios* are knock-down on their own—showing credence and thus credal-based belief have gone drastically wrong—while large *reductios* are no such thing.

When someone is hit with a *reductio*, of course, they have not normally lent equal credence to beliefs used against them. And the lower the belief-making threshold turns out to be the more scope there will be for divergence from our idealising assumptions. But the relevant lesson here is clear: our *reductio*-based practice is best explained by the view that belief is grounded in confidence.[13]

*The Pointlessness Worry*
Suppose rational credence is structured like a probability function. Then there will be a coarse-grained threshold-based set of facts much like those discussed by credal-based Lockeanism. After all, threshold-based states come for free once credal states are in place. This leads to a substantive worry for credal-based Lockeanism. The worry is expressed well by Stalnaker:

One could easily enough define a concept of belief which identified it with high subjective or epistemic probability (probability greater than some specified number between one-half and one), but it is not clear what the point of doing so would be. Once a subjective or epistemic probability value is assigned to a proposition, there is nothing more to be said about its epistemic status. Bayesian decision theory gives a complete account of how probability values, including high ones, ought to guide behaviour... So what could be the point of selecting an interval near the top of the probability scale and conferring on the propositions whose probability falls in that interval the honorific title 'believed'?[14]

The worry is simple: if a kind of state springs from credence via a threshold—if it's Lockean in our terms—the kind will be basically pointless, nothing but residue entailed by genuine explanatory theory (i.e. Bayesianism).

This is a serious worry.

Defenders of credal-based Lockeanism must do more than explain their point of view. They must also explain the point of their view. This won't be easy, of course, since Stalnaker is right: one *can* easily define a kind of state by appeal to a

---

[13] A nice discussion of the technical issues here can be found in (Hawthorne & Bovens, 1999).
[14] (Stalnaker 1984; 138). I've put 'belief' in for 'acceptance' to bring the quote into line with our terminology.

credal-based threshold, it is *not* clear what the point of doing so would be given the bona fides of the Bayesian account of rational credence. One wonders what's left to be done: what is the point of credal-based Lockeanism?

I want to answer the pointlessness worry in two steps. One of them will deal with the role of confidence-based belief in our behavioural life. The other will deal with its role in our cognitive life. The first topic will be dealt with here, but the second must wait till Chapter 13, where inference is discussed in detail as well as our overall cognitive architecture. Before getting to that, though, we may sketch here the role of confidence-based belief in everyday action.

To see how, consider an analogy. Suppose you are forced to watch an evil experiment cooked-up by a coach. He's built a hallway 400 metres long with doorways every few metres. The doorways are rather short: 5'5" (just over 167cm). Suppose the evil coach kidnaps a large number of runners, places them at one end of the hallway, administers poison to kill them in 60 seconds, informs them that the antidote is at the other end of the hallway, and then let's them run for their lives. Suppose his victims all have personal-best times of about one minute for the 400m. Who will survive the experiment?

Without knowing more it's difficult to say, but one thing's certain already: short runners will have a decided advantage over middling-height runners, and a very decided advantage over tall runners. Any victim of the experiment like Usain Bolt height-wise—an exceedingly tall sprinter—with a personal-best of about one minute for the 400m, will stand basically no chance of surviving the experiment. She'll need to bend *way* down repeatedly while running for her life. This will slow her down more than enough to ensure death, and so it will be for tall runners in general.

Consider Stalnaker's line applied to the case:

One could easily define concepts like being tall, being short, being middling in height—by appeal to specific height thresholds in a chosen range of values. But it is not clear what the point of doing so would be. Once specific heights are fixed for runners in the hallway, there is nothing more to their height-theoretic status, and the physics of very-specific heights gives a complete account of how height values, including high ones, account for which runners can pass through doorways in the hall. What could be the point of selecting intervals in the continuum of specific heights and conferring on them honorific titles like 'tall', 'short', or 'middling'?

The answer to this question is two-fold.

First, there are epistemic and/or practical reasons for chunking fine-grained heights into categories like being tall, being short, or being middling in height. It is often expensive and/or next-to-impossible to discover the specific height of a particular thing. This can easily happen when it is both cheap and obvious how to discover whether the item in question is tall, short, or middling in height. One need only glance to make the latter determination. In this way coarse-grained categories are much easier to work with—both epistemically and practically—than fine-grained categories in the height continuum.

Similarly, there are epistemic and/or practical reasons for chunking states of credence into strong, weak, and middling-strength varieties. It is often difficult or next-to-impossible to discover credence lent by a particular agent. This is often the case when it is easy to discover whether an agent lends strong, weak, or middling-strength credence. One need only ask them (or watch them a bit) to make the latter determination. In this way coarse-grained categories are much easier to work with—both epistemically and practically—than fine-grained categories in the Bayesian attitudinal continuum.

Second—as the poison-hallway example makes clear—there are important generalizations which turn on whether an object is tall rather than short (say). Tall runners stand next-to-no chance in the poison-hallway scenario, yet short runners stand a good chance of survival. Truths like this make a great deal of difference when played out over stretches of time, across large populations, or both. That is why biological laws are often couched in gradable terms: being long, being sharp, being fast, and so forth.

Similarly, there are important generalizations which turn on whether an agent lends high, medium, or low-level credence. Agents who lend high credence, after all, behave much more like one another—everything else being equal—than do like agents who lend low- or middling-strength credence; and vice versa. Those who lend strong credence to their success in life, for instance, stand a better chance of doing well in life than those who lend only low- or medium-strength credence to their success—the power of positive thinking! But general truths like this make a great deal of difference in the social world. Credal-based Lockeanism naturally sees this as one of the key reasons why many psychological laws are couched in gradable terms of belief, disbelief, and suspended judgement. And Chapter 13 makes likewise clear why confidence-based belief is crucial to our inferential practices. All in all, then, the pointlessness challenge can be answered head-on.

## 10.4 Deeper Challenges for Credal-Based Lockeanism

In this section we lay out two deeper worries for credal-based Lockeanism, worries which show that the view is not correct as it stands. We've seen that it generates enough good news to make plausible that something is deeply right about the position. So we end with a puzzle about credal-based Lockeanism: if the view is wrong as it stands, but something in the neighbourhood is right, what does that something look like?

### The Psychology Worry
Credal-based Lockeanism is built from three bi-conditionals. In short form they are

(B)  Belief                ↔  Strong credence
(D)  Disbelief             ↔  Weak credence
(S)  Suspended Judgement   ↔  Middling credence.

Credence counts as strong exactly when it does not fall below the belief-making threshold, weak exactly when it does not fall above the disbelief-making threshold, and middling in strength exactly when it falls between such thresholds. Credal-based Lockeanism is the conjunction of (B), (D) and (S).

Unfortunately, the left-to-right direction of each bi-conditional is false. To see this, focus on an obvious fact about our mental life (discussed at length in Chapter 5):

we do not always invest credence when we invest confidence. Since credence is point-valued subjective probability, investing credence is configuring an exact spread of confidence across every niche of epistemic possibility, it's adopting a hyper-precise epistemic attitude. We do manage it from time to time but mostly we don't invest credence when we invest confidence. Mostly our take on things is attitudinally fine-grained but less exact than credence.

For instance: suppose a given coin has a 95% bias to heads, I know this, and I consider whether the coin will land heads on its next toss (H). In the event, I will invest 95% credence in H. This does not seem to be metaphor or literally untrue idealization. It seems plainly the case that in these circumstances I will be 95% sure that the coin will land heads on the next toss. I will in fact adopt that very attitude to H, investing a particular credence, and manifesting its exactness in my functionality.

But consider the claim that it will be sunny in Tucson tomorrow (T). As it happens I am highly confident that it will be sunny in Tucson tomorrow. Indeed I would go further and say that I believe that it will be sunny in Tucson tomorrow, and, that I do so precisely in virtue of being so confident that it will be sunny in Tucson tomorrow. But there is no credence that I invest in T, no precise confidence that I invest in the claim that it will be sunny in Tucson tomorrow. My take on the issue is rougher than any state of credence. I am highly confident that it will be sunny in Tucson tomorrow; but no real number $r$ is so that the strength my confidence in T is $r$% of certainty's strength. Yet I invest credence in T only if there is such an $r$. Hence I invest no credence in T. My high confidence is no state of credence at all, though it nevertheless makes for belief in T. So it is possible to believe in the absence of credence. The left-to-right direction of **(B)** is false.

A similar point holds for **(D)**. Just think of the claim that it will not be sunny in Tucson tomorrow (¬T). Being clear-headed and investing high confidence in T, I invest low confidence in ¬T. Again I would go further and say that I disbelieve that it will not be sunny in Tucson tomorrow precisely in virtue of investing such low confidence in ¬T. But just as there is no credence that I lend to T, there is no credence that I lend to ¬T, no precise confidence invested in the claim that it will not be sunny in Tucson tomorrow. My take on the matter is rougher than any state of credence. I do invest low confidence in the claim that it will not be sunny in Tucson tomorrow. But no real number $r$ is so that the strength my confidence in ¬T is $r$% of certainty's strength. I invest credence in ¬T only if there is such an $r$, so I invest no credence in ¬T. My low confidence in ¬T is no state of credence at all, though it nevertheless makes for disbelief in ¬T. It is possible to disbelieve in the absence of credence. The left-to-right direction of **(D)** is false.

And a similar point holds for **(S)**. Just think of the claim that there is a smelly vinegar factory in Slough (V). I have no idea if this claim is true, having no evidence on the matter to speak of. I do lend some kind of confidence to V, though—now that I think of it, at least—and it is clear that the confidence I lend is neither strong nor weak. I would go further and say that I suspend judgement in V precisely in virtue of lending such middling-strength confidence to the claim that there is a smelly vinegar factory in Slough. But there is no credence that I invest in the matter, no hyper-precise confidence that I lend to V. My take on things is rougher than any investment of credence. I do have middling-strength confidence in V. But no real number $r$ is so that the strength of that confidence is *r*% of certainty's strength. I invest credence in V only if there is such an *r*, so I invest no credence in V. My middling-strength confidence in V is no state of credence at all, though it makes for suspended judgement in V. It is possible to suspend judgement in the absence of credence. The left-to-right direction of (S) is false.

The left-to-right directions of (B), (D) and (S) entail, contrary to manifest psychological fact, that belief/disbelief/suspended judgement require the investment of credence. Nothing of the sort is true. It is possible to believe, disbelieve, or suspend judgement without investing credence, and it is psychologically common to do so. The point does nothing to suggest that belief, disbelief, or suspended judgement can occur in the absence of confidence. It simply means that hyper-precise confidence is not needed for any of the coarse-grained attitudes. As a matter of psychological fact, any of them can be adopted without adopting credence. This psychological fact about us directly conflicts with credal-based Lockeanism.

## *The Epistemology Worry*

There are epistemic worries for credal-based Lockeanism as well as psychological ones. And just as the former spring from obvious psychological aspects of our life, so the latter spring from obvious epistemic aspects of that life. Specifically, they spring from the incompatibility of credal-based Lockeanism and an intuitive epistemic principle I call the 'Norm of Character Match'. This principle says that one should adopt an attitude to a content only if that attitude's character matches the character of evidence used in its formation. Of course the sense of match at work in the norm is best gleaned by example, and in Chapter 12 we'll systematize intuitions about it to make the norm more transparent, tractable, and theoretically fecund. For now, though, we work with intuition on a case-by-case basis.

For instance: when your weather-related evidence comes solely from a fully trusted source, and that source says that there is an 80% chance of rain, then, on that basis, you should be 80% sure that it will rain. If your source says only that it is likely to rain, however, or only that there is a strong chance of rain, or anything even roughly like that, then, on that basis, your take on the weather should be appreciably rougher as a result. You *should* be confident that it will rain in such evidential circumstances, on the basis of your source's less exact testimony, but there is no credence that you should have in such circumstances that it will rain.

The point is well known in the literature.[15] Everyday evidence is often meagre and vague, too weak to rationalize credence. The view that belief-making confidence should always be credence conflicts with the Norm of Character Match, for credence is a hyper-precise spread of conviction ranging over every niche of epistemic possibility. Quotidian evidence routinely fails to rationalize such hyper-detailed conviction, even under idealization. Such evidence routinely demands an attitude which is decidedly confidence-theoretic in nature yet coarser in grain than credence, something we called *thick confidence* in Chapter 3. The Norm of Character Match

---

[15] Classic discussion can be found in (Hacking, 1995), (Jeffrey, 1983) and (Levi, 1974). More recent discussion can be found in (Christensen, 2004), (Halpern, 2003), (Joyce, 2005), (Kaplan, 1983), and (Walley, 1991).

ensures that everyday evidence often warrants the adoption of such confidence rather than credence. To adopt the latter on the basis of routine everyday evidence is to outrun one's evidential headlights. It is to do so precisely with respect to the character of the attitude adopted on the basis of one's evidence.

Fortunately, common sense recognizes states of confidence untethered to credence, states such as being non-credally confident that it will rain. Both credence and thick confidence are manifest components of everyday psychology, manifest elements of our attitudinal repertoire. This is an epistemic good thing, too, for both types of confidence are mandated by evidence routinely in our possession. Credal-based Lockeanism is incompatible with the fact that non-credal confidence is very often mandated.

The position insists that coarse-grained attitudes spring from credence. This is false as a matter of psychology and wrong as a matter of epistemology. It is possible to believe, disbelieve, and suspend judgement without lending credence. Very often our evidence mandates that we do so. Yet credal-based Lockeanism generates a great deal of good news: it underwrites a robust realism about coarse- and fine-grained attitudes, fits well with how we talk about the former as gradable, underwrites intra-level irreducibility of both coarse- and fine-grained attitudes, makes sense of the ways in which coarse- and fine-grained attitudes coordinate in the causal production as well as the rationalization of action. And so on.

This makes it hard to believe that credal-based Lockeanism is barking up the wrong tree. The good news surrounding the view makes it plausible that there is something right about the position. When faced with the psychological and epistemic worries, therefore, it is natural to augment credal-based Lockeanism, to generalize the view in the hope that we may handle the worries. This is our next task. We'll see that a liberalized Lockeanism not only sidesteps the psychological and epistemic worries sketched here, it also edifies a huge range of central topics in the book.

# 11
# Force-based Attitudes

## 11.1 Building Epistemic Attitudes

In this chapter we present and defend a new metaphysics of confidence. The position to be developed maintains that all types of confidence—point-valued subjective probability (i.e. credence), interval-valued subjective probability (i.e. sharp thick confidence), mushy credence (i.e. vague thick confidence)—are all built from mixtures of what we'll call *cognitive force*.[1] We'll see that this latter ingredient is a recognizable element of our everyday conception of mind, though it hasn't been used before in a reductive theory of confidence. By doing so we'll be able to do a number of things well for the first time.

In this chapter we lay out the view and show how it makes for a truly satisfying confidence-based approach to the coarse-grained attitudes. In the next chapter we use the view to

- diagnose when and why the standard kinematics for thick confidence breaks down;
- explain why kinematics is forward-looking (or ahistorical);
- define powerful notions of propositional and doxastic justification in a confidence-theoretic setting;
- use them to explain how and why the character of an attitude should match the quality of evidence used in its formation; and
- explain the restricted circumstances in which confidence is subject to content-based accuracy even though (a) belief and disbelief are always subject to them, and (b) confidence-based Lockeanism about them is true.

The fact that all of this can all be done—in a relatively short space, and a relatively straightforward way, solely by appeal to cognitive force—is itself the most powerful reason to think that the story told here is on the right track; for that story generates non-trivial explanatory payoffs which are otherwise missing from our epistemology. This is good reason to think the story is on the right track.

However, years of presenting this material has shown that there are two main reactions to it. Some accept straightaway that there are cognitive forces at least roughly in line with the sketch to follow, while others have little-to-no feel for cognitive force at the outset. Those in the first camp are normally delighted to see that cognitive force can be put to such widespread and non-trivial work in epistemology. Those in the second camp tend to reject from the beginning any

---

[1] See Chapter 3 for a detailed discussion of these types of confidence.

*The Rational Mind*. Scott Sturgeon, Oxford University Press (2020). © Scott Sturgeon.
DOI: 10.1093/oso/9780198845799.001.0001

story built on cognitive force, and so do not warm immediately to such force being put to that work. A central hope of this chapter is that philosophers of the latter sort will work through everything to follow, minimally register its strong internal coherence and explanatory unity, and then take these theoretical virtues to indicate that a force-based metaphysics of confidence has something positive going for it.

## 11.2 Cognitive Force

We begin with a warm-up analogy. I should say at the outset that it is not an exact or perfect analogy. But it does provide a finger-hold on the notion of cognitive force for those who need one from the outset. Experience has shown that this finger-hold often grows into a firm grip as the discussion unfolds.

To begin, suppose a waiter asks you to sample a piece of Limburger cheese. Since you are aware that such cheese is not to everyone's taste, and you've never had Limburger before, you inspect the cheese carefully before tasting it. You prod the cheese with a finger, sniff it with your nose, and so forth. It is then likely that one of three things will happen:

- You are drawn to the cheese;
- You are repelled by the cheese;
- You are neutral about the cheese.

The first upshot involves gustatory attraction: a force which drives you to the cheese in action, prompting a taste, a sniff, a bite. The second upshot involves gustatory repulsion: a force which drives you from the cheese in action, prompting avoidance behaviour. The third upshot involves gustatory neutrality: active indifference between you and the cheese which makes for laissez-faire interaction with the cheese. Each of these reactions comes in degrees, of course, but set that aside for the moment. Focus here on the fact that there is good pre-theoretic reason to recognize three kinds of gustatory force: attraction, repulsion, and neutrality.[2]

There is also such reason to insist that these forces can cohabit, that they can arise side-by-side in reaction to food. A chunk of Limburger can attract and repel at the same time, for instance, and when this occurs the result can be instability. There can be gustatory battle between elements of one's reaction to food, gustatory tension which makes for behavioural instability. In the event, no strong or stable disposition to act with respect to the food springs from one's gustatory reaction to it. If prompted to choose whether to eat, no stable disposition will manifest itself in action. Resulting behaviour will be closer to random than systematic.

Yet there needn't be such instability generated by gustatory reaction to food. There may be no gustatory conflict at all: one's reaction to Limburger may be solely one of

---

[2] Note that gustatory neutrality is not merely the absence of gustatory attraction and repulsion. Napoleon was neither attracted to nor repelled by a Big Mac. But nor was he neutral about such food: it was not on his radar at all. This is the gustatory analogue of an important point in the theory of suspended judgement. Such judgement is not merely the absence of belief and disbelief, but rather its own kind of attitude: *committed neutrality*. See Chapter 6, (Friedman, 2013), (Friedman, 2013), (Hájek, 1998) or (Sturgeon, 2010) for related discussion.

attraction or repulsion or neutrality, in which case an easy behavioural equilibrium is reached. Or there may be functionally harmonious *mixtures* of gustatory force, stable blends of attraction tempered by a whiff of repulsion, or repulsion muted by a whiff of neutrality. These are complex ways of achieving functional stability with respect to food, complex ways of generating stable dispositions to react.

For example, suppose there is a very particular way that you like your first coffee in the morning: a certain type of bean should be used, ground a certain way; a certain type of milk should be used, heated a certain way; a certain type of combining process should be used; etc. I present you with your first coffee of the day and almost everything is right about it: the beans, the milk, the combinatorial process. But I've put the result of my efforts in the wrong kind of *cup* (say one that's too small or not heated right). Then it is likely that you will be largely attracted and slightly repelled by your coffee, with the blend of gustatory forces making for a stable disposition to drink my offering (with a whiff of reservation, so to say).

We may think of gustatory equilibria as functional stability points which arise from the interaction of gustatory attraction, repulsion, and neutrality. To a rough first approximation, stability points are strong and stable dispositions to eat a given piece of food, to push it away, or to interact with it neutrally. The key idea is that the overall disposition itself springs from a mixture of three gustatory forces: attraction, repulsion, and neutrality, with each force carrying its own signature way of driving food-related activity, and all three working in concert to make for a strong and stable disposition to act in a full range of culinary possibilities.

The main contention of this chapter is that all of this carries over, *mutatis mutandis*, to the cognitive domain. Suppose you are asked about a particular claim C: say the claim that Mars is larger than Venus. You understand the claim fully but have not considered it before. You comb through your information for evidence relevant to C's truth-value. It is then likely that one of three things will happen:

- You are drawn to C;
- You are repelled by C;
- You are neutral about C.

The first upshot involves intellectual attraction: a force driving you to C in thought, promoting embrace of the claim with your mind. This is the intellectual analogue of gustatory attraction, something worthy of description as an intellectual pull in the direction of a claim's hitting the facts. And just as gustatory attraction promotes the ingestion of food, so, by analogy, intellectual attraction promotes interaction with a claim—in behaviour, practical and theoretical reasoning, and so on—as if it is true. When one speaks of feeling the force of a reason for a claim one thereby references, at least in part, intellectual attraction. At least part of what one expressly talks about in making the remark is a kind of psychological pull. In effect the remark suggests that this pull is triggered by appreciation of the evidential force displayed by an epistemic reason. In the next two chapters we'll use this sort of match between psychological and epistemic force when theorizing about the epistemology of confidence. The point here is just that common sense already recognizes the first sort of psychological force: intellectual attraction.

The second upshot from above involves intellectual repulsion: a force driving you away from C in thought, promoting rejection of the claim with your mind. This is the intellectual analogue of gustatory repulsion, something worthy of description as an intellectual push from a claim's marking the facts. And just as gustatory repulsion promotes the avoidance of food, so, by analogy, intellectual repulsion promotes interaction with a claim—in behaviour, practical and theoretical reasoning, and so on—as if it is false. When one speaks of feeling the force of a reason against a claim one thereby references, at least in part, intellectual repulsion. At least part of what one expressly talks about in making the remark is a felt psychological push-from. In effect the remark suggests that this push-from is triggered by appreciation of the evidential force displayed by an epistemic reason. In the next two chapters we'll use this sort of match between psychological and epistemic force in theorizing about the epistemology of confidence. The point here is just that common sense already recognizes the second sort of psychological force: intellectual repulsion.

The third upshot from above involves intellectual neutrality: active mental indifference which sits between you and claim C, promoting a laissez-faire stance between the two of you. This is the intellectual analogue of gustatory neutrality, something worthy of description as purposeful intellectual neutrality about a claim's truth-value. And just as gustatory neutrality promotes neutral behaviour with respect to food, so, by analogy, intellectual neutrality promotes *refraining* from use of a claim—in behaviour, practical or theoretical reasoning, and so on—as if the claim is true or as if it is false. When one speaks of feeling the absence of effective reason for or against a claim one thereby references, at least in part, intellectual neutrality. At least part of what one expressly talks about in making the remark is a felt psychological reserve. In effect the remark suggests that such reserve about a claim is triggered by appreciation of an unhappy circumstance concerning the evidence relevant to the claim. In the next two chapters we'll use this sort of match between psychology and evidential circumstance in theorizing about the epistemology of confidence. The point here is just that common sense already recognizes the third kind of psychological force: intellectual neutrality.

These cognitive forces also come in degrees—a fact we'll use later in this chapter to serious effect—but the first thing to say about them is that there is good pre-theoretic reason to recognize three: attraction, repulsion, and neutrality. It is then important to emphasize that reflection on cases provides strong pre-theoretic reason to insist that cognitive forces, like their gustatory analogues, can cohabit. They too can spring up side-by-side in reaction to a piece of information. There can be cognitive battle or dissonance between elements of one's intellectual reaction to a given claim; and such battle can also lead to a kind of instability—intellectual instability. This entails an absence of strong or stable disposition to adopt an overall take on a claim.

For example, suppose John is hair-wise midway between a clear case of baldness and a clear case of hairiness. You inspect his head thoroughly, in good daylight, and consider whether John is bald. This is a borderline case par excellence. As Wright has observed of such cases, the 'absolutely basic datum' about them is that they come across as [cases] where we are baffled to choose between conflicting verdicts about which polar verdict applies, [true or false], rather than as cases which we recognize as enjoying a status inconsistent with both.[3]

We are baffled in such a case, I submit, precisely because borderline cases induce strongly conflicting psychological forces (in a distinctive way). Once we possess all canonical evidence for a penumbral case of vagueness—once we know exactly how John is hair-wise, for instance—we are intellectually drawn to and repelled by the penumbral claim, with conflicting reactions being prompted by the very *same* canonical evidence.

The result is a special kind of attitudinal instability, the kind which results from conflicting cognitive forces springing from sensitivity to a single corpus of evidence. When John is a borderline case of baldness, and you know exactly how he is hair-wise, you will be intellectually drawn to the claim that John is bald by way of reaction to how he is hair-wise, and you will also be intellectually repelled by that claim on that basis. This cognitive situation generates the distinctive intellectual vibe of a borderline case of vagueness—the cognitive mood music, so to say. That vibe consists in overall cognitive instability resulting from force-based conflict brought on by equivocal evidence.

On the other hand, distinct intellectual forces working on a single mind and a single claim do not always lead to attitudinal instability. To see this, consider a familiar example. Let us call a feature 'well understood' when there are circumstances in which it is fully clear that the feature in question applies to something, or circumstances in which it is fully clear that the feature in question fails to apply to something. It is then tempting to say that for any well understood feature there exists a set of things—empty or otherwise—which satisfy that well understood feature. And it is easy to be attracted to this claim. After all, instances of the claim manifestly apply in everyday cases, and it's hard to see how the claim could be false in the first place. Yet the tempting claim leads directly to paradox, as we know, and that makes it easy to be repelled by it too. In my own case I still feel both sorts of intellectual force even after having reflected on the matter for years. I nevertheless end up with a con-attitude to the tempting thought. This is a case in which robustly conflicting intellectual forces make for a stable epistemic attitude, a situation which squares perfectly with the force-based view of confidence developed here.

## 11.3 Picturing Force-Based Confidence

The major proposal of this chapter is that levels of confidence are nothing but stable configurations of cognitive force. This is a view about the metaphysics of confidence rather than its rationality. Later we'll see how the proposed metaphysics can be used to shed considerable light on the latter topic, but for now we focus on the metaphysics rather than the epistemology.

The basic idea is that levels of confidence are functional stability points grounded in blends of cognitive force: each type of confidence is a stable mixture of attraction,

[3] (Wright 2001: 70).

repulsion, and neutrality. I assume here without argument that there are two kinds of confidence to be woven into the force-based framework. One is familiar point-valued credence idealized in Bayesian epistemology. The other is thick confidence idealized in various generalizations of the Bayesian framework. The former involves the kind of state you enjoy when you are 50% sure that the coin will land heads, for instance, the latter involves the kind of state you enjoy when you are fairly confident that it will rain (and that's all). First we'll explain how the force-based approach works for credence, then we'll generalize our story to thick confidence.

To begin, our proposal is that credence is the result of mixing attraction, repulsion, and neutrality in a way that involves *no* neutral force. Put another way: each grade of credence involves a level of neutrality that is literally nothing, mixed with blends of other cognitive force. We further propose that this is what sets credence apart from thick confidence: the latter involves non-zero neutrality potentially mixed with blends of other cognitive force. As we'll see in a moment, such neutrality is anathema to credence (and this is why suspended judgement marches in step better with heavily thick confidence than it does middling-strength credence).

There are several ways to picture and develop the line being proposed. Take any type of credence and let its strength be represented with unit-real $n$.[4] The suggestion is that this type of credence is composed of a blend of attraction and repulsion. We may picture this idea in Figure 11.1.

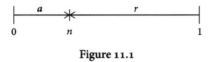

Figure 11.1

Of course there are two degenerate cases of credence: 0% and 100%. The suggestion is that they involve a nil component of neutrality as well as one other cognitive force. When credence is 0% such a nil component is mixed with a nil component of attraction, plus some kind of repulsion or other. The result will be a full attitudinal ruling-out of a claim. When credence is 100% a nil component of neutrality is mixed with a nil component of repulsion and some kind of attraction or other. The result will be a full attitudinal embrace of a claim. Non-degenerate types of credence are then mixtures of a nil component of neutrality with a bit of attraction and a bit of repulsion. For any unit real $n$, we might say, $n$-level credence occurs exactly when two things are true: the neutrality component of the attitude equals zero; and the strength of its attraction component equals $n/(1-n)$ times the strength of its repulsion component.

From this perspective credence is a special kind of confidence, the result of zero neutrality mixed with non-zero attraction or repulsion. The perspective gracefully generalizes to thick confidence too: we need only add the idea that such confidence involves the cognitive force of neutrality. As we'll see, this thought is both initially

---

[4] For excellent discussion of idealizations like this see (Cook, 2002), and (Edgington, 1997).

plausible, easy to motivate by philosophical reflection on cases, and generates a number of edifying points in the epistemology of confidence.

To begin, note that thick confidence can wear precision on its sleeve like a credence, and also that it can fail to do so. There is such a thing as being non-credally very confident full stop—*just* very confident, as it were—and there is such a thing as being 95%-to-98% confident exactly.[5] Both types of confidence are thick, but the functional thrust of the first type of state is much more vague than is the second. It is easy to extend the picture behind Figure 11.1 to thick confidence which wears precision on its sleeve. It is not easy to extend it to thick confidence which fails to do so. This has nothing to do with the thickness of vague thick confidence but only to do with its vagueness. Since there is no easy way to model the relevant sort of vagueness—confidence-theoretic or otherwise—it is no strike against the approach developed here that it does not extend easily to thick confidence with no transparent precision. The same is true of every precise representation of phenomena with manifestly imprecise edges. For this reason we set vague thick confidence aside in what follows.[6]

Our main suggestion about confidence is that it results from the combination of attraction, repulsion, and neutrality. Take any sharp thick confidence $[l,u]$—say 30-to-40% confidence, 80-to-85% confidence, whatever. We can easily picture it as composed of attraction, repulsion, and neutrality.

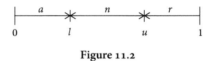

Figure 11.2

Figures 11.1 and 11.2 make visually clear that on the present approach thick confidence and credence are highly unified, arising from stable configurations of cognitive force. This is the root idea behind the force-based approach to confidence. It involves four inter-related claims:

- Levels of confidence are functional stability points.
- They arise from the mixture of attraction, repulsion, and neutrality.
- Credence is nil neutrality mixed with attraction and/or repulsion.
- Thick confidence is non-nil neutrality potentially mixed with attraction and/or repulsion.[7]

Our next task is to sketch a formal model of the force-based conception of confidence. After doing so we will put that model to use in formal and informal epistemology.

---

[5] See Chapter 5 and its references for further discussion.
[6] See (Edgington, 1997), and (Sainsbury, 1996).
[7] The caveat is needed for the fully dilated case in which one is totally neutral about a claim. This will be explained over the next two sections and plays a central role in our discussion of the kinematics of confidence.

## 11.4 Modelling Force-Based Confidence

We can also picture credal-making combinations of cognitive force with a two-dimensional plane. We start with an origin $\underline{o}$, an attraction axis running from $\underline{o}$ up the page, say, and a repulsion axis running from $\underline{o}$ to the right

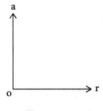

Figure 11.3

Lengths up the $\underline{a}$-axis represent amounts of attraction, those up the $\underline{r}$-axis represent amounts of repulsion, and points in the plane represent combinations of attraction and repulsion. The origin corresponds to a lack of cognitive force altogether.[8]

In this depiction, the $\underline{a}$-axis is an open ray consisting of points $<\underline{a},\underline{r}>$ with $\underline{r}$ equal to zero and $\underline{a}$ greater than zero. Each such point represents a combination of non-zero attraction and nothing else, so each point in the $\underline{a}$-axis may be thought to represent a way of fully ruling-in a claim, a way of maintaining some level of attraction so that the overall doxastic effect is the stable ruling-in of the claim in question. The $\underline{a}$-axis itself may be thought to represent 100% credence.

Similarly, the $\underline{r}$-axis is an open ray consisting of points $<\underline{a},\underline{r}>$ with $\underline{a}$ equal to zero and $\underline{r}$ greater than zero. Each such point represents a combination of non-zero repulsion and nothing else, so each point in the $\underline{r}$-axis may be thought to represent a way of fully ruling-out a claim, a way of maintaining some level of repulsion so that the overall doxastic effect is the stable ruling-out of the claim in question. The $\underline{r}$-axis itself may be thought to represent 0% credence.

Now think of the open ray halfway between the $\underline{a}$- and $\underline{r}$-axes. It consists of points <a,r> with a equal to r. Points in the ray represent ways of mixing equal amounts of attraction and repulsion, and, for this reason, the ray into which they form sits at a 45° angle from the $\underline{a}$-axis. Intuitively, the ray built from $<\underline{a},\underline{r}>$ with $\underline{a}$ equal to $\underline{r}$ sweeps out half the space from the ray which represents no credence to the one which represents full credence. We can think of the ray as representing 50% credence. This is the attitudinal stability point generated by exact match of attraction and repulsion (with no neutrality in the mix). Points in the relevant ray represent different ways that cognitive force can mix to yield 50% credence.

There is an obvious generalization of this perspective to each credence. For any non-origin point $\underline{p}$ in the attraction/repulsion plane, there will be a unique open ray $\underline{R}$ from the origin through $\underline{p}$. And there will be an angle θ between the $\underline{r}$-axis and $\underline{R}$. θ will be

---

[8] Since the axes in Figure 11.3 extend indefinitely, the picture is an idealization. This is the force-theoretic analogue of the idea that credal strength is well-represented by an infinite decimal expansion.

## 280 FORCE-BASED ATTITUDES

some percentage of the 90 degrees that exist between the attraction and repulsion axes. $\underline{R}$ will represent the credence matching that percentage, and points in $\underline{R}$ will represent ways that attraction and repulsion can be mixed to generate that credence.

Now consider a sharp thick confidence $[l,u]$. Earlier we depicted it in the following way

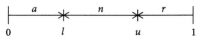

Figure 11.4

We can also represent this sharp thick confidence by adding a neutrality axis to the attraction/repulsion plane. This makes for a three dimensional volume (Figure 11.5).

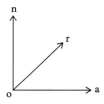

Figure 11.5

As before lengths along the $\underline{a}$-axis represent amounts of attraction and those along the $r$-axis represent amounts of repulsion; but now lengths up the $n$-axis represent amounts of intellectual neutrality too. Once again points in the space represent combinations of cognitive force, only now there are three kinds of force in the mix: attraction, repulsion, and neutrality.

To model sharp thick confidence built from these forces we need a function from triples $<a,r,n>$ to intervals $[l,u]$ in the unit interval. Figure 11.2 suggests we use

(*) $\quad a/(a+r+n) = l \quad$ and $\quad (a+n)/(a+r+n) = u.$

Since expressions on the left-hand sides of these equations scale linearly, we may solve for the case where $(a+r+n)$ equals one. This yields natural results:

$$a = l \quad r = 1 - u \quad n = u - l.$$

These latter equations correspond to the left-hand, right-hand, and middle bits of the unit interval, respectively, when that interval is chunked with lower-bound $l$ and upper-bound $u$. This matches Figure 11.2 of course, and it's intuitively what you'd expect when the open ray fixed by (*) intersects the plane corresponding to $(a+r+n)=1$. In essence the ray to that plane _is_ the unit interval in the three-dimensional volume.

Now, the interval $[l,u]$ is itself represented by the full ray built from triples $<a,r,n>$ so that for positive $x$

$$<a, r, n> = <xl, x(1-u), x(u-l)>.$$

And since the interval $[l,u]$ represents a certain sharp thick confidence—namely, the one with *minima* represented by $l$ and *maxima* represented by $u$—it follows that the ray just described represents the sharp thick confidence too. We can thus represent states of sharp thick confidence with open rays in the attraction/repulsion/neutrality quadrant. Points in a ray represent mixtures of cognitive force which generate kinds of functional stability, namely, those kinds identical to the cash-value of types of sharp thick confidence.

So we have before us a three-dimensional representation of confidence as such—vagueness aside—one which captures each type of credence and each type of sharp thick confidence. The former are represented by rays in the two-dimensional attraction/repulsion plane at the base of the volume depicted in Figure 11.5 The latter are represented by rays shooting up into the volume depicted.

Orthodox norms for credence readily translate into the ray-theoretic framework. Consider the view that a measure of strength for credence—invested across cells of a partition—should add-up to 100%. This is the 'additivity thought' at the foundation of probability-based approaches to rational credence. It generates structure needed to define coherence for unconditional probabilities, and, thereby, structure needed to define conditional probabilities. In turn conditional probabilities—plus a certain conception of learning, as we saw in Part I—are enough to define orthodox kinematics for rational credence. This is why the additivity thought is the bedrock of the Bayesian model discussed earlier in the book. We'll see in the next section that it is likewise the bedrock of orthodoxy about thick confidence.

The principle is easy to capture in ray-theoretic terms. Here is one way to do so. For any content $\Phi$, let $\theta_\Phi$ be the angle between the credal-ray for $\Phi$ and the rejection axis. The additivity thought then corresponds to the injunction that for any partition $\Phi_1$, $\Phi_2$, etc.,

$$\sum_{\theta_{\Phi i}} = 90°.$$

Instances of this thought are entirely intuitive:

$$(\theta_\Phi + \theta_{\neg\Phi}) = 90°$$
$$(\theta_{AB} + \theta_{A\neg B} + \theta_{\neg A}) = 90°,$$
etc.

There is thus a ready expression of probability-based norms for confidence in ray-theoretic terms. Probability-based approaches to ideally rational confidence conservatively extend the ray-theoretic framework: nothing can be done in the former that cannot be done in the latter.[9]

---

[9] Unorthodox norms for credence—e.g. those of Dempster–Shafer Theory or Ranking Theory—can also be translated into the ray-theoretic framework. Bayesian norms are used in the text for illustrative purposes, since they are most widely understood and thought to apply to ideally rational confidence. See (Shafer, 1976) for Dempster–Shafer Theory, and (Spohn, 2012) for Ranking Theory.

## 11.5 Force-Based Lockeanism

The force-based approach to confidence sees credence and thick confidence as deeply unified. This helps to sort out the relation between coarse- and fine-grained attitudes in a number of ways. Specifically, it makes for a graceful successor to the credal-based Lockeanism discussed in the previous chapter.

Recall that such Lockeanism maintains that belief is sufficiently strong credence, disbelief is sufficiently weak credence, and suspended judgement is credence of intermediate strength. The view generates a non-trivial amount of good news, as we have seen, but it also flouts manifest aspects about our psychology and epistemology. This is because credence is itself unnecessary for belief, disbelief, or suspended judgement, and because everyday evidence very often rationalizes a take on things which is fine-grained but nevertheless coarser than credence. Happily, the force-based approach to confidence underwrites a version of Lockeanism which makes for even better news than its credal-based cousin.

To see this, consider the view that belief is a mixture of cognitive force which makes for sufficiently strong confidence, disbelief is a mixture of cognitive force which makes for sufficiently weak confidence, and suspended judgement is a mixture of cognitive force which makes for sufficiently thick confidence.[10] This is a force-based version of Lockeanism about coarse-grained attitudes. To appreciate its intuitive appeal, note the force-based approach to confidence entails that mixtures of cognitive force which generate high confidence are exactly those dominated by the force of attraction, mixtures of cognitive force which generate low confidence are exactly those dominated by the force of repulsion, and mixtures of cognitive force which generate rather thick confidence are exactly those dominated by the force of neutrality. The force-based approach to confidence thus folds into a Lockean approach to the coarse-grained attitudes to generate a position on which belief springs from stable mixtures of cognitive force dominated by attraction, disbelief springs from stable mixtures of cognitive force dominated by repulsion, and suspended judgement springs from stable mixtures of cognitive force dominated by neutrality. The resulting position is a confidence-first approach to coarse-grained attitudes significantly more intuitive than any on which coarse attitudes are grounded in explanatorily basic states of confidence.[11]

Like other forms of Lockeanism, the force-based approach reduces a tripartite space of attitudes to an indefinitely large space of confidence-theoretic states. The force-based version of the approach then reduces such confidence-theoretic states to an indefinite number of ways that a tripartite range of cognitive forces mix together. This means that force-based Lockeanism sees belief as a mixture of cognitive force almost all of which is attraction, disbelief as a mixture of cognitive force almost all of which is repulsion, and suspended judgement as mixture of cognitive force almost all of which is neutrality. This may be the wrong story about coarse-grained attitudes.

---

[10] As presented here force-based Lockeanism says very little about which mixtures of cognitive force lead to confidence. Those details are left for another occasion.

[11] To be worked out any such view will have to take a stand on how thick confidence relates to the thresholds used in the approach. We needn't take a stand on this here.

But it is a more edifying thought than the bald-faced remark that belief/disbelief/ suspended judgement are high/low/middling-strength confidence.

In the previous chapter we saw that credal-based Lockeanism manifests a number of good-making features. We'll end this chapter by showing how its force-based cousin manifests those features too, often more cleanly or to a higher degree. We'll also see here how the force-based view manifests some further good-making features; and in the next chapter we'll put the view to sustained explanatory work.

To begin, consider the following aspects of force-based Lockeanism:[12]

(1) The view underwrites a hearty realism about coarse- and fine-grained attitudes in line with common sense, and in this it is similar to credal-based Lockeanism. But the force-based approach goes further: not only does it ground belief/disbelief in strong/ weak confidence respectively, it underwrites the idea that we lend thick confidence as well as credence. Hence force-based view puts forward a better version of Locke-style realism about the attitudes than does its credal-based cousin.

(2) The force-based view also does a better job of matching how we ordinarily talk about belief, disbelief, and their degrees. Both credal- and force-based Lockeanism underwrite ordinary remarks like

- Sascha believes that snow is white less firmly than Fritz does

or

- Arno disbelieves that Trump will be re-elected but not fully.

Every version of Lockeanism fits with remarks like these. Like the thick-confidence-using version of the approach, though—and contrary to credal-based Lockeanism—force-based Lockeanism well supports our sense that often, when asked *exactly* how sure we are if a given claim is true, while being able to say honestly that we believe the claim in question, or that we're very confident in the claim in question, nonetheless we're at a loss for how to respond with a credence, for it just doesn't seem that we invest any particular credence in the claim. In turn this means that force-based Lockeanism does a better job of squaring with our ordinary talk of the attitudes than does its credal-based cousin, for like other thick-confidence-using versions of the approach it explains why we are often at a loss to say what our credence is. We're at a loss because we have no credence in the cases to hand.

(3) Force-based Lockeanism does a better job of making sense of the inter-level irreducibility of coarse-grained attitudes than does its credal-based cousin. After all, the force-based view locates three basic types of cognitive force: pro, con, and neutral in flavor. The view then uses these forces to mix into confidence so as to make sense of why we chunk confidence into three categories: belief, disbelief, and suspended judgement. The resulting picture is one on which the first category is confidence dominated by pro cognitive force, the second is confidence dominated by con cognitive force, and the third is confidence dominated by neutral cognitive force. Whenever I teach credal-based Lockeanism, some clever student objects that belief

---

[12] For more discussion of some of these issues see Chapter 10.

simply does not seem to be what you get when you start with ingredients for disbelief and then merely add *more* of them. The objection is phenomenologically probative, for what it's worth, and applicable to any Lockean approach which takes confidence as explanatorily basic. But the objection has no purchase on force-based Lockeanism, since that version of the approach does not take confidence as basic. It reduces all forms of confidence to pro, con, and neutral cognitive force. This makes for a decidedly more satisfying form of Lockeanism about the coarse-grained attitudes, unsurprisingly, since it grounds them ultimately in a coarse-grained collection of similar cognitive forces.

(4) The force-based view does a better job of knitting together the causal roles of coarse- and fine-grained attitudes than does its credal-based cousin. After all, it is common for belief, disbelief, and suspended judgement to spring from thick confidence rather than credence; yet thick confidence and credence function differently. This means that force-based Lockeanism can do a more realistic job of characterizing the functional fit between coarse- and fine-grained states than its credal-based cousin, for the fine-grained functional profiles we normally enjoy— the ones which normally make for belief, disbelief and suspended judgement—are themselves *more* detailed than functional profiles which individuate coarse-grained attitudes, but they are all the same *less* detailed than those which individuate credence. Put another way: fine-grained states which normally make for belief, disbelief, and suspended judgement are coarser than credence but finer than belief, disbelief, or suspended judgement. All thick-confidence-using versions of Lockeanism get right this aspect of how the attitudes fit together functionally. No credal-based version of the approach does. Since force-based Lockeanism is a thick-confidence view par excellence, it does a better job of explaining how coarse- and fine-grained attitudes functionally march in step than does a credal-based version of the approach.

(5) Force-based Lockeanism does a better job of knitting together the rational roles of coarse- and fine-grained attitudes than does its credal-based cousin. Since our evidence is often imprecise in various ways, confidence-theoretic states which rationally ought to make for belief, disbelief, and suspended judgement are often coarser than credence. Like other thick-confidence-using versions of Lockeanism, the force-based view squares with this fact well. Unlike other versions of Lockeanism, though, the force-based view recognizes a layer of mental fact below the confidence-theoretic, so to say, a force-based layer of mental fact. That layer of fact directly echoes the myriad ways in which evidence supports, rebuts, and is neutralized by further evidence (so-called 'defeaters'). This makes the ultimate layer of attitude-generating mental fact, on the force-based view, both structurally and functionally like evidence used in everyday life. Hence the force-based version of Lockeanism does a good job of clarifying how quotidian evidence rationalizes the attitudes.[13]

(6) Force-based Lockeanism can easily locate a functionally minimal sufficient condition for belief, for disbelief, and for suspended judgement. With respect to the

---

[13] This point is discussed a great deal more in the next chapter.

first kind of state: the view need only point to thick confidence running from the belief-making threshold to certainty (Figure 11.6).

Call this the 'b-spread' of confidence. Since propositional attitudes are individu-

**Figure 11.6**

ated functionally—in line with our Cash-Value assumption—manifesting the b-spread of confidence requires exactly two things: one must manifest the positive function shared by all and only believers, and one must fail to do so by manifesting a more fine-grained determinate of that positive function. In this sense the b-spread of confidence is belief and only belief yet distinct from belief as such.

On all Lockean approaches to belief (which recognize credence), one can end up believing by adopting a sufficiently strong credence. Doing so is functionally incompatible with adopting the b-spread of confidence.[14] Since propositional attitudes are individuated functionally, adopting a belief-making credence is incompatible with adopting the b-spread of confidence. On the Lockean approach to belief, then, the b-spread of confidence makes for belief, b-or-stronger credence does so as well, yet adopting the b-spread of confidence is incompatible with adopting any such credence. Adopting the b-spread of confidence is the functionally weakest manifestation of belief. Adopting the b-spread of confidence is enough for belief and nothing psychologically more than belief, but adopting the b-spread of confidence is not identical to believing as such.

Similarly, force-based Lockeanism can easily locate a functionally minimal sufficient condition for disbelief. The view need only point to thick confidence running from no confidence to the disbelief-making threshold (Figure 11.7).

**Figure 11.7**

---

[14] This point is spelled out further in §5.2ff.

Call this the '**db**-spread' of confidence. Since propositional attitudes are individuated functionally, manifesting the **db**-spread of confidence requires exactly two things: one must manifest the positive function shared by all and only disbelievers, and one must fail to do so by manifesting a more fine-grained determinate of that function. In this sense the **db**-spread of confidence is disbelief and only disbelief yet distinct from disbelief as such.

On all Lockean approaches to disbelief (which recognize credence), one can end up disbelieving by adopting a sufficiently weak credence. Doing so is functionally incompatible with adopting the **db**-spread of confidence. Since propositional attitudes are individuated functionally, adopting a disbelief-making credence is incompatible with adopting the **db**-spread of confidence. On the Lockean approach to disbelief, then, the **db**-spread of confidence makes for disbelief, **db**-or-weaker credence does so as well, yet adopting the **db**-spread of confidence is incompatible with adopting any such credence. Adopting the **db**-spread of confidence is the functionally weakest manifestation of disbelief. Adopting the **db**-spread of confidence is enough for disbelief and nothing psychologically more than disbelief, but adopting the **db**-spread of confidence is not identical to disbelieving as such.

And finally, force-based Lockeanism can give a *much* better story about suspended judgement than its credal-based cousin. Such judgement was always the coarse-grained attitude which gave credal-based Lockeanism the hardest time, for suspended judgement is a kind of considered reserve. Yet the hallmark of reserve is a refusal to take a stand, yea- or nay-wise, so to say, on the truth of a claim. Yet nothing like that seems to be involved with any level of credence, for they all seem to involve an exact spread of confidence across every niche of epistemic space. Being 50% sure that it will rain, for instance, is tantamount to a thumbs-up for rain in half your epistemic possibilities and a thumbs-down for rain in the other half. There's no hesitation or reserve in that, so it looks as if credence as such—and thus middling-strength credence—is something rather the opposite of suspended judgement, rather than anything which could make for such judgement. Since credence involves a pro- or a con-stance across all of epistemic possibility, just like a truth-value, it is the wrong sort of thing to make for suspended judgement.

What's needed is something which builds into overall stable reserve about the truth-value of a claim. That is precisely what we find in thick confidence, on a force-based view of the phenomena. What makes for thickness in a given kind of thick confidence, on the approach, is the relative proportion of neutrality in the attitude-generating mixture of cognitive force. On the forced-based approach, then, fully dilated thick confidence consists solely of neutral cognitive force, credence consists solely of attraction and/or repulsion—and thus no neutrality at all—and types of thick confidence in between the extremes consist of mixtures of attraction, repulsion, and neutrality.

A good way to think of suspended judgement, on this approach, is by appeal to a thickness threshold. For every level of confidence there will be an amount of thickness associated with that level, ranging from 0% with credence to 100% with fully thick confidence. We can say that suspended judgement is thick confidence that happens to be thick enough, just as Lockeans say that belief is confidence that is strong enough, and disbelief is confidence that is weak enough. On this force-based approach to suspended judgement, such judgement is thick confidence that involves proportionally enough neutrality to make the grade. Just as we have belief- and disbelief-making thresholds for confidence, then, we have a suspended-judgement threshold too. The former have to do with strength of the relevant attitude maker. The latter has to do with its level of thickness, i.e. the relative proportion of reserve or neutrality involved in its constitution.

This is a satisfying Lockean story about suspended judgement, far superior to any credal-based version, or indeed any Lockean version which takes confidence as fundamental. The force-based view puts reserve at the heart of our conception of suspended judgement. This is exactly in line with its everyday phenomenology; and the story fits well with the idea that suspended judgement is something over and above the mere absence of belief and disbelief.

(7) Force-based Lockeanism leads to a natural understanding of epistemic compartmentalization. For our purposes, this occurs when someone has functionally-dissonant psychological states: perhaps they act as if $\Phi$ is true in one context, as if $\neg\Phi$ is true in another context, and in no stable way elsewhere. Large amounts of behaviour can then be used to motivate an attribution of belief in $\Phi$, an attribution of disbelief in $\Phi$, and an attribution of cognitive unsettledness about $\Phi$. Force-based Lockeanism sees each of these conditions as involving unstable mixtures of cognitive force, functionally competing forces dominating within different contexts, with no force dominant across contexts. Hence the view has the resources to put forward a clean explanation of why it is natural to think that there are compartmentalized attitudes: there really are, by its lights, functional states very like differing epistemic attitudes taken to $\Phi$. Those states are writ small, as it were, functionally pointed at disjoint regions of ordinary life (and potential action). Such 'mini-attitudes' make for functionality very like epistemic attitudes, merely tailoring their functionality to smaller portions of epistemic space.

This may not be the correct way to think about compartmentalization, of course, but it is a promising way to think about it. Force-based Lockeanism thus makes it easy see how compartmentalized mental states resemble functionally similar but more globally stable states—i.e. states the stable functional thrust of which spreads across larger and larger portions of practical possibility—thereby making sense of our inclination to attribute the kinds of states said to be compartmentalized. The view also makes it easy to see how compartmentalized mental states resemble functionally similar but less stable states—i.e. states the functional thrust of which spreads across an even smaller portions of practical possibility—thereby making sense of our disinclination to attribute the kinds of states said to be compartmentalized. Force-based Lockeanism clarifies why compartmentalization is puzzling to begin with. This is a significant mark in its favour.

Now, points (1)-thru-(7) form into a highly non-trivial amount of good news. Jointly they suggest that something is deeply right about force-based Lockeanism. It is my view, however, that the strongest pieces of evidence in its favour are yet to come. They are topics of the next chapter.

# 12
# Force-Based Confidence at Work

## 12.1 Preview

In this chapter we explain and discuss three major topics: dilation within a representor-based kinematics of confidence, doxastic and propositional rationality within a confidence-theoretic setting, and accuracy within a confidence-first epistemology. In all three cases we find that the force-based view helps make sense of what's going on.

In the next section, we discuss the tendency of representors to *dilate* in a technical sense to be explained from scratch. It is shown why this fact about representors makes orthodox kinematics of thick confidence subject to counter-example. The dilation-based worry is generalized and a systematic-yet-puzzling pattern of intuition is revealed. The force-based view is used to explain the pattern of intuition. Along the way new types of counter-example to representor-based kinematics are presented, and the force-based view is used to make sense of them too, in exactly the ways that it made sense of dilation-based worries. The resulting story exposes a deep link between the metaphysics of confidence and the nature of rational kinematics. That force-based metaphysics is then used to explain how propositional and doxastic rationality work out within a confidence-theoretic setting, and why confidence seems sometimes-but-not-always to be subject to content-based accuracy.

## 12.2 Thick Confidence and Representors: Pesky Dilation

We saw in Chapters 3, 4, and 11 that there is more to rational confidence than credence, that there is such a thing as rational thick confidence too. This fact about our psychology leads to a generalization of classic Probabilism. On that generalization, credence is modelled with a probability function and thick confidence is modelled with a complex set of such functions. The formal theory of states deploys richly membered sets of probability functions to model the rational configuration of confidence at a time, and Jeffrey's rule applied to members of those sets in its transition theory. For our purposes that will be the representor framework.[1]

In what follows we'll only be considering limit-case instances of Jeffrey's rule, instances in which an agent becomes rationally certain of new input. The rule

---

[1] See Chapter 3 for details.

*The Rational Mind*. Scott Sturgeon, Oxford University Press (2020). © Scott Sturgeon.
DOI: 10.1093/oso/9780198845799.001.0001

describing exactly those transitions—which Jeffrey aimed to generalize in putting forward his own rule—is Conditionalization. It says in essence that once a rational agent becomes sure that a claim A is true—where A is the logically strongest claim of which the agent becomes certain—then, for any claim C, her new credence for C should equal her old conditional credence for C given A. From this point forward we'll only be considering situations in which thick-confidence needs revising because a rational agent in equilibrium stops being in equilibrium by virtue of becoming certain of something. The orthodox transition theory for thick confidence in such a case applies Conditionalization to members of the agent's representor.[2]

This approach to a general transition theory for confidence is challenged by a technical aspect of representors, namely, their pesky disposition *to dilate* in a sense to be explained. It turns out that this aspect of representors renders them ill-suited to model thick confidence, as we'll see. But reflecting on why this is so helps to confirm the basic nature of confidence as well as its relation to the project of kinematics itself, which in turn helps us see in a deep way what's going on in a kinematics of confidence. In this chapter we'll lay out the dilation bother in detail and then reflect on its significance for confidence and kinematics. Along the way we'll discover new worries for a representor-based transition theory, worries which have not been discussed in the literature.

The standard dilation-based difficulty faced by the orthodox transition theory for thick confidence is illustrated in the following case:

### EGGS

Let *eggs* be a claim about which you are clueless, perhaps a claim about the price of eggs in medieval Tuva. You have no evidence about *eggs* at all, let us suppose, or at least you come as close to this as is humanly possible. Suppose also you realize that I know for sure whether *eggs* is true. Then you write the word 'sign' on one side of a fair coin to stand for *eggs* being true, and the phrase 'not sign' on the other side to stand for *eggs* being false. Then you close your eyes, toss the coin, and ask me how it lands. You are rationally sure that I'll be honest. Then I report: the coin lands with its true side up.[3]

---

[2] Or throws them out of an agent's representor if Conditionalization is undefined. See (Kaplan, 1983) or (Joyce, 2010) for the details.

[3] This thought experiment was constructed by reflecting on a similar one developed by David Christensen in correspondence. In turn Christensen's thought experiment was constructed by reflecting on a similar one found in White's influential 'Evidential Symmetry and Mushy Credence' (2009). White's thought experiment involves an *eggs*-knowledgeable coin labeller. This leads some to think that by digesting the details of White's case one can somehow gain an indirect epistemic grip on *eggs*. Though not of this view, Christensen worried that this fact about White's thought experiment might skew intuitions of many about it, and, thereby, ruin the scenario's dialectical efficacy. So he built a new scenario to avoid the bother. In all essentials his case is just like ours, save that *eggs* and *sign-up* are reversed in the proceedings. This does rule out any whiff that an epistemic grip on *eggs* can be got by digesting details of the case; but for reasons that exceed the scope of this chapter it does not seem obvious that Christensen's case poses a real challenge to the orthodox model of thick confidence. Once it is tweaked to yield the thought experiment in main text, however, both things are true at once: there is no whiff that one gains an epistemic grip on *eggs* by digesting details of the case; and the case to hand poses a real challenge to the orthodox model of thick confidence. Hence the essentials of White's problematic are preserved without background noise.

Let *sign-up* be the claim that the word 'sign' lands up on the toss, and *truth-up* be the claim that the side of the coin which is true lands up. A challenge to the orthodox approach to thick confidence can then be mounted as follows.

Proponents of orthodoxy see your initial take on *eggs* as something other than credence of ½. Since you are clueless about whether *eggs* is true, they typically use the unit interval to model your attitudinal reaction to your lack of evidence about *eggs*:

(1) **old**(*eggs*) = [0, 1].

But your **initial** take on *sign-up*—in line with the Principal Principle—should match its pre-toss chance:

(2) **old**(*sign-up*) = ½.

When you learn that *truth-up* is correct, however, you learn nothing to make for a shift in your take on *eggs* or on *sign-up*. So your view of those claims looks reasonably constant in light of your new information:

(3) **old**(*eggs*) = **new**(*eggs*)
(4) **old**(*sign-up*) = **new**(*sign-up*).

But once you learn that *truth-up* is correct you can be rationally sure that *eggs and sign-up* have the same truth-value: either both true or both false. Once you learn that *truth-up* is correct, after all, you can be sure that the coin lands with 'sign' up while *eggs* is true *or* with 'sign' down while *eggs* is false. This means we have

(5) **new**(*sign-up*) = **new**(*eggs*).

Now we face contradiction: if you haven't changed your mind about *eggs* or about *sign-up*—as (3) and (4) jointly ensure—but you have ended with the same view of them—as (5) ensures by itself—you must have started with the same view of those claims. That is jointly ruled out by (1) and (2).

By way of reaction: let a *case* be any scenario like the one above, save that your initial take on *eggs* can vary. Let us think carefully about the update of confidence upon learning that *sign-up* is true in the full range of cases. This will make several things clear, three of which are emphasized in what follows:

(A) Cases with initial thick confidence for *eggs* immediately generate a prima facie puzzle;
(B) Intuition about the full range of cases generates a much deeper puzzle;
(C) Respecting that intuition leads not only to a principled critique of the orthodox model of thick confidence, but also to a better understanding of the nature of confidence and its relation to kinematics.

We take these lessons in turn.

To begin, note that thick confidence is central to any puzzle there might be in the area. Purely credal cases—i.e. cases with initial credence for *eggs* rather than initial thick confidence—present no puzzle at all. Consider three of them diagrammed as in Figure 12.1, with boxes for your epistemic space. Think of horizontal lines in a box as dividing that space so that its upper half contains *sign-up*-worlds while its lower half contains ¬*sign-up*-worlds; and think of vertical lines in a box as dividing your epistemic space so that its left half contains *eggs*-worlds while its right half contains ¬*eggs*-worlds.

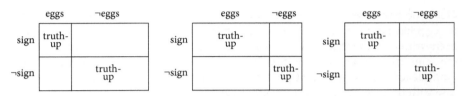

Figure 12.1

old(*eggs*) = 1/3              old(*eggs*) = 2/3              old(*eggs*) = 1/2
old(*sign-up*) = 1/2           old(*sign-up*) = 1/2           old(*sign-up*) = 1/2
new(*sign-up*) = new(*eggs*)   new(*sign-up*) = new(*eggs*)   new(*sign-up*) = new(*eggs*)
old(*eggs*) = new(*eggs*)      old(*eggs*) = new(*eggs*)      old(*eggs*) = new(*eggs*)
old(*sign-up*) > new(*sign-up*)  old(*sign-up*) < new(*sign-up*)  old(*sign-up*) = new(*sign-up*)

In cases like these it is clear—after reflection, at least—that you should conditionalize on *truth-up*. For this reason fully credal cases pose no difficulty for the Bayesian model, since the model handles them well, predicting exactly in line with strong, considered, pre-theoretic intuition.

But think of the full range of cases with an initially balanced attitude taken to *eggs*—call these 'balanced cases'. Let the full range start with the case exhibiting 50% initial credence for *eggs*, move into cases with greater and greater initial thick confidence for *eggs*—always centered on 1/2 to preserve balance, of course—and then end with the case actually used above: the case with maximally thick initial confidence in *eggs*. As we have just seen, there is no difficulty about the initial case in the range. It is clear in the fully credal balanced case that you should conditionalize on *truth-up*. The moment we step away from that case, however—the moment we look at balanced cases with initial *thick* confidence for *eggs*—we face a prima facie puzzle. This is because three principles are true in any such case, yet their joint truth is definitely puzzling.

The first principle concerns your initial take on *sign-up* and on *eggs*. In all balanced cases exhibiting initial thick confidence for *eggs*, the following will be true by stipulation:

(Diff-Attitude)   Different initial attitudes will be taken to *sign-up* and to *eggs*.

In any such case you will start with 50% confidence in *sign-up* and a balanced thick confidence for *eggs*. Your initial take on the claims will be distinct, so (Diff-Attitude) will be true by stipulation.

The second principle concerns a conditional certainty you should have once the description of a balanced case is absorbed. After all, any case whatsoever—and thus any balanced case—will be described so that the following is true:

> (Cond-Equivalence)  The correctness of *truth-up* will be initially seen as conditionally sufficient for the equivalence of *eggs and sign-up*.

Once you have digested the details of a case—once you have absorbed that a name for *eggs* has been written on one side of a fair coin and a name for its negation has been written on the other—you should be initially certain that *eggs and sign-up* have the same truth-value, on condition the correct side of the coin lands up. (Cond-Equivalence) follows from that description straightaway. The principle applies to any case with balanced initial thick confidence for *eggs*.

The third principle concerns whether the truth of *truth-up* has any bearing—by your lights in a case—on the truth-value of *sign-up* or of *eggs*. The following principle will be true of any case:

> (No-Relevance)  The correctness of *truth-up* will be initially seen as irrelevant to the truth-value of *sign-up* and the truth-value of *eggs*.

It is part of our description of a case, after all, that the truth-values of *eggs* and *sign-up* have nothing at all to do with one another. But the truth-value of *truth-up* has solely to do with them: whether *truth-up* is correct in a case is fixed metaphysically by the truth-values of *eggs* and *sign-up*. This is why (No-Relevance) is true for any case with initially balanced thick confidence for *eggs*. The principle follows from the description of any such case.

Now we can locate a prima facie puzzle about any balanced case with initial thick confidence in *eggs*. In any such case you begin with differing takes on *eggs* and *sign-up*, you begin fully certain that *eggs* and *sign-up* have the same truth-value on condition that *truth-up* is correct, but you also begin fully certain that *truth-up*'s correctness has no bearing on *sign-up* or on *eggs*. It is no wonder that balanced cases with initial thick confidence for *eggs* call into question the epistemic bona fides of thick confidence. One wants to ask: 'How can it be that distinct attitudes are rational for a pair of claims which are equivalent on a certain condition, when that very condition is itself manifestly of no bearing when it comes to the two claims in question?' It is not obvious that this is possible, to put it mildly, and thus balanced cases with initial thick confidence for *eggs* generate a serious prima facie puzzle.

There is a deeper puzzle in the neighbourhood, though, which can be drawn to the surface of discussion by reflection on the full range of cases. When spelling it out the first thing to notice is this: the representor approach to rational thick confidence entails that initial thick confidence for *eggs* is automatically *inherited* in a case by the new view for *sign-up*. To see this consider a representative case with initial thick confidence for *eggs*: suppose you start out exactly 1/4th-to-1/3rd sure *eggs* is true. Then your epistemic space will be pictured as follows

# THICK CONFIDENCE AND REPRESENTORS: PESKY DILATION 293

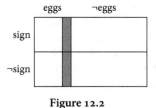

**Figure 12.2**

Since you begin with 50% credence for *sign-up*, there is a horizontal line halfway up the box. Since you begin with sharp thick confidence of 1/4th-to-1/3rd for *eggs*— and since you take *sign-up* and *eggs* to be unrelated—there is an orthogonal grey band stretching from 1/4th to 1/3rd of the way along epistemic space from left-to-right. But since orthodoxy about thick confidence models it with a set of credence functions, we may also picture its take on your view with a set of boxes

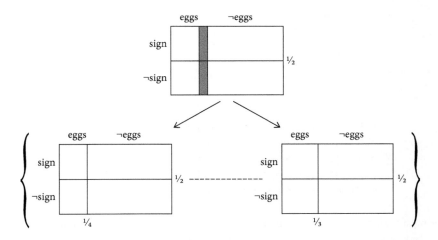

**Figure 12.3**

When you learn solely in effect that *eggs* and *sign-up* have the same truth-value, moreover, the orthodox model will construct a new representor for you by conditioning elements of your old representor on the news. Hence the model predicts that your new take on *sign-up* will *thicken*, that it will shift from a credence to a thick confidence.

This thickening-of-attitude results from the fact that orthodoxy builds a representation of your new take on *sign-up* by appeal to probability values got through conditioning functions used to represent your old take on *sign-up*. Those functions see your old view of *sign-up* conditional on the news as ranging from 1/4th to 1/3rd. This ensures that orthodoxy sees your new view of *sign-up* as itself 'spread out' across this range. The new thick confidence for *sign-up* is got by conditioning elements of your old representor on the news that *sign-up* and *eggs* have the same truth-value.

Years of experience with this type of thought experiment—in both teaching and colloquia—have shown that many find such thickening-of-attitude acceptable—or at any rate, as Jim Pryor put it to me in 2007, that they can grow 'comfortable' with the thickening upon reflection. My own view is that such thickening-of-attitude is not perforce irrational, but there are cases in which it *is* manifestly irrational to thicken in the way obliged by orthodoxy. In these cases the model simply goes wrong in its prescriptions. We'll see different sorts of scenarios about which the model goes wrong later on in this chapter, but here we should be clearer on which cases (in our technical sense of a case) the model seems to mishandle.

To begin, consider a pair of unbalanced cases which exhibit tiny amounts of initial thick confidence for *eggs*

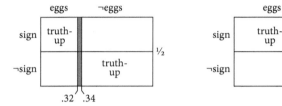

**Figure 12.4**

old(*eggs*) = [.32, .34]         old(*eggs*) = [.65, .67]
old(*sign-up*) = 1/2             old(*sign-up*) = 1/2
new(*sign-up*) = new(*eggs*)     new(*sign-up*) = new(*eggs*)
old(*eggs*) = new(*eggs*)        old(*eggs*) = new(*eggs*)
old(*sign-up*) > new(*sign-up*)  old(*sign-up*) < new(*sign-up*)

Being unbalanced cases, of course, neither falls within the range of balanced cases glossed earlier. But in each case above no detailed story about the update of thick confidence is needed—certainly no formal *model* is needed—to see that your new information is relevant to *sign-up*. Specifically, it is pre-theoretically clear that your new information is negatively relevant to *sign-up* is the first case above, and it is likewise clear that your new information is positively relevant to *sign-up* in the second case above. In each of these unbalanced cases it is pre-theoretically obvious that your new take on *sign-up* should be shaped, somehow, by your old take on *eggs*, your old take on *sign-up*, your initial view that the truth-values of *eggs* and *sign-up* have nothing to do with one another, and so forth. In a nutshell: it is pre-theoretically clear, in the unbalanced cases above, that your new take on *sign-up* should be shaped by your old take on the set up. Yet that clarity is not itself based on theory or fidelity to model. It is just common sense. In the unbalanced cases above, therefore, it is pre-theoretically plausible that your new view of *sign-up* should *inherit* some thickness from your old take on *eggs*.

This story applies to any case involving small amounts of unbalanced initial thick confidence for *eggs*. In any such case it is clear that your new information is actively relevant—either pro or con—to the truth-value of *sign-up*. In any such case it is obvious that your new take on *sign-up* should be shaped by your old take on the set up. But this very obviousness does not itself come from theory or fidelity to model. It comes from common sense. In any unbalanced case which exhibits tiny amounts of initial thick confidence for *eggs*, therefore, it is pre-theoretically plausible that your new view of *sign-up* should inherit some thickness from your old take on *eggs*.

This suggests that your new view of *sign-up* should be likewise fixed in cases with tiny amounts of *balanced* initial thick confidence for *eggs*. For example, consider a case like Figure 12.5.

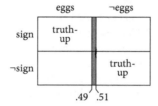

**Figure 12.5**

old(*eggs*) = [.49, .51]
old(*sign-up*) = 1/2
new(*sign-up*) = new(*eggs*)
old(*eggs*) = new(*eggs*)
old(*sign-up*) ??? new(*sign-up*),

In my view the replacement of questions marks here is a spoils-to-the-victor issue. After all, it is plausible that cases which exhibit a given level of balanced initial thick confidence for *eggs* should be treated the same way as cases which exhibit that same level of unbalanced initial thick confidence for *eggs*. Whatever the best story turns out to be, for updating very small amounts of initial thick confidence un-spread symmetrically around ½, it is plausible that *that* is the story to be told about cases with such confidence spread symmetrically around ½; for it is plausible that balanced cases should be treated like unbalanced cousins. The latter, after all, are like the former in all relevant respects. There is strong, stable pre-theoretic intuition concerning the latter that your new view of *sign-up* should inherit its character from your old take on the set up. Whatever story best codifies intuition about that should be applied to cases which exhibit tiny amounts of balanced initial thick confidence for *eggs*. If that is right, however, then tiny amounts of balanced initial thick confidence for *eggs* are insufficient for a serious worry about the epistemic propriety of thick confidence.

Let me be explicit about the diagnostic line at work here:

(D) In every case with a tiny amount of unbalanced initial thick confidence for *eggs*, it is pretheoretically plausible that your new take on *sign-up* should be unequal to your old take on *sign-up*; for in every such case it is pre-theoretically plausible that your new information is positively or negatively relevant to *sign-up*, and in turn this is so precisely because of your old take on the set up—and most saliently, of course, your old take on *eggs*. But every case with a tiny amount of balanced initial thick confidence for *eggs* matches members of a class of similar cases exhibiting just its level of unbalanced initial thick confidence for *eggs*. All members of that class intuitively lead to updating of *sign-up* which thickens your initial take on the claim. So that is what should happen in balanced cases which match them. In every case with a tiny amount of balanced initial thick confidence for *eggs*, therefore, it is pre-theoretically plausible that your new take on *sign-up* should be unequal to your old take on *sign-up*. What to do about *sign-up* in such cases is a spoils-to-the-victor issue.

This diagnostic line of thought leads to the view that in every balanced case with tiny amounts of initial thick confidence for *eggs*, your update of *sign-up* should result in a *thickening* of your take on that claim.

The next question is whether every balanced case with initial thick confidence for *eggs* can be treated this way? Can we generalize fully from balanced cases which exhibit tiny amounts of initial thick confidence for *eggs*? Is it always pre-theoretically clear—or even mostly clear after considered reflection, or even a tiny bit clear after such reflection—that in every balanced case whatsoever your new take on *sign-up* should be thickened by appeal to your old take on the set up?

I don't think so.

To see why, recall the range of balanced cases sketched earlier. Let us go through it and say how updating of *sign-up* should proceed. When we do that, our initial verdict will be clear to the last detail; for the range sketched earlier begins with the case which exhibits 50% initial credence for *eggs*. Our first verdict will thus be that *sign-up* should be updated by Conditionalization; and that verdict will seem very obvious indeed. Our next verdicts, however, will not be so clear, though we have seen that their general shape will be clear enough to work with. After all: when it comes to balanced cases exhibiting tiny amounts of initial thick confidence for *eggs*, the diagnostic line (D) applies: in any such case the update of *sign-up* should yield a thickened attitude toward *sign-up* by appeal to your initial take on the set up. The exact details of this are certainly not pre-theoretically clear. The basic shape of the update is pre-theoretically clear.

But consider what happens as we move further down the range of balanced cases, shifting our gaze from those with tiny amounts of initial thick confidence for *eggs*, focusing instead on cases with larger and larger amounts of thick confidence. As we do so, it seems obvious that the diagnostic line (D) becomes less and less intuitive; for as we shift our gaze further down the range it becomes less and less clear that your new take on *sign-up* should be fixed by your old take on the set up. This is not because cases which come before us fail to match a relevant class of unbalanced cases. It is rather because intuition about the relevance of new information peters out *in those very unbalanced cases*.

Let me be clear about the way I see intuition panning out across the full range of cases sketched earlier. I shall do this by describing intuition in two stages. The first will concern movement from balanced cases with tiny amounts of initial thick confidence for *eggs* to the balanced case with 50% initial thick confidence for *eggs*. The second will concern movement from the balanced case with 50% initial thick confidence for *eggs* to the balanced case with 100% initial thick confidence for *eggs*.

As we go from balanced cases with tiny amounts of initial thick confidence for *eggs* to the balanced case with 50% initial thick confidence for *eggs*, intuition seems to shift from strongly supporting the diagnostic line at (D) to full neutrality about it. As we move down this bit of the range, in other words, intuition seems to shift from strongly supporting the idea that your new take on *sign-up* should be thickened by your old take on the set up to full neutrality about that idea. But this change in intuition does not result from the cases in question failing to match a relevant class of unbalanced cases—namely, those with identical levels of initial thick confidence for *eggs*—for the cases to hand <u>do</u> match such unbalanced cases in all relevant respects. What happens instead is that as we go from balanced cases with tiny amounts of initial thick confidence for *eggs* to the case with 50% initial thick confidence for *eggs*, support for the diagnostic line at (D) goes to ground with respect to the unbalanced cases mentioned in (D). That is why supporting intuition for (D) peters out with respect to the balanced cases before us, why intuition shifts from full support for (D) to neutrality towards it as we move down this bit of the range.

Moreover, as we go from the balanced case with 50% initial thick confidence for *eggs* to such cases exhibiting ever larger amounts of initial thick confidence for *eggs*—arriving eventually at the exemplar case used above—intuition seems to shift from full neutrality about the diagnostic line at (D) to full rejection of that line. But here too the change does not result from cases before us failing to match relevantly-similar unbalanced cases. Cases before us <u>do</u> match such unbalanced cases in all salient respects. What happens instead is that as we go from the balanced case with 50% initial confidence for *eggs* to the case actually used in the text above, pull toward rejection of (D) builds up a head of steam concerning the unbalanced cases mentioned in (D). That is why intuition cuts against (D) more and more strongly as we move across balanced cases before us, why intuition shifts from full neutrality about (D) to complete rejection of the line.

The facts sketched in the previous two paragraphs make for a deep puzzle about the transition theory of cases. Consider the one in the middle of the mess: the case with 50% balanced initial thick confidence for *eggs*. By my lights, *no* approach to the update of *sign-up* is intuitively compelling in this case—not even after very considered reflection. But at least we can say something systematic about the way that intuition pans out as we proceed from this neutral starting point. After all, we can say that thickening your old view of *sign-up* by appeal to your initial take on the set up seems more and more intuitive as a case exhibits less and less initial thickness in confidence for *eggs*; and we can say that thickening your old view of *sign-up* by appeal to your initial take on the set up seems less and less intuitive as the case in question exhibits more and more initial thickness in confidence for *eggs*. A systematic point can be made about the way intuition plays out across cases:

(↔) The level of pre-theoretic plausibility which attaches to the idea that your new view of *sign-up* should inherit its character from your old take on the set up, in a given case, is itself inversely proportional to the case's level of initial thickness in confidence for *eggs*.

When the level of initial thickness in confidence for *eggs* is low in a given case, the level of pre-theoretic plausibility which attaches to the idea that your new view of *sign-up* should inherit its character from your old take on the set up is itself high. When the level of initial thickness in confidence for *eggs* is high in a given case, the level of pre-theoretic plausibility which attaches to the idea that your new view of *sign-up* should inherit its character from your old take on the set up is itself low. And so on.

When it comes to the orthodox model's prescriptions for the full range of cases, then, considered intuition shifts *systematically*. It fully endorses orthodoxy when the range of values for one's initial take on *eggs* is a credence. It fully (or almost-fully) endorses orthodoxy when the range of values for one's initial take on *eggs* is vanishingly small. Considered intuition hesitates more and more about orthodoxy when the range of those values grows in size, intuition tends to disagree with orthodoxy when the range in question becomes large. And in the case where your initial take on *eggs* is maximally dilated, considered intuition flatly rejects the orthodox model. After all, when you begin certain that *sign-up*'s truth-value is fixed entirely by the flip of a fair coin, and you begin with maximally thick confidence for eggs, it is dead-obvious that *sign-up* and *eggs* have nothing to do with one another, and then you learn solely that *sign-up* and *eggs* have the same truth-value, well, it would be madness to *thicken* your take on whether *sign-up* is true. In those circumstances you should end-up 50% sure that *sign-up* is true, and, in light of the news, 50% sure that *eggs* is too. Yet the orthodox model prescribes a fully thick confidence for both claims. That prescription is plainly wrong.

In a nutshell: the degree of agreement we find across the full array of cases, between orthodox prescription for thick confidence and considered intuition, is inversely proportional to the degree of initial thickness in one's take on *eggs*:

- no thickness → perfect agreement
- small thickness → strong agreement
- middling thickness → intuition falls silent
- large thickness → strong disagreement
- full thickness → absolute rejection.

Why on earth should *that* be so? Why is the level of pre-theoretic plausibility to do with the model's prescriptions inversely proportional to the level of initial thickness in confidence for *eggs* in a case? That is very puzzling indeed.

The answer these questions springs directly from the force-based view of confidence put forward in the previous chapter. In the next section we'll see how that view can be used to explain the systematic shift of intuition sketched above, intuition surrounding entirely new types of difficulty for representor-based kinematics, and a very deep point of contact between the nature of confidence and the project of kinematics. In subsequent sections we'll see how the force-based view can be used to explain the distinction between doxastic and evidential justification, and the way in which accuracy applies to confidence.

## 12.3 Force-Based Confidence and Rational Kinematics

The force-based view of confidence can be used to diagnose why the orthodox kinematics for confidence breaks down in a systematic way. In particular, it can be used to explain why that kinematics yields correct prescriptions in a range of interesting cases and mistaken ones in a range of others. This lends considerable

# FORCE-BASED CONFIDENCE AND RATIONAL KINEMATICS 299

support to the idea that confidence is a mixture of attraction, repulsion, and neutrality.

The key point to be explained is the following:

(↔) In a given EGG-like case, the level of pre-theoretic plausibility which attaches to the idea that your new view of *sign-up* should inherit its character from your old take on the set up is itself inversely proportional to the case's level of initial thickness in confidence for *eggs*.

We can picture the situation as shown in Figure 12.6. Consider the full array of EGG-like cases.

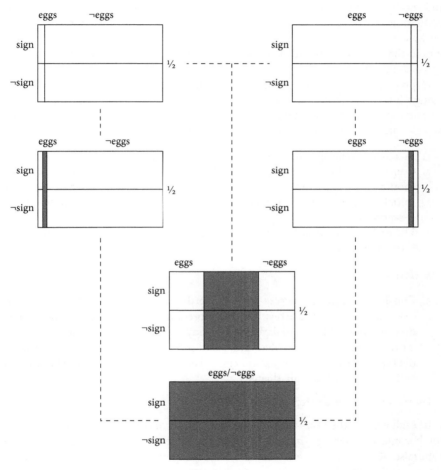

**Figure 12.6**

The top of the array represents the full range of credence-only versions of the template scenario before us. These are all cases handled gracefully by orthodox approaches to rational credence. In each of them you start out rationally certain that the relevant coin is fair, and thus 50% certain that *sign-up* is true. In each of them you lend a credence to *eggs*. Lower stages of the array represent ranges of locations for greater and greater thickness in your initial take on *eggs*, intuitively, based on greater and greater inexactness in your initial information about the price of eggs in medieval Tuva. The bottom of the array represents the unique case in which your initial take on *eggs* is fully dilated: you begin with a fully-neutral take on *eggs*, because you begin with no information about the price of eggs in medieval Tuva.

The key point about considered intuition is then this: it shifts rather dramatically as one descends in the array. Considered intuition agrees with the orthodox approach when considering credal EGG-like cases (at the top of the array). But it disagrees more and more with orthodoxy as one goes down the array. And at the bottom—when pondering the unique EGG-like case in which initial confidence for *eggs* is fully thick, considered intuition is flat-out against the orthodox approach. But why should that be? Why should there be variance like this as we descend the array of EGG-like cases?

Happily, the force-based approach to confidence explains this variation quite well, though it takes a moment to see what's going on. First we'll state the explanation of the variance explicitly, step-by-step, and then we'll explain its major moving parts, to make clear how the explanation works. Here it is in step-by-step form:

1. In a sense to be specified, EGG-like cases are *orthogonal tug-of-war cases*.
2. Considered intuition insists that attitudes grounded in cognitive neutrality should give way in such cases precisely to the extent that they are so grounded.
3. Initial thick confidence for *eggs* involves more and more neutrality as we descend in the array.
4. The orthodox approach to rational confidence forbids it from giving way in an orthogonal tug-of-war.

Therefore,

5. Considered intuition agrees with the orthodox approach about fully-credal cases at the top of the array, but cuts more and more against orthodoxy as we descend to the fully-dilated case at the array's bottom. This is because the initial attitude taken to *eggs* involves more and more neutrality as we so descend: at the top of the array one's take on *eggs* involves no neutrality, at the bottom it is entirely neutral (i.e. fully dilated).

Let me flesh out each step of this explanation.

1. In each case in the array you become sure that *truth-up* is correct, which means you become sure that *sign-up* and *eggs* have the same truth-value: either both true or both false. Receipt of the news thus sets off a competition between your old view of *sign-up* and your old view of *eggs*. And the set-up—about which you are always rationally certain, in every EGG-like case—ensures that whether *sign-up* is true never has anything to do with whether *eggs* is true, and vice versa. To learn that *sign-up* and *eggs* have the same truth-value, therefore, sets off a tug-of-war between views about topics known to have nothing to do with one another. By stipulation that is an orthogonal tug-of-war situation. Hence the array of EGG-like cases is filled with orthogonal tug-of-war situations.

2. Intuition is clear that substantive attitudinal neutrality should give way in orthogonal tug-of-war cases like those found in the array. In cases like that, such attitudes should not help shape your new view of things after updating on the news. Instead they should melt away without trace, leaving no forward-looking impact on your epistemic life. To see this vividly suppose you have investigated $\Phi$ and $\Psi$ thoroughly, and, as a result, your rational configuration of attitudes ends-up having three salient features: it fully respects that $\Phi$ and $\Psi$ have nothing to do with one another, it lends a heavily-neutral attitude to $\Phi$ (i.e. a heavily dilated confidence), and it lends an 85% credence to $\Psi$. Then you learn solely that $\Phi$ and $\Psi$ have the same truth-value. How should you update on the news?

Considered intuition is crystal clear: you should bring your new view of $\Phi$ into line with your old take on $\Psi$, <u>not</u> create a new take on $\Psi$ by appeal to your old take on $\Phi$ (not even in part). Neutrality like this should give way in an asymmetric tug-of-war pitting credence against a seriously thick attitude. When credence can lead the way in a rational update, serious amounts of neutrality should vanish in reaction to the news. Step 2. of the explanation above simply generalizes this idea to each case in the array of EGG-like cases. (Later on we'll see *why* this intuitive aspect of rational kinematics is true.)

3. The top of the array consists in purely credal EGG-like cases. In each of them you begin with reasonable credence for *sign-up* and *eggs*. Then you become sure that the two claims have the same truth-value. The result is a symmetric tug-of-war. In purely credal cases like this, your new take on each claim should be shaped by your old take on each claim; and it should be so shaped exactly as orthodoxy maintains: you should form a new view of things in line with conditioning on the news. Neither your initial take on *sign-up* nor your initial take on *eggs* should give way. Intuition agrees fully with the orthodox approach to top-end cases of the array.

As we descend from those cases, however, we encounter cases involving thick confidence for *eggs* rather than credence. This means greater and greater neutrality is involved in the case before us as we move down the array. As we descend from purely credal cases at the top, therefore, we move further and further into cases where the lessons of point 2. apply. This means we move further and further into a range of cases in which initial thick confidence for *eggs* should give way in a tug-of-war with initial credence for *sign-up*.

4. This conflicts with the orthodox approach to confidence. For any claims $\Phi$, $\Psi$, and any probability function **p**: the probability that **p** gives to $\Phi$ or to $\Psi$, on the assumption that $\Phi$ and $\Psi$ have the same truth-value, is itself shaped by the probability that **p** gives $\Phi$ and the probability that **p** gives $\Psi$.[4] This means that for any $\Phi$, $\Psi$ and **p**: building a new probability function by conditioning **p** on the news that $\Phi$ and $\Psi$ have the same truth-value results in a new function whose take on each claim is shaped by the old function's take on $\Phi$ and its take on $\Psi$. The old function's take on neither claim will give way. Neither take will defer to the other.

This fact about probability functions shapes how sets of them behave. It entails that whenever a range of values is allotted to $\Phi$ or to $\Psi$ by a set of probability

---

[4] See Chapter 2 for a detailed explanation of all this from scratch.

functions, a range of values will be assigned to both claims when members of the set are conditioned on the news that Φ and Ψ have the same truth-value. So when sets of probability functions are used to model thick confidence, and the update rule for such sets is Conditionalization, it follows that whenever one lends thick confidence to Φ, conditioning solely on the news that Φ and Ψ have the same truth-value automatically results in a new thick view of Ψ, no matter how the run-up to the update plays out.

5. This is wrong. The array is filled with orthogonal tug-of-war cases, and, aside from its top level, cases involving initial thick confidence for *eggs*. Since that thick confidence increases as we move down the array, the relative amount of neutral cognitive force involved with one's initial take on *eggs* also increases. This means the loudness with which intuition insists that orthodoxy goes wrong increases as we descend in the array. There is a tiny whiff of it just below purely credal cases at the top, a bit louder worry about orthodoxy as we go down the array, and full-throated rejection of the approach as we reach the full-dilation case. This is because the neutrality of one's initial take on *eggs*—that very cognitive force, the one which grows to full domination as we descend to the bottom of the array—should play no role in the update brought on by the news to the effect that *sign-up* and *eggs* have the same truth-value. In a moment we'll see why this is true—and that explanation is itself rather interesting—but for now we note merely that intuition recognizes perfectly that the cognitive force of neutrality should not influence the way forward in updates like those in the array. The orthodox approach to rational confidence has no room for this sentiment. Since it insists that your initial view of *eggs* should always shape your new view of *sign-up*, intuition about how the update should go cuts ever more loudly against orthodoxy as we descend in the array of EGG-like cases.

This is a clean diagnosis of one area in which orthodox kinematics goes wrong. The fundamental mistake it makes is to insist that thick confidence play the kind of role in updating that credence plays. Since thick confidence involves the cognitive force of neutrality, that is not right. To the extent that neutrality is involved in one's initial attitudinal equilibrium, reached by way of reaction to total evidence, attitudes so lent should give way to the kinds of update situations found in the array.

The force-based approach to confidence makes good sense of this. It maintains that confidence is a mixture of attraction, repulsion, and neutrality; and it sees the degree of thickness involved in a given type of confidence as itself a measure of the relative strength of neutrality making for that type of attitude. Confidence involving only a whiff of thickness is made from mixtures of cognitive force with a relative whiff of neutrality. Confidence involving a modicum of thickness is made from mixtures of cognitive force with a relative modicum of neutrality. And so on. High levels of thickness in confidence involve mixtures of cognitive force strongly dominated by neutrality. Whenever evidence prompts such a state, intuition rightly insists that the prompted state defer to attitudes grounded in better evidence. The force-based approach to confidence explains why intuition moves, in a systematic way, from full support for orthodox kinematics to full rejection of it. This is strong indication that something is right in the force-based metaphysics of confidence.

Now, these last thoughts prompt an edifying objection to the force-based story about points 1 thru 5. Although the objection ultimately fails, unearthing *why* it fails leads directly to an edifying story about one of the most important aspects of kinematics. To see why, suppose you have ideally rational thick confidence for T, ideally rational credence for C, and a view on which T and C have nothing to do with one another. Then you learn solely, to your surprise, that T and C have the same truth-value. This sets off a tug-of-war between your old take on T and your old take on C. We have seen in cases like this that intuition indicates your old take on T should give-way to your credence for C—or at least it does so to the extent that your old take on T is relatively infused with neutrality (i.e. thick). But the worry is that it is not the *nature* of your old take on T which explains why it is intuitive that that take should give way in the tug-of-war, but, rather, that your give-way intuition is explained by the degree to which there is an absence of information about T in the set-up of the case. The reason it seems intuitive that your old take on T should give way to your credence for C, the objection goes, is because you realize that your initial thick confidence for T is itself a rational reaction to little-or-no evidence about T in the set-up. When the lack of such evidence is small—and only a whiff of initial thickness for T is rational—we have a mild and wavering intuition that your initial take on T should give way to your credence for C; but when the lack of such evidence is large—and a great deal of initial thickness for T is ideal—we have a strong and stable intuition that your initial take on T should give way to your credence for C. When learning solely that orthogonal contents have the same truth-value, then, the objection has it that intuition saying thick confidence should give way to credence is explained by awareness of the absence of evidence to hand, not the nature of thick confidence. This looks to conflict with the view that such give-way intuition is explained by the nature of the attitude in question. Since the force-based explanation of give-way intuition was itself being offered in support of the forced-based metaphysics of confidence, the fact that lack of evidence can itself be used to explain give-way intuition undermines the support for that metaphysics.

There is much to be learned about the kinematics of confidence from seeing why this objection fails. Before that can be made clear, however, a faulty assumption made by the objection must be identified and moved to the background of discussion. I call it the paucity-of-evidence principle:

(PE)  give-way intuitions can always be explained by the paucity of evidence in the set-up of a case.

It should be clear straightaway that something is wrong with this principle. After all, nothing was said about whether there *is* a paucity of evidence in the T-and-C case discussed—indeed nothing was said about the evidence in that case at all. We did say enough to generate a strong and stable give-way intuition about thick confidence, but nothing was said about whether that confidence was adopted by way of reaction to an absence of evidence.

Explanation in line with the paucity-of-evidence principle can be put forward in cases like those in the array discussed earlier. But other cases generate strong and stable give-way intuitions—of precisely the sort we're discussing—even though they manifest *no* lack of evidence in their set-up. Those cases show that give-way intuitions cannot always be explained by awareness of an evidential absence in the set-up of a case. The paucity-of-evidence principle is not always true in a case, and, for this reason, the difficulty for orthodox updating we're discussing extends beyond EGG-like cases.

To see this, consider the following two non- EGG-like cases:

(A) Suppose you are faced with the toss of a biased coin. Let H be the claim that it lands heads. Suppose you know the coin is 75% biased to heads, and, as a result, you begin with a 75% credence for H. Let Φ be a claim evidence about which comes through a pair of trusted advisors. Each is known by you to be a stellar expert on whether Φ is true, and also such an expert on who should be trusted about whether Φ is true. The pair give you their news in a bundle: source-1 claims that Φ is true and that source-2 should not be trusted about whether Φ is true; source-2 claims that Φ is not true and that source-1 should not to be trusted about whether Φ is true. This is your total evidence.

The set-up contains information relevant to Φ, but the information suffers from full collective defeat.[5] It is thus useless as guide to whether T is true. This is why your initial take on Φ should be thick. After all, a stellar expert has told you that Φ is true, such an expert has told you that Φ is not true, and for each of those pro/con testimonials there is further stellar testimony that the pro/con testimonial itself should not be trusted. Despite having non-trivial evidence about Φ in the case— there is no lack of such evidence here—your Φ-relevant evidence is collectively undercut.[6]

Next suppose the Oracle tells you that Φ and H have the same truth-value. Then we have a strong and stable intuition that your initial take on Φ should give way to your credence for H. This is exactly the kind of intuition we've seen before, though it does not spring from sensitivity to an evidential absence in the set-up before us. There is no such absence and we know it. In undercutting scenarios of this sort, give-way intuition springs from sensitivity to the manner in which initial evidence is undercut. Intuition registers that a region of the initial evidence, so to say, should not be used in an update brought on by the news. This has nothing to do with the absence of initial evidence. It has everything to do with the presence of undercutting evidence.[7]

(B) Suppose you are faced with the toss of a biased coin. Let H once again be the claim that the coin lands heads. Suppose you know the coin is 75% biased to heads, and, as a result, you begin with a 75% credence for H. This time there is a difficult life-choice before you: you must choose between pursuit of a career in philosophy and one in firefighting. You are strongly

---

[5] See (Pollock, 1986), (Pollock, 1987), and (Lasonen-Aarnio, 2010).

[6] One can easily augment the case so that undercutting defeat generates any level of thickness for P desired. Just leave undefeated information which pins down the desired level of thickness for P, with the remainder of one's information about P being undercut by other information to hand. The resulting level of initial thickness on P will match intuition about the extent to which that initial take on P should give way to initial credence for H. This won't be due to an initial lack of information relevant to P. It will be due to the character of the collection of undefeated information relevant to C.

[7] A new approach to undercutting evidence is presented in (Sturgeon, 2014).

drawn to each life-path, so you investigate the matter. You talk to philosophers about what it is like to work in the academy—salaries, activities and so forth—gathering piecemeal and contradictory information. You talk to firefighters about what it is like to work in a stationhouse—salaries, activities and whatnot—gathering similar sorts of information. Then you realize that the primary goods in a philosopher's life seem incommensurable with those in a firefighter's life. Whenever you compare them seriously you become hopelessly confused.

Let Φ be the claim that philosophy is the best path before you (i.e. the one which generates maximal value). You have a great deal of information about Φ in the set-up, but that information is *unruly*: it contains guesstimates and approximations, contradictory sketches of unpredictable factors, seemingly incommensurable values. Despite having copious *pro tanto* considerations relevant to Φ—both pro and con, both precise and imprecise—your initial evidence is simply unmanageable. This is why you begin with a rational thick confidence for Φ.[8]

The Oracle then tells you that Φ and H have the same truth-value. Intuition about updating on the news is then strong, stable and familiar: your initial take on Φ should give way to your credence for H. You should become 75% sure that philosophy is the best way forward. This intuition does not spring from sensitivity to an evidential absence in the set-up. There is no such absence and you know it. Rather, intuition here springs from sensitivity to the unruly nature of evidence. Such evidence should fall away in a tug-of-war, play no role in the update brought on by input, for the evidence is entirely unmanageable. This fall-away feel to the evidence, and the give-way intuitions it creates, has nothing to do with the absence of initial evidence in the case. It has everything to do with the presence of unruly evidence.

Cases like (A) and (B) are similar in many ways. In each of them the agent begins with a great deal of information relevant to whether a given claim is true. In each of them the agent rationally reacts to that evidence by lending a thick confidence. In each of them the *character* of initial information about the claim to which thick confidence is lent precludes that information from rightly influencing update on the news.

Something similar happens in the array of EGG-like cases discussed earlier. Since they begin with little-to-no evidence about the claim to which thick confidence is taken, and it is intuitive that such confidence thereby plays no role in shaping update brought on by the Oracle, in EGG-like cases too intuition about update is driven by sensitivity to the quality of initial evidence. One way for that evidence to be poor is for it to be undercut, another way for it to be poor is for evidence to be unruly, yet a third way for evidence to be poor is for it to be absent.

This suggests a more general worry for the line on thick confidence being defended. After all, in dilation cases like those in the array, as well as undercut and unruly cases like (A) and (B), give-way intuitions can be explained by the character of the evidential set-up. Sometimes that character involves a paucity of evidence, other times it involves a defect in fully-present evidence. In each case intuition about

---

[8] For a related discussion of unruly cases see (Rayo, 2011). One can easily augment them so that unruliness generates any level of thickness for P desired. To do so one need only 'dial down' the level of unruliness in the initial evidence.

update can be explained by the character of the evidence to hand. This motivates the character-of-evidence principle:

(CE)  give-way intuitions can be explained by the character of the evidential set-up in a case.

It is difficult to see how this principle could fail. Were it to do so, after all, intuition about updating would detach from the character of evidence in a case, which hardly seems likely.

The challenge before us, therefore, is to show how it can be true that give-way intuitions can always be explained by the character of the evidential set-up—as the character-of-the-evidence principle rightly insists—but *also* true that such intuitions can be explained by the thickness of thick confidence. We need a story about how the character-of-evidence principle can be true alongside the character-of-confidence principle:

(CC)  give-way intuitions can be explained by the degree of thickness manifested by the attitudes involved.

Seeing why both these principles are true reveals something extremely important about the nature of rational kinematics.

Note that in all cases before us—and doubtless in others we've not seen—the evidential set-up manifests some kind of defect rendering it sub-optimal in shaping an update brought on by the Oracle. When the defect in the initial evidence is significant, its presence generates a strong and stable intuition that the initial take anchored to defective evidence should give way to the initial take anchored to credal-making evidence. This intuition reflects the fact that new input ties a content to which thick confidence was rightly lent to a content to which credence was rightly lent.

But notice: when attitudes are adopted by way of ideal reaction to evidence, the kinematic effect of evidential character is *marked* by intrinsic aspects of the attitudes involved. Specifically, it is marked by degree of thickness displayed by an attitude taken in reaction to the evidential set-up. In all of the cases explicitly before us, for instance—EGG-like or otherwise—the thickness of your initial take on a claim functions as a surface-level marker for something prudently marked on the surface of your attitudes, namely, the level of defect displayed by evidence used in the formation of your take. And in all of those cases the maximally thin character of your initial take on H functions as a surface-level marker for something prudently marked on the surface of your attitudes, namely, the full absence of defect in the evidence used in the formation of your take.

This leads to a pair of thoughts: how things should proceed in an update is intuitive in light of the character of the evidential set-up—there is no denying the character-of-evidence principle—but also how things should proceed in an update is intuitive in light of the character of your initial attitudes—there is no denying the character-of-confidence principle either. When dealing with rational confidence, its character directly indicates the quality of evidence to hand, and, for this reason, the surface-level character of attitudes *codes* for the extent to which evidence used in their formation should influence the way forward upon receipt of news linking the relevant contents. This is why the character of attitudes can be used to explain whether it is intuitive that your new take on a claim should fall into line with your old take on H once news from the Oracle is absorbed.

The fact that attitudinal character codes for quality of evidence explains why we can generate strong and stable give-way intuitions about a case, as we did earlier, *before* saying anything about evidence in its set-up (something taken as read earlier in our description of a case). We need only insist that thick confidence is taken by way of rational reaction to the set-up. Since the character of a rational attitude codes for the general quality of evidence used in its formation, the fact that an attitude is rational, together with its thickness, is enough to make for strong and stable intuition concerning how it should influence the way forward in an update. Such intuition reflects that the character of well-formed attitudes itself echoes the character of evidence used in their formation.

When updating on orthogonal news relevant to whatever thick confidence is taken, the degree of thickness involved in a type of thick confidence marks—on the surface of the attitudinal type—the degree to which evidence used in the ideal adoption of thick confidence should be ignored when updating. The relevant point is not that initial information should be ignored upon receipt of any news whatsoever, of course; news may be relevant to initial evidence or vice versa. The relevant point is that when no such relevance occurs, when new input is orthogonal to initial evidence yet relevant to whatever thick confidence grounded in that evidence is taken, then, in those circumstances, degree of thickness in attitude functions as code for the extent to which evidence warranting thick confidence should be disregarded upon receipt of the news. <u>The Face of Confidence Itself Codes for Prior Defect in Evidence</u>.

This coding makes good sense on a force-based treatment of confidence. Recall that on such a treatment confidence is a mixture of cognitive force: attraction, repulsion, and neutrality. On such a treatment the degree of thickness involved in an attitude type is itself determined by the relative amounts of neutrality involved in the force-mixture generating that type. The key point is then this: evidential relevance and cognitive neutrality are anathema to one another. Relevance in evidence should lead to non-neutral reaction to content. Greater and greater net levels of relevance in an evidential set-up should lead to less and less thickness in attitude taken by way of reaction to that set-up.

When there is entirely crisp evidence about $\Phi$ in a given situation—say because $\Phi$'s chance is known, or its frequency of truth in a salient reference class of situations, or some other clear balance of factors like those is to hand—then, in that sort of case, neutrality about $\Phi$ is an inapt reaction to the evidence. One should not be neutral about $\Phi$ but drawn to or repelled by the claim (or both). One's confidence in such a case should spring solely from mixtures of attraction and repulsion. To exactly the extent that this happens, however, the force-based approach sees one's take on $\Phi$ as a credence. The approach underwrites the idea that crisp evidence normatively precludes thickness in one's take on a content, and, thereby, that the face of confidence should code for the quality of evidence to hand.

When there is defective evidence about Φ in the set-up—say because there is little-to-no information about Φ, or the information about Φ undercuts itself to some degree, or that information is unruly to a certain extent—then, in these circumstance, non-trivial amounts of neutrality are the apt reaction to evidence. And the extent to which a neutral cognitive force aptly dominates one's overall confidence-making mixture will be exactly the extent to which the overall evidence is defective. In this way levels of confidence growing from mixtures of cognitive force dominated by neutrality function as markers for degree of evidential defect in the set-up, and levels of confidence growing from mixtures of force dominated by attraction/repulsion function as markers for degree of evidential precision in the set-up. When levels of confidence are formed rationally, then, their characters reflect the nature of evidence used in their formation.

This is why rational update is a forward-looking affair. When new information arrives, rational agents have no need to re-litigate everything that has evidentially gone before. There is no need to put all their old evidence and all their old attitudes together with new input. They need only put attitudes with the input. If the character of the attitudes did not reflect the character of past evidence, the forward-looking feel to updating would be puzzling. We'd wonder why old evidence should not—in the ideal, at least—be consulted when new input arrives. Since the nature of ideal attitudes echoes the character of evidence, however, re-litigation is unnecessary. This is why rational kinematics is a forward-looking affair.

In a nutshell: precision involved in a credence rationally lent to a claim marks the high quality of overall evidence to do with that claim; and imprecision involved in a thick confidence rationally lent to a claim marks defect in overall evidence to do with that claim. The face of our attitudes generates intuition about how new input should be absorbed. Those intuitions are ultimately grounded in the quality of our evidence. But the quality of evidence should itself be echoed in the character of attitudes taken by way of reaction to it. Hence the character-of-evidence principle explains the character-of-confidence principle. The latter is true because the former is true.

## 12.4 Force-Based Confidence and Evidence

The forced-based view of confidence can be used to shed considerable light on the idea that one should adopt a level of confidence only if the character of that confidence matches the quality of evidence used in its formation. This idea is crucial to understanding why rational kinematics is forward-looking—why new input need only be put with extant attitude—and so the force-based view can also be used to shed light on the nature of kinematics.

This can be done by using the formal picture developed earlier to spell out, within a confidence-theoretic setting, notions of propositional and doxastic justification. To do *that*, however, we must *blanche* our formal notation of its standing cognitive interpretation. Then we can apply an evidence-based interpretation to it and compare the two readings of the formalism side-by-side. This will expose a good deal of useful structure inside the idea that quality of evidence should match character of attitude. That structure will also prove useful in understanding how kinematics works.

To begin, suppose there are orthogonal parameters $x$, $y$, and $z$ associated with an arbitrary claim $\Phi$, and that amounts of them can be measured with positive real numbers. We have seen that the open ray consisting of triples $<x,y,z>$ so that for positive r

$$<x, y, z> \ = \ <rl, r(1-u), r(u-l)>$$

can be used to represent the interval $[l,u]$. This was exploited to model cognitive forces mixing into levels of confidence. Representations of credence result from $z$ taking a zero value, and representations of thick-confidence result from $z$ taking larger values (vagueness aside).

This formalism can be usefully interpreted in a different way. Rather than $x$, $y$, and $z$ representing three types of cognitive force, we may take them to represent three types of evidential significance. Specifically: $x$ and $y$ can be said to represent levels of pro and con evidential relevance; and $z$ can be said to represent levels of evidential defect. This renders our three-dimensional framework capable of generating a map from combinations of three values for evidential significance to *total support intervals*. Representations of unit-real-valued total support results from $z$ taking a zero value, and representations of unit-interval total support results from $z$ taking larger values (vagueness aside).

These two interpretations of the formalism—targeting three types of cognitive force and three types of evidential significance—can jointly be used to expose theoretically-relevant structure within the idea that evidence and attitude should match in character. When doing so it proves useful to mark differences of theoretical role with differences of font. So let '**att**($\Phi$)', '**rep**($\Phi$)', and '**neut**($\Phi$)' be variables standing for amounts of cognitive force: attraction, repulsion, and neutrality to do with $\Phi$; and let '*pro*($\Phi$)', '*con*($\Phi$)', and '*def*($\Phi$)' be variables standing for amounts of evidential significance: directly supporting force, cutting-against force, and some kind of defect to do with whatever to hand directly supports or cuts against $\Phi$.

Now consider the useful and well-known distinction between a belief's being justif*ied* and its being justifi*able*. Suppose Holmes and Watson jointly investigate a murder, sharing and discussing all aspects of their evidence along the way. Suppose they jointly gather a huge amount of data which proves that the butler is guilty, they both end up believing that the butler is guilty, but they do so for differing reasons: Holmes believes on the basis of the overwhelming evidence they both possess, Watson believes on the basis of prejudice against butlers. In the event, Holmes and Watson each have justifi<u>able</u> belief in the butler's guilt, since they each have (and fully appreciate) evidence proving that guilt. But only Holmes' belief in the butler's guilt is justifi<u>ed</u>, for only he bases that belief on the evidence in his possession. Justifiable belief requires only that an agent possess good evidence for a belief they happen to have. Justified belief requires also that an agent's belief be grounded or based in the evidence she happens to have. The distinction is often drawn with technical terms—'propositional' and 'doxastic' justification respectively—but it's a distinction of common sense through and through.[9]

To my knowledge, this important distinction has not yet been drawn in the epistemology of confidence. We can easily do so, however, by appeal to our three-dimensional framework and its two interpretations. The result can then be used to explain the forward-looking nature of rational kinematics.

To see how this works, just begin with the following idea:

(1) A level of confidence invested in $\Phi$ is justifiable iff
  (i) its strength matches the strength of support for $\Phi$ generated by one's total evidence.

This is a confidence-theoretic analogue of justifiable belief. It concerns the kind of situation in which degree of support generated by total evidence matches strength of confidence lent to a claim. Our formalism can be used to codify it gracefully:

(2) A level of confidence invested in $\Phi$ is justifiable iff
  (i) for some $l$ and $u$ in [0,1]: confidence($\Phi$) = $support(\Phi)$ = $[l,u]$.

Justifiable credence results from $l$ being identical to $u$, and, vagueness aside, justifiable thick confidence results from $l$ being distinct from $u$. This is a simple and obvious way to spell out propositional justification within a confidence-theoretic setting.

But note how our three-dimensional formalism, plus its two readings, jointly lead to a stronger kind of match between attitude and evidence than any captured by (1) or (2). After all, our formalism and those readings can be used to expose a deep kind of match between attitude and evidence, one which consists in a component-by-component match across types of three-dimensional phenomena. This leads to a significant strengthening of (1):

(3) A level of confidence invested in $\Phi$ is component justifiable iff
  (i) its strength matches the strength of support for $\Phi$ generated by one's total evidence, because
  (ii) cognitive forces which mix into the level of confidence each match analogue aspects of evidential significance which mix into one's total support for $\Phi$.

Component justifiability involves a match in strength between attitude and evidence, plus a match in strength between components of attitude and evidence. Our formalism can be used to capture it gracefully:

(4) A level of confidence invested in $\Phi$ is component justifiable iff
  (i) for some $l$ and $u$ in [0,1]: confidence($\Phi$) = $support(\Phi)$ = $[l,u]$, because
  (ii) for some **att**($\Phi$), **rep**($\Phi$), **neut**($\Phi$), $pro(\Phi)$, $con(\Phi)$ and $def(\Phi)$:
    (a) **att**($\Phi$), **rep**($\Phi$) and **neut**($\Phi$) mix into confidence($\Phi$), and
    (b) $pro(\Phi)$, $con(\Phi)$ and $def(\Phi)$ mix into $support(\Phi)$, and
    (c) **att**($\Phi$) = $pro(\Phi)$, **rep**($\Phi$) = $con(\Phi)$, **neut**($\Phi$) = $def(\Phi)$.

---

[9] These terms come from (Kvanvig & Menzel, 1990). In effect literature to do with the basing relation concerns the relevant distinction. See (Pollock, 1986) or Chapter 12.

Component justifiability requires that the match in strength between attitude and evidence results from a component-by-component match between elements which build into confidence and those which build into total evidential support. This is a highly non-trivial matching condition. It occurs exactly when the amount of cognitive attraction one has for a claim matches the amount of pro tanto support there is for it in one's total evidence, the amount of cognitive repulsion one has for a claim matches the amount of pro tanto counter-support there is for it in one's total evidence, and the amount of cognitive neutrality one has for a claim matches the amount of evidential defect there is for it in one's total evidence.

Now, principles (1) thru (4) concern confidence-theoretic analogues of propositionally justified belief. We have seen that such belief turns into doxastically justified belief when it is based on appropriate evidence. A strengthening of (1) thru (4) can be used to construct confidence-theoretic analogues of this crucial idea. The first relevant thought is

(5) A level of confidence invested in $\Phi$ is justified iff
  (i) its strength matches the strength of support for $\Phi$ generated by one's total evidence; and
  (ii) the level of confidence is based on one's total evidence.

This is a confidence-theoretic analogue of doxastically justified belief. Principle (5) targets situations in which confidence is appropriately grounded in total evidential support. Our formalism can be used to capture it in a straightforward way:

(6) A level of confidence invested in $\Phi$ is justified iff
  (i) for some $l$ and $u$ in [0,1]: confidence($\Phi$) = $support(\Phi)$ = $[l,u]$; and
  (ii) confidence($\Phi$) is grounded in $support(\Phi)$.

Justified credence results when $l$ is identical to $u$, and, vagueness aside, justified thick confidence results when $l$ is not identical with $u$.

It would be theoretically good, though, to elucidate condition (6ii) further. What is it for a level of confidence to be grounded in a level of support generated by total evidence? We can drill into the phenomena with our three-dimensional picture and its two readings. Doing so leads directly to a strengthening of (3):

(7) A level of confidence invested in $\Phi$ is component justified iff
  (i) its strength matches the strength of support for $\Phi$ generated by one's total evidence,
  because
  (ii) cognitive forces which mix into the level of confidence each match aspects of evidential significance which mix into one's total available support for $\Phi$, and
  (iii) cognitive forces in play are each based on the evidential aspects in play.

Component justification involves a match in strength of attitude and evidence, plus a match in strength of components which build into attitude and evidential support, plus a component-by-component basing of cognitive force in its matching evidential echo. Our formalism can be used to capture the idea cleanly:

(8) A level of confidence invested in Φ is component justified iff
   (i) for some $l$ and $u$ in [0,1]: confidence(Φ) = support(Φ) = [$l,u$], because
   (ii) for some **att**(Φ), **rep**(Φ), **neut**(Φ), *pro*(Φ), *con*(Φ) and *def*(Φ):
       (a) **att**(Φ), **rep**(Φ) and **neut**(Φ) mix into confidence(Φ), and
       (b) *pro*(Φ), *con*(Φ) and *def*(Φ) mix into *support*(Φ), and
       (c) **att**(Φ) = *pro*(Φ), **rep**(Φ) = *con*(Φ), **neut**(Φ) = *def*(Φ); &
   (iii) (a) **att**(Φ) is based on *pro*(Φ),
       (b) **rep**(Φ) is based on *con*(Φ), and
       (c) **neut**(Φ) is based on *def*(Φ).

Component justification happens when one is attracted to a claim, to the extent that one is, precisely because and in virtue of possessing relevant amounts of supporting evidence, and when one is repelled by a claim, to the extent that one is, precisely because and in virtue of possessing relevant amounts of rebutting evidence, and when one is cognitively neutral about a claim, to the extent that one is, precisely because and in virtue of possessing relevant types of defective information. Each of these matching conditions is itself non-trivial, and each of the basing requirements is too. Together component matching and basing requirements add into a highly non-trivial link between confidence and evidence.

We can now draw everything together. One should adopt a confidence only if its character matches that of the evidence used in its formation. Our discussion of justifiable and justified confidence makes clear that this thought involves a number of moving parts, parts which can be understood in a surface-level and a deeper compositional way. The former makes for a very weak norm in the neighbourhood:

> One should lend confidence only if it is justifiable while the latter makes for a stronger-but-related norm:

> One should lend confidence only if it is component justifiable.

> But the idea that evidence and attitude should aptly fit together also relies on the thought that evidence be used in the formation of confidence. Neither of the weak norms just mentioned depend on how evidence is used.

> We have seen, though, that by adding such use into theory we can move gracefully from the domain of justifiable confidence to that of justified confidence. This leads to a stronger normative thought:

> One should lend confidence only if it is justified, and to the strongest thought in the neighbourhood.

> One should lend confidence only if it is component justified.

> In this way our three-dimensional framework, along with its two readings, lead to a good deal of edifying structure within the idea that confidence can be both propositionally and doxastically justified.

This internal structure can be used to explain further why rational kinematics is a forward-looking affair. The key point is this: kinematical rules have no purchase on epistemically sub-optimal agents—they apply only to those who manifest no epistemic blemish. To see why, note that kinematical rules have to do with what is obligatory rather than merely permissible. The rule of Conditionalization, for instance, describes how posterior credence should look when one begins in a certain way and then receives new input. The idea is not that the movement-of-mind described by the rule is merely permissible. It is rather that that movement is outright obligatory. If an agent starts out in a sub-optimal position, however—say if her credences are incoherent or not component justifiable—then, the down side of flouting a rule like Conditionalization might well be less important epistemically than the up-side of correcting flaws in the prior-to-input position. When this is so it will be worth paying the price associated with flouting a given kinematical rule. Since those rules are meant to make for straight obligations, however, it follows that they weren't in play to begin with: kinematical rules have purchase only on blemish-free agents. They do not apply to those who are anything less than perfect upon receipt of new input.

As a result, kinematic rules apply to an agent only if her attitudes are *component justifiable*. We have seen that such justifiability requires not only that there be a match in strength between attitude and evidence, but also that this match be the result of a component-by-component match between elements which build into confidence and those which build into total evidential support. Component justifiability occurs exactly when the amount of cognitive attraction one has for a claim matches the amount of pro tanto support there is for it in one's total evidence, the amount of cognitive repulsion one has for a claim matches the amount of pro tanto counter-support there is for it in one's total evidence, and the amount of cognitive neutrality one has for a claim matches the amount of defect there is for it in one's total evidence. Since kinematical rules apply to an agent only if her attitudes are component justifiable, such rules apply only if her attitudes already reflect, in their very metaphysics, the contours and details of the evidential situation to hand. This is why there is no need to consult old evidence when new input arrives. Antecedent-to-learning attitudes are component justifiable. The details of extant evidence are reflected in their metaphysics. Kinematical rules need only put new input with extant attitudes to mandate a new configuration of doxastic states.

## 12.5 Force-Based Confidence and Content-Based Accuracy

This section deals with a complex-but-systematic pattern of intuitive verdict about the relation between one type of accuracy and confidence. The type of accuracy relevant here—which we call *content-based accuracy*—is found at the heart of cutting-edge work on the theory of states as well as the theory of state-transitions.[10] An assumption running through the work is that levels of confidence are routinely subject to content-based accuracy. Once we unpack the notion, however, we'll see that the opposite is intuitively true. Very few levels of confidence are subject to content-based accuracy. We'll also see that the force-based view of confidence underwrites the complex deliverance of intuition about the relation between this sort of accuracy and confidence.

Our discussion begins with the notion of accuracy found in everyday life—not the specific idea of content-based accuracy toward which we are working, but the

---

[10] See (Fitelson & Easwaran, 2015), (Greaves & Wallace, 2005), (Joyce, 1998) and (Joyce, 2005).

ordinary (or undifferentiated) notion of accuracy found in everyday life. One interesting thing about this notion is its wide range of application: rifles, thoughts, maps, and quarterbacks are subject to accuracy—in the everyday sense, at least—and so are conjectures, theorems, marks on a board, strikers in football, and Mike Tyson's upper-cut. The ordinary notion of accuracy applies to a huge range of things. But it does not apply to everything: Dallas and dirt and do-dos are not in the accuracy business—in the ordinary run of things, anyway—and neither are comets or cupids or commands. The everyday notion is wide in its scope but it does not apply to everything.

A primary reason for this is less emphasized in accuracy-based epistemology than it might be. This is the fact that everything subject to accuracy has a *target* of some kind. That target will be an object, event, or other kind of phenomena, and the relation between the item in the accuracy business and its target will *fix* the item's level of accuracy. For instance: quarterbacks have their accuracy fixed by how well their passes connect with receivers; strikers have their accuracy fixed by how well their shots connect with goal-areas; remarks have their accuracy fixed by how well their contents convey the facts; Mike Tyson's upper-cut has its accuracy fixed by how well his fists connect with an opponent; and so on. The pattern is perfectly general. Everything subject to accuracy has a target of some kind. Only by having one can an item be in the accuracy business.[11]

The sort of accuracy relevant to our discussion though—content-based accuracy—requires more than merely having a target. It also requires that the goal or function of the item in the accuracy business is to engage with a content by way of *reaction* to a target. Put another way: content-based accuracy requires that the item in the accuracy business aims to hit its target, at least in part, *with* its content. Just think of maps, assertions, portraits, or states of acceptance or denial. All of them involve a proprietary kind of engagement with content. They differ in what kind of content is involved, of course, but they all engage with some kind of content or other, and they do so by way of reaction to a real-world target, aiming to hit their target with content had or possessed or manifested by the thing in the content-based accuracy business. That target may be a coastline, the facts, a person, or some combination of these. But each time we find an item in the content-based accuracy business, the item in that business manifests a content with some sort of target in view. Each time the item manages to be accurate—to whatever degree it manages to be accurate—*by* hitting its target (to some degree or other) with its content. That is the essence of content-based accuracy: lassoing a target with a content.

It is assumed here that levels of confidence satisfy at least part of the picture needed for content-based accuracy. When someone is sure that it rains, for instance, it is assumed that their mental state is an attitude lent to the proposition that it rains. And when someone is 80% sure that it rains, it is likewise assumed that their mental state is a weaker attitude lent to the very same proposition. The general thought being taken for granted, then, is that levels of confidence are propositional attitudes. Hence they satisfy at least part of what's needed for content-based accuracy: the

---

[11] See (Cummins, 1996) and (Millikan, 2000) for useful discussion of accuracy and targets.

manifestation of content. If levels of confidence do so with a real-world target in view, therefore—if their function or aim is to hit or lasso such a target with their content—there should be no difficulty in seeing them as subject to content-based accuracy.[12]

The question before us is thus simple: *do* levels of confidence manifest content with a worldly target in view? When a level of confidence L is lent to content P, is that lending of confidence a way of registering, via the L-to-P link, how a worldly target is P-wise?

Well, the answer depends on which type of confidence we're talking about. Certain levels of confidence—roughly, the very weak ones and very strong ones—*do* seem clearly to be lent to a content by way of reaction to a target. This is why those levels of confidence self-present as clearly in the content-based accuracy business, why it seems stably obvious upon reflection that they are subject to content-based accuracy. But other levels of confidence—roughly, the middling-strength ones and very thick ones—seem clearly *not* to be lent to a content by way of reaction to a target. This is why they self-present as clearly not in the content-based accuracy business, why it seems stably obvious upon reflection that they are not subject to content-based accuracy. And still other levels of confidence—those which fall outside the categories just mentioned—do not self-present as clearly one way or the other. When one of them is lent to a content, it turns out to be stably unclear whether the resulting (kind of) mental state is a way of registering, with a confidence-to-content link, how the world is. Hence we are faced once again with a complex-but-systematic pattern of intuitive verdict. This one has to do with the interaction of content-based accuracy and levels of confidence.

The pattern is easy to picture. First we represent all types of confidence with a two-dimensional array, then shade-in the array to reflect considered judgement about when a given type of confidence is subject to content-based accuracy. The first step involves letting strength of confidence increase left-to-right in a representational array. The second step involves letting thickness of confidence increase top-to-bottom in that array. This makes for a two-dimensional confidence map.[13]

---

[12] From a certain philosophical perspective it is natural to say that strength of confidence aims at reflecting strength-of-evidence *in situ*; and from another it is natural to say that strength of confidence aims at reflecting chance-of-truth *in situ*. Each of these perspectives underwrites the idea that levels of confidence target something. Hence each of them satisfy the root idea of accuracy: namely, that levels of confidence can do better or worse when it comes to hitting their target. But neither of these perspectives supports the view that confidence hits its target with its content. Since that is what's needed for content-based accuracy—the sense of accuracy relevant here—neither of them entails that confidence is subject to such accuracy. Instances of the first perspective can be found in (Swinburne, 2001) or (Williamson, 2000). Instances of the second can be found in (Mellor, 2012), (Beebee & Papineau, 1997) or (Pettigrew, 2012). Much work in accuracy-first formal epistemology looks to be motivated, at least in part, by conflating the bona fides of rifle-like accuracy for confidence—the kind apt for the two perspectives just sketched—with the bona fides of content-based accuracy for confidence. For a discussion of accuracy-first epistemology which uses rifle-like accuracy, see my 'Epistemology, Pettigrew style' (2018) in *Mind*.

[13] The box isn't quite right as it stands, since there is a unique type of maximally thick confidence. If we ignore a rather natural link between two-dimensional area and cardinality, an inverse pyramid might then be a better depiction of what we are after.

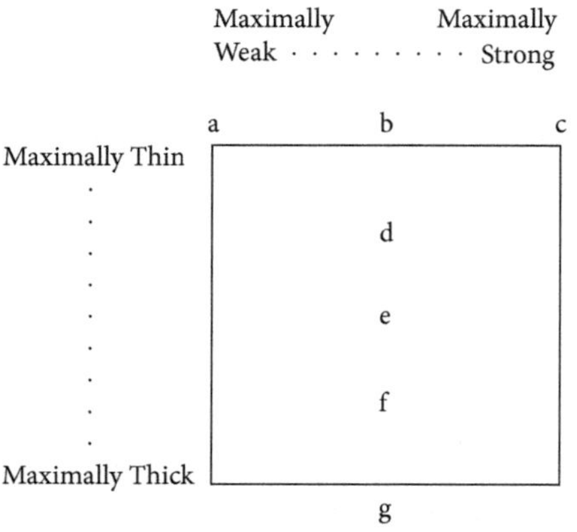

316   FORCE-BASED CONFIDENCE AT WORK

```
              Maximally           Maximally
              Weak  · · · · · · · · Strong

              a         b         c
Maximally Thin  ┌─────────────────┐
              ·                   │        Point  =  Level of Confidence
              ·         d         │         a     =  0%
              ·                   │         b     =  50%
              ·                   │         c     =  100%
              ·         e         │         d     =  40–60%
              ·                   │         e     =  25–75%
              ·                   │         f     =  10–90%
              ·         f         │         g     =  0–100%
              ·                   │
Maximally Thick └─────────────────┘
                        g
```

**Figure 12.7**

Levels of credence are represented in the map by points forming into its northern edge. The weakest one—0% confidence—is represented by the map's northwest tip. The strongest one—absolute certainty—is represented by the map's northeast tip. Non-degenerate credence is represented by points lined up between these extremes, weakest to strongest left-to-right. Thick confidence is represented by points below the northern edge of the map. The very thinnest types of thick confidence is represented by points crowding up against the credal northern edge, and thicker types of confidence are represented by points located further south in the map. Fully dilated confidence—0-to-100% certainty—is represented by the g-point at the very bottom of the array.[14]

With our confidence map in place it is easy to shade in the complex pattern of intuitive verdict about content-based accuracy and confidence. We use light grey for types of confidence which self-present as clearly in the content-based accuracy business, medium grey for those which self-present as clearly not in that business, and dark grey for types of confidence which fail to self-present in either of these way (Figure 12.8).

Figure 12.8 makes visually manifest that considered intuition endorses the application of content-based accuracy to only a small amount of the confidence map. Only points which represent extremal types of confidence—very weak or very strong confidence—are light grey, with most of the map being medium grey. This reflects the fact that considered intuition sees most every type of confidence—those which are middling in strength or contain substantive amounts of thickness—as *not* subject to content-based accuracy. So epistemology which uses content-based accuracy for all types of confidence rests on a faulty projection. It applies to all types of confidence a content-based notion which is intuitively apt only to extremal varieties of confidence.

Now, the question of whether a given type of confidence is sufficiently weak or sufficiently strong to be clearly in the content-based accuracy business it itself a vague

---

[14] Similar remarks apply here as in the previous footnote.

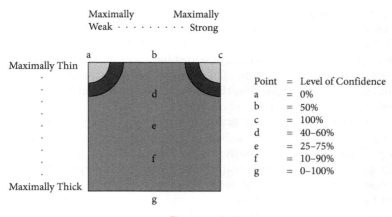

**Figure 12.8**

matter. And the question of whether a given type of confidence is sufficiently middling in strength or sufficiently thick to be clearly not in that business is likewise a vague matter. This is why dark grey areas are sandwiched between light and medium-grey zones of Figure 12.8. Points in those areas represent types of confidence which self-present in no clear way when it comes to whether or not they are subject to content-based accuracy.

Figure 12.8 codes a complex pattern of intuitive verdict about content-based accuracy and confidence. The pattern it makes visually vivid is exactly the one you'd expect to find on the force-based approach to confidence. To see why, recall how that approach puts forward three crucial claims about the generation of confidence: low-strength confidence is built from mixtures of cognitive force dominated by repulsion, high-strength confidence is built from mixtures of cognitive force dominated by attraction, and thickness of confidence is pinned down by relative amounts of neutrality in an attitude-making mixture of cognitive force. These claims join with intuitions coded in Figure 12.8 to entail a key correlation between how intuitive it is that a given type of confidence is subject to content-based accuracy and how cognitive force mixes to make for the level of confidence in question. Specifically:

(*) It is intuitive that a given level of confidence is subject to content-based accuracy exactly to the extent that its force-based metaphysics is dominated by attraction or repulsion.

The nature of cognitive force explains this key correlation.

To see how, consider a novelist wondering if a character in her book should commit a terrible crime. When doing so she might find herself attracted to or repelled by a claim describing her character's behaviour. In the event, her reaction would echo cognitive forces used in our metaphysics of confidence. But it would not be an engagement with content by way of reaction to a real-world target. Put another way: the author's reaction would not be engagement with content aimed at hitting an actual target with its content. Rather, it would be engagement with content by way of reaction to a fictional universe, the one created by the author's work. When someone is attracted to P in the sense which makes for confidence, however—or is repelled by P in that sense—the cognitive force emanating from P, so to say, is an engagement with P triggered by taking P to capture something about the real world. This is how the psychology of such cognitive force makes use of ingredients sufficient for content-based accuracy: it involves the manifestation of content by way of reaction to a real target, something in the actual world.

It is thus intuitive that mental-states dominated by attraction or by repulsion are subject to content-based accuracy. Being so dominated entails that a state is predominantly a manifestation of content taken by way of reaction to the world, that the state in question aims predominantly to hit its real-world target with its content. Such mental states self-present as in the business of content-based accuracy. Hence we find light grey at the northwest and northeast corners of Figure 12.8. Credence represented by points in those regions is dominated by attraction or by repulsion. It is thus clearly a manifestation of content with the actual world in view. This is why it is clear that such confidence is in the content-based accuracy business.

On the other hand, consider being 50% sure that P. This credence appears in the middle of the northern edge of our confidence map. Intuition is firmly against the idea that it is in the content-based accuracy business. This is just as you'd expect if the force-based metaphysics of confidence were true. After all, that view maintains that 50% credence is built from equal parts attraction and repulsion. We have seen that each of these forces involves the manifestation of content by way of reaction to the world. We have also seen, though, that each of them involves opposing reactions to a content. Attraction occurs when an agent's intellectual pull to a claim aims at hitting a real-world target with a content. Repulsion occurs when an agent's intellectual push from a claim aims to reflect that such a target is missed by a content. Since 50% confidence springs from equal part attraction and repulsion, 50% confidence involves no predominant reaction to how a content relates to a real-world target at all. A fortiori it involves no such reaction dominated by attraction or by repulsion. This is why it is intuitive that middling-strength credence is not subject to content-based accuracy.

Now glance across the northern edge of the confidence map. Shades there shift systematically as credence moves from weakest to strongest left-to-right. There is light grey when credence is at or near 0%, which shifts to dark grey as credence increases to 25%, which shifts to medium grey as credence moves on to 50%, which shifts back to dark grey as credence increases to 75%, which shifts back to light grey as credence moves to certainty. This is exactly what you'd expect if the force-based metaphysics is true. After all, the metaphysics entails that a given type of credence is dominated by attraction or by repulsion to just the extent that it approximates a degenerate value (i.e. to just the extent that it is very strong or very weak). Hence the force-based view explains why it is clear that credence tending to degenerate value is subject to content-based accuracy, why it is clear that credence tending to middle-strength value is not so subject, and why credence between the extremes self-presents in no clear way at all when it comes to whether it's in the content-based accuracy business. The latter occurs when it is essentially unclear whether a given type of confidence is dominated by attraction or by repulsion. This is why we find light grey toward the top corners of our confidence map, medium grey toward the middle of its northern edge, and dark grey along that edge between these three areas. The shades represent when it is clear that a given type of credence is subject to content-based accuracy, when it is clear that a given type of credence is not so subject, and when it is unclear that a given type of credence is in the content-based accuracy business at all.

Now recall one of the main lessons of §12.3: the raison d'etre of cognitive neutrality is to mark defect in evidence. We have seen that such defect may come in at least three different flavours: the existence of little-to-no evidence, the existence of collectively undercut evidence, the existence of unruly evidence. Since the point of cognitive neutrality is to mark such defect, it is not a cognitive force triggered by way of reaction to the world. It is rather a cognitive force triggered by way of reaction to the quality of one's evidence. Unlike its force-theoretic cousins, therefore, neutrality does not involve ingredients needed for content-based accuracy. This is why levels of confidence dominated by neutrality self-present as not in the content-based accuracy business.[15]

We are now well placed to explain shades of grey below the credal northern edge of our confidence map. This involves a medium-grey region flowing ever more widely south from points which represent middling-strength credence, and a dark grey region occupying space between outer edges of the medium-grey region and light grey zones in the northwest and northeast corners of the confidence map. Each of these areas is exactly what you would expect if the force-based metaphysics of confidence is true. Consider them in turn:

1. The force-based metaphysics of confidence entails that a given point in Figure 12.8 will be medium grey exactly when it represents a type of confidence which obviously fails to be dominated by attraction or by repulsion. This can happen in one of two ways: either the force-based metaphysics of that type of confidence is obviously similar to the force-based metaphysics which makes for middling-strength credence—as we find toward the middle-top of the map—or, the force-based metaphysics of that type of confidence is dominated by neutrality—as we find more and more going south from the top-middle of the map. In each type of case it will be clear that the confidence in question is not built largely from attraction or largely from repulsion. So in each type of case it will be clear that that the confidence in question is not subject to content-based accuracy. This is why medium-grey flows south ever more widely from points representing middling-strength credence.

2. The force-based metaphysics of confidence entails that a given point in our confidence map will be dark grey exactly when it represents a type of confidence which fails to be obviously built predominantly from attraction or from repulsion, and which also fails to be obviously not so built. In other words, the force-based metaphysics entails that dark grey points represent types of confidence which are penumbral in both strength and thickness. When it comes to those types of confidence it is unclear if they are very weak or very strong or very thick, and, as a result, it

---

[15] This meta-level character of neutrality fits well with how undercutting defeaters work. See (Sturgeon, 2014).

is unclear if they are subject to content-based accuracy. In this way dark grey slots between light- and medium-grey in the confidence map.

When it comes to content-based accuracy and confidence, therefore, the situation is both clear and systematic. Considered intuition affirms that a given type of confidence is subject to such accuracy exactly to the extent that it is very strong or very weak. This means intuition affirms that a given type of confidence is not subject to content-based accuracy exactly to the extent that it clearly is not very strong or very weak, either because it is clearly middling in strength or because it is clearly quite thick. But considered intuition remains unclear about what is going on in all other cases. Since attraction and repulsion involve ingredients needed for content-based accuracy, while neutrality has to do with the quality of one's evidence, and since the three cognitive forces ground confidence as suggested above, reflection on cases generates a complex pattern of intuitive verdict about confidence and content-based accuracy. That pattern is exactly the one predicted by the force-based metaphysics of confidence. This is strong reason to think that the force-based view is on the right track.

# 13
# Inference and Rationality

## 13.1 Preview

In this chapter we end our journey by focusing on inference and rationality. We start with the idea of rational shift-in-view and construct a space of salient options for handling it. Then we focus on a particular kind of rationality—often called 'doxastic' rationality—and argue that it places strong constraints on how causation and epistemic relevance fit together. This leads to the idea of a *coordinated epistemic reason*: a reason where causal and epistemic efficacy fuse into one. It is argued that such reasons are central to rational inference, and, as a result, that a certain kind of everyday, non-ideal rationality is the proper home of such inference. This leads to a pair of puzzles: one motivates a novel picture of human rational architecture, the other forces incorporation of lessons drawn earlier in the book. We close the chapter by dealing with each of them.

## 13.2 Rational Shift-in-View: a Space of Theories

Let us end our discussion as we began it, at the outset of the book, with a segmented-cylinder picture of mental life (Figure 13.1).

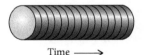

Figure 13.1

The starting view is that mental states exist at a time, that they persist through time, and that there is change of mental state in both senses of the phrase: which mental states an agent has can change across time, and persisting mental states can change as they persist across time.

Examples of the first sort of thing are legion: one might be a libertarian in youth but give up the view in later life. This involves a persisting agent changing which mental states she has. Examples of the second sort of thing are also legion: religious belief may be fragile when begun but set in stone after years of practice. Inter alia this would involve a single mental state—belief in God, say—changing across time, transitioning from a view easily dropped to something like a cornerstone of epistemic life. We represent both sorts of change with cross-sections of the cylinder, thinking of

*The Rational Mind.* Scott Sturgeon, Oxford University Press (2020). © Scott Sturgeon.
DOI: 10.1093/oso/9780198845799.001.0001

them as snapshots of a mental life. Persistence and change of mental states are then represented by the way that cross-sections are strung together.

We also begin with a neutral conception of epistemic norms, insisting only that such norms involve rules for epistemic evaluation. We presuppose nothing about what sorts of things are subject to epistemic evaluation, nor anything about what makes such evaluation correct. The initial commitment—in thinking that there are epistemic norms—is just that there are rules for the epistemic evaluation of something or other.

This commitment makes contact with our cylinder picture in two spots:

(a) In the evaluation of its cross-sections,

and

(b) In the evaluation of how they string together.

So we start with the view that a full-dress theory of rationality has (at least) two moving parts: one concerned with the evaluation of synchronic aspects of a mental life, the other concerned with the evaluation of diachronic aspects of that life.

There is a lot to like in this initial picture. I want to dig deep into one of its components, though, the idea that there is such a thing as rational shift-in-view. Consistent with the Rationality-of-Transitions assumption of Chapter 1, we shall take it as read that there is such a thing in what follows, and we shall make two further assumptions about it. First, we assume that epistemic factors of some kind figure into rational shift-in-view—as their prompt, origin, source, or something like that—and second, we focus exclusively on shift between *basic* epistemic commitments, looking only at shift-in-view between states which are explanatorily fundamental to the theory of rationality. The phrase 'shift-in-view' will stand only for such transitions in what follows.

Our starting picture is something like this:

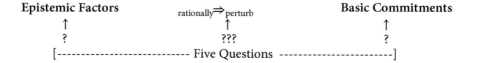

As the picture indicates we'll press five questions about rational shift-in-view. Reflection on them will lead to a space of theoretical options for understanding the nature of rational inference.

*Question 1: which factors play into rational shift-in-view?*

By stipulation a factor plays into rational shift-in-view when it is a prompt or source of that shift-in-view. Most philosophers agree that there are such things. But if you ask ten of them about epistemic factors, a blizzard of answers will result. There is no useful way to bundle those answers into a manageable choice-point, so far as I can see, for too many answers are plausibly defended in the literature: perceptual experience, intuition, conflict in outright commitment, conflict in suppositional commitment, states of knowledge, facts in the world, etc. All of these have sensibly been thought to prompt rational shift-in-view. This means it's best to leave open the topic of epistemic factors in our discussion, for tackling it directly would take us too far afield from present concerns.

*Question 2: What kind of transitions are covered by epistemic norms?*
When discussing rational inference it is important to emphasize a distinction between two types of state transition. There are what we might call *agential* transitions and *impersonal* ones. The former make for agency when they occur. Their existence constitutes their owner *doing* something, acting in some way. In the non-cognitive domain agential transitions include episodes like standing-up, walking, and so forth. In the cognitive domain agential transitions include episodes like supposing, shifting one's attention, etc. In both cases the transitions are constitutive of some kind of agency, and when states figuring in them are cognitive, the resulting agency is too. It is cognitive agency.

Impersonal transitions do not function this way. When they occur their owner is not thereby doing something. In the non-cognitive domain impersonal transitions include episodes like shift in blood sugar, temperature, and so on. In the cognitive domain impersonal transitions include episodes like sub-personal shift in sub-personal commitment—a change in one's implicit bias, for instance—or sub-personal shift in personal commitment—say a subconscious shift in anger at one's boss. The former occurs when both the transition itself and states which undergo it are non-agential, i.e. not constitutive of agency. The latter occurs when the transition itself is non-agential despite the states which undergo it being standard person-level phenomena.

It would be a mistake to equate the agential/impersonal distinction with a difference between conscious and unconscious transitions. Both directions of the following bi-conditional are false:

(*)   Transition from state-1 to state-2 is agential ↔ it is conscious.

There are non-agential transitions between conscious states, and there are agential transitions between non-conscious states. When you get socked in the eye and experience a sequence of starry visual episodes, the transition between those episodes is not constitutive of agency despite being fully conscious. So the right-to-left direction of (*) is false. When a rational detective consciously comes to accept that a suspect wasn't at the scene of the crime, she'll go on then to adjust other views, right below the surface of consciousness, on a host of other topics relevant to that fact—concerning whether various bits of evidence are misleading, say, whether other suspects are more likely to be guilty, etc. But none of that happens on the surface of consciousness. It's done below that surface despite being part of what it is for the agent to be a rational detective. So the left-to-right direction of (*) is false too.[1]

---

[1] Or consider a driver in the middle of nowhere. She has been driving all day, lost in thought, she looks up and notices much to her surprise that she's 20 miles down the road. It is clear that she has been driving the car across those 20 miles, equally clear that agential transitions have been involved in the effort, but there do not seem to have been conscious transitions involved in her agency.

*Question 3: What kind of transition theory do epistemic norms fit into?*
At several points in previous chapters we've had reason to distinguish two components of a transition theory: its *dynamics* and its *kinematics*.[2] When discussing rules for rational shift-in-view, this is a distinction of first importance. It matters a great deal whether a rule of rationality is supposed to be part of a theory's dynamics or its kinematics.

Recall that a theory's dynamics explain the overall shape of its target—both at a time and across time—by appeal to forces which generate that shape. The dynamics within a theory of rationality, therefore, detail epistemic forces which interact across an agent's states and transitions to generate facts about rationality. A theory's kinematics, on the other hand, describes the overall shape taken by its target without detailing forces which generate that shape. The focus is entirely on structural aspects of facts within the theory's domain. The kinematics of rationality, therefore, systematize structural features of the phenomena, leaving aside epistemic forces responsible for those structural details.

As we have seen, various dynamical and kinematic rules are to be found in literature on epistemic rationality. Conditionalization and Jeffrey's rule are kinematic prescriptions for credence. Partial meet contraction is a kinematic prescription for belief. The theory of defeasible reasoning contains dynamic rules for revision of belief, and so on.[3] It is important to keep clear on the distinction between these rules, since dynamic and kinematic phenomena relate asymmetrically: the former explain the latter, the latter do not explain the former. This proves important in the theory of rational inference.

*Question 4: What kind of rationality is involved in shift-in-view?*
Although this question turns on a distinction in the theory of rationality the importance of which cannot be easily over-estimated, the distinction is rarely drawn in the literature. In a nutshell: the relevant choice-point here is between *ideal* and *everyday* rationality.

An effective way to introduce this distinction is by analogy. Take any morally good person you know—say my eleven year old son Fritz. He's a great guy morally speaking—I promise!—but like everyone he is not morally perfect. It is natural and common sense to draw a distinction, then, between the everyday moral goodness which Fritz manifests in spades and the moral goodness he would manifest were he morally perfect. Plenty of folks manifest the former sort of moral goodness. No ordinary human being in history ever has, currently does, or ever will manifest the latter sort of moral goodness. There is a significant distinction to be drawn, then, between everyday moral goodness and moral perfection. No one can manifest the latter, though plenty of 'good'uns' manifest the former.

---

[2] See Chapters 5, 6, and 9.
[3] Conditionalization and Jeffrey's rule are primarily discussed in Chapters 4 and 6. Partial meet contraction is primarily discussed in Chapters 2 and 3. See (Horty, 2014) or (Pollock, 1987) for examples of dynamical rules for the update of belief.

So it goes in epistemology. It is natural (and perhaps even common sense) to draw a distinction between everyday epistemic goodness—which the commitments of ordinary rational people routinely manifest—and ideal epistemic goodness—which they always entirely lack. Our rational beliefs, states of confidence, and shifts-in-view routinely manifest the former sort of epistemic goodness—they *are* often rational in the everyday sense, after all—but none of them ever manifests the latter sort of epistemic goodness, none of them are ideally rational. The great physicist on the cover of this book, Lise Meitner, was a very smart cookie indeed, but even she wasn't *ideally* rational.

Ideal rationality is the sort of rationality manifested by a commitment-laden mind which is blemish-free when viewed from an epistemic point of view. Everyday rationality is the sort of rationality manifested by beings who are epistemically good in quotidian sorts of ways. Ideal rationality is often thought to require full logical consistency in one's epistemic commitments, the closure of those commitments by many-premise entailment, probabilistic coherence, and so forth.[4] Everyday rationality is not subject to those things—which is good, since no one can satisfy demanding constraints like that. The relevant point is often put by saying that everyday rationality is 'bounded' in various ways. But that way of putting it indicates a perspective on further issues—to be discussed in a moment—which should *not* be taken as settled when simply stating the distinction between everyday and ideal rationality.

With common sense, then, we start with the assumption that there is such a thing as ideal versus everyday rationality, just as there is such a thing as ideal versus everyday moral goodness. This assumption raises a deep question about rationality rarely discussed in the literature. What is the explanatory relationship, if any, between ideal and everyday rationality?

There are four notional possibilities:

(a) Ideal rationality explains its everyday cousin;
(b) Everyday rationality explains its ideal cousin;
(c) Each partially explains the other;
(d) There are no explanatory relations between them.

It is uncommon for epistemologists to take an explicit stand on this topic, which means an important aspect of their approach goes unspecified. My sense is that no one holds—or at least no one would hold, were they to consider it explicitly—the last position listed above, the view on which there are no explanatory relations between ideal and everyday rationality. But this is most definitely a view one might take, for instance, if one thought that both everyday and ideal rationality were each fully explained by some deeper phenomenon. John Pollock commits to (b) for the epistemology of belief—calling everyday rationality 'justification' and ideal rationality 'warrant'—and he defines the latter notion via a fixed-point construction which makes appeal to the former. Those who work on 'bounded' rationality normally do the reverse.

---

[4] See Chapters 2 and 5 for a detailed explication of these notions.

Although this is one of the most important issues in the theory of rationality, it is also one of the least well explored. There is a flowering literature in the theory of political justice, however, centring on an analogous distinction. In a nutshell, the relevant divide in the theory of justice is this: some say that the most important thing to sort out theoretically is the absolute best case scenario justice-wise, while others say that the most important thing to sort out is how to take do-able local steps to improve (but not perfect) one's situation justice-wise. John Rawls is the parade-case theorist of the former sort. Amartya Sen is the parade-case theorist of the latter sort. In recent decades there has been vigorous and fruitful debate in the theory of justice about which approach is best and why. Epistemology would benefit from a similar debate about rationality.

My sense is that those drawn to formal epistemology are often Rawlsian by instinct—though I may be wrong about this. They certainly tend to write as if ideal rationality is explanatorily basic in the ballpark, with everyday rationality being explicated, if at all, by appeal to bounds placed on the ideal. My sense is also that those drawn to informal epistemology are often Senian by instinct—though I may be wrong about this too. They certainly tend to write as if everyday rationality is the basic notion in the area, with its ideal counterpart to be explicated, if at all, by appeal to everyday rationality. It would be nice to see the issues explored fully.[5]

*Question 5: What are basic epistemic commitments?*
This is the framing question of Part II of the book, of course, a question which probes the relation between coarse- and fine-grained attitudes. Are belief, disbelief, and suspended judgement more fundamental within the theory of rationality than levels of confidence? Is something like the reverse true? And so on. With common sense we assume that there are states of belief, disbelief, and suspended judgement, as well as levels of confidence. The key issue turns on the relation between these coarse- and fine-grained attitudes—perhaps better put the issue turns on which of the attitudes is most fundamental to rational shift-in-view.

We've canvassed five questions about rational shift-in-view. All but the first have been regimented with a two-way choice-point. The un-regimented question—the one about factors which prompt rational shift-in-view—has been left open, since there is no consensus about its answer in the literature (and common sense seems to recognize a huge range of epistemic factors). For any agreed-upon factor, though, regimenting choice-points guarantee that we face a sixteen-fold space of theoretical options. The story we tell about rational shift-in-view prompted by that very factor could fit into any of the theoretical options.

For example, we henceforth accept that visual experience is an epistemic factor which prompts rational shift-in-view. Not everyone in philosophy believes that, of course, but it's a plausible view and we'll take it for granted in what follows. With the assumption in our pocket we face the following space of options for visual-based shift-in-view:

---

[5] See (Rawls, 1999), (Sen, 2009), (Schmidtz, 2011), (Stemplowska & Swift, 2012), (Valentini, 2012).

## RATIONAL SHIFT-IN-VIEW: A SPACE OF THEORIES 327

| Visual-based Shift-in-View | TYPE of TRANSITION | TYPE of NORM | TYPE of RATIONALITY | TYPE of ATTITUDE |
|---|---|---|---|---|
| 1 | Agential | Dynamic | Everyday | Coarse |
| 2 | Agential | Dynamic | Everyday | Fine |
| 3 | Agential | Dynamic | Ideal | Coarse |
| 4 | Agential | Dynamic | Ideal | Fine |
| 5 | Agential | Kinematic | Everyday | Coarse |
| 6 | Agential | Kinematic | Everyday | Fine |
| 7 | Agential | Kinematic | Ideal | Coarse |
| 8 | Agential | Kinematic | Ideal | Fine |
| 9 | Impersonal | Dynamic | Everyday | Coarse |
| 10 | Impersonal | Dynamic | Everyday | Fine |
| 11 | Impersonal | Dynamic | Ideal | Coarse |
| 12 | Impersonal | Dynamic | Ideal | Fine |
| 13 | Impersonal | Kinematic | Everyday | Coarse |
| 14 | Impersonal | Kinematic | Everyday | Fine |
| 15 | Impersonal | Kinematic | Ideal | Coarse |
| 16 | Impersonal | Kinematic | Ideal | Fine |

It is not possible to locate with high confidence every notable theorist within the chart, for too many are inexplicit about what they are up to when theorizing about visual-based shift-in-view. But it is possible to locate a number of well-known theorists.

For instance: Mike Martin, John McDowell, John Pollock (for visual-based justification), Jim Pryor, Crispin Wright, and Martin Davies (with respect to transmission) all belong to line 1 of the chart. When it comes to visual-based rationality, they all theorize about the agential dynamics of everyday rationality for belief. Pollock also belongs to line 3 when he writes about visually warranted belief. Wright and Davies belong on line 5 when speaking about closure conditions for visual-based rationality. Mark Kaplan and Richard Jeffrey* belong to line 12 when writing about visually-induced shift of credence. Rudolph Carnap, Hartry Field, and Roger White belong on line 16 when speaking of that topic. And so on.[6]

For our purposes the key question is simple: when we shift our focus from rational shift-in-view prompted by visual input to rational shift-in-view which is inferential in character, where does fundamental theory fit into the analogue chart? Put another

---

[6] Richard Jeffrey* is the non-actual philosopher who is as much like Richard Jeffrey as it is possible to be consistent with thinking (contra Jeffrey) that there *are* rational links from visual experience to credence.

way: when a rational shift-in-view is a sensibly-taken inferential step, and we've settled on fundamental rationality displayed by that step, where in the relevant chart does our story of that rationality fit in?

In the next section we sketch a conception of visual rationality which lands squarely on a particular line of the chart. In the following section we argue that relevant aspects of that story apply to rational inference. This will lead to our answer to the end-question of the previous paragraph.

## 13.3 Rational Steps

I want to paint a particular picture of visually based rational shift-in-view. The picture I have in mind is easy to state but less easy to understand. In a nutshell, it is the view that visual states are *coordinated epistemic pro tanto reasons*. This is a mouthful, of course, but the description captures crucial elements needed for a good understanding of rational inference. We'll get clear on the highlighted description first with respect to visual-based shift-in-view, by unpacking the mouthful-description notions by notion, and then we'll apply the elucidated theoretical resources to the topic of inference. When doing so it helps to unpack the target description's constitutive notions in reverse order.

1. In the intended sense we'll use here, a *reason* is a state which generates normative bias concerning action or activity. When $x$ is a reason to $\Phi$, for instance, $x$ cuts in favour of $\Phi$-ing, and when $x$ a reason not to $\Phi$, it likewise cuts against $\Phi$-ing. This is to say in the first case that $\Phi$-ing is a good idea at least with respect to $x$, and it's to say in the second case that $\Phi$-ing is a bad idea at least with respect to $x$. Anything we might do—in virtually any sense of 'do'—is something for which there can be reasons, and something against which there can be reasons. You might have reason to run to the shop, or to live carefully, or to respect your elders, or to grow old gracefully. Then again you might have reason not to do any of those things. Reasons are states which generate normative bias in this intuitive way.

2. In the intended sense we'll use here, a pro tanto reason is a reason which makes for non-decisive normative bias concerning action or activity. When $x$ is a pro tanto reason to $\Phi$, for instance, $x$ favours $\Phi$-ing in a way that is not guaranteed sufficient to make $\Phi$-ing a good thing to do all things considered. Similarly, when $x$ is a pro tanto reason not to $\Phi$, $x$ disfavours $\Phi$-ing in a way that is not guaranteed sufficient to make not $\Phi$-ing a good thing to do all things considered. This sounds obscure but really it's simple: think of how we often decide whether to perform an ordinary action (like buying or cleaning a house). Often we list pros and cons associated with the action in question. This amounts to listing the pro tanto reasons for, and the pro tanto reasons against, the action. Our hope is that the contemplated act will stand out as obviously the right thing to do if the pros outweigh the cons significantly, or it will stand out as obviously the wrong thing to do if the opposite is the case. This is why we list and reflect on pros and cons. They make for non-decisive bias concerning the action we're contemplating. They are thereby pro tanto reasons.

3. In the intended sense we'll use here, *epistemic* reasons play their reason-like role specifically with respect to action or activity subject to epistemic appraisal. These are reasons which make for distinctively epistemic bias concerning action or activity.

When $x$ is an epistemic reason to $\Phi$, for instance, $x$ cuts in favour of $\Phi$-ing specifically qua action evaluable from an epistemic point of view. And when $x$ is an epistemic reason not to $\Phi$, $x$ cuts against $\Phi$-ing qua action so evaluable. Relevant examples are the formation of new belief, the update of credence, the increase or decrease in how entrenched or resilient a given epistemic commitment is, and so on. These are episodes for which there can be epistemic reason.

4. In the intended sense we'll use here, a *coordinated* reason is a reason which leads a particular sort of double life. When $x$ is a reason to $\Phi$, that will be so in virtue of some reason-investing feature R of $x$. But when $x$ is a causal prompt to $\Phi$, that will be so in virtue of some causal-prompt-investing feature C of $x$. The entity $x$ itself is coordinated in our sense if R and C are identical features. When that happens the aspect which explains $x$ being a causal prompt with respect to $\Phi$-ing is identical to aspect which explains $x$ generating positive normative bias with respect to $\Phi$-ing. And the same story holds for $x$ being a coordinated reason not to $\Phi$ *mutatis mutandis*.

For example, suppose $x$ is the state consisting in an itchy chin. Then $x$ will be a coordinated reason to chin-scratch. After all, having an itchy chin is a reason to chin-scratch: the state makes for normative bias in favour of such scratching. But having an itchy chin is also a causal prompt to chin-scratching: those with itchy chins are thereby causally disposed to scratch their chin. Yet the feature in virtue of which having an itchy chin is a *reason* to chin-scratch is identical to the feature in virtue of which having an itchy chin is a causal prompt to chin-scratch, if the set-up is taken at face value at least. In both cases it is the itchiness of the chin that is relevant. Having an itchy chin is thus a coordinated reason to chin-scratch. The causal and normative roles of the state are driven by the very same thing: the property of being itchy.

Coordinated reasons promote or inhibit activity through aspects of their character, aspects which make for reasonable pro or con bias. When $x$ is a coordinated moral reason to $\Phi$, $x$'s causal and moral 'oomph to $\Phi$' springs from the very same features of $x$. When $x$ is a coordinated practical reason to $\Phi$, $x$'s causal and practical 'oomph to $\Phi$' springs from the very same features. And so on. When $x$ is a coordinated epistemic reason to $\Phi$, therefore, $x$'s causal and epistemic 'oomph to $\Phi$' springs from the very same features of $x$ too—and so it goes for every other type of reason.

Drawing all this together, then, the hypothesis I want to push is that visual experiences are coordinated epistemic pro tanto reasons. They make for non-decisive normative bias concerning shift-of-view activity. They are causal prompts to that activity as well, and the features in virtue of which they are such prompts are identical to the features in virtue of which they make for normative bias to shift-in-view.

One final bit of terminology is helpful: let's stipulate that a mental-state transition is *reckoning* when its input is a coordinated epistemic reason. This leaves open whether the reason in play generates decisive or non-decisive bias, of course, so the terminology leaves open whether reckoning is defeasible or otherwise. But it does permit a crisp statement of the main hypothesis to be defended about inference, namely, that inference in the ordinary sense is reckoning in the stipulated sense. This is our next topic.

## 13.4 Inference and the Basing Relation

The first thing that should be said about inference—as we mentioned in §6.2.—is that not every systematic mental-state transition is inferential in character. Classic examples come from associative links in the mind: thought of salt can be systematically linked to thought of pepper without the connection between those thoughts being inferential in character. Despite its being entirely predictable that thought of pepper will occur after thought of salt, the connection between them may be associative rather than inferential.

To get a feel for inference it helps to consider a bog-standard case, so recall the example discussed in Chapter 6. You have no idea whether Sascha is in Paris or in Barcelona but you rationally believe she's in one place or the other. Then you receive news that Sascha is not in Paris (and no other news). Your Paris-or-Barcelona belief then joins forces with your not-Paris belief to produce a new belief, namely, belief to the effect that Sascha is in Barcelona.

The key transition in the example involves a couple of input states—your belief that Sascha is either in Paris or Barcelona, and your belief that she is not in Paris—and it involves a single output state—the belief that Sascha is in Barcelona. Not only is it true that the latter state of belief is based on the former states of belief in the case, it's also true that the basing itself seems to reflect some kind of sensitivity to the input contents in the example *evidentially supporting* the output content. This is what bog-standard inference always seems like. It always seems to involve a small clutch of input states of a certain kind producing an output state of that kind, with the production itself displaying sensitivity to how input content supports output content.

In our previous discussion this led us to the *Core Inference Principle*:[7]

(CIP)    A mental-state transition is inferential if

1. Its input is a small number of instances of an attitude taken to contents.
2. Its output is an instance of that attitude taken to a new content.
3. The output is formed on the basis of the input.
4. The shift from input to output reflects sensitivity to the fact that input-contents evidentially support output-content.

It is natural to think that each clause of this principle captures something essential to bog-standard cases of inference. I do not think, though, that the Core Inference Principle captures the heart of inference as such; and I have two reasons for thinking it does not.

The first is probably a spoils-to-the-victor issue—i.e. an issue resolution of which is best adjudicated by whichever approach conquers most other topics on the table—but the second worry I have for thinking that the Core Inference Principle fails to capture the heart of inference is more serious. We'll definitely need to correct the Principle in light of the second consideration if we want to capture the heart of inference as such, and we may need to in light of the first issue as well.

---

[7] See 6.2ff.

The potential spoils-to-the-victor issue results from a simple fact, namely, *not* all inference-like mental-state transitions satisfy Core Inference Principle. Once a flat-out contradiction is proved in a bit of reductio reasoning, for instance, the opposite of what's initially supposed is endorsed. But that transition—the endorsement of the logical opposite of what has been supposed at the outset of the reductio—looks inferential in character (or at least it does on initial inspection). It's certainly a mental-state transition subject to epistemic appraisal. It's also a crucial element in *some* kind of reasoning. But the last psychological step in a reductio fails clause 4 of the Core Inference Principle. After all, contents which figure upstream in reductio conflict with the output content endorsed at the end of the reasoning—perhaps they conflict with it as a group, but still, they conflict with it—so they don't support the content eventually endorsed. The last step of reductio fails clause 4 of the Core Inference Principle.

Consider another example. Suppose a friend is standing behind you within earshot and asks how many fingers they're holding up. You turn, look, and it visually seems plain as day that your friend is holding up three fingers. This leads you to believe that they are holding up three fingers, and, on that basis, to say as much in reply. Consider the shift from visual experience to belief in the case and ask yourself this: is the shift inferential in character? Well, it's a mental-state transition subject to epistemic appraisal. Since it looks to you as if your friend is holding up three fingers—and everything else in the case is normal, by hypothesis—it is perfectly rational that you come to believe that your friend is holding up three fingers. After all, this is exactly what your visual evidence indicates.[8]

It's not clear the transition from your visual experience to belief itself satisfies clause 1, 2, or 4 of the Core Inference Principle (though it satisfies clause 3 by stipulation). For one thing, the input to the transition involves visual experience itself. It is contentious whether such experience is a propositional attitude at all, hence it's contentious that clause 1 of the Core Inference Principle is satisfied. Even if clause 1 of that Principle is satisfied, though, the transition from visual experience to belief fails clause 2 of the Principle, for its input and output states are not instances of the same type of attitude. And finally—when taken at face-value, anyway—clause 4 of the Principle is also not satisfied by visually-based belief like yours in the case, since input- and output-contents are one and the same thing in the case. When it looks to you as if your friend is holding up three fingers, and on that basis you come to believe that your friend is holding up three fingers, you literally believe what you see. Output content and input content are identical. But no claim evidentially supports itself, so when you come to believe that your friend is holding up three fingers, on the basis of its looking to you that way, clause 4 of the Core Inference Principle is not satisfied.

These sorts of worries make it unclear that the Core Inference Principle captures the essence of inference. To the extent that the Principle goes wrong—due to phenomena like those found in the visual case—the problem is that steps in the phenomena turn out to be different than bog-standard cases of belief-to-belief

---

[8] Actually we should be more careful about which notions figure in the subject-place, so to say, when it comes both to the content of your visual experience and the belief formed on its basis. Since that thorny issue is not relevant to present concerns, we leave it aside.

inference. But there's a much deeper worry about the Core Inference Principle that we still need to flag, a worry which applies even to bog-standard cases of inference.

To see this, note there is an obvious difference between having evidence for some conclusion drawn and drawing a conclusion on the basis of the evidence had. This difference turns on the basing relation, of course, something central to clause 3 of the Core Inference Principle. We've seen that the difference between merely having evidence for a conclusion drawn, and actually drawing a conclusion the basis of the evidence had, is directly relevant to two types of rationality: evidential and doxastic rationality.[9]

Consider a case in which Holmes believes that the butler is guilty on the basis of clues he and Watson have jointly uncovered (and understood), though Watson believes that the butler is guilty solely on the basis of bias toward servants. In circumstances like these both Holmes and Watson have adequate evidence to believe that the butler is guilty, yet Holmes' belief is rational in a way that Watson's is not. This can be put by saying that both Holmes and Watson have evidentially rational (or 'justified') belief in the butler's guilt, whereas Holmes alone has doxastically rational (or justified) belief in that guilt. Basically evidential rationality requires only the possession of suitable evidence, whereas doxastic rationality requires also that epistemic commitment be based on suitable evidence in one's possession. Epistemologists are led to wonder about the nature of the basing relation itself, inter alia, because they are interested in the difference between evidential and doxastic rationality.

Most think the basing relation is some kind of causal relation.[10] This is one reason why epistemologists tend to see paradigm cases of inference as some kind of causal transition between mental states. But the key issue about inference before us turns on *how* causation plays out in the phenomena. Consider the following platitude connecting the philosophy of mind and the theory of rationality:

*The Bridge Principle*: the epistemic status of a bit of reasoning depends, among other things, on the content of the mental states involved.

When an inferential move is well taken, this normative fact will itself be determined, at least in part, by the contents had by the mental states in play. Of course the caveat is needed for the reason just noticed: not only does the content have to fit together evidentially, the connection between the content-bearing states has to be appropriate as well. Causal-basing theorists say the appropriate connection is causal—and that seems basically right—but a complete theory demands more detail. It turns out the crucial detail leads to serious revision in the Core Inference Principle.

Intuitively, the content of one's evidential states determines which conclusion, if any, should be drawn. Conjoining this with a causal perspective on the basing relation suggests a metaphysically potent position. Specifically, it suggests that inferences are causal steps which unfold between mental states because of (or in virtue of) the contents displayed by their *relata*. When contents relate properly to one another rational inference is the result. When contents do not relate properly to one

---

[9] See (Kvanvig & Menzel, 1990) and §11.7.
[10] There are naysayers about this as with everything in philosophy. For an overview see (Korcz, 1996).

another irrational inference is the result. Reflection on the basing relation leads directly to the idea that inference involves causation-because-of-content, something we might aptly term *content-causation*.

This is a non-trivial position, for it is a straightforward affirmation of the causal efficacy of content. Roughly speaking, feature F will count as causally efficacious when states which have it cause other things in virtue of their having it.[11] When I was a teenager, for instance, I drank a whole bottle of cheap purple wine—Mad Dog 20/20, if memory serves—which immediately caused me to redesign the back seat of a friend's car. The purple colour of the wine had nothing to do with my redesigning efforts. The acidity, sugar, and alcohol in the wine were doubtless the culprits. These latter features were causally efficacious with respect to my design efforts. The purple colour of the wine was not. The colour was 'epiphenomenal': a feature of a cause which is causally irrelevant to that cause generating its effects. The view that content is causally efficacious in inference, therefore, is the view that inferential inputs give rise to such outputs because of (or in virtue of) each having the contents they do. Reflection on the basing relation leads directly to the idea that possession of content does causal-explanatory work in inference, directly to a rejection of content epiphenomenalism.

Perhaps an unwarranted leap has been made from the fact that there is content-sensitivity in some sense, when it comes to inference, to the metaphysically charged idea that there is content-causation in inference. Perhaps we can explain this sensitivity by appeal to something more anodyne than content-causation, thereby removing a commitment to content-causation from our approach to inference. The most natural way to do this is to emphasize counterfactual relations between mental states when one of them is based on another. Let's see if that strategy can be used to avoid commitment to content-causation.

As we might put it, then, suppose you base conclusion C on evidence E. According to the content-causation story, this involves the following elements: two mental states $M_1$ and $M_2$, the former having content C and the latter having content E, and the former causing the latter in virtue of these content-theoretic facts. We might deny this story while preserving some semblance of content-sensitivity by noting that counterfactual dependence between $M_1$ and $M_2$ is itself a function of content. There are several ways to flesh out the idea.

The most wooden runs as follows: for $M_2$ to be based on $M_1$ we require only that $M_2$ depend counterfactually on $M_1$. Such a view will count you as basing $M_2$ on $M_1$ if you would lack the former were you to lack the latter. This leaves room for the causal inertia of content, of course, but it misconstrues the basing relation. After all, one mental state may counterfactually depend on another without the basing relation

---

[11] The literature on mental causation is vast. It's not too far wrong to think that its modern state came by way of reaction to Davidson's initial attempts to reject epiphenomenalism (the thesis, roughly, that the mind is causally inert). See his influential 'Mental Events' (1970). The standard worry for Davidson's line is that it secures, at most, the causal efficacy of mental events; it does nothing to secure the efficacy of mental features or properties involved in those events. This influential worry seems first to appear in (Hopkins, 1978), then picked up by (Honderich, 1982), and then discussed widely after influential and independent discussion in (Kim, 1984). See also (Crane, 1995), (Ehring, 1996), (Sturgeon, 1994), with (Yablo, 1992) being the must-read in the area.

entering the picture. This would happen were each of them to be the effect of a common cause. If I flip a switch which causes you first to believe E and then to believe C, your latter belief will counterfactually depend on your former belief—if you hadn't believed E you wouldn't have believed C, since I wouldn't have flipped the switch (we may suppose)—but neither belief will cause the other, and neither will be based on the other. And the lack of causation between them at least partly explains the absence of basing: one sign that your coming to believe C is not based on your belief in E is the fact that the latter did not cause the former to exist. This is why causal-basing theories are motivated.

Simply adding an unfettered causal requirement will not solve the difficulty. One mental state may be caused by another, upon which it counterfactually depends, without the former being based on the latter. Suppose your belief in E causes you to bump your head, which in turn causes you to form a belief in C. Then your belief in E will have caused your belief in C, and the latter will depend counterfactually on the former, we may suppose—if you hadn't believed E you wouldn't have believed C, for you wouldn't have bumped your head—but scenarios like this plainly lack the causal use of evidence we find in bog-standard cases of inference.

In fact belief in E may even cause belief in C because of the former belief's content without it being the case that belief in C is based on belief in E. Suppose you believe that Donald Trump is stuck to the ceiling, and, as a result, you look up and bump your head on a low-hanging light. The collision causes you to form a belief that Nigel Farage should retire. In the event, the content of your belief about Trump will be causally relevant to the production of your belief about Farage—you looked up, after all, because and in virtue of believing that Trump was stuck to the ceiling—but it will not be the case that you base your belief about Farage on your belief about Trump. What is lacking is not causation, of course, nor even causation which springs in some sense from the content of the causal antecedent. What is lacking is that causation in the case isn't explicable by appeal to the contentful features of each *relatum*. Since the effect qua Farage-should-retire belief is not explicable in terms of the cause qua Trump-is-stuck-to-the-ceiling belief, the former is not based on the latter in the sense relevant to the theory of inference. The causal relation needed for a good understanding of inference requires that inferential *relata* stand in a causal relation to one another because of their content. We are thus led full circle back to content-causation: when it comes to inference, rationality requires the causal efficacy of content.

Several wrinkles in the dialectic suggest as much. For one thing the hypothesis that rational inference involves content-causation is the most intuitive thing to say in the area. If the content of our thoughts causally explains anything, after all, it's how we reason. Then there's the fact that counterfactual dependence is insufficient for basing in exactly the way that counterfactual dependence is insufficient for causation, which strongly suggests that the basing relation is causal. Then there's the fact that unconstrained causation is itself insufficient for basing, which suggests that the basing relation isn't merely causal. And then there's the fact that content-efficacy of cause is insufficient on its own for basing, which strongly suggests that the basing relation is causally constrained by content on both ends. Content-theoretic features of cause and effect appear to be essential ingredients to inference as such.

This is in line with the picture of reckoning sketched in the last section. Recall that steps in reckoning were driven by coordinated epistemic reasons (by stipulation). In light of what's gone before it's natural to propose, then, that inference is one kind of step in reckoning. After all, it's natural to think that inferential inputs are coordinated epistemic reasons: states which make for proprietary epistemic bias, which causally prompt a shift-in-view, and which do so precisely in virtue of features which generates their proprietary epistemic bias—features individuated by content.

For example: when your belief that Sascha is either in Barcelona or Paris joins with your belief that Sascha is not in Paris, and the two inferentially produce the new belief that Sascha is in Barcelona, input belief-states function as a *triggered* coordinated epistemic reason. They are a causal prompt of new belief—which prompt is actually set off *in situ*—they prompt as they do because of their content—perhaps together with interest in where Sascha is—and they generate epistemic bias in favour of believing that Sascha is in Barcelona precisely in virtue of that content. Input belief-states are a causal prompt of a cognitive action in favour of which they generate epistemic bias; and both roles are played in virtue of the same contentful features.

*This* is how doxastic rationality gets off the ground. Since inference is run on coordinated epistemic reasons, outputs are based on inputs so as to create doxastic rationality. If inputs were merely uncoordinated epistemic reasons, evidential rationality would result, but not the best kind of rationality, not doxastic rationality. The better kind of rationality requires coordinated epistemic reasons. The basing relation associated with such rationality is a causal relation driven by coordinated epistemic reasons. The fundamental role of such reasons is to push reckoning along in virtue of what makes it evidentially kosher.

This means we should replace the Core Inference Principle with a view which makes use of content-causation. We are thereby led to the *Better Inference Principle*:

(BIP)  A mental-state transition is an inference iff

1. Its input is a small number of instances of an attitude taken to contents.
2. Its output is an instance of that attitude taken to a new content.
3. The output is formed on the basis of the input via content-causation.

This new Principle has one great advantage over the Core Inference Principle. It allows bad inference as well as good inference. Clause 4 of the Core Inference Principle requires that an inferential shift reflects sensitivity to the fact that input-contents evidentially support output-content. The clause actually requires, therefore, that input-contents evidentially support the output-content. That always happens in the bog-standard cases of inference considered by philosophers, because they always involve reasonable inference, but it does not always happen in all cases of inference. After all, there are bad inferences as well as good ones, and the input contents of bad inferences fail to support their output content. That's why they're bad.

The correct theory of inference will then recognize good and bad inferences as bona fide examples of its subject matter. It is the theory of epistemic rationality which will go on to discriminate good from bad qua inference, not the theory of inference as such, for the theory of inference as such is a non-normative bit of philosophy of mind. Our Nature-Before-Norms assumption thus applies directly to the case: just as the theory of action should not individuate its target phenomena by appeal to conditions which make action prudent or moral or wise, so the theory of inference should not individuate its target phenomena by appeal to conditions which make inference rational or irrational or wise.

## 13.5 A Puzzle about Shift-in-View: Visual Update and Inference

We are left, then, with a proposal about visual-based updating and a hypothesis about inferential updating. The first counts as a proposal because it's not been argued for strongly—more put forward as a plausible view—and the second counts as an hypothesis (rather than a proposal) because it has been argued for strongly, by reflection on the basing relation and related phenomena. The proposal is that visual-based shift-in-view is a type of *reckoning*—in the stipulated sense of that term introduced earlier—and the hypothesis is that inference is likewise a type of reckoning. The key thought in both cases is that shift-in-view is driven by coordinated epistemic reasons. If that's correct—if the proposal and the hypothesis are true—visual and inferential updating have a great deal in common.

The next thing to note is that they have all this in common in what I shall call a *principal* sort of way. Let me explain what I have in mind with this thought. We'll say that a feature principally applies to a transition if the transition manifests that feature in virtue of aspects which have to do with its nature or point. Consider some examples:

> (a) Suppose we both suffer from neutropenia (i.e. chronically low white blood cell count). Suppose also that I'm a huge fan of neutropenia, since I love everything about myself and I am aware that I suffer from the condition. For this reason I will only be friends with those who also have neutropenia. Suppose finally that you and I have a close friendship. But you start eating your spinach and your white blood cell count starts to recover. We both know about this, so, as your heath improves our friendship deteriorates. The neutropenic transition will be a good-making feature from a health-theoretic point of view and bad-making feature from a friendship point of view. Yet these normative features do not apply to the transition in the same way. The former principally applies to the uptick in your white blood cells, the latter does not so apply. After all, health-theoretic goodness has to do with the very point or nature of the transition in question—i.e. it has something to do with your physical well-being—but friendship-theoretic badness has only to do with aspects of the uptick in your white blood cells which are extrinsic to its nature or point. Intuitively put: white blood cells are meant to foment good health, and, for this reason, health-related normative aspects of their flux apply principally to that flux; but white blood cells have nothing to do in themselves with friendship, so, for that reason, friendship-related normative aspects of their flux do not apply principally to that flux.
>
> (b) Suppose you sell cheese at the local market and one day I buy some with a particular coin. Unbeknownst to either of us the coin has a crazy history which

involves it being infused with mild radiation. The coin causes anyone who keeps it in their possession to have an upset tummy. From a vender-theoretic point of view, then, giving you the coin is a good thing, since you're trying to exchange cheese for money. From a health-theoretic point of view giving you the coin is a bad thing, since it causes you to have an upset tummy. Normative features apply differently to the case: the vendor-theoretic one applies principally to the financial transaction, the health-theoretic one does not. Vender-theoretic goodness is fixed by aspects of the financial transaction which have to do with its nature or point. Health-theoretic badness is fixed by aspects of the transaction extrinsic to that nature or point.

A feature applies principally to a transition, then, when the feature is manifested in virtue of aspects of the transition which have to do with its nature or point.

There are a number of features that visual and inferential shift-in-view share principally. For one thing, they each principally concern everyday rationality rather than ideal rationality. It is the very point of each kind of transition to take the agent from a state that is less than ideal—since it is not fully worked out, since it does not contain commitments which reflect all evidence to hand—to a state that is better worked out, to one that better reflects the available evidence. When an agent's epistemic commitments are updated on the basis of new visual input, for example, there is visual evidence before the transition that has yet to be epistemically absorbed. That is the point of the visual-based update. The agent's epistemic state before the update is sub-optimal, and the update is meant to make it better. The kind of rationality that principally applies to visual-based shift-in-view is everyday rationality, not ideal rationality.

Similarly, when an agent's epistemic commitments are updated by inference, a new epistemic commitment is formed on the basis of old ones. Before the update there are epistemic commitments that have not been fully exploited, otherwise there would be nothing new to infer from them. Yet exploiting unexploited commitment is raison d'etre of inferential update. The agent's epistemic state before the inference is sub-optimal, and inference is meant to better her epistemic position. Hence the kind of rationality that principally applies to inference is likewise everyday rationality, not ideal rationality.

For another thing, both visual and inferential updates principally involve doxastic rationality. Both types of mental-state transition are driven by coordinated epistemic reasons, so both are driven by the very features which generate their proprietary epistemic bias. Doxastic rationality is the kind of rationality produced by coordination between causation and normative bias. It is a principal feature of each kind of update, for this reason, that the transition in question is a transition of a kind that produces doxastic rationality. This is neither a bug nor a side-effect of these types of shift-in-view. It is a feature shared by their nature, point, or purpose.

For yet another thing, both visual and inferential updates principally involve dynamic rationality. Since it is the nature or point of each to be driven by coordinated epistemic reasons, each process is driven by factors which make for normative bias. That is precisely what it is for normative forces to play out, of course, so visual and inferential updating are principally subject to doxastic rationality. That sort of rationality is manifested by each process in virtue of aspects central to its very nature or point.

Putting all this together, then, visual and inferential update have principally to do with the everyday dynamics of doxastic rationality. That is a lot to have in common! One could be forgiven for thinking that visual and inferential shift-in-view are really the same kind of thing deep down, as far as rationality is concerned, that the theory of rationality should see them as covered by the very same norms, that the only difference between them as far as rationality is concerned involves differences in their input *relata*.

But that ignores an important asymmetry between them which might be thought to show that each process really has a distinct essence, a difference so significant that visual and inferential updating manifest distinct kinds of rationality. What kind of asymmetry does the line in the previous paragraph ignore? The asymmetry captured with these two claims:

(V) Visual updating is an *impersonal* process: something that happens to us rather than something we do.

(I) Inference is an *agential* process: something we do rather than something which happens to us

Recall the distinction in §13.2 between agential and impersonal norms. (V) and (I) jointly suggest that norms for visual and inferential update are drawn from differing areas of epistemology, that norms for visual update come from the theory of impersonal rationality, and norms for inference come from the theory agential rationality.

If that's right we face a puzzle, for there seems to be a mismatch between the fundamental theory of rational visual update and the fundamental theory of rational inference. Yet it is also plausible to suppose that whatever theory is basic to one kind of shift-in-view is basic to the other. The puzzle is to explain how one set of norms covers visual-based shift-in-view while another covers inference.

There is a natural general strategy for responding to this puzzle which can itself be fleshed out in three ways. One of these ways looks pretty implausible—the first one we'll discuss below—but the other two look promising as solutions to the puzzle before us. We'll take no stand on which of them is correct—noting solely that one or the other of them must be—but we note here that the last strategy to be discussed is our ultimate favourite (largely because it comports best with my first-person sense of cognitive life).

The general strategy for answering the puzzle is simple: reject the presupposition made by the question which generates it. When asked to explain how it could be that one set of norms applies to visual updating while another set applies to inference, the general move is to insist that in the relevant sense only one set of norms is in play, namely, norms which apply both to visual and inferential update.

There are three obvious ways to flesh out this move:

- The impersonal strategy accepts (V) and rejects (I), arguing that all norms in the area are impersonal;

- The agential strategy rejects (V) and accepts (I), arguing that all norms in the area are agential; and
- The no-worries strategy accepts (V) and (I), insisting that this leads to no trouble.

Consider each option in turn.

The least plausible of the three options is the impersonal strategy. This view agrees that visual update is an impersonal matter—that it is something which happens to us rather than something we do—but the strategy denies that inference is any different. The thought is that inference is something that happens to us too, not something we do, and hence that norms of inference are impersonal just as norms for visual update are impersonal. Of course if that is right there is no puzzle in the area since all rational shift-in-view is impersonal.

It must be admitted that there *is* such a thing as flash-of-insight phenomenon—when a conclusion hits you as a bolt from the blue—but that is very unusual. Indeed it is so exceptional that its exceptional nature proves the general rule: normally, when conclusions are reached by a rational agent, they are drawn *by* the agent via inference, with the process looking decidedly agential. This is why it is difficult to believe that (I) is false, and thus why it is difficult to endorse the impersonal reaction to the puzzle before us. A better bet would be to deny that flashes of insight are inferential in the first place, holding on to the idea that inference is agential, and rejecting the present reaction to the puzzle.

The personal reaction agrees that inference is agential—something we do rather than something which happens to us—but it denies that visual update is anything different. The thought is that visual update is something we do as well, and that norms for visual update are agential like those for inference. If that is right then once again there is no puzzle in the area before us, since all rational shift-in-view within it is agential. And here the proposal is not *so* hard to believe; for it must be admitted that at least sometimes the imprint of visual experience on epistemic commitment is got in an agential manner. When you start out non-trivially unsure whether to take visual experience at face value, for instance, and work out explicitly by thinking things through that you should in fact take your visual experience at face-value, then, in those circumstances, visual experience will rationally imprint on epistemic commitments via agential steps. You will purposefully take your experience at face value, or at least in a certain way (say as mostly trusted), and when you do this the upshot will be agential visual update. The key question is whether all visual updating is likewise agential.

Recall our truck-driver from §4.5. Anyone who has driven (or hiked) long distances will have gotten lost in thought while doing so. All of a sudden you realize—with a start, of course—that you're miles down the road and you've paid no attention to what you've been doing. It is nevertheless plausible to think that it is you who have been doing it. In such a case it is not as if someone else or no one at all has been driving (or hiking)! Agential norms have been in play even when you're attention has been unfocused on your activity. There has been such activity to be sure, it has just happened without conscious attention.

A defender of the agential strategy could say, with a modicum of plausibility, that the same sort of thing happens with ordinary visual updating. The thought would be that we normally pay no attention to such updating—or at least very little attention—even though it is something we do all the time, and that this lack of attention gives off the impression that ordinary visual updating is automatic or impersonal, more like something run by auto-pilot than by pilot. But the thought would be that this impression is wrong, that it is always pilots in charge of visual updating, so to say, that such updating is always an agential matter. If that's true, though, there is no unresolved puzzle before us. Both visual and inferential shift-in-view is agential in character. The same area of theory applies to them both.

The final strategy we'll consider is the no-worries move, which takes its cue from the first insight of the personal strategy. The move notes that some visual updates are agential. The no-worries strategy then admits that other visual updates are non-agential, but insists that agents have the power—within limits, of course—to take charge of their visual-based updating pretty much whenever they think it a good idea. No-worries defenders point out that this makes visual-based shift-in-view like *breathing*. They note that in both cases the phenomenon normally runs on auto-pilot, but that in both cases agents generally have the power to turn off the auto-pilot, so to say, and take charge of the process. The thought is that it's normally within an agent's gift to ensure that breathing and visual updating are agential rather than impersonal in character. Proponents of the no-worries strategy point out that this suggests there is no conflict between agential and impersonal norms.

The line goes something like this. There are meta-epistemic norms for when visual updating should run on auto-pilot and when it should be agential in character (the auto-pilot is not an agent). Those meta-epistemic norms turn on background commitments about what sort of environment one is in, how well vision works in that environment, and so on.[12] Unless a mistake has been made in flouting such meta-epistemic norms, however—which would be a different kind of mistake than a ground-level mix-up in visual updating—there is no conflict in how the auto-pilot should exploit visual experience and how the agent should do so. Put another way: unless there is a mistake and the wrong sort of thing is in charge of the visual update, agential norms and impersonal ones agree in how updating should proceed. Even if it turns out that applicable norms come from different areas of epistemology, therefore, advice from one area about a visual update will be kosher by the other's lights. There is no worry in having norms for visual update deriving from two areas of theory. The areas agree when meta-norms are satisfied.

## 13.6 A Deeper Puzzle: Inference and Confidence

We close out the chapter with a second puzzle about rational shift-in-view. This puzzle takes shape when a consequence of the primary lesson of Part II of the book is put together with the conception of inference defended here. After setting up the

---

[12] These issues are directly relevant to whether dogmatism is true of visual updating, and to the nature of undercutting defeater. See (Pollock, 1986) for both issues, (Pryor, 2000) and (Pryor, 2013) for the first issue, and (Sturgeon, 2014) for the second.

puzzle, we'll consider two reactions: one inspired by Steve Yablo's important work on mental causation, the other inspired by reflection on our cognitive machinery. Throughout we'll take it to be an adequacy condition on any reaction to the puzzle that it can explain why puzzle-generating claims look attractive in the first place.

To begin, the major lesson of Part Two is that confidence-first epistemology is correct, that epistemic commitments are at bottom states of confidence, that coarse-grained attitudes are grounded in their fine-grained cousins. In the previous two chapters we defended a particular version of the general approach, but the particulars involved in that defence are not relevant to the puzzle before us. All we need here is the view that belief is at bottom a state of confidence, something we'll take as read in what follows.

The other piece of the puzzle comes from the conception of inference defended in this chapter. The key thought, recall, is that inference is driven by coordinated epistemic reasons. We've seen this ensures a number of important things about inference, three of which play a central role here:

- Whenever a state transition is driven by a coordinated epistemic reason, the transition is pushed along by aspects of the reason which causally prompt its owner to do something. This means the thing for which the coordinated epistemic reason *is* a reason is itself a thing its owner can do. We're dealing with agential rationality whenever a state transition is driven by a coordinated epistemic reason.
- Whenever a state transition is driven by a coordinated epistemic reason, the transition is pushed along by aspects of the reason which generate epistemic bias concerning the output. The process is principally subject to dynamics rather than kinematics—i.e. the bit of theory detailing forces which generate evidential and doxastic rationality.
- Whenever a rational state transition is driven by a coordinated epistemic reason, its output is a new epistemic commitment. The set of commitments prior to the transition, then, could not have been fully worked out. They could not have contained everything supported by the agent's evidence, for then the inference would have been otiose. When dealing with coordinated epistemic reasons, we're principally dealing with everyday rather than ideal rationality.

Drawing all this together, inference is a step-wise process subject to the agential dynamics of everyday rationality, pushed forward by coordinated epistemic reasons. That is the heart and soul of inference.

Neither the view that confidence-first epistemology is correct nor the view that inference is driven by coordinated epistemic reasons is uncontentious. We've seen, though, that each of these views can be supported by a range of powerful considerations. It is clear at a glance that the most natural thing to say about the relation between belief and confidence is that belief is sufficiently strong confidence. When you confess that you believe in the Easter Bunny, after all, and I ask you how strongly you do so, it is not as if I've changed topics. It is likewise natural to think that inference is something we do, and that when going in for it our aim is to form new views on the basis of old ones precisely because the old views support new ones. A fancy way of putting this is that reasoning is a step-wise process undertaken to exploit coordinated epistemic reasons. But the relevant point needs no fancy language. It is just that inference is cognitive action prompted by old commitments supporting new ones.

Let us accept this conception of inference and place it alongside a confidence-first approach to epistemic attitudes. In the event, we face a new puzzle straightaway, for states of confidence do not seem to be inferential *relata*. They do not seem to play the right cognitive role to ground our inferential activity. We thus look to be faced with an inconsistent triad:

- We reason with states of belief. (R-with-SoB)
- States of belief are deep down states of confidence. (Locke)
- We do not reason with states of confidence. (¬R-with-SoC)

If we reason with states of belief, though—in line with the first claim above—and states of belief are deep down states of confidence—in line with the second—it seems we must reason with states of confidence, a view which conflicts with the third claim above. All three of the claims are readily defensible yet they seem to conflict with one another. What to do?

## 13.7 Inference, Causation, and Confidence-Grounded Belief

There are many ways to introduce the deep motivations behind Steve Yablo's ground-breaking work on mental causation. One of them is to explain, by appeal to his work, how three plausible claims about mental causation can all be true, even though they look to conflict with one another. After seeing Yablo's way with that putative conflict it will be clear how one might reconcile confidence-first epistemology with the view that inference is driven by coordinated epistemic reasons.

In a nutshell, Yablo is concerned to underwrite the following three claims:

- Mental states cause things like doorbells to ring. (M-cause)
- Mental states are deep down micro-physical states. (Ground)
- Micro-physical states do not cause things like doorbells to ring. (¬Micro-Cause)

If mental states have everyday effects like the ringing of doorbells, though—in line with the first claim above—and mental states are deep down micro-physical states—in line with the second—it seems that micro-physical states must have everyday effects like the ringing of doorbells too, which conflicts with the third claim above. All three of the claims about mind and causation seem plausible to many in the philosophy of mind, and each of them have been vigorously defended in the literature. But the claims do seem to conflict with one another. What to do?

Yablo's reaction is a three-part affair.

First, he points out that philosophers' commitment to (Ground) is actually a commitment to the view that mental facts are constituted by microphysical facts in just the way that statues are constituted by matter, that cars are constituted by car-parts, that teams are constituted by players, and so forth. The relevant point here is an obvious one (at least on reflection): the notion of constitution in play allows for copies of the same kind to be built from different kinds of shaping material. One copy of Michaelangelo's _David_ might be built from marble, for instance, while another is built from bronze. One Dodge Dart might be built with red pieces of metal, while another is built with blue. One copy of England's football team might have David Beckham as a member while another does not. And so on. The kind of metaphysical building-up-from involved with (Ground) thus allows for a given mental kind to be built-up-from one kind of brain-state in humans, another kind of material state in Martians, and so on. In a nutshell: those who accept (Ground) endorse the idea that mental facts are *multiply realized* by micro-physical facts.

Second—and independently of his first point—Yablo argues that we should approach causation in broadly Humean terms. This means we should think of causation (give or take a bit) as some sort of *counterfactual dependence*. Whenever event C causes another event E, Humeans say basically that this consists in E depending on C counterfactually. And whenever event E depends on event C counterfactually, Humeans say basically that this consists in it being the case that E wouldn't have happened had C not happened. On this view—which is a tinker-toy version of a much more sophisticated story[13]—one event causes another event exactly when the other event wouldn't have happened had the one not occurred.

Third—and independently of his first two points—Yablo points out not only that everyday effects of mental events counterfactually depend on those events, but, also, that everyday effects of mental events do *not* counterfactually depend on the very precise micro-events which ground mental causes. Consider a real-world case which happened as I was writing this paragraph: my doorbell rang because a delivery woman decided to ring it. That decision was the cause of the ringing. But the decision itself was constituted by a complex array of very precise micro-events in the delivery woman's brain. Yablo's third point is then the following. The doorbell ringing counterfactually depends on the delivery woman's decision to ring it. Had she not decided to ring my doorbell, the ringing of my doorbell would not have occurred. But the ringing of my doorbell does *not* counterfactually depend on the very precise micro-events in the delivery woman's brain, the events which in fact ground her decision to ring my bell; for if those very precise grounding events had not occurred, similar micro-events would have occurred, and, as a result, would have constituted a decision to ring my doorbell (since decisions like that are multiply realized by distinct-but-similar brain events). If the delivery woman's brain had been different at the very precise micro-level, in other worlds, it would not have been so different that a different decision was taken on her part (say a decision to knock on the door rather than ring its bell, or to walk away altogether). If the delivery woman's brain had been different at the very precise micro-level, therefore, the bell would still have been rung. This means the ringing of my doorbell does not counterfactually depend on the very precise micro-events in the brain of the delivery woman who decided to ring the bell, even though her decision was metaphysically grounded in those very precise micro-events.

---

[13] This is very rough of course. Yablo has led the investigation of what kinds of counterfactual dependence are plausible candidates for causation, on a Humean approach to the phenomenon. See (Yablo, 1992), (Yablo, 1992), (Yablo, 2004), and other Yablo papers.

Yablo duly concludes that three things are true in the case: the delivery woman's decision to ring the doorbell caused the doorbell to ring; the delivery woman's decision to ring the doorbell was grounded in very precise micro-events in her brain; those grounding micro-events do not cause the doorbell to ring. Yablo reconciles these seemingly conflicting claims by appeal to multiple realization of the mental, a Humean approach to causation, and the fact that causal patterns of counterfactual dependence do not automatically 'flow down' the grounding relation.

Confidence-first epistemology is set up precisely to allow for the multiple realization of belief. Put another way: the position is designed to allow for situations in which two subjects each believe a particular claim—have belief-states with matching contents, but which are nothing but states of confidence deep down—yet lend distinct levels of confidence to the claims in play. Confidence-first epistemology sees coarse-grained attitudes (like belief) as nothing but multiply realized levels of confidence. This is one of its signature features. We might adopt a Yablo-style approach to causation, then, and craft a reaction to the puzzle before us in line with his reconciliation of (M-cause), (Ground), and (¬Micro-cause).

The position would begin with the thought that states of belief are multiply realized by states of confidence. It would then insist that causation is a particular pattern of counterfactual dependence, and, for this reason, that the exploitation of coordinated epistemic reasons involves exploitation of this pattern of dependence. The view would go on to note that such dependence does seem to play out between new states of belief and old ones on the basis of which they are inferred, but, crucially, that the relevant pattern of counterfactual dependence does *not* seem to hold between new states of belief and the confidence-theoretic grounds of old states of belief from which new ones are inferred.

For example, suppose you infer Q from P. On the conception of inference we're working with this fact about you involves two states of belief: belief in P and belief in Q. The conception also involves your belief in Q being based on your belief in P. This is the triggering of a coordinated epistemic reason—which in turn is just a fancy way of saying that your belief in Q is caused in the right way by your belief in P. Now suppose we add confidence-first epistemology to the mix and a Humean approach to mental causation. Then the following three things will be true:

- your belief in P causes your belief in Q
- your belief in P is deep down a state of confidence in P
- your state of confidence in P does not cause your belief in Q.

To see this in a working example, suppose that the realizers of your belief in P and your belief in Q are states of 99% credence. Then we can work up to a feel for the relevant theoretical move here by asking the following two questions:

Q1: would you have believed Q had you not believed P?
Q2: would you have believed Q had you not lent 99% credence to P?

The first question asks if belief in Q counterfactually depends on belief in P. The second question asks if belief in Q counterfactually depends on 99% credence being lent to P. It is plausible that the questions get different answers—or, at any rate, that this is so if a confidence-first epistemology is true which permits multiple realization of belief in confidence.

If you hadn't believed P, after all, confidence-first epistemology suggests you wouldn't have had confidence in P much like the confidence you actually have, since your confidence in P would have fallen below the belief-making threshold (rather than being healthily above it, we may suppose in the case). Were your confidence for P significantly lower than it actually is, however, you wouldn't have ended-up with a strong confidence in Q, so you wouldn't have ended-up with a confidence for Q which makes for belief. Hence confidence-first epistemology suggests that you wouldn't have believed Q had you not believed P.

On the other hand, if you hadn't lent 99% credence to P, confidence-first epistemology suggests that you would nevertheless have had a very similar credence for P. If you hadn't lent 99% credence for P, after all, the scenario most like the actual one in which you didn't lend 99% credence to P is a scenario in which you have basically the same evidence for P and basically the same reaction to it, only ever-so-slightly different, say because you lend 98.5% credence to P rather than 99% credence (or whatever). In those circumstances, though, you would have lent something exquisitely close to 99% credence to Q, since you would have had basically the same evidence for P and basically the same reaction to it. By confidence-first epistemology, therefore, if you hadn't lent 99% credence to P, you would still have believed Q, for you would still have lent a belief-making credence to P.

So the approach can say the following: when you infer Q from P your belief in Q counterfactually depends on your belief in P, but your belief in Q does not counterfactually depend on the confidence-theoretic ground of your belief in P. Hence we can put a Humean approach to causation with confidence-first epistemology and locate causal facts which play out between states of belief but not play out between states of confidence and states of belief. Although it may be true that mental-state-1 causes mental-state-2, and also true that mental-state-1 is grounded in very precise mental-state micro$_1$, it is nevertheless *not* true that micro$_1$ itself causes mental-state-2.

On this picture, belief-to-belief transition may in fact be the agential exploitation of a coordinated epistemic reason at the level of belief, and states of belief may in fact be fully realized by states of confidence, yet *no* transition from confidence to belief is the exploitation of a coordinated epistemic reason. It may be true that we reason with states of belief, therefore, and also true that states of belief are deep down nothing but states of confidence, yet it may be false that we reason with states of confidence. And if things work out this way, the puzzle before us is solved.

I am sympathetic to this reaction to the puzzle.[14] Naturally a thorough defence of Humeanism about causation is beyond the scope of this work. But there is obviously something right about the view that macro-states depend counterfactually on one another in ways that macro-states do not depend on micro-states (because of multiple realization). It ought to be possible, for this reason, to exploit the asymmetry

---

[14] For similar thoughts about macro-causation, developed independently, see the last section of (Sturgeon, 1994); and for further thoughts about this general topic see chapter 6 of (Sturgeon, 2000).

of counterfactual dependence and find truth in the idea that inference is a relation between belief states which does not hold between states of belief and very precise belief-makers, i.e. very precise states which ground belief. This means it ought to be possible to construct a Yablo-style reaction to the puzzle before us.

## 13.8 Rational Architecture

Having said that, I actually prefer an entirely different reaction to the puzzle before us, one which denies a puzzle-generating claim with which we began. Recall the three puzzle-generating claims:

>We reason with states of belief. (R-with-SoB)
>States of belief are deep down states of confidence. (Locke)
>We do not reason with states of confidence. (¬R-with-SoC)

My favoured reaction to the puzzle generated by the putative conflict between these claims rejects the view that we reason with our states of belief. As soon as we reject that view, of course, we no longer face a contradiction between three of our commitments. But we do still face a difficulty, for it's an adequacy condition on any reaction to the puzzle before us that our reaction to it be capable of explaining why puzzle-generating claims looks true in the first place. After rejecting the view that we reason with our states of belief, therefore, we must explain why it seemed that we reason with our states of belief in the first place.

The relevant thought about that is simple. The view that we reason with our states of belief is actually a *misreading* of an entirely different claim, a claim which looks obvious but is in fact ambiguous. The thought continues that this latter claim—the one which looks obvious but is in fact ambiguous—has a reading which *is* clearly true but leads to no difficulty in light of our other commitments, yet the ambiguous claim also has reading which is *not* clearly true and leads to contradiction when placed with those commitments. We're seduced into a puzzle, the story goes, because we mistakenly accept the claim which isn't clearly true and place it with our other commitments, thereby seeming to generate a contradiction, when really we're attracted only to the claim which is clearly true, the one which leads to no trouble in light of our other commitments. Why do we make this mistake? Because the claim which isn't clearly true sounds very like the claim which is clearly true. The puzzle gets off the ground, the story goes, because talk of belief is systematically ambiguous.

To see how this works consider the *reason-with-beliefs* principle:

>We reason with our beliefs. (R-with-B)

At first glance this principle looks pretty good, but it's really an equivocal piece of English. This is because talk of belief is ambiguous: sometimes it stands for the state of believing, other times it stands for the item believed (when one is in a state of believing). This is the notorious act-object ambiguity in talk of belief. On the former understanding of that talk it concerns the psychological state of belief—or, as it's sometimes put, the psychological act of believing. On the latter understanding of belief-talk it concerns the propositional content of the psychological state of belief. The reasons-with-belief principle can be heard in either of these ways. It has two salient interpretations.

Those interpretations are not equivalent. One of them contributes to the puzzle before us, the other one does not. One way to hear the claim that we reason with our beliefs, after all, is via the claim that we reason with our states of belief, in which case belief-states are inputs and outputs of inference. This claim looks to generate conflict when placed with our other commitments, since we think of belief-states as really states of confidence deep down, and we deny that we reason with states of confidence. Another way to hear the claim that we reason with our beliefs, though, is via the claim that we reason with propositions believed. Heard in this way the thought amounts to the reason-with-things-believed principle:

We reason with things believed.   (R-with-TB)

This is the view that we reason with propositions believed, that inference involves mental-state transition indexed by contents believed.

It is hard to see how *that* could be wrong (at least in bog-standard cases). Yet the agreeable view (R-with-TB) does not involve the hypothesis that inference itself is transition between psychological states of belief. It is rather only the weaker (and commensurately more agreeable) thought that inference is transition between psychological states indexed (i.e. individuated) by things believed, by propositions believed. It is not difficult to see how this latter view might be correct even though inference fails to be transition between psychological states of belief. Or at least it is not difficult to see this once a bit of elbow grease has been put to the task.

The first step in doing so is noticing that the theory of rational inference is but a tiny slice of a much larger story about rational shift-in-view. Even bog-standard cases of inference routinely involve more than inference-like transition between beliefs (no matter how beliefs are understood), for they routinely involve transition between perceptual states and epistemic commitment. This is what happens in the Sascha-Barcelona story told earlier, for instance, when you *become* convinced that Sascha is not in Paris. It is on the basis of testimony to that effect that you become so convinced. Yet the shift from reception of testimony to new opinion about its subject matter is not inference-like shift from belief to belief (again, no matter how belief is understood). It is rational transition from something-other-than-belief to belief.

Similarly, there are other types of rational shift-in-view which are not shifts from belief to belief. There are rational transitions from states of confidence to states of confidence, for instance, rational transitions from suppositional states to non-suppositional states (as in the last step of *reductio*). There are rational transitions from states of imagination to epistemic commitment (say when you work out how something will happen by pretending to see it happen); and perhaps rational transitions in the reverse direction (say when understanding something for the first time bestows and triggers the capacity to visualize it). In humans like us, anyway, there are multifarious kinds of rational shift-in-view. Epistemology's theory of inference is but a slice of a much larger pie.

Once you think about it, in fact, our rational architecture seems to manifest four major moving parts:

- *Perceptual States*— visual, tactile, auditory states, etc.
- *Standing Attitudes*— point-valued states of credence, thick confidence, belief, disbelief, suspended judgement, states of supposition, conditional states, etc.
- *States of Reasoning*—more on which anon.
- *Interest/Affect*—states of wonder if something is/has been/will be the case; states of worry if something is/ has been/will be the case; states of worry if something would happen were something else the case, etc.

And notionally, at least, this architecture can involve rational transition between each of its moving parts. So we can picture the set up with a box-like structure.

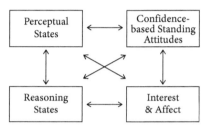

**Figure 13.2**

Each of the arrows here marks a notionally-possible type of rational shift-in-view. Many of them represent paths of influence which obviously occur in humans. Others represent paths hotly debated in psychology and in philosophy.

For instance, consider the direction of traffic which flows from perceptual states to states of confidence. It's clear that states of confidence are rationally influenced somehow by conscious perception of the world, though it's unclear how this works in detail. Do perceptual states connect directly to the world? If so, does that fact explain their rational impact on states of confidence? Do perceptual states rationally influence confidence only in tandem with background commitments? And so forth. No matter how these questions work out, it's clear that in some sense perceptual states rationally influence states of confidence. This is one of the most important and most obvious rational links in our cognitive life, a real driving force of everyday rationality. It is something of a scandal, then, that we do not have worked out theories of the rational path in question. An absolute must on our list of further topics in epistemology is the rational link *from* conscious experience *to* states of confidence.

Now consider the reverse direction of traffic, the one which flows from states of confidence to perceptual states. It is not at all obvious that the former rationally influence the latter. But it is notionally possible that there is such influence in that direction. Whether this notional possibility is more than merely notional is itself an on-again/off-again topic in psychology and in philosophy. For what it's worth I find empirical and philosophical work supporting the idea that there is rational influence—supporting, as one might put it, the existence of epistemically salient 'top-down' effects in human psychology, cases where background attitude and affect rationally influence how one perceives the world—very persuasive. But this is a contentious area of psychology as well as its epistemology. Whether we exhibit top-down effects at all in our cognitive architecture is an empirical issue for science to sort out (not a philosophical issue for us to sort out). If it turns out that we do undergo such effects, psychology will face a raft of further empirical questions about how those effects play out. But even if it turns out we do not undergo top-down effects, as a matter of empirical fact, it is still logically possible that we do, and, thus, it is philosophy's job to think through the epistemic significance of that logical possibility. It is not a priori that perceptual states are insulated from epistemic commitment or affect, after all, so philosophers should explore what it would mean for the theory of rationality if that insulation fails. This is another important element of our list of further topics in epistemology: we need a developed range of approaches to the rational impact that attitude and affect might have on the epistemic role of conscious experience.[15]

So it goes for each notionally-possible direction of traffic in Figure 13.2. The rational architecture depicted in that figure—box architecture, we'll call it—is not meant to answer every question we'd like to ask about sources of everyday rationality. It's meant only to make use of a richer conception of our mind than is often deployed in discussion of rational shift-in-view. In addition to perceptual states and standing propositional attitudes, for instance, box architecture makes use of standing reasoning states. One of the major goals of this chapter is to place lessons drawn earlier in the book, lessons about standing attitudes, with a sketch of autonomous reasoning states. So consider the topics in turn.

Earlier we defended a confidence-based approach to standing attitudes. We were liberal in our conception of confidence, of course—admitting multiple types of thick confidence, point-valued credence, and so on—but we were conservative in our approach to coarse-grained attitudes. In particular, we defended the view that belief is nothing but strong confidence of some kind. To a rough first approximation, the approach put forth maintained that what it is to believe a proposition is to invest sufficiently strong confidence in that proposition. But if that is right, belief is like being tall: just as one ends up being tall by manifesting a fine-grained height which is sufficiently large *in situ*, so it is on the view defended earlier that one ends up believing by investing confidence which is sufficiently strong *in situ*. States of belief are states of confidence deep down.

We need to place this approach to belief alongside an approach to autonomous reasoning states. This is easily done if we recall our friend Creda from §2.7:

Creda invests credence in whatever functional sense we do, and her states of credence are psychologically basic. Creda thinks in a language-like system of inner representations—a language-of-thought, so to say—and she has a gigantic transparent head. Within that head there are one hundred and one smaller transparent boxes, marked '0', '1', '2', etc. These are the

---

[15] For a philosophically sophisticated discussion of the psychological literature on top-down effects, see (Firestone & Scholl, 2016). For a trailblazing discussion of the epistemic issues surrounding that topic see (Siegel, 2017).

credence boxes of Creda's psychology. She lends $n$% credence to a claim C by placing a C-meaning sentence of her language-of-thought in the '$n$-box', i.e. the credal box marked '$n$'. We stipulate that whenever a C-meaning sentence is in Credas's $n$-box, she thereby manifests the signature function of $n$% credence lent to C. But this is just a fancy way of saying that Creda's boxes have a functional cash-value identical to that of credence.

Creda is a credence-based agent. She's unlike us in being able to lend only 101 varieties of credence, in contrast with the nuanced varieties we can lend. She's unlike us in failing to lend thick confidence too, in contrast with the varieties of thick confidence we lend all the time. In other key respects, though, Creda is very like us, for she is a confidence-based agent.

On the confidence-based approach to belief, therefore, Creda is capable of lending belief as well as investing credence, for Creda is capable of lending credence which is strong enough to ground belief. Not only does Creda invest credence as a matter of basic psychology, then—just as we do if the arguments of this book are sound—she also believes when credence is sufficiently strong—just as we do if those arguments are sound. In this way Creda is very like us when it comes to coarse- and fine-grained attitudes.

But how does she manage to infer or reason?

Here we add a new piece of architecture to Creda's psychology, something meant to mimic a crucial component of the box architecture proposed as our own. In addition to Creda's 101 credal boxes, then, we stipulate that she has a Reasoning Box too. And we think of this as a self-standing update mechanism. We see reasoning in Creda as computation on sentences in her language-of-thought, and we see that computation as taking place inside a Reasoning Box. We stipulate that whenever a sentence which means P is placed in Creda's Reasoning Box, a bit of reasoning is thereby sparked off, reasoning which launches from some kind of commitment to P.

Since there are various kinds of reasoning humans can go in for—belief-to-belief inference, for example, suppositional reasoning as in *reductio*, imagination-based reasoning as in thought-experiments, and so forth—and since Creda is meant to mimic our rational architecture in key respects, we add further details to the Reasoning-Box story. Those details make explicit the types of reasoning Creda can go in for. Naturally, we sculpt the whole thing to echo our types of reasoning.

We stipulate that whenever a sentence is put into Creda's Reasoning Box it is prefaced with a subscript. The subscript marks the kind of reasoning sparked off by the sentence being placed in Creda's Reasoning Box. When $\sigma$ is a sentence of her language-of-thought which means that it will snow tomorrow, for instance, not only does Creda lends $n$% credence to the claim that it will snow tomorrow by placing $\sigma$ in the credal box marked '$n$' in her head, we stipulate that when $\sigma$ is placed in her Reasoning Box, something of the form '$\_\sigma$' goes in there. We likewise stipulate that in such a case the subscripted blank is filled in with notation to make explicit the variety of reasoning undertaken by the subscripted $\sigma$ placed in the Reasoning Box.

For example, when Creda supposes it to be true that it will snow tomorrow, and then reasons from that supposition, we stipulate that she begins the unfolding sequence of mental states by placing '$_{sit}\sigma$' in her Reasoning Box. Since $\sigma$ means that it will snow tomorrow, the truth-theoretic content of the resulting psychological state—the state got by placing '$_{sit}\sigma$' in the Reasoning Box—is stipulated to be nothing but the claim that it will snow tomorrow. Since $\sigma$ is subscripted with 'sit', its placement in the Reasoning Box (so subscripted) is stipulated to yield a state the truth-theoretic content of which is treated as *supposed actually true*, rather than a content treated as accepted as true, or treated in some other way.

This is how we make explicit what occurs when a bit of suppositional reasoning in the indicative mood is sparked off in Creda.[16] The process begins with a sentence in her language-of-thought being placed in the Reasoning Box. The subscript 'sit' is attached to the front of the sentence to indicate that the sentence's content is taken in the indicative suppositional mood, so to say. Downstream reasoning (in that mood) takes place when new claims are inferred from old ones within the Reasoning Box. This occurs when new sentences of Creda's language-of-thought are tokened on the basis of old ones in her Reasoning Box, with everything chasing back to the placement of '$_{sit}\sigma$' in that box.

Consider a case in which Creda supposes it *were* true that it snows tomorrow, as opposed to one in which she supposes that it *is* true that it snows tomorrow. We stipulate that this involves Creda sparking-off a bit of suppositional reasoning by placing '$_{swt}\sigma$' in her Reasoning Box. Once again $\sigma$ means that it will snow tomorrow, so once again the content of the resulting psychological state is stipulated to be that it will snow tomorrow. This time $\sigma$ is subscripted with 'swt' rather than 'sit', though, so the relevant content is being treated as if it supposedly were true rather than as if it supposedly is true (or treated in some other way).

This makes explicit what occurs when a bit of suppositional reasoning in the subjunctive mood is sparked off in Creda. The process begins with a sentence of her language-of-thought being placed in the Reasoning Box. The sentence is subscripted to mark how its content is being taken. Downstream suppositional reasoning (in the subjunctive mood) then occurs when new claims are inferred from old ones in the Reasoning Box. This happens when new sentences of Creda's language-of-thought are tokened on the basis of old ones in the Reasoning Box, with everything chasing back to the placement of '$_{swt}\sigma$' in the box.

Suppose Creda lends strong credence to the claim that it will snow tomorrow. Since $\sigma$ is the sentence of her language-of-thought which means that it will snow tomorrow, Creda manages to lend strong credence to this claim by placing $\sigma$ in a strong credal-box. Just to illustrate, let that box be marked '99' in her head. Then Creda lends strong credence to the claim that it will snow tomorrow by lending 99% credence to that claim. Suppose this is enough to ground belief *in situ*. Then not only does Creda lend strong credence to the claim that it will snow tomorrow, she believes that it will snow tomorrow as well. Her credal state will ground a belief-state too.

The most important stipulation we'll make about Creda is then this: the fact that she believes something—by lending it sufficiently strong credence—is what *qualifies*

---

[16] See Chapters 3, 4, and 7 for suppositional reasoning and its relation to conditional credence.

the item believed for use in her Reasoning Box; and when that use happens the vehicle in Creda's language-of-thought which has the item believed as its content will be subscripted to indicate that the content is to be treated as actually true, and the resulting subscripted sentence will itself be injected into the Reasoning Box. We may suppose that this is what happens when Creda becomes interested, for whatever reason, in chasing down the upshot of one of her beliefs.

This all means that we're thinking of Creda as a sub-optimal agent. Like us she is someone who has neither the time nor the capacity nor the inclination to work out all of the (potentially defeasible) consequences of what she believes. From time to time, though, she is prompted to better her epistemic position, for whatever reason, to work through some of those consequences. When this happens she goes in for a bit of reasoning. She chains together steps of inference in her Reasoning Box.

Let's work through an example.

We've stipulated that Creda is 99% sure that it will snow tomorrow, that her confidence in this claim is sufficient for belief *in situ*, and that $\sigma$ is the sentence in her language-of-thought which has this claim as its content. Suppose Creda becomes interested in the upshot of her view that it will snow tomorrow—in particular, suppose she wonders how long it's been since it snowed on tomorrow's date. We stipulate that Creda also believes two further things: that tomorrow is in the year 2019, and that it hasn't snowed on tomorrow's date since 1900. In the event, she reasons from three extant commitments to a view which answers the question interest in which sparks off the reasoning. Creda puts together her view that it will snow tomorrow with her view that tomorrow is in the year 2019, throws into the mix her view that it hasn't snowed on tomorrow's date since 1900, and infers from these ingredients that it hasn't snowed on tomorrow's date for 119 years. This latter claim answers the question interest in which prompted inference in the first place.

Three sentences in Creda's language-of-thought drive the example:

- $\sigma$, which means that it will snow tomorrow;
- $\sigma^*$, which means that tomorrow is in the year 2019;
- $\sigma^{**}$, which means that it last snowed on tomorrow's date in 1900.

Creda invests belief-level credence in claims which are the meanings of these sentences, for she places each of them in a strong-enough credal box. Then Creda becomes interested in how long it has been since it last snowed on tomorrow's date. We think of this as an interrogative sentence being placed in her Interest Box. This new state of interest prompts Creda to inject $_{true}\sigma$, $_{true}\sigma^*$, and $_{true}\sigma^{**}$ into her Reasoning Box. From there she tokens a new sentence in that box—subscripted with 'true'—on the basis of the three sentences placed in the Reasoning Box. This new sentence means that it hasn't snowed on tomorrow's date for 119 years. It's placement in the Reasoning Box, subscripted with 'true', on the basis of $_{true}\sigma$ and $_{true}\sigma^*$ and $_{true}\sigma^{**}$, amounts to an inference by Creda to the view that it hasn't snowed on tomorrow's date for 119 years. This inference is taken from three of Creda's beliefs: that it will snow tomorrow, that tomorrow is in 2019, and that it last snowed on tomorrow's date in 1900.

If we assume that Creda has perceptual states like we do, we can see her as strongly approximating the box architecture proposed here as our own. Recall that architecture has four major elements.

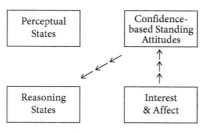

Figure 13.3

Arrows above indicate how elements of Creda's architecture interact in the case before us. Interest in the answer to a particular question prompts three states of confidence-grounded belief to inject their contents into the Reasoning Box. In turn this then sparks off an inference to a content which answers the question prompting cognition in the first place.

Creatures like Creda manifest rational architecture built from four basic ingredients: perceptual states, levels of confidence, states of affect or interest, states of reason. It is a matter of stipulation that Creda manifests psychological architecture like this. It is one of the major proposals of this book that we do so as well. When it comes to everyday rationality, then—the kind humans perforce chase via inference—my proposal is that we are creatures like Creda. We make use of perceptual states, states of confidence, states of affect and interest, and states of reasoning. Inference takes place between tokens of the last kind of state. Reasoning-states are the *relata* of inference.

If this picture of our rational architecture is on the right track, we reason with our beliefs in one sense but not in another. Our states of reasoning do very often have contents which we believe, so, in that sense, we reason with our beliefs. But we do not reason with our beliefs in the sense that our states of belief are inferential *relata*. That cuts against the picture of rational architecture defended here.

## 13.9 Rational Shift-in-View

Note how this picture makes for a nice reply to a powerful worry about confidence-based belief. Here is Stalnaker expressing the worry:

One could easily enough define a concept of belief which identified it with high subjective or epistemic probability (probability greater than some specified number between one-half and one), but it is not clear what the point of doing so would be. Once a subjective or epistemic probability value is assigned to a proposition, there is nothing more to be said about its epistemic status. Bayesian decision theory gives a complete account of how probability values, including high ones, ought to guide behaviour... So what could be the point of selecting an interval near the top of the probability scale and conferring on the propositions whose probability falls in that interval the honorific title 'believed'?[17]

I am sympathetic to the motivation behind this worry. Defenders of confidence-based belief must do more than articulate their point of view. They must also articulate the point of their view. Inter alia this means they must specify the explanatory work done by confidence-based belief. The worry is that there is no work to be done, that confidence-based belief is an explained non-explainer, so to say, something which explains nothing but is itself explained by confidence.

Let us grant that this is so for ideally rational agents, just to get the ball rolling. Even granting this much it is decidedly *not* so for sub-optimal agents like Creda. After all, we have defined her mental capacities so that she cannot approximate the Bayesian model: not only is it psychologically impossible for her to lend credence even roughly in line with that model, it is psychologically impossible for her to update credence that way too. By stipulation Creda is far from capable of being accurately described by the Bayesian theory of states or the Bayesian transition theory.

This is important.

When it comes to everyday rationality, after all—the kind of rationality central to the epistemology of inference—psychological capacities limit how agents should be if they're to be rational. It is unclear how psychological capacities do this, of course, but we can say this about that without lapsing into worrisome hostage to fortune. Whenever an agent's credence should turn out a certain way—whenever it should satisfy a given structural constraint, for instance, or be shifted in line with a given update rule—the agent must be psychologically capable of at least roughly configuring credence as it's supposed to be configured, and the agent must be psychologically capable of at least roughly changing credence as it's supposed to be changed. For any condition C whatsoever, that is to say, if an agent must satisfy C to be rational in the everyday way, the agent must be capable of coming close to the satisfaction of C. So if an agent cannot come even remotely close to approximating C, that condition is no constraint on her everyday rationality.

This has sharp implications for Creda's everyday rationality. After all, it entails that each way credence cannot even roughly be for Creda—each way ruled far out of bounds by her psychological capacities—is a way for credence to be which it needn't be if Creda is to be everyday rational. If Creda cannot even remotely come close to being a certain way psychologically, in other words, that way of being isn't required for her everyday rationality. Similarly, each way credence cannot even roughly be updated by Creda—each type of update ruled far out of bounds by her psychological capacities—is a way for credence to be updated which it needn't be updated if an update by Creda is to be everyday rational. If Creda cannot even remotely come close to updating a certain way psychologically, in other words, that way of updating isn't required for her everyday rationality.

By stipulation, though, it is not possible for Creda to distribute credence in a way which comes remotely close to satisfying the laws of probability. We have defined her

---

[17] (Stalnaker, 1984: 138).

so that this condition far outstrips her psychological capacities. The only circumstances in which she can roughly approximate probabilistic laws are those in which she is dealing with a tiny number of claims, and even then the approximation is super rough. In all other cases we've stipulated that she is entirely incapable of even roughly approximating probabilistic laws. The claims involved in her doing so are simply too great for her to manage the task. Hence those laws do not specify structural constraints on the everyday rationality of credence in Creda. They may specify structural constraints on her credence in some hyper-idealized way; and it may be that restrictions on them specify structural constraints on her everyday rationality. But the laws of probability as such do not constrain her everyday rationality, for she cannot come remotely close to satisfying them.

Similarly, it is not possible for Creda to update credence in a way which comes remotely close to satisfying Jeffrey's rule, for we have made sure that such an update far outstrips her psychological capacities. The only circumstances in which she can remotely approximate the rule are those in which she's dealing with a tiny number of claims, and even then the approximation is likewise super rough. In all other cases we stipulate that Creda is utterly incapable of coming remotely close to approximating a Bayesian update. The mental-movements needed to do so are simply too great for her to manage. Hence Jeffrey's rule does not specify a structural constraint on the everyday rationality of update in Creda. It may specify a structural constraint in some hyper-idealized way; and it may be that restriction on Jeffrey's rule yields constraints on her everyday rationality too. But Jeffrey's rule itself does not constrain her everyday rationality, for Creda cannot come even remotely close to its approximation.

To the extent we think general rules like those found in the Bayesian model have something to do with rational credence for Creda, therefore—in the everyday sense of rationality central to the theory of inference—we should think of those rules as applying via some kind of principles of restriction. And we should insist that such principles satisfy two desiderata:

- they should yield clear, workable constraints on the configuration or update of credence;
- those constraints should be close to psychologically possible for Creda, i.e. she should be roughly capable of satisfying them.

Principles of restriction like this will yield workable constraints on how Creda is permitted to be credence-wise. They will also generate methods for determining how far from heavily-idealized norms—like those found in the Bayesian model—Creda is permitted to go, so to say, consistent with her being rational in the everyday way. Hence principles of restriction like this will amount to a theory of everyday rationality for Creda.

But what goes for Creda goes for humans as well.

It is a matter of empirical fact that we cannot distribute credence in a manner which comes even remotely close to satisfying the laws of probability. As it happens our psychological capacities fall far short of that demand. We can sometimes lend credence roughly in line with the theory, but only when dealing with a tiny number of claims (and thus a tiny fraction of theory). In all other cases we are utterly incapable of approximating probabilistic laws. Hence those laws do not specify structural constraints on the everyday rationality of our credence. Restrictions on them may do so, of course—or they may not, as the case may be—but the actual laws themselves, the laws of probability theory as such, are not laws of our everyday rationality.

Similarly, it is a matter of empirical fact that humans cannot update credence remotely in line with Jeffrey's rule. As it happens our psychological capacities fall far short of that demand. We can sometimes update roughly in line with the rule, but only when dealing with a tiny number of claims (and hence not actually much in line with the rule). In all other cases we happen to be utterly incapable of approximating Jeffrey conditionalization. Hence Jeffrey's rule does not state a constraint on the everyday rationality of our shift in credence. Restrictions on it may do so, of course—or they may not, as the case may be—but Jeffrey conditionalization itself is no law of our everyday rationality.

To the extent we think general rules like those found in the Bayesian model have something to do with our rational credence, therefore—in the everyday sense of rationality central to the theory of inference—we should think of those rules as applying via some kind of principles of restriction. And here too we should insist that such principles satisfy two desiderata:

- they should yield clear, workable constraints on the configuration or update of our credence;
- those constraints should be close to psychologically possible for us, i.e. we should be roughly capable of satisfying them.

Principles of restriction like this will yield workable constraints on how we are permitted to be credence-wise. They will also generate methods for determining how far from heavily-idealized norms—like those found in the Bayesian model—we are permitted to go, so to say, consistent with our being rational in the everyday way. Hence principles of restriction like this will amount to a theory of our everyday rationality. In my view concocting such principles is the most important task to be done in epistemology.

# Bibliography

Adams, E. W. (1996). *The Logic of Conditionals: An Application of Probability to Deductive Logic*. D. Reidel Publishing Company.
Adams, E. W. (1998). *A Primer of Probability Logic*. Stanford: Csli Publications.
Baker, L. R. (2009). Non-Reductive Materialism. In A. Beckermann, B. P. McLaughlin, & S. Walter (eds), *The Oxford Handbook of Philosophy of Mind*. Oxford University Press.
Beebee, H., & Papineau, D. (1997). Probability as a Guide to Life. *Journal of Philosophy*, 94(5), 217–43.
Bennett, J. (2003). *A Philosophical Guide to Conditionals*. Oxford: Oxford University Press.
Chalmers, D. (2012). *Constructing the World*. Oxford: Oxford University Press.
Chang, R. (2015). *Making Comparisons Count*. Routledge.
Chisholm, R. M. (1966). *Theory of Knowledge*. Englewood Cliffs, NJ: Prentice-Hall.
Christensen, D. (2004). *Putting Logic in its Place: Formal Constraints on Rational Belief*. Oxford: Oxford University Press.
Cook, R. T. (2002). Vagueness and Mathematical Precision. *Mind*, 111(422), 225–47.
Correia, F., & Schnieder, B. (eds). (2012). *Metaphysical Grounding: Understanding the Structure of Reality*. Cambridge University Press.
Crane, T. (1995). The Mental Causation Debate. *Proceedings of the Aristotelian Society*, 69, 211–36.
Crane, T. (2001). *Elements of Mind: An Introduction to the Philosophy of Mind*. Oxford: Oxford University Press.
Cummins, R. C. (1996). *Representations, Targets, and Attitudes*. MIT Press.
Davidson, D. (1970). Mental Events. In L. Foster, & J. W. Swanson (eds), *Essays on Actions and Events* (pp. 207–24). Clarendon Press.
Dorr, C. (2010). The Eternal Coin: A Puzzle about Self-locating Conditional Credence. *Philosophical Perspectives*, 24(1), 189–205.
Edgington, D. (1986). Do Conditionals Have Truth-Conditions. *Critica*, 18(52), 3–30.
Edgington, D. (1995). On Conditionals. *Mind*, 104(414), 235–329.
Edgington, D. (1996). Lowe On Conditional Probability. *Mind*, 105(420), 617–30.
Edgington, D. (1997). Commentary. In M. Woods, *Conditionals* (pp. 95–137). Oxford University Press.
Edgington, D. (1997). Vagueness by Degrees. In R. Keefe, & P. Smith (eds), *Vagueness: A Reader*. MIT Press.
Edgington, D. (2014, 2 October). Indicative Conditionals. Retrieved from *Stanford Encyclopedia of Philosophy*, https://plato.stanford.edu/entries/conditionals/
Ehring, D. (1996). Mental Causation, Determinables, and Property Instances. *Noûs*, 30(4), 461–80.
Enderton, H. B. (1977). *Elements of Set Theory*. Elsevier Science.
Field, H. (2003). No Fact of the Matter. *Australasian Journal of Philosophy*, 81(4), 457–80.
Fine, T. L. (1973). *Theories of Probability: An Examination of Foundations*. Academic Press.
Firestone, C., & Scholl, B. J. (2016, January). Cognition Does Not Affect Perception: Evaluating the Evidence for 'Top-Down' Effects. *Behavioral and Brain Sciences*, 39, 1–72.
Fitelson, B. (2013). Gibbard's Collapse Theorem for the Indicative Conditional: An Axiomatic Approach. In M. Bonacina, & M. Stickel (eds), *Automated Reasoning and Mathematics: Essays in Memory of William W. McCune*. Springer.

Fitelson, B., & Easwaran, K. (2015). Accuracy, Coherence, and Evidence. *Oxford Studies in Epistemology*, 5, 61–96.
Fodor, J. A. (1975). *The Language of Thought*. Harvard University Press.
Fodor, J. A. (1990). Making Mind Matter More. In J. A. Fodor, *A Theory of Content and Other Essays*. MIT Press.
Foley, R. (1992). The Epistemology of Belief and the Epistemology of Degrees of Belief. *American Philosophical Quarterly*, 29(2), 111–24.
Frankish, K. (2009). Partial Belief and Flat-out Belief. In F. Huber, & C. Schmidt-Petri (eds), *Degrees of Belief* (pp. 75–93). Springer.
Frege, G. (1948, May). Sense and Reference. *The Philosophical Review*, 57(3), 209–230.
Friedman, J. (2013a). Rational Agnosticism and Degrees of Belief. In T. S. Gendler, & J. Hawthorne (eds), *Oxford Studies in Epistemology* (Vol. 4). Oxford: Oxford University Press.
Friedman, J. (2013b). Suspended Judgment. *Philosophical Studies*, 162(2), 165–81.
Gardenfors, P. (1986). Belief Revisions and the Ramsey Test for Conditionals. *Philosophical Review*, 95(1), 81–93.
Gardenfors, P. (1988). *Knowledge in Flux: Modelling the Dymanics of Epistemic States*. MIT Press.
Gibbard, A. (1981). Two Recent Theories of Conditionals. In W. Harper, R. C. Stalnaker, & G. Pearce (eds), *Ifs* (pp. 211–47). D. Reidel Publishing Company.
Greaves, H., & Wallace, D. (2005). Justifying Conditionalization: Conditionalization Maximizes Expected Epistemic Utility. *Mind*, 115(459), 607–32.
Hájek, A. (1998). Agnosticism Meets Bayesianism. *Analysis*, 58(3), 199–206.
Hacking, I. (1995). *The Emergence of Probability*. Cambridge: Cambridge University Press.
Halpern, J. Y. (2003). *Reasoning About Uncertainty*. MIT Press.
Harman, G. H. (1970). Induction: A Discussion of the Relevance of the Theory of Knowledge to the Theory of Induction (with a Digression to the Effect that neither Deductive Logic nor the Probability Calculus has Anything to Do with Inference). In M. Swain (ed.), *Induction, Acceptance, and Rational Belief* (pp. 83–99). Dordrecht: D. Reidel Publishing Company.
Harman, G. H. (1986). *Change in View*. MIT Press.
Hawthorne, J., & Bovens, L. (1999). The Preface, the Lottery, and the Logic of Belief. *Mind*, 108(430), 241–64.
Holton, R. (2014). Intention as a Model for Belief. In M. Vargas, & G. Yaffe (eds), *Rational and Social Agency: Essays on the Philosophy of Michael Bratman*. Oxford University Press.
Honderich, T. (1982, January). The Argument for Anomalous Monism. *Analysis*, 42(4), 59–64.
Horty, J. F. (2014). *Reasons as Defaults*. New York: Oxford University Press.
Jeffrey, R. (1965). *The Logic of Decision*. University of Chicago Press.
Jeffrey, R. (1970). Dracula Meets Wolfman: Acceptance vs. Partial Belief. In M. Swain (ed.), *Induction, Acceptance, and Rational Belief* (pp. 157–85). D. Reidel Publishing Company.
Jeffrey, R. (1983). Bayesianism with a Human Face. In J. Earman (ed.), *Testing Scientific Theories* (pp. 133–56). University of Minnesota Press.
Joyce, J. (1998). A Nonpragmatic Vindication of Probabilism. *Philosophy of Science*, 65(4), 575–603.
Joyce, J. (2005). How Probabilities Reflect Evidence. *Philosophical Perspectives*, 19(1), 153–78.
Joyce, J. (2010). A Defense of Imprecise Credences in Inference and Decision Making. *Philosophical Perspectives*, 24(1), 281–323.
Kaplan, M. (1983). Decision Theory as Philosophy. *Philosophy of Science*, 50(4), 549–77.
Kaplan, M. (2005). Decision Theory and Epistemology. In P. K. Moser (ed.), *The Oxford Handbook of Epistemology*. Oxford University Press.
Keynes, J. M. (1921). A Treatise on Probability. *Journal of Philosophy*, 20(11), 301–6.

Kim, J. (1984). Epiphenomenal and Supervenient Causation. *Midwest Studies in Philosophy*, 9(1), 257-70.
Kolmogorov, A. N. (1933). *Grundbegriffe der Warscheilichkeitsrechnung*. Berlin: Springer.
Korcz, K. A. (1996). *The Epistemic Basing Relation*. Dissertation, The Ohio State University.
Kripke, S. A. (1980). *Naming and Necessity*. (M. Gilbert, ed.) Cambridge, MA: Harvard University Press.
Kvanvig, J. L., & Menzel, C. (1990). The Basic Notion of Justification. *Philosophical Studies*, 59(3), 235-61.
Kyburg, H. E. (1998). Interval-Valued Probabilities. Henry E. Kyburg, Jr. and the Imprecise Probabilities Project: http://www.sipta.org/documentation/interval_prob/kyburg.pdf
Lance, M. N. (1995). Subjective Probability and Acceptance. *Philosophical Studies*, 77(1), 147-79.
Lasonen-Aarnio, M. (2010). Is There a Viable Account of Well-Founded Belief? *Erkenntnis*, 72(2), 205-31.
Lehrer, K. (1974). *Knowledge*. Clarendon Press.
Leitgeb, H. (2014). The Stability Theory of Belief. *Philosophical Review*, 123(2), 131-71.
Levi, I. (1974). On Indeterminate Probabilities. *Journal of Philosophy*, 71(13), 391-418.
Levi, I. (1977). Subjunctives, Dispositions and Chances. *Synthese*, 34(4), 423-55.
Lewis, D. (1966). An Argument for the Identity Theory. *Journal of Philosophy*, 63(1), 17-25.
Lewis, D. (1976). Probabilities of Conditionals and Conditional Probabilities. *Philosophical Review*, 85(3), 297-315.
Lewis, D. (1980). A Subjectivist's Guide to Objective Chance. In R. C. Jeffrey (ed.), *Studies in Inductive Logic and Probability, Volume II* (pp. 263-93). Berkeley: University of California Press.
Lewis, D. (1994). Humean Supervenience Debugged. *Mind*, 103(412), 473-90.
Lewis, D. (1994). Reduction of Mind. In S. Guttenplan (ed.), *Companion to the Philosophy of Mind* (pp. 412-31). Blackwell.
List, C., & Pettit, P. (2011). *Group Agency: The Possibility, Design, and Status of Corporate Agents*. Oxford: Oxford University Press.
Loar, B. (1981). *Mind and Meaning*. Cambridge University Press.
Maher, P. (2008). *Betting on Theories*. Cambridge University Press.
Matthews, R. J. (1994). The Measure of Mind. *Mind*, 103(410), 131-46.
McGee, V. (1989). Conditional Probabilities and Compounds of Conditionals. *Philosophical Review*, 98(4), 485-541.
McGee, V. (1994). Learning the Impossible. In E. Eells, & B. Skyrms (eds), *Probability and Conditionals: Belief Revision and Rational Decision* (pp. 179-99). Cambridge University Press.
McGinn, C., & Hopkins, J. (1978). Mental States, Natural Kinds and Psychophysical Laws. *Aristotelian Society Supplementary Volume*, 52(1), 195-236.
McLaughlin, B. P. (1995). Varieties of Supervenience. In E. E. Savellos, & Ü. D. Yalçin (eds), *Supervenience: New Essays* (pp. 16-59). Cambridge University Press.
Mellor, D. H. (2012). *Mind, Meaning, and Reality: Essays in Philosophy*. Oxford: Oxford University Press.
Millikan, R. G. (2000). Review: Representations, Targets and Attitudes. *Philosophy and Phenomenological Research*, 60(1), 103-11.
Moore, R. E. (1966). *Interval Analysis*. Prentice-Hall.
Nozick, R. (1990). *The Normative Theory of Individual Choice*. Garland.
Pettigrew, R. (2012). Accuracy, Chance, and the Principal Principle. *Philosophical Review*, 121(2), 241-75.
Pollock, J. L. (1986). Contemporary Theories of Knowledge. *Philosophy and Phenomenological Research*, 49(1), 167-71.

Pollock, J. L. (1987). Defeasible Reasoning. *Cognitive Science*, 11(4), 481–518.
Pollock, J. L. (1995). *Cognitive Carpentry*. MIT Press.
Popper, K. R. (1959). *The Logic of Scientific Discovery*. Routledge.
Pryor, J. (2000). The Skeptic and the Dogmatist. *Noûs*, 34(4), 517–49.
Pryor, J. (2013). Problems for Credulism. In Chris Tucker (ed.), *Seemings and Justification: New Essays on Dogmatism and Phenomenal Conservatism*. Oxford University Press.
Ramsey, F. P. (1925/1990). Truth and Probability. In F. P. Ramsey, & D. H. Mellor (eds), *Philosophical Papers* (pp. 52–109). Cambridge: Cambridge University Press.
Ramsey, F. P. (1990). General Propositions and Causality. In F. P. Ramsey, & N.-E. Sahlin (eds), *The Philosophy of F.P. Ramsey*. Cambridge University Press.
Rawls, J. (1999). *A Theory of Justice*. Harvard University Press.
Rayo, A. (2011). A Puzzle About Ineffable Propositions. *Australasian Journal of Philosophy*, 89(2), 289–95.
Rinard, S. (2017). Imprecise Probability and Higher Order Vagueness. *Res Philosophica*, 94(2), 257–73.
Ripley, D. (2011). Negation, Denial, and Rejection. *Philosophy Compass*, 6(9), 622–29.
Rosen, G. (2009). Metaphysical Dependence: Grounding and Reduction. In B. Hale, & A. Hoffmann (eds), *Modality: Metaphysics, Logic, and Epistemology* (pp. 109–36). Oxford University Press.
Rumfitt, I. (2000, October). 'Yes' and 'No'. *Mind*, 109(436), 781–823.
Sainsbury, R. M. (1996). Concepts Without Boundaries. In R. Keefe, & P. Smith (eds), *Vagueness: A Reader* (pp. 186–205). MIT Press.
Schiffer, S. R. (1981). Truth and the Theory of Content. In H. Parret (ed.), *Meaning and Understanding*. De Gruyter.
Schiffer, S. R. (1987). *Remnants of Meaning*. MIT Press.
Schiffer, S. R. (2003). *The Things We Mean*. Oxford: Oxford University Press.
Schmidtz, D. (2011). Nonideal Theory: What It Is and What It Needs to Be. *Ethics*, 121(4), 772–96.
Schnieder, B., Hoeltje, M., & Steinberg, A. (eds). (2013). *Varieties of Dependence: Ontological Dependence, Grounding, Supervenience, Response-Dependence (Basic Philosophical Concepts)*. Philosophia Verlag.
Schoenfield, M. (2013). Permission to Believe: Why Permissivism Is True and What It Tells Us About Irrelevant Influences on Belief. *Noûs*, 47(1), 193–218.
Sen, A. (2009). *The Idea of Justice*. Belknap Press of Harvard University Press.
Shafer, G. (1976). *A Mathematical Theory of Evidence*. Princeton University Press.
Siegel, S. (2017). *The Rationality of Perception*. Oxford: Oxford University Press.
Spohn, W. (2012). *The Laws of Belief: Ranking Theory and its Philosophical Applications*. Oxford: Oxford University Press.
Stalnaker, R. (1984). *Inquiry*. Cambridge University Press.
Stanley, J. (2005). *Knowledge and Practical Interests*. Oxford: Oxford University Press.
Stemplowska, Z., & Swift, A. (2012). *Ideal and Nonideal Theory*. In D. Estlund (ed.). Oxford University Press.
Stich, S. P. (1996). *Deconstructing the Mind*. New York: Oxford University Press.
Sturgeon, S. (1987). Foley on Causation and Rationality. *Analysis*, 47(1), 62–4.
Sturgeon, S. (1994). Good Reasoning and Cognitive Architecture. *Mind and Language*, 9(1), 88–101.
Sturgeon, S. (1998). Visual Experience. *Proceedings of the Aristotelian Society*, 72(2), 179–200.
Sturgeon, S. (2000a). *Matters of Mind: Consciousness, Reason and Nature*. Routledge.
Sturgeon, S. (2000b). Michael Woods: 'Conditionals' (Book Review). *Mind*, 109(433), 179.
Sturgeon, S. (2002). Conditional Belief and the Ramsey Test. *Royal Institute of Philosophy Supplement* (51), 215–32.

Sturgeon, S. (2008). Disjunctivism About Visual Experience. In A. Haddock, & F. Macpherson (eds), *Disjunctivism: Perception, Action, Knowledge* (pp. 112-43). Oxford University Press.
Sturgeon, S. (2010). Confidence and Coarse-Grained Attitudes. In T. S. Gendler, & J. Hawthorne (eds), *Oxford Studies in Epistemology* (pp. 3-126). Oxford: Oxford University Press.
Sturgeon, S. (2019). Undercutting Defeat and Edgington's Burglar. In L. Walters, & J. Hawthorne (eds), *Conditionals, Probability & Paradox: themes from the Philosophy of Dorothy Edgington*. Oxford: Oxford University Press.
Sturgeon, S. (2018). Epistemology, Pettigrew Style. *Mind*.
Swinburne, R. (2001). *Epistemic Justification*. Oxford: Oxford University Press.
Trommershauser, J., Kording, K., & Landy, M. (eds). (2011). *Sensory Cue Integration*. Oxford: Oxford University Press.
Urbach, P., & Howson, C. (1993). *Scientific Reasoning: The Bayesian Approach*. Open Court Publishing Company.
Valentini, L. (2012). Ideal vs. Non-ideal Theory: A Conceptual Map. *Philosophy Compass*, 7(9), 654-64.
van Fraassen, B. (1985). Empiricism in the Philosophy of Science. In P. Churchland & C. Hooker (eds), *Images of Science*. Chicago: University of Chicago Press.
van Fraassen, B. (1989). Symmetries of Probability Kinematics. In B. van Fraassen, *Laws and Symmetry* (pp. 318-48). Oxford: Clarendon Press.
van Fraassen, B. (1990). Figures in a Probability Landscape. In J. Dunn, & A. Gupta (eds), *Truth or Consequences* (pp. 345-56). Kluwer Academic Publishers.
Walley, P. (1991). *Statistical Reasoning with Imprecise Probabilities*. London: Chapman & Hall.
White, R. (2005). Epistemic Permissiveness. *Philosophical Perspectives*, 19(2), 445-59.
White, R. (2009). Evidential Symmetry and Mushy Credence. In T. S. Gendler, & J. Hawthorne (eds), *Oxford Studies in Epistemology* (pp. 161-86). Oxford: Oxford University Press.
Williamson, T. (2000). *Knowledge and its Limits*. Oxford: Oxford University Press.
Wilson, J. (2017, 7 February). Determinables and Determinates. *Retrieved from Stanford Encyclopedia of Philosophy:* https://plato.stanford.edu/entries/determinate-determinables/
Woods, M. (1997). *Conditionals*. Oxford: Oxford University Press.
Wright, C. (2001). On Being in a Quandary. *Mind*, 110(437), 45-98.
Yablo, S. (1992). Cause and Essence. *Synthese*, 93(3), 403-49.
Yablo, S. (1992). Mental Causation. *Philosophical Review*, 101(2), 245-80.
Yablo, S. (2014). *Aboutness*. Princeton University Press.

# Index

*Note*: Figures are indicated by an Italic '*f*', respectively following page numbers.

Adams, E. 111 n., 262 n.
AGM (Alchourrón-Gärdenfors-Makinson) Model, *see* Belief Model
agreement strategy 94–5
Alchourrón, Carlos 3, 155, 175
alethic items 211–16
ALIEN THREAT 137–42
antecedents 109, 119, 120, 132, 135, 136, 138, 139, 141, 177, 199, 207, 211
  alethic items associated with 212
  causal 334
  conjunctive 121
  explicitly contradictory 122
  fact-stating 108
  *see also* Unconditional Antecedents Assumption
APA (American Philosophical Association) 224 n.
assumptions:
  alignment 159, 160–2
  binary-attitude 5, 9, 11, 78 n., 109, 110
  cash-value 5, 183, 237–9, 251, 253, 285
  matching-models 8–9
  nature-before-norms 4, 335
  plausible 261
  rationality-of-states 6
  rationality-of-transitions 6–7, 322
  specific 4
  standard 261
  unconditional antecedents 123–4, 127, 128
  updating 113, 133, 134
Attitude box 238–9
attitudes:
  antecedent-to-learning 313
  eliminativism about 229
  force-based 272–87
  heavily-neutral 301
  realism about 256
  talk of 257
  *see also* coarse-grained attitudes; epistemic attitudes; fine-grained attitudes; propositional attitudes; tertiary attitudes
attraction and repulsion 277, 279–80, 307, 318, 320
  gustatory 273 n.

Baker, L. R. 240 n.
Ball Game 25–48
  *see also* Red-spotted balls

basing relation 104, 310 n.
  inference and 330–6
Bayes, Thomas 3, 19
Bayesian Credence 9, 22, 59, 86
  Ball Game and 40–5
Bayesian kinematics 101
  conditionality and 124–9; restricted-vision 142–7
Bayesian Model 3, 7, 8*f*, 11, 19–61, 75–7, 80–2, 101, 102, 110, 118, 126, 150, 152, 156, 198, 200, 208, 291, 354
  adding left-out bits of common sense to 67
  additivity thought is the bedrock 281
  bad news for 125, 131
  basic assumption of 62
  basic introduction to 9
  conditional credence in 10; role of 111
  conditional probability derivative in 146 n.
  conditionality in 111–16; restricted-vision and 124, 154
  confidence found in 13
  counter-instance to 132
  general rules found in 355, 356
  generalizing 85, 86; initial strategy discussed for 83; interval-based 87, 90
  Jeffrey's Rule for updating confidence in 10
  major problems raised for 10
  putting a human face on 65
  Ramsey's norm and 121, 125, 127
  ratio norm of 109
  rigidity in 111–16, 128
  Updating Assumption of 133
Bayesian theory of states 19–25, 28, 29, 44, 47, 55, 61–100, 111, 354
  backbone of 27, 45
  Creda far from capable of being accurately described 354
  credence function in 59, 60
  critical discussion of 9
  full 48
  fundamental law in 42–3
Bayesian transition theory 9–11, 41*f*, 245, 354
  critical discussion of 101–54
  equation central to 51
  game used to develop feel for 48
  Jeffrey's Rule 53–8
  principle central to 56
Beebee, H. 315 n.
belief-first creatures 237, 238, 241, 242

Belief Model 3, 7f, 25, 59 n., 155-79, 198
  basic introduction to 9
  critical discussion of 11, 180-96
  guiding principles of conservatism in 11
  rationality in an agent matches 11
  transition theory 11, 155, 158-63, 165, 173-80, 189-96
Belief Model's theory of states 155-8, 176-80, 186
  discussion of how to revise 11
  fine-grained analogue of enrichment of 63 n.
  norms used in 187
beliefs 185, 206, 239, 241
  appeal to 228
  changing 165; rich and 157
  conditional 11, 175-8, 212, 235
  configuration of 155-6
  conflicting 263
  consistent and closed by logic 162
  correct 156
  Creda's 352
  explicit 247
  extraordinary 176
  firmly-established 262
  indicative 210
  initial 164
  input 103
  investigator's set of 263
  lack of 12
  Lottery 264
  metaphysics of 221
  not enough to go around 236-7
  rational 155, 224, 265, 325
  reasoning with 15, 353
  *reductio* set of 264, 266
  see also Reason-with-Beliefs Principle
Bella 11, 58-60, 237, 241, 244
  belief-box of 178-9, 238
  beliefs psychologically basic to her mind 178
  credence-as-belief is true of 239-40
  like-mindedness of Creda and 239, 242
Bennett, J. 108 n., 111 n., 213 n., 216 n.
Berker, Selim 182 n.
Binary-Attitude Assumption 5, 9, 11, 78 n., 109, 110
black boxes 78
  see also Fuzz-only-box versions; Interval-box evidence; Point-box rules; Reasoning box
bog-standard cases of inference 246, 335, 347
  input and output content 103
  scenarios that plainly lack the causal use of evidence found in 334
  something essential to 330
  worry which applies to 332
Bovens, L. 266 n.
Box Partition Principle 31, 32
Brown University 87 n.
Brown-Blackwell Lectures 144 n.

Canada Case 190-2, 194-5
Cantor, Georg 21-2
Carnap, Rudolph 327
Cartesian epistemology 227 n.
Cash-Value Assumption 5, 183, 237-9, 251, 253, 285
Chalmers, D. (udwlh) 141 n.
Chang, R. 72 n.
Character-of-Evidence Principle 306, 308
Chisholm, R. M. 2
Christensen, D. (fuzzy jumper) 270 n., 289 n.
coarse-grained attitudes 2, 3, 9, 11-15, 180-9, 194, 195, 198, 200, 221-3, 228-32, 235, 252 n., 270, 273, 349
  aim to ground 248
  confidence-based approach to 272
  confidence-first epistemology and 344
  everyday description of 257
  formal approaches to 257
  inter-level irreducibility of 283
  intra-level reductionism about 257
  major puzzle for Lockeans about 253 n.
  satisfying form of Lockeanism about 284
  tacit 237
  unacceptable to endorse eliminativism about 230
  see also fine-grained and coarse-grained attitudes
Coarse View 224, 225, 227, 228, 230-1
cognitive force 13, 14, 273-84, 286, 286, 287, 302, 307-11, 317-20
Commanding Oracle 45-6
conditional commitment 3, 19, 116, 128, 132
  binary approach to 101, 129
  critical discussion of 11
  Ramsey Test and 197-217
  restricted-vision conception of 120
  tertiary approach to 101
  unconditional credence and 10
Conditional Credence 9, 10, 26 n., 45-8, 55-61, 83, 86, 99 n., 101, 112-16, 118-20, 125, 126, 128, 132, 138, 143-7, 149, 151-4, 200, 202 n., 209, 213-16, 235, 289, 351 n.
  contra Bayesian 75-82
  role in the Bayesian model 111
Conditional Credence Rule 47, 48f, 78, 79, 82-3
  see also Indicative Credence; Midpoint Conditional Confidence Rule
conditional probability 47, 48, 76-7, 79, 95
  derivative 59
  metaphysical life of 80
  orthodox 77, 82
conditionality 82, 86, 107, 211-16
  Bayesian kinematics and 124-9
  binary view of 110, 129, 142, 213
  confidence-theoretic 214
  dualism about 142, 213

restricted vision 10, 11, 101, 116–24, 127–8, 142–7, 149, 151, 152, 154
  rigidity and 111–16, 128
  suppositional view of 144
  tertiary approach to 129, 142, 214, 215, 216
  Updating Assumption about 133
  $y$-place theory of 11
confidence:
  appeal to states of 228
  comparative 90
  face of 307, 308
  found in Bayesian model 13
  high 20
  justifiable and justified 312
  kinematics of 278 n.; representor-based 288
  low 20
  metaphysics of levels of 221
  see also force-based confidence; spread of confidence; thick confidence
confidence-theoretic states 72, 94, 213, 214, 223, 253, 270, 272, 278, 282, 284, 288, 308, 310, 311, 344, 345
Conjunction-Introduction rule 130–1, 260 n.
Conjunction Rule 51, 55, 224–6, 261–3
consequents 109, 119, 120, 126–7, 136, 137, 139, 177, 199, 207, 211, 212
  fact-stating 108
content-based accuracy 288
  force-based confidence and 313–20
contextism 213
  about conditionals 212, 214
contraction 162–73, 174, 175, 177, 189
  partial meet 11, 324
Contradiction Avoidance 199–200, 205, 206
Cook, R. T. 62 n., 67 n., 277 n.
COPPER WIRE 136–7
Core Inference Principle 104, 244–7, 330–2, 335
Correia, F. 77 n.
Crane, T.(t-daddy) 210 n., 333 n.
Creda 237, 238, 240–2, 244, 349–55
  like-mindedness of Bella and 239, 242
  matching psychology of 9, 58–60
Creda's psychology:
  adding a new piece of architecture to 350
  basic mental element in 59
  Bayesian model matches 60, 61
  credence boxes of 59
Credal-based Lockeanism 255
  challenges for: answerable 260–8; deeper 268–71
  strengths of 256–9
Credal-Import/Export Law 136, 146
Credal-Import/Export norm 121, 123, 124
Credal Partition Principle 83, 85, 86, 113
credence 25, 282
  bogus notion of 228
  point-valued states of 348, 349
  positive 120
  rational distributions of 120
  reasoning with 244–8
  sensible 228
  states of 72
  sub-agential 92 n.
  unconditional 10, 48$f$, 78–80, 83, 86, 107, 109–11, 147
  unorthodox norms for 280 n.
  see also Bayesian Credence; Conditional Credence; Credence Function; Credence Partition Principle; Indicative Credence; Rational Credence
credence-as-belief 235–54
Credence Function 59, 60, 66, 112, 209, 293
  conditional 118, 120, 146
  perturbed 8$f$
Credence Partition Principle 28–9, 42–5, 48$f$, 54, 55, 58$f$, 59, 82
  additive spirit of 83
Cummins, R. C. 314 n.

Davidson, D. 333 n.
Davies, Martin 327
Dempster-Shafer Theory 281 n.
Disjunctive Syllogism 130, 131, 132
Dorr, C.(c-dog) 66, 250 n.
Dovetail Puzzle 14
DROP-ZONE 45–6, 80–2

Easwaran, K. 313 n.
Edgington, D.(dot) 29 n., 62 n., 67 n., 108 n., 118 n., 119 n., 143, 144, 199 n., 213 n., 216 n., 277 n., 278 n.
eggs 289–302
Ehring, D.(dougie fresh) 333 n.
either-or strategy 95–6
eliminativism 228, 229, 230, 231
Enderton, H. B. 22 n.
Entailment Rule 132, 187, 224
  two-part 131
epistemic appraisal 328
  certain propositional attitudes are subject to 6
  derivative propositional attitudes subject to 179
  epistemic attitude shifts are subject to 6
  mental-state transition subject to 331
  proprietary 187
  psychological states become subject to 20
epistemic attitudes 102, 157–8, 176, 184, 199, 287
  building 272–3
  coarse-grained 155, 158, 230
  confidence-first approach to 342
  fine-grained 163, 198, 216; reality of 230

reality of (cont.)
  hyper-precise 269
  puzzling about 221–32
  rational shift of 163
  shifts in 6–8
  stable 276
  various constraints on 158
Epistemic Conservatism 10, 163–5, 199–200, 205, 206
epistemic entrenchment 171, 173
epistemology:
  accuracy-first 315 n.
  belief-first 12, 14, 233–54
  Cartesian 227 n.
  coarse-grained 198, 199
  confidence-first 12, 245, 288, 341, 342, 344–5
  credence-first 12–13, 255–71
  informal 9–11, 278
  see also fine-grained epistemology; formal epistemology
Expansion-as-Deduction Theorem 175
expansion postulates 174, 175, 189–90, 194
  Belief Model 191–2, 195

face-value strategy 92–4
Field, H.(hbomb) 179 n., 255 n., 327
Fine, T. L. 77 n.
fine-grained attitudes 3, 9, 11–15, 198, 221–3, 228–32, 235, 252 n., 273
  best strategy for grounding 248
  epistemology of 181
  formal approaches to 257
  intra-level irreducibility of 257
  move from point-based to interval-based 86
  one type of 61–75
  popular models of 180
  rational 19, 61
  rational flux across time 107
  unacceptable to endorse eliminativism about 230
fine-grained and coarse-grained attitudes 341
  causal harmony between 258
  Creda is very like us when it comes to 350
  Credal-based Lockeanism sees them relating to one another 259
  epistemology of asymmetry in 180
  folk psychology shot through with 256
  hearty realism about 283
  help to sort out the relation between 282
  intra-level irreducibility of 271
  knitting together causal roles of 284
  metaphysical integration of 255
  relation between 326
  symmetry between 186
  very intimate link between 255
fine-grained epistemology 198, 199, 200, 227, 257
  Bayesian 202

fine-grained opinion:
  distribution of: restricted-vision 118–19, 120, 128; unrestricted-vision 138
  supposition-dependent 139
Fine View 215, 225, 227, 228, 231
Firestone, C.(chazmataz) 349 n.
Fitelson, B.(brando) 87 n., 120 n., 123 n., 313 n.
Fitting Character Thesis 62
Fodor, J. 179 n., 229, 231
Foley, R. 255 n.
folk psychology 229, 256
  causal-explanatory power of 230
force-based confidence 288–320
  content-based accuracy and 313–20
  evidence and 308–13
  modelling 279–81
  picturing 276–8
  rational kinematics and 298–308
formal epistemology 1, 3, 8, 9–11, 87, 90, 103, 198, 278
  accuracy-first 315 n.
  Gärdenfors Bombshell dropped on 200
  leading figures in 92
  Rawlsians drawn to 326
  running theme throughout 197
  see also Ramsey Test
Frankish, K. 240 n.
Frege, G. 4 n.
Friedman, J. (moneybags) 273 n.
full rationality 91, 158
  Bayesian model's take on 29
  inference-based efforts to regain 103
Functional Equivalence 237–44
FUZZ-ONLY-BOX versions 74–5

games, see Ball Game; Marble Game
Gärdenfors, Peter 3, 11, 155, 164 n., 165–7, 171–7, 195, 197
Gärdenfors' Bombshell 199–200, 202, 206
Gibbard, A. 120 n., 208
Greaves, H. 313 n.

Hacking, I. 65 n., 270 n.
Hájek, A. 273 n.
Halpern, J. Y. 65 n., 91 n., 270 n.
Harman, Gilbert 129, 234 n.
  see also Nozick-Harman Point
Harvard 87 n.
Hawthorne, J. 266 n.
Hoeltje, M. 243 n.
Holton, R. 227 n., 236 n.
Honderich, T. 333 n.
Hopkins, J. 333 n.
Horty, J. F. 245 n., 324 n.
Howson, C. 227 n.
Humeans 343, 344, 345
HURT LOCKER 134–6

## INDEX

impossible agents 9, 11, 244
incompleteness 147
  logical 156
Incompleteness Worry 116, 120, 124, 128, 142, 145, 147
indicative conditionals 101, 108, 111 n., 134, 144, 200, 203
  Import-Export law for 208
  Ramsey Test for 198
Indicative Credence 128, 138
  binary 142, 213
  conditional and 107–13, 115, 116, 119, 120, 142, 143, 146, 200, 210, 214
  high 140, 141
  low 140, 141
  *raison d'être* of 122
  Suppositional Ramsey Norm and 139
induction and deduction 203
inference 106, 267
  basing relation and 330–6
  Bayesian 103
  fundamentals of 103
  key ingredient of 105
  mental-state transitions and 104, 105
  obligatory patterns of 141
  rationality and 321–56
  rules of 10, 105, 107, 129–31, 142
  standard cases of 104, 244
  theory of 101
  *see also* bog-standard cases of inference; Core Inference Principle; rational inference
Inference Puzzle 15
informational economy 165–7, 170, 171, 174, 175, 189
inter-level irreducibility 283
interval arithmetic 72 n.
INTERVAL-BOX evidence 63–4, 69, 73
Intervalish-box evidence 73–4
intra-level irreducibility 257, 259, 271
irrationality 26
  credal 266

Jeffrey, Richard 3, 12, 57, 65, 92, 227, 234, 327
Jeffrey Conditionalization 57–8, 58*f*, 59, 101–5, 107, 116, 132, 147, 150–1, 202 n., 244, 245, 356
  connection between *Modus Ponens* and 131
  counter-instance to 134
Jeffrey's Rule 9, 10, 53–8, 102–5, 107, 112, 114, 120, 121, 124, 127, 128, 129 n., 131, 132, 134, 148–9, 245, 246 n., 288–9, 324, 355, 356
Joyce, Jim 65 n., 87 n., 91, 92, 94 n., 270 n., 313 n.
judgement 122, 315
  *see also* suspended judgement
Judy Benjamin Problem, 153–54, *see also* REACT

justification 325
  component 310–11
  doxastic 105 n., 272, 298, 308, 310, 311, 312
  evidential 105 n., 298
  propositional 272, 308, 310, 311, 312

Kant, Immanuel 158
Kaplan, Mark (marky mark) 65 n., 91 n., 92, 263, 264 n., 270 n., 289 n., 327
Keynes, J. M. 65 n.
Kim, J. 333 n.
kinematics 9–10, 129 n., 214, 217, 245, 272, 278 n., 289, 290, 313, 324, 327, 341
kinematics:
  orthodox 281, 298, 302
  probability 105 n.
  rational 105, 106, 107, 288, 310, 312;
    force-based confidence and 298–308
  representor-based 288, 298
  understanding how it works 309
  *see also* Bayesian kinematics
Korcz, K. A. 104 n., 332 n.
Kording, K. 103 n.
Kripke, S. A. 4 n.
Kvanvig, J. L.(thanks!) 310 n., 332 n.
Kyburg, H. 86 n., 225

Lance, M. N. 236 n.
Landy, M. 103 n.
language-of-thought 59–60, 178–9, 237–8, 248, 349–52
Lasonen-Aarnio, M.(tree hopper) 304 n.
Lehrer, K. 2
Leitgeb, H. 240 n.
Levi, I. 65 n., 164 n., 270 n.
Levi identity 11, 164, 174, 175, 189
Lewis, David 11, 61–2, 94 n., 185 n., 197
List, C. (fire warden) 92 n.
Loar, B. 185 n.
Locke, John 342, 346
Lockeanism:
  confidence-based 272
  force-based 282–7
  *see also* Credal-based Lockeanism
lotteries 260, 263, 264, 266
Lottery Paradox 225, 226, 232, 264 n.

Maher, P. 65 n., 228 n., 263 n.
Makinson, David 3, 155, 175, 225
Marble Game 9, 48–53, 54, 133*f*, 200–1
Marching-in-Step Phenomenon 232, 252–4, 258–9
Martin, Mike 327
Matching-Models Assumption 8–9
Matthews, R. J. 5 n.
McDowell, John 327

McGee, V. (thanks!) 118 n., 120 n.
McLaughlin, B. P. 240 n.
Mellor, D. H. 315 n.
mental-state transitions 2, 3, 103
  inference and 104
Menzel, C. 310 n., 332 n.
Michigan 87 n.
Midpoint Conditional Confidence Rule 86
Midpoint Partition Principle 85-6
Millikan, R. 314 n.
minimal-revision function 204, 205
*Modus Ponens* 10, 101, 129, 132, 134-8, 141, 142, 214, 217
  double-whammy application of 131
Moore, R. E. 72 n.

Naïve Principle 84-5
Nature-Before-Norms Assumption 4, 335
NBA (National Basketball Association) 224 n.
neutrality 274, 279, 281, 282, 286, 287, 299, 303, 309, 317, 320
  attitudinal, substantive 301
  cognitive 300, 307, 311, 313; *raison d'être* of 319
  cognitive force strongly dominated by 302
  committed 182, 183, 185-6, 273 n.
  full 297
  gustatory 273, 275
  intellectual 184, 275, 280
  nil 278
  non-nil 278
  non-trivial amounts of 308
  non-zero 277
  settled 184
  stable 188
  zero 277
Norm of Character Match 270
Nozick-Harman Point 129-42

Oracles 81, 205, 206, 304-7
  *see also* Commanding Oracle;
    Strange Oracle
Original Probability Distribution Pold 50
Oxford 87 n.

Papineau, D. 315 n.
parity 72 n.
Partition Principle 30, 118, 119, 150, 225 n.
  Ball Game and 25-9
  *see also* Box Partition Principle; Credal Partition Principle; Credence Partition Principle; Midpoint Partition Principle; Probability Partition Principle
Partition Rule 33, 40, 224-6
  credence 45
pesky dilation 288-98

Pettigrew, R. 315 n.
Pettit, P. 92 n.
phenomenology 265, 284, 287
  dialectical 264
Plato 1
POINT-BOX rules 62, 63, 73
Pollock, John 2 n., 131 n., 135 n., 236 n., 245 n., 304 n., 310 n., 324 n., 325, 327, 340 n.
Popper, Karl 12, 234-5
postulates 66, 67, 69, 73, 144, 173, 177
  Belief Model 11
  contraction 174
  likewise-motivated 175
  revision 174, 195
  *see also* expansion postulates
Preface Paradox 225, 226, 232, 264 n., 266
Presumption-of-Non-Contradiction thesis 125
presupposition 23, 111, 122, 165, 210, 222, 338
  false 215
  mandatory 215
  psychological 65, 230, 232
probabilism, *see* Bayesian model
Probabilistic Coherence 8f, 325
probability 50, 55, 236
  claims about 9
  classic 9, 91, 288
  comparative 59, 60, 95
  conjunction rule for 51
  laws of 40, 354, 355, 356
  original 51, 52
  orthodox approach to 76, 77
  percentage bits to play with 34
  positive 37
  unconditional 76, 77
  *see also* conditional probability; subjective probability
probability distribution 34, 35, 36, 38-40, 51
  original 53; *see also* Original Probability Distribution Pold
probability functions 9, 13, 59, 75, 95
  classic 91, 92
  finitely additive 29 n.
  fully rational credence structured like 28-9
  interval-valued 61
  multiple; appeal to 61; classic 91
  procedure for changing 65
  richly membered sets of 92
Probability Partition Principle 36, 40
probability theory 27, 29, 44, 65, 76
  Ball Game and 33-40
  basic rule of 40
  laws of 39-40; basic 36
  orthodox 77, 79, 80
probability values 59, 60, 91, 94

propositional attitudes 4, 6, 76, 104,
    178, 182, 212, 221, 246, 285–6,
    314, 331, 349
  attitude-focused part of theory of 210
  binary 109
  *bona fide* 187
  derivative 179
  kind of functionalism about 5
  tertiary 61
propositions 41, 111, 116, 155, 158, 159 n., 162,
    165, 166, 173, 192, 210, 215, 266
  attitude lent to 341
  believed 347, 349, 354
  binary relations between thinkers and 5
  claims for 211
  conjunctive 201
  construed 4, 117
  contingent 206 n.
  epistemic status of 353
  false 261
  input 74
  true 4, 201
Pryor, Jim (jp) 135 n., 294, 327, 340 n.
psychology 21, 76, 99, 238, 239, 251 n., 268–70,
    282, 288, 318
  basic 350
  Bayesian 67
  common-sense 65, 69, 73
  contentious area of 349
  everyday 271
  made-up 69
  matching 9, 11, 58–60, 177–9, 187, 275
  mirror-image 227 n.
  on-again/off-again topic in 348
  over-developed 19
  precision in 68
  rational 9, 77–8
  specific assumptions about 4
  sub-optimal 81
  target 58, 178
  under-developed 20
  underlying 25, 158–9
  worry 268–71
  *see also* Creda's psychology; folk
    psychology
Putnam, Hilary 179 n.

Ramsey, F. P. 2, 3, 10, 11, 65 n., 107, 138–9, 176,
    179, 198, 200, 202, 209, 217
Ramsey norm 108–9, 111–16, 119–29, 142,
    146, 214
  suppositional 139–41, 143
Ramsey Test 7f, 139, 176–7, 177f, 178
  coarse-grained 199, 203, 204, 205, 206, 210
  conditional commitment and 197–217
  fine-grained 200, 202, 207–10, 213, 214, 216
RANDOM SUPPER 89–90

Ranking Theory 281 n.
Rational Credence 25, 28, 41, 43, 78, 80 n., 81,
    104, 109, 111 n., 112, 225, 226, 262, 265–7,
    281, 303, 355, 356
  Bayesian transition theory for 53
  distributions of 109, 118, 121, 128, 208;
    Ramsey's norm holds in all 138
  fully 28–9, 48, 54, 55, 73, 75; Bayesian rules
    for 40
  investing 223
  orthodox approaches to 299
  perturbed 107
  standard assumptions about 261
  vigorous appeal to intuition concerning 61
  well-known thought about 224
rational inference 9, 15, 105, 323, 332–3, 334
  crucial elements needed for good
    understanding of 328
  idealized 10
  nature of 14; understanding 322
  reasons central to 321
  theory of 14, 324, 338, 347
rational shift-in-view 10, 176, 190, 192, 353–6
  conditional commitment and 11, 19, 197
  contact-point of 111, 115, 116, 142, 202 n.
  developing a theory of 6
  fully 194, 195
  obligatory path forward in 214
  purely logical constraints on 196
  puzzle about 340
  sixteen-fold classification of approaches to 14
  space of theories 321–8
  types of 347–8
rational transitions 116, 147, 178, 348
  claims about 163–5
  states undergo 102
rationality 5 n., 11, 82, 155, 160, 178, 223, 235
  agential 338, 341
  basics of 87
  bounded 325
  doxastic 14, 288, 321, 332, 335, 337–8, 341
  dynamic 337
  epistemic 4, 65, 66, 157, 324, 335, 353
  everyday 14, 324–7, 337, 341, 348, 349,
    354–6
  evidential 332, 335, 341
  fine-grained 87
  formal work on/models of 1, 2, 7, 8–9,
    197, 198
  fundamental 328
  human fallibility and its relation to 225
  ideal 14, 321, 324–7, 337, 341
  impersonal 338
  inference and 321–56
  informal work on 1, 2
  kinematics of 324
  less-than-full 102

rationality (*cont.*)
  non-ideal 14
  propositional 288
  rule of 324
  structural demand on 83
  super-human 158
  theory of 4 n.
  visual-based 327
  warm-up for tackling general aspects of 180
  *see also* full rationality; irrationality; theory of rationality
Rationality-of-Transitions Assumption 6–7, 322
Rationalizing-in-Step Phenomenon 259
Rawls, John 326
Rayo, A. 305 n.
REACT (Recovery of Equilibrium After Conditional-credence Transfer) 153–4
Reason-with-Beliefs Principle 346–7
reasoning 12, 15, 171, 195, 210, 214–16, 244–8, 332, 341–2
  defeasible 324
  non-monotonic 2
  practical 185, 274, 275
  *reductio* 331
  states of 348*f;* autonomous 349
  suppositional 139, 140, 144, 350, 351
  theoretical 185, 274, 275
Reasoning box 350, 351, 352, 353
RED-SPOTTED BALLS 78–9
RESTAURANT CHOICE 79–80
restricted vision 10, 11, 101, 116–24, 127–8, 142–7, 149, 151, 152, 154
Revision Theorem 11, 175
rigidity 101, 125, 146
  conditionality and 111–16, 128
rigidity worry 116, 120, 124, 128, 142, 145
Rinard, S. 87 n.
Ripley, D. 185 n.
Rosen, G. 243 n.
Rumfitt, I. 185 n.

Sainsbury, R. M. 278 n.
Schiffer, S.(tl) 59 n., 179 n., 185 n., 210 n., 238 n., 255 n.
Schmidtz, D. 326 n.
Schnieder, B. 77 n., 243 n.
Schoenfield, M.(mim) 63 n., 106 n.
Scholl, B. J. 349 n.
Sen, Amartya 326
Shafer, G. 281 n.
shift-in-view 150, 263, 335
  conditional commitment and 147, 209
  indicative belief and 210
  inferential 340
  puzzle about 336–40
  visual-based 329, 340
    also rational shift-in-view

Siegel, S.(robo) 349 n.
snazzy features 77
Spohn, W. 281 n.
spread of confidence 285–6
  exact 67, 269, 286
Stalnaker, R. 266–7, 353–4
Stanley, J. 257 n.
Steinberg, A. 243 n.
Stemplowska, Z. 326 n.
Stich, S. P. 229 n.
STRANGE ORACLE 87–9, 90, 96–9
Sturgeon, S. 104 n., 108 n., 120 n., 131 n., 135, 136, 259 n., 273 n., 304 n., 319 n., 333 n., 340 n., 354 n.
subjective probability 2, 29
  point-valued 61, 64–5
  real-valued 64, 65, 66, 67
supposition 46, 129, 140, 347
  explicit 139
  *see also* Suppositional Ramsey Norm
suppositional credit 139, 142–3
  conditional commitment reduces to 144
  sub-surface 145
Suppositional Ramsey Norm 139–41, 143
suspended judgement 1, 2, 10–13, 157–9, 161–4, 180–9, 192, 194, 198, 221–3, 223*f,* 229–31, 235, 253 n., 256*f,* 257, 268–71, 273 n., 277, 282–4, 286–7, 326, 348
Swift, A. 326 n.
Swinburne, R. 315 n.

tertiary attitudes 96, 98, 99–100, 110
  intervals and 87–91
  *sui generis* 111
theory of rationality 4 n., 116, 324, 332, 338, 349
  dynamics within 324
  full-dress 6, 7, 19, 20, 58, 177, 322
  one of the most important issues in 326
  shift-in-view between states which are explanatorily fundamental to 322
theory of states 6, 197*f,* 313
  formal 288
  roles that correspond to 7
  *see also* Bayesian theory of states; Belief Model's theory of states
thick confidence 64–7, 87–93, 99, 223 n., 233, 270–2, 277, 282–7, 300–3, 306–9, 315 n., 316, 348–50
  conditional 82, 83, 86
  fully dilated 286
  fuzzy 75
  justifiable 310, 311
  multiple types of 349

open 96, 97, 98
orthodox kinematics of 288
orthodox transition theory for 289
rational 73, 85, 92, 288, 305
representors and 288–98
sharp 69–73, 95, 272, 278, 280, 281
THREE DOORS 183
Threshold View 223–8, 232
tinker-toy theory 25, 69, 70, 167, 343
transition theory 6, 7, 58, 197, 288, 297, 324
  forward-looking/ahistorical nature of 14
  orthodox 289
  popular 13
  representor-based 289
  see also Bayesian transition theory; also under Belief Model
transitions 7f, 8, 58f, 162
  conditional credence is rigid in, described by Jeffrey rule 147
  epistemic 6
  rational state 91 n.
  states and 19, 59; linking 175–7
  see also Bayesian transition theory; mental-state transitions; rational transitions
Trommershauser, J. 103 n.
truth tables 9, 34–6, 42, 54
  three-letter 101
truth-values 39, 80 n., 183–5, 188, 215, 274, 275, 286, 290, 292–5, 298, 300–5

Unconditional Antecedents Assumption 123–4, 127, 128
ungrammatical claims 123

Update-Disposition 203
  credence as 234–5
Updating Assumption 113, 133
  counter-instance to 134
Urbach, P. 227 n.

Valentini, L. 326 n.
Van Fraassen, B. 65 n., 91 n.
Venn diagrams 9

Wallace, D. 313 n.
Walley, P. 65 n., 91 n., 270 n.
Wedgwood, Ralph 260 n.
White, R. 63 n., 289 n., 327
Williamson, T. 315 n.
Wilson, J. 258 n.
Woods, M. 108 n., 111 n., 199 n., 213 n.
Worry 236–8, 245, 246
  analogue 61
  conflict 262–6
  conjunction 260–2
  dilation-based 14, 288, 289
  epistemology 270–1
  incompleteness 116, 120, 124, 128, 142, 145
  influential 333 n.
  over-generation 99
  pointlessness 266–8
  psychology 268–70
  rigidity 116, 120, 124, 128, 142, 145
  under-generation 96
Wright, C. 275–6, 327

Yablo, S. 210 n., 259 n., 333 n., 343, 344, 346